THE MORAL CHOICE

THE MORAL CHOICE

by
Daniel C. Maguire

Library of Congress Cataloging in Publication Data
Maguire, Daniel C.
The moral choice.
Includes bibliographical references and index.
1. Ethics.   I. Title.
BJ1012.M34   170
ISBN: 0-86683-771-X (previously ISBN: 0-03-053796-7)
Library of Congress Catalog Card Number: 77-76248
Published by arrangement with Doubleday & Co., Inc.

Printed in the United States of America

First Winston Press printing, August, 1979

Biblical excerpts are from the Jerusalem Bible, copyright © 1966 by Darton, Longman & Todd, Ltd., and Doubleday & Company, Inc. Used by permission of the publishers.

Permission to quote material from the following sources is gratefully acknowledged:

"Nichomachean Ethics" from The Oxford Translation of Aristotle, translated and edited by W. D. Ross, Vol. 9, 1925, by permission of Oxford University Press. The Idea of National Interest, by Charles A. Beard and G. H. E. Smith, 1934, The Macmillan Company; copyright 1934 by Charles A. Beard. "Anthropology and the Abnormal," by Ruth Benedict, in The Journal of General Psychology 10, No. 1 (1934), pp. 59–80; copyright 1934 by The Journal Press. The Two Sources of Morality and Religion, by Henri Bergson, 1935, Henry Holt and Company, Inc.; copyright 1935 by Henry Holt and Company, Inc. History of Ethics, by Vernon J. Bourke, 1968, Doubleday & Company, Inc.; copyright © 1968 by Vernon J. Bourke. Science and Human Values, by J. Bronowski, 1959, Torchbooks, Harper & Row; rev. ed., 1965, Harper & Row; copyright © 1956 by J. Bronowski; rev. ed. copyright © 1965 by J. Bronowski; reprinted by permission of Julian Messner, a Simon & Schuster division of Gulf & Western Corporation. Morality and the Language of Conduct, by Hector-Neri Castaneda and George Nakhnikian, 1963, Wayne State University Press; copyright © 1963 by Wayne State University Press. Ethics, by John Dewey with John H. Tufts, 1932, Holt, Rinehart and Winston, Inc.; copyright 1908, 1932 by Holt, Rinehart and Winston, Inc.; reprinted with the permission of the Center for Dewey Studies, Southern Illinois University at Carbondale. The Firmament of Time, by Loren Eiseley. Copyright © 1960 by Loren Eiseley, © 1960 by the Trustees of The University of Pennsylvania. Reprinted by permission of Antheneum Publishers. Beyond Right and Wrong, by Harry K. Girvetz, 1973, The Free Press; copyright © 1973 by Harry K. Girvetz. An Inquiry into the Human Perspective, by Robert L. Heilbroner, 1975, W. W. Norton & Company, Inc.; copyright © 1974 by W. W. Norton & Company, Inc. "The Dialectic of the Sacred and the Comic," by M. Conrad Hyers, in Cross

Winston Press, Inc.
430 Oak Grove
Minneapolis, Minnesota 55403

5   4   3   2

To my father and mother, who
kept me in touch with my roots . .

ACKNOWLEDGMENTS

I am heavy with debt and gratitude to many: to Margie, my wife, loving critic-in-residence and colleague in ethics, for innumerable suggestions and for patience in her role as manuscript-widow; to Berard Marthaler, former chairman and permanent friend, who made me the beneficiary of both his brilliance and his support; to Maurice Duchaine, Charles E. Curran, Gerard Sloyan, Quentin Quesnell, John Hunt, Terence Connelly, and Kenneth Schmitz, whose friendship and influence have significantly affected the course of my intellectual and professional story; to my dear sons, Danny and Tommy, who interrupted me frequently and happily with their gentle and insistent love; to the baby-sitters and friends of Danny and Tommy, Monica Lemon and Therese Deshotels, who kept those interruptions at an appropriate level; to my invaluable teaching assistants at Marquette University during these years of writing, Fred Kreuziger, Ed Oates, Nick Fargnoli, and Regina Hall; to my typists, whose genius in deciphering my manuscript verged on infinity, Camille Slowinski, Romilia Powell, Cece Bauer, Agnes Johnson, Maggie Halleman, and Carolyn Worm; to Kathy Weissmueller, Paul Johnson, and Steve Price, who saved me from my own proofreading; to Michael A. McNiel, my student, for his work as illustrator; to all my students present and past for the stimulation and instruction they have given me; and to Doubleday's Bob Heller and Jan Waring, who have perfected the art of the painless prod.

CONTENTS

PRELUDE

This book presents a theory of moral knowledge, a theory of how it is that we moral beings may most sensitively know and evaluate. The theory is one that I have developed over twenty years of teaching and researching about the phenomenon of human morals. Since moral values constitute us as persons, the work I address here is awesome in its importance. Morality is certainly too important to be left to the professional moralists, and since everyone is a moralist in his fashion, this abandonment of morals to the experts has never really happened. There is, however, a service due from the moralist to all the other valuing animals of his species, and that service is theory. The alternative to theory is whimsy and caprice at the individual level and shallowness and incongruity at the level of culture. Life is a series of moral choices, and each and every one of us is at it all the time. There is no area of deliberate human behavior that lacks a moral dimension. The value questions are everywhere—in politics, in sex, in business, in the rearing of children, and in the realm of what one owes to one's self. Each of us has, in effect, his own little method for moral evaluation. If, however, we have never visited our method with reflection, the chances are that our method is biased and imperfect. The chances are too that we underestimate our moral freedom and our potential as persons. There is no one who is not in need of the critical pause for theory.

Since most people who address ethics formally in philosophy or theology, or who skirt it in the social sciences, underestimate its complexity, there is a compelling need to address it in its depth and breadth. For too many professional moralists, ethics has been seen as a matter of principle, language and reason. It is all of that, but it is much more. Moral understanding also unfolds in the exquisite power of creative imagination, in feeling and affectivity, in mind-forming relationships with various authorities, in the special perspectives of comic and tragic experience, in ways that are unique to the individual and in ways that bear the mark of the group. And all of us moral knowers have a history and a social matrix (with all of its myths and moods) out of which our thinking grows with more organic continuity and dependency than we are disposed to concede. Anyone who would discuss the "art-science of moral choice" must address all of this.

In doing this, I have attempted to give full vent to the theoretical needs of my subject while attempting not to join those moralists whom Schopenhauer indicted for rendering unintelligible the simplest relationships of life. I have also attempted to face with thoroughness the theoretical challenges of ethics without falling under the shadow of philosopher H. A. Prichard's lament about "the comparative remoteness of the discussions of Moral Philosophy from the facts of actual life." Thus my theory is interlaced with copious examples and applications. There is an obvious mercy in this, since unrelieved theory is at the least unkind. But aside from motives of gentleness, unrelieved theory might easily also be dishonest. If one is unwilling to illustrate the applicability of his theory to "the facts of actual life," it may be that his theory is irrelevant to those same facts. Ethics is about life and that should be visible when one addresses it. Be advised, however, that my examples may not do justice to my theory. They may reflect my bias more than my method. With such failures human thinking is fatally fraught. So if you disagree with a position I defend in offering an example, return to the theory which may be more generous with you than it was with me in its yield of truth.

My language has been crafted with an eye to mercy, but I cannot say that I have always avoided obscurity or tough and turgid prose. No serious work, I allege defensively, could really be free of these hazards. Easy and constant clarity is cheap and suited, in Kant's phrase, only for "shallowpates." I can say at least that I worried about joining my book to those books on ethics that Adam Smith found "dry and disagreeable, abounding in abstruse and metaphysical distinctions, but incapable of exciting in the heart any of those emotions which it is the principal use of books of morality to excite." I was attentive too to the warning of John Dewey that ours is a culture notoriously insensitive to the aesthetic aspect of the morally good. But with all of this attention and worry, like Adam Smith and Dewey too, I could not avoid what may be dry and disagreeable to some and unduly abstruse to others, for the roads to understanding are not always straight or smooth. Insight is often like the birth of a child—painful for a time, but well worth it when the price is paid.

Some will wonder whether this is a book in philosophy or theology. My answer is that in the traditional sense of the term, this is a book in philosophy. This, however, does not cut me off from religious experience as a bearer of moral insight. It is my belief that good ideas need no passport to enter an open mind, and if much moral insight is housed in the major religious traditions, I make room for that in my theory of ethics. The book, however, is not a confessional book representing only one philosophical or religious tradition. It is basically a book on the epistemology of ethics which seeks in as full a way as possible to illustrate how we know in matters moral so that our knowing might be more sensitive.

I am aware as I write that, in the words of philosopher Harry Girvetz, there is an "ought phobia" in the land. Ethics as a formal discipline of the mind has been out of style for a time. But I write with hope, since the strange fairy tale of "value-free objectivity" is slowly being laid to rest. The Positivistic poisons are abating and a value-full world is awakening to the need for ethical reflection. This book seeks to serve that awakening.

THE MORAL CHOICE

CHAPTER ONE

MUDDLE IN THE MORALSCAPE

Young buoyant America is all at once looking wizened. Its star-spangled self-assurance is spent. The amazing thought has dawned that everything might be wrong; there is a feeling of the ubiquity of iniquity.

Granting that every age is prone to thinking its own times the worst (an ancient cuneiform tablet is said to bear the inscription: "Alas! The times are not what they used to be!"),[1] our age seems to have impressive grounds for claiming a unique moral chaos.

Ours is a naked and brittle condition in which no value seems secure. Businessmen defend as essential to their competitive position practices which an older ethic reserved to liars and thieves. Permanent marriage seems to many to be simply quaint. Pornography can scarcely keep ahead of real life in imagining new adventures in sexual calisthenics and intrigue. Politics has lost all remnants of innocence as political scandals reveal the depth and breadth of corruption in political and corporate life. Bribes, chicanery, and cheating range from the tower suite to the soap-box derby. Walking some of our urban streets requires the courage of a frontiersman. And some see our youth reacting like Bolsheviks to all the established values of the quiet America so recently deceased.

The system of justice is no longer trusted. It now seems that the blindfolded lady with the scales of justice in her hand can see through her blind. She must see that the scales do not balance. Wealth, whiteness, and good connections make for different stories in the courtroom. Psychiatrist Karl Menninger, an elder in our land, has studied the court system and concluded that "it commits more crime than it punishes."[2]

Attendant to the apparent collapse of morals, science has normalized surprise and we are badgered daily by new and awesome moral questions. Should we do some of the things that we suddenly and terrifyingly can do? Should we manipulate the genetic code of man? Should we do research on externally growing human embryos or unborn fetuses?

And what about our mounting capacity for suicidal war? As one observer puts it: "We have invented the end of the world and we are keeping it in storage in our arsenals."[3] As nuclear and biological weapons potential spreads, the question arises as to how much moral intelligence is operating on planet earth or is thought-free, unmanageable momentum in charge. The power to kill and overkill increases with no obvious link to rationality.

Our sudden value quake perhaps best compares to what happened in Japan more than a century ago. An epochal upheaval began there in 1853 when Commodore Perry and his ships steamed into Yedo Bay and roused Japan from its long and soporific occlusion. Japan had been hiding from the world and from the tumult of colliding values. Contact ended this retreat. Despite their commercial intentions, the principal cargo of these ships was questions. And this was jarring to a Japan which had become a land of answers. The political and commercial consequences of Perry's visit command most of the historians' attention, but it was the importation of new questions that changed Japan forever.[4]

Culturally and morally, we too had practiced the art of the enclosed mind and we are now meeting our Yedo Bay. Meaning and answers were tidily, if artificially, imposed, and subversive questions were drummed out of court without a trial. Before the value tumult of recent decades, the United States was remarkably successful in projecting as its national image the simplicities of a Norman Rockwell magazine cover. Here man and dog behaved as expected, or, at least, there was no admitted doubt about what they should have been up to if they were not.

But now a thousand ships have found our Yedo Bay. Suddenly, the unquestionable is questioned, the unthinkable is not only thought but done. The intruding ships were such things as mass society, mobility, the power of communications media to invade cultural enclaves, the countercultural blitzkriegs against tradition in any form, and the discrediting of oracles in Church, State, and Academe.

There is much that is new in all of this, but there is also something that is not new. The human race has always teetered between barbarity and morality, with morality only slowly establishing its claims. This dramatic dialectic continues. The stakes, of course, are higher and more definitive now. Technological barbarians are more dangerous. But the gateway to an alternative to barbarism is, as it always was, ethical reflection. The ancients said: "He who reflects not in his heart is like the beast that perishes." That really is not true. The beasts are better off. Even without reflection, they have instinct which imbues them with the wisdom of survival. We have no such advantage. We will neither survive nor flourish by instinct, but only by the activation of our moral consciousness. As Nietzsche correctly says, we are "the valuing animal"; we are not essentially programmed. We have to think and opt amid competing values. And our most fundamental thinking and valuing is at the level of morals.

to rise or be deeply

do we really?

Moral values are more basic than all other values, because moral values touch, not just on what we do or experience or have, but on what we *are*. It is admittedly unfortunate if a person is not gifted with the values of wealth, gracefulness, beauty, education, and aesthetic sophistication. But it is a qualitative leap beyond the merely unfortunate if a person is a murderer, a liar, or a thief. Here the failure is at the level of what a person is and has to be *as a person*. Confusion at this level is intolerable and often lethal. Thoughtful evaluation is the only alternative to this confusion.

Ethics is the art-science which seeks to bring sensitivity and method to the discernment of moral values. Sad to tell, at this time when ethical reflection is critically needed, it is not enjoying a high noon. The intellectual and cultural atmosphere is not friendly to it.

Ethics is not the consuming passion of our time as it has been in the past. In classical times the giants of genius were most teased by the great moral questions. To probe the sense and meaning of the moral was the supreme intellectual challenge. The philosopher Arthur Schopenhauer could write in 1840 that "all philosophers in every age and land have blunted their wits on it."[5]

Some of those philosophers, before and after Schopenhauer (and including Schopenhauer), have managed to blunt ethics as well as their wits. Because of this, and for a variety of other reasons, ethics stands in recession and in disrepute, and the society that needs this kind of reflection to realize its humanness could not care less. In a day of bogus crises, here is the real thing. The disease is potentially terminal and the only remedy is unknown or suspect.

To show that all of this is true, and to show the need for the resur-
rection of a reflective ethics, we turn now to a sampling of some of
the wracking value questions that are upon us in the contemporary
moralscape in the areas of sex, science, business, and politics. Then
we will look at the formidable barriers that block our addressing and
possibly answering those questions. In spite of these barriers, showing how to address these questions in a way most likely to produce
sensitive ethical answers is the precise aim of this book.[6]

Sex Rampant . . .

Traditionally, sex has had ethical reflection lavished on it with
prodigality. It has almost seemed that sex is what morality is all
about. "She is an immoral woman" would usually be taken to mean
that the woman was looser than the mores permitted in her sex life.
The charge would not raise the question of whether this woman was
anti-Semitic, or whether she had vast holdings in General Motors
and took no notice of the corporation's doings, or whether she was
politically disinterested. Yet a solid case for gross immorality in all
these instances could be made.[7] Similarly, the recent term "the new
morality" is regularly freighted with sexual connotations, although it
describes a vastly broader phenomenon.

This, at least, is the way it has been. Even if people did not live up
to the moral standards, sex was clearly a moral matter—that is, a
matter on which moral judgment could be passed. Sex is now becoming in many segments of society a moral free zone. Consenting
adulthood is the moral passport to any sexual act. All further questions are the product of unwarrantable "hang-up." Some would say
that even weird sexual behavior should be spared the burden of evaluation. As Albert Ellis writes in *The American Sexual Tragedy:*

> If a human being, from time to time, enjoys unusual sex
> participations, such as being beaten while he is having sex
> relations, or copulation with animals . . . we may justifiably
> call him odd, or peculiar, or statistically unusual. But we
> may not, from a psychological (or biological) standpoint
> justifiably call him abnormal, perverted, or deviant.[8]

Notice that Ellis does not even consider *moral* evaluation. In this,
he is not unusual. Morality has been prescinded from for so long in
the name of a "value-free" objectivity that a recessive reaction to

moral categories is statistically normal even though it is intellectually freakish. Such a phobic reaction to moral evaluation is a strange and radical ailment for the valuing animal. But there it is and the sexual scene is illustrative of much of it.

The tragedy of this is seen in the observation of May and Abraham Edel when they write in *Anthropology and Ethics*: ". . . sex is nearly everywhere highly charged morally, for in addition to its high emotional potential, it is part of the most central nexus of human social interrelationships."[9] Sex is no fringe activity for the human animal. In any society it symbolizes and affects to a significant degree the patterns of social existence. Therefore, if there is something new in the sex life of a people, it deserves our questioning attention. Sex is too serious both for individuals and for social existence to be left to the vagaries of fad or unexamined whim.

Sometimes an incident is more revealing about the temper of the times than a thousand concepts. In April 1974 an organization known as Face to Face with the 70's sponsored a conference on human sexuality at a small Catholic college in the Midwest. During a discussion on sex education one gentleman rose and announced that he and his wife had allowed their young daughter to watch them having intercourse as a way of teaching "the facts of life." Their daughter was greatly impressed and requested to have intercourse with the father also. The gentleman allowed to the now gasping conference that he, of course, could not do that, adding, somewhat anticlimatically, that he too was looking for answers.[10]

It would seem safe to say that this sort of parental sex theater is novel—at least with a view to recent times. It is not, however, lonely or without explicit defenders. In a book entitled *Show Me: A Picture Book of Sex for Children and Parents*, authors Will McBride and Helga Fleischhauer-Hardt urge parents to welcome the children during love-making.[11] Others suggest that it is both wholesome and progressive for mothers to teach their pubescent daughters how to masturbate as a relief for menstrual tension. The question is whether these innovators are in the moral vanguard or are deviant outriders. How do we know that making love for the edification of our young is morally deviant? In the past it was considered wrong to have intercourse during pregnancy, to have intercourse in any but the classical position with the male on top, or to masturbate in any circumstances.[12] While these opinions reigned, anyone advocating anything else would presumably have been greeted by gasps of indignation. In these cases, however, the innovators seem to have corrected past errors. Is there nothing more that we can do in the face of today's innovations but wait in a "let's see who wins" attitude?

There is another area of sexual ethics where the innovators have moved ahead at a brisk pace—premarital coitus. In one of the most extensive studies of sexual mores in the United States done since Kinsey, Morton Hunt offers statistical data on sexual trends in this country. He reaches the following judgment:

> It now appears likely that within another five to ten years only a tiny minority of females and an even smaller one of males, consisting of the deeply religious, the emotionally disturbed and the personally undesirable, will remain virginal through their teens or will be virginal at the time of marriage.[13]

Hunt is saying that this is what appears likely given what is happening now. He is not saying or denying that this ought to happen. He is describing, not prescribing. But it is reasonable to ask the ethical *ought* question. Is this what *should* be happening? *Should* we be as calm as feminist Eleanor Garst, who asks: "Will life be the same when every girl at the onset of puberty takes The Pill as routinely as she sees her dentist?"[14] *Should* we follow Nena and George O'Neill, authors of *Open Marriage*, and Anna and Robert Francoeur, authors of *Hot and Cool Sex*, when they argue for the moral normalcy of satellite sexual relationships which are had with the spouses' consent?[15] According to these authors, the primary relationship—that is, the marriage—does not exclude, nor should it, other sexual, romantic relationships.

As humanist Corliss Lamont writes:

> . . . since it is clear that one can be sincerely in love with at least two persons at the same time, a husband or wife may feel free to go the whole way with another person whom he or she truly loves. . . . To limit the supreme sexual experience to just one member of the opposite sex for an entire lifetime represents an unreasonable restraint and a killjoy ethics.[16]

These positions cannot be presumed right because current, or wrong because new. Who is to say that they are not the prescient heralds of the future? Ethics must speak to that. Ethics is the *votum* of the present regarding the shape of the future. It is for ethics to provide a method for judging these and other realities right now.

Still on the subject of sex: Is there anything morally wrong with sex clinics which employ a surrogate partner to help persons who are sexually troubled? We tend to think that that which is customary is right and such clinics are too new to be customary. But does that make them wrong?

Should homosexual persons, who appear to be positively and irreversibly homosexual, marry? Should these marriages be legally recognized for tax and social security purposes? Should churches provide religious marriage services for homosexuals? Should homosexuals be permitted to adopt children? Why, or why not?

Should pornography be viewed more positively? Should prostitution involving two consenting adults be presumed wrong or criminal? Maybe prostitution provides a socially basic service which should be decriminalized and regulated. Could it be that the evils attendant upon prostitution derive from its criminal association and not from prostitution itself? However persons may feel inclined to answer these questions, do they know why they feel that way? Is their opinion rooted in prejudice, in the inability to cope with the new or the inability to cope with anything but the new; or does it have deeper and defensible grounding? All fair questions. All grist for ethical inquiry.

The Lordship of Science . . .

"Science has made us gods," exclaimed the French scientist J. Rostand, "before we were even worthy of being man."[17] Rostand's remark has the makings of a valedictory address to an era. It does, however, make two points more quickly than any valedictory on record. First, scientists can now do routinely what reasonable men of the recent past would have thought could only be done by divine intervention. His second point: Our heads are more developed than our consciences; our skills outstrip our moral sensitivities. As an awesome result, our new potential is as lethal as it is grand.

Like any valedictory, however, Rostand's gets wafted aloft by its own rhetoric. A comment on his "science" and his "gods" is needed. Science, as such, has not really made us anything. Science as such is an abstraction. What exists concretely is men and women doing scientific research and applying it. It is they, or, we can say, *we* who have made ourselves whatever we are. We cannot blame what we are on some numinous and inexorable power called "science" which shapes us according to its own arcane purposes. Granting that scientific and technological achievements have a way of collecting and generating a momentum to which we can easily submit, and granting that scientific changes affect our moral setting qualitatively, still, more basic than what we call "science" are the moral agents who do science. Scientists are persons first. And if we persons make a mess, it is our mess. We cannot indict faceless science or technology in our stead.

Furthermore, is it true that we have made ourselves gods? No. What is true is that we have been forced to realize that we are *persons* who, as such, cannot forever avoid the moral questions that are inherent in everything we do and are. The era from which we are taking leave is the one where scientists could dream of plowing their turf contentedly, untroubled by moral value questions. Such things could be left to sentimentalists, religionists, and ethical dons. This illusion of value-free science is melting. Moral questions complicated or created by our science are everywhere. As Robert Veatch, of the Hasting Institute of Society, Ethics and the Life Sciences, says: "We have begun to recognize that the value-free science is a machine running wild."[18] The ought question has returned with a vengeance. *Should* we do all the things we newly *can* do?

There are a number of areas we could turn to illustrate how moral questions burgeon forth from scientific achievement. The mastery of nuclear power, whether for destruction or for energy, presents enormous moral problems, as does the technological transformation of human society. Increasing technological control brings increasing moral responsibility. Medicine, however, is a fitting part of the scientific sphere to illustrate the insistence with which moral questions are pressing us in the contemporary moralscape, and so we will turn to it for examples.

Anthony Shaw, M.D., reports this case in the *New England Journal of Medicine:*

> Baby A was referred to me at 22 hours of age with a diagnosis of esophageal atresia and tracheoesophageal fistula. The infant, the firstborn of a professional couple in their early thirties, had obvious signs of mongolism, about which they were fully informed by the referring physician. After ex-

plaining the nature of the surgery to the distraught father, I offered him the operative consent. His pen hesitated briefly above the form and then as he signed, he muttered, 'I have no choice, do I?' He didn't seem to expect an answer, and I gave him none. The esophageal anomaly was corrected in routine fashion, and the infant was discharged to a state institution for the retarded without ever being seen again by either parent.[19]

Commenting on this case, Dr. Shaw says it was mishandled since the father should have been told that there was an alternative—not signing the consent for operation. Shaw is parting company here with some of his surgical colleagues who feel there is "no alternative to attempting to save the life of every infant, no matter what his potential."[20] However, the case is more *morally* complex than Shaw allows. There are other alternatives to be questioned.

If the parents do not believe they have the stamina to raise a seriously affected Down's child (the term "mongolism" is a medical crudity), and if they do not wish to turn the child over to the inadequacies of a state institution and so choose to let the child die, they have to face the fact that death might come to the child in a painful and ghastly way as the child slowly dehydrates and starves to death. By what reasoning is it more moral to let a child die in such torture? Strangely enough this brutal option is one that is open and used under current law.[21] If death is seen as preferable in the face of some drastic deformity (Down's syndrome is often compatible with considerable development), why is it more moral to allow a torturous death than to induce death painlessly by the administration of drugs?[22]

Other moral questions arise in these kinds of cases. Should the state have a system for finding persons who are willing to adopt genetically damaged children? Probably there are many persons, single and married, heterosexual and gay, who have the maturity required of adopting parents, who would do this. In that event, the parents could choose death only in the absence of all possible adoptive parents.

Other cases in the biomedical field: *abortion*; it is now possible to tell by a process known as amniocentesis[23] what the sex of a fetus is. By this method, the determination of sex could be made and the fetus of undesired sex could be aborted late in the second trimester. Is a late abortion justified merely by the desire for a certain sex?

Simpler methods may make it possible to choose sex by inexpensive techniques, not involving abortion, and no more complex than contraception.[24]

The moral considerations here are multiple. For one thing, this could affect male-female balance in the population. As Peter Steinfels, of the Institute of Society, Ethics and the Life Sciences, writes: "If present correlations remained the same, a United States with many more males would have lower life expectancy, fewer churchgoers, higher crime rates and more Democratic voters!"[25]

On the abortion question more generally, it would appear to be neither the best of times nor the worst of times for fetuses. On the ominous side (from the presumed perspective of the fetus) we might reflect back just to the year 1962 when Mrs. Sherri Finkbine made international headlines by flying to Sweden to have her fifth pregnancy legally ended. Abortion was illegal in the United States. She aborted because she had taken thalidomide before she knew it could cause serious deformities in a fetus. She verified after the abortion that her child would have been deformed. Afterward, she received an avalanche of hate mail and she lost her job as hostess of a TV show.

We have come a long way from Finkbine to the Supreme Court's decisions in *Roe* v. *Wade* and *Doe* v. *Bolton* where it was established that abortions during the first two trimesters are within the law. States may prohibit abortions only in the stage "subsequent to viability."[26] As H. Tristram Engelhardt, Jr., a physician and ethicist, writes in support of the Supreme Court decisions: "No one else's personal rights are intimately involved; the fetus has no personal rights."[27]

Aside from being declared a nonperson and thus being despoiled of "personal rights," the fetus is also, in these days, called "a parasite" and "a cannibal" that feeds on the mother's body.[28] One need not speculate long on how few rights a parasite or a mother-eating cannibal might be conceded. Clearly these stinging metaphors are not glad tidings for the fetal community.

On the other side, however, feverish right-to-life movements, fixated primarily on the value of prenatal life, have become a vocal citizens' lobby, pushing, among other things, for an amendment to the Constitution which would negate the effects of the Supreme Court's libertarian position. At any rate the legal situation is still unsettled, as is indicated by the conviction of a Boston physician, Dr. Kenneth C. Edelin, on February 15, 1975, and then reversed a year later in an abortion case, which came within the permissive precincts of the Supreme Court's ruling but which involved an "abortus" which apparently could have lived. As medical technology pushes the moment of viability back into the earlier stages of pregnancy, the Court's guidelines would seem to allow for infanticide—if one grants that a viable fetus can be described as a baby. Thus many hospitals on their own, chastened by the Edelin case, are turning to more conservative guidelines.

In all of this, it is unfortunate that the defense of the rights of the fetus has been taken on by ethical absolutists who deny categorically the possibility of any moral abortion. Their position, as I shall argue, is not compatible with sound ethics.

Another word that rears its head regularly on the biomedical frontier is *triage*, the process by which we attempt to decide who among many claimants will receive limited medical resources. A formidable triage problem looms with the development of the artificial heart, which may be available by the mid-1980s.[29] As many as fifty thousand people a year might benefit from such a device. That number of artificial hearts would not be available for some time. In the meantime, what criteria would be used for the moral choice of who gets the few available hearts? Since the cost would probably be near $25,000, would the hearts be reserved for the rich? Some say it should be in terms of "social worth criteria," but could we expect real justice in judging the social worth of a poor black farmer and a rich, white, and well-connected business executive? A distinguished panel, convened by the National Heart and Lung Institute, course, will not resolve all problems, since there might be many who can best benefit physically from the artificial heart. These criteria, of course, will resolve all problems, since there might be many who meet the medical specifications. The panel then favored random selection by lottery.[30] Is a lottery the best process of discernment achievable by the human mind?

Another problem coming to the fore especially in biomedicine is the problem of *who gives consent* for children and minors when it comes to operations and various medical procedures. For example, do parents who find their thirteen-year-old daughter pregnant have a right to order an abortion over the objections of the daughter? Could parents authorize the removal of a kidney from a five-year-old child for implantation in an identical twin? Can the organs of the se-

verely mentally retarded be removed for transplantation? Should
mentally retarded boys and girls be sterilized at puberty?

The question is being asked whether there is not a need for a special Bill of Rights for children and especially for handicapped children who may be too easily allotted the status of chattel.[31] The old
rubric of "parental consent" can no longer be adduced as an easy answer in making moral decisions for children. It could be used to justify unwarranted invasions of privacy and bodily integrity. It could
be a shield for conflicts of interest in which the child is the loser.
When we drop the convenient shield of parental consent, however,
we pick up innumerable moral dilemmas.

Medical experimentation is another area of moral quandaries. We
are all the beneficiaries of medical experimentation. At a certain
point, experimentation with animals can no longer help and human
subjects are needed to determine whether, and in what dosage, a particular new treatment will help. In the rush to get this information,
medical researchers, in many instances, are acting on the principle
that the end justifies the means—a principle that has no moral respectability but is widely used in every walk of life. Some of these
cases are atrocious: Cancer cells are injected into patients without
their permission; poor San Antonio women are given placebos instead of the Pill, as a result of which ten of them become pregnant;
treatment is withheld from certain syphilitic patients in a group experiment; asthmatic attacks are simulated in children to test the
effectiveness of certain treatment; at Willowbrook in Staten Island
in New York a number of mentally retarded children are given a live
hepatitis virus in an experiment, etc.[32] The obvious moral need for
consent from those experimented on has often been bypassed. The
atrocities of medical experimentation on nonconsenting subjects
should serve as a searing example of what happens when scientists ignore the moral dimension of their work.

Other moral questions confront editors of medical journals.
Should they publish the results of rather obviously immoral experiments if those results are scientifically important, or would they be
implicated in helping to legitimate the shady methods of the experi-
menters?

The flow of moral questions is relentless. Is it right to do experiments on a fetus, which is going to be aborted anyhow, to discover
the effects of certain drugs on fetal life? What if the mother
changed her mind after the experiments? Could she be legally bound
in advance of the experiment not to change her mind afterward?

Does a husband have a right to veto his wife's plans for an abortion if the abortion is in no way therapeutic, and if the wife and husband both originally intended to have the child? Does the husband have a right to consent to conception but not to termination of a pregnancy? Would an alert masculine liberation movement assert such a right and refuse to let the man be reduced to stud status, or does the bearer always outrank the inseminator in such a conflict?

Is it ever moral to control behavior by affecting the brain pharmaceutically, surgically, or electronically? Are carriers of serious genetic disorders morally bound not to reproduce? Should law reinforce this?

It is, of course, not only in medicine that science and ethics meet. Recognition of this is evinced today by the formal efforts being made to draw ethics into the custody of science. In his widely and intensely discussed book *Sociobiology: The New Synthesis*, Edward O. Wilson tries to draw all aspects of social behavior, animal and human, under the mantle of the form of science that he calls sociobiology.[33] He feels that not only ethics but also aesthetics, politics, culture, and religion need biologization and he wants to understand such things as altruistic behavior in terms of evolution and selection acting upon genes.[34] Science is also moving in on ethics imperiously in the field of ethology where efforts are made to explain moral behavior by reference to animal behavior. Thus certain behavior such as aggression or homosexuality is considered in positive moral terms because it is found as adaptive behavior in animals. There is what could be called high and low ethology regarding just how much ethically relevant continuity is postulated in moving from animals to men—high postulating more, and low, less continuity.[35]

The temptation in ethology is to a simplistic reductionism, to missing the qualitative leap involved in moving from animal to person; its value can be in its defeat of an angelism which would treat us as disincarnate minds who have shuffled off all linkage with our evolutionary forebears. In any event, ethology is another explicit contact point between ethics and science and can be seen as an effort to restore value questions to the realm of intellectually respectable inquiry.

Though efforts to reduce ethics to science must be rejected as shallow and naïve in the face of the depth and breadth of the moral phenomenon, the concern with ethics represents a move toward realism on the part of science. As Gunther S. Stent, a professor of molecular biology, writes: "Since scientists are human beings rather than Mar-

tians, since they and the phenomena they observe necessarily interact, and since they use language to communicate their results, it follows that scientific statements, particularly in biology, are rarely free
of terms which imply functions, roles, and values."[36] These "functions, roles, and values" are replete with moral significance, and this
is what scientist Stent is recognizing. Since science throughout is top-
heavy with moral value implications, science and ethics are bedfellows by unavoidable lot. They have no choice but to be introduced.

The Morality of the Dinosaurs . . .

History in our day has turned a corner.[37] We are battered by the
recurring discovery that our understanding even of basic things must
incessantly die and be born again. This is complicated by the fact
that in some parts of the planet history lags. It has not yet and may
not ever reach the same corner.

Thus we witness a bumper crop of new nations and a florid expression of nationalism in some parts of the world. Elsewhere (and there
is some overlap) the significance of the nation is receding in confusion before the onset of the modern dinosaur, the multinational corporation (MNC). The appearance of this creature creates problems
that make the problems of biomedicine look trivial. The moral problem here is, in fact, so great that most people dismiss the possibility
of morally evaluating something so mammoth and so complex. That,
of course, is part of the problem, since moral evaluation is just what
the supercorporation instinctively avoids and desperately needs. In
the absence of moral evaluation, which must eventually be enfleshed
in political action, the corporate entities will follow what some sees
as their mindless primary passion to grow for the sake of growing. As
Douglas Sturm, of Bucknell University, writes of the corporation:
"Growth is its basic orientation, continued growth without any purpose or end beyond sheer growth."[38] If this is correct, the supercorporations, in growing, will feed upon human and material resources,
and upon each other, with no intrinsic concern for such moral and
human needs as justice or peace. The needs of justice and peace may
at times be in conflict with the needs of growth.

It has been suggested that by 1980 three hundred supercorporations will control 75 per cent of the world's manufacturing assets.[39]
It will be difficult for any nation, new or old, to escape the influence

of these superpowers who will, if present trends continue, change and dominate the quality of our existence. They will do this without our consent and with relative immunity to constraint. If man, "the valuing animal," is not valuing here, he will be party to a catastrophic default.

Power, even corporate power, is not per se good or evil. But it will be good only if it is ensouled with the distinctively humanizing qualities of wisdom, reason, and meaningful directedness. The power of the supercorporation must be made *sapiens* or it will be good only by accident, and that, given the dimensions of that power, is not enough.

The formidable thing about morality is that it allows for no neutral ground in deliberate human affairs. Pure goodness or pure evil are, of course, metaphysical abstractions, and moral goodness and evil always exist in mixed proportions where life is lived.[40] Nevertheless, it remains true that morality is a dimension of human existence whether that existence is in private, interpersonal, or corporate form.

Corporations, like individuals, do not have moral immunity. However, judging these entities is fantastically more complex—as corporations are more complex than individuals. With that obvious fact in view, it remains true that corporations *can* be described in terms of morality or immorality. What they achieve is in many ways geared toward what humans call good (i.e., what humanizes) or evil (i.e., what dehumanizes). They are not neutral. They cannot be hidden from moral scrutiny. They are lively and influential agents which operate in morally describable terms within the human community. It is a lethal illusion to treat them as existing in a moral vacuum because of their enormity, as though morality could be sequestered and consigned to the simpler matters of private life.

Moral evaluation has begun. The specifically moral dimensions are emerging. On the negative side of the emerging debate, moral consciousness, especially in the United States, is being shocked by the realization that the supercorporation is not a democracy. Its governmental models are normally feudal and dictatorial. Romantic, democratic thought patterns would fain see employees, stockholders, and consumers as citizens. They are not. As one professor of business administration puts it, the structure of the corporation "tends to disregard human beings and to treat them as inventories of machined parts on a shelf, to be used only as the computer commands."[41] As the corporation grows, it laughs at yesterday's toylike legal weapons against monopoly and the suppression of competitive free enterprise. Of the American business scene, with all of its avowed devotion to free competition, it is now said that "only a small segment remains in any sense competitive free enterprise."[42] Through price fixing and the calculated limitation of production to raise prices and profits, the corporation achieves taxation without representation.[43] Corporations have no discernible center of loyalty. What obtains is what Professor Capitman, of Florida International University in Miami, calls "multinational colonialism."[44] The MNC treats all nations, including the mother country, as colonies. Financial depression will be encouraged in one country, even the mother country, if this condition maximizes over-all profits and enhances growth.

The MNC does not usually challenge capitalist governmental systems. It need not. It is strong enough to subvert, co-opt, and indenture governmental agencies and to sell the idea that what is good for the corporation is good for the nations that host it. If (as in Chile) a socialist government is elected, the offended MNC will work to subvert it (as did ITT). Thus, the MNC, which is more powerful than most nation-states, has a foreign policy, or, if you will, a colonial policy, but has no politically legitimated constitution or parliament.

Because it has the power to profoundly affect the unalienable rights to life, liberty, and the pursuit of happiness of many, the MNC is a kind of government but it is not one which, in the words of the Declaration of Independence, derives its "just powers from the consent of the governed."

Contemporary criticism sees the MNC, again in the words of the Declaration, as guilty of "a long train of abuses and usurpations." Affected peoples will have to ask themselves one of the largest moral questions of our day. Is it "their right," is it "their duty, to throw off such Government, and to provide new Guards for their future security?"

Using the moral idealism of the American Revolution, writer William O'Toole underscores the irony of American corporations effectually declaring their independence of the mother country. Taking aim at the oil MNCs, he writes in part:

We, the Largest Oil Companies in the United States . . .
in order to form a more perfect Cartel, establish Oil prices,
insure domestic shortages. . . .
When in the Course of selling Energy it becomes Neces-

sary for a Cartel to dissolve the Political Bonds which have connected them to their Government and to assume among the Powers of the Earth, the separate and equal Station to which the Laws of Nature and of Nature's Oil entitles them . . . etc.[45]

The crux of the criticism is that the supercorporations are successfully superseding the structures of justice that men developed within the framework of the nation-state. The result is a power that is unrestrained by law or conscience. By classical definition, such power is tyranny.

If all of this criticism is true, are we not in the presence, at last, of something on the moralscape that is ethically simple? *How* the MNCs should be reduced presents problems, but *whether* they should be moved on seems to be ethically clear. Nothing is quite so evident, however, in modern ethics. The MNCs do not lack defenders. They are "the most constructive force in the world economy," says J. Stanford Smith, chairman of International Paper.[46] (Of course, Mr. Smith may be perceived as a biased witness.) George Ball, former Undersecretary of State with a reputation for independent judgment, says : "It is not accidental that the peoples of the West have largely left the acquisition and transformation of raw materials to the masters of commerce, for they alone have possessed the incentive and flexibility to discover and develop these resources quickly and efficiently."[47]

Ball sees the solution of conflicts among MNCs and nations as solvable, not by the destruction of the MNCs, but by the creation of supernational authority. In other words, solve the conflict, not by dismantling one of the litigants, but by moving to superior forms of governance through the recognition of international common interest. What seems commendable in this view is that the genuine problems presented by the growth of the MNCs could lead to a qualitative improvement in the international picture due to the perception of new and permanent supernational needs.

Those who agree with Arnold Toybee that nationalism is a luxury that cannot be afforded in the atomic age[48] should, perhaps, applaud the creative possibilities of the MNC epoch. Some of the complaints against the MNC only serve to add force to this. It is lamented that the MNC ships jobs overseas. So it does. A legitimate question is "So what?" Although well outside the intentions of the MNC, a benign effect may be appearing here which is moving jobs, skills, and economic growth possibilities from the wealth-glutted industrial nations to the economic late starters in the family of nations. The pursuit of greed in this case may have accidentally opened a new avenue of distributive justice. Of course, greed, whatever good process it may unwittingly precipitate, cannot govern the equitable unfolding of that process. Mind and moral sensitivity, if they can find expression in international politics, must supervene. Still, from this more positive viewpoint, the MNC is an opportunity, not a nemesis; or, at the least, it is a nemesis which may, by the alchemy of human creativity, be proved opportune.

The debate on the MNCs will continue at every level of expertise and discourse. If the omnipresent moral dimensions are not recognized and explored in these debates, the debate will be left in the hands of mental mechanics, those who function skimmingly at the surface level of human knowing experience, where computers do better than men, where accumulation and superficial connections are preferred to penetration and depth, and where good and bad value assumptions work like busy invisible hands without the benefit of test or intelligent direction. This kind of cerebral friction will easily be taken for knowledge wherever serious ethical inquiry is in disrepute.

Though the MNCs are the largest problem on the business side of the moralscape, they do not have a monopoly on moral questions. All businesses large and small have to face the question whether their operating respect for the moral dimension of all human life is adequate, if they are concerned only to avoid blatant violations of accepted moral norms. It is observably true that businesses are more interested in doing well than in doing good. More cynically it could be said that businesses are interested in doing well while not getting caught doing evil. However, is it enough to avoid price fixing and the repression of genuine competition, false advertising, the rapacious engulfing of small businesses, racist and sexist discrimination, the shipping of oil in defective vessels, kickbacks, etc.? Is this kind of minimalism (which is itself regularly breached) an adequate basis for the building of a humane society? Can business only contribute to the common weal by avoiding statutorily forbidden harm? Does business power have any positive obligations to the common weal? Is it hopelessly idealistic to think that business could be a force for creative moral influence in the national and international human community? If this is hopelessly idealistic, if business can only follow its dominant principles of profit and growth, is there any practical alternative to greater governmental control so that the need of the common good can be met? In no sense is the business suite a moral vacuum. Moral questions face the businessman at every step. He cannot ignore them and then wonder why a more value-conscious age has ever lower regard for the business community.

Labor is also a highly charged moral area in business ethics. It is fair to ask whether labor functions as a competing corporation with its own fat hierarchy monistically geared to the pursuit of its own growth. Can labor proceed in its demands as though it were absolved of the foundational human requirement of sensitivity to the common good?

All of these issues have moral dimensions. When the moral dimension of any behavioral matter is ignored, dehumanizing results will in some way ensue. The meeting of business and ethics is not just an edifying ideal. It is, humanly speaking, indispensable.

Politics vs. Morality . . .

The politician Count Cavour of Italy once said that if he and his political colleagues were to do for themselves what they do for Italy, they would be jailed as rogues and scoundrels. There is a perennial dilemma surrounding the relationship of good politics and good morals. As Reinhold Niebuhr saw it:

> Politics will, to the end of history, be an area where conscience and power meet, where the ethical and coercive factors of human life will interpenetrate and work out their tenative and uneasy compromises.[49]

The fact is that it is necessary and moral to do things in politics that would be unjustifiable in the circumstances of private life. In the political sphere, war might have to be waged, punishment inflicted, personal freedoms limited, properties appropriated by way of eminent domain, etc. The political order has exigencies and complexities that have no part in private life. Thus, moral behavior there will be correspondingly more difficult to judge.

The problem is that because it is more difficult, the moral dimension tends to be dropped. As a result, politics often gets done without conscience. Moral values get relegated to "questions of last resort," as Arthur M. Schlesinger, Jr., writes in his revealingly entitled article "The Necessary Amorality of Foreign Affairs."[50] Outside of last-resort matters, then, it appears that one enters a moral free

zone where conscience can be dropped before entering. It is unfortunately within that supposed moral free zone—and not just in rare
"questions of last resort"—that decisions are made about who shall
live and who shall die, about who shall remain malnourished, and
who well fed. Since these issues are intrinsically moral in their
significance, it is malignant to caricature morality as irrelevant to the
normal business where such decisions are made. The tendency to
create this moral vacuum is the prime problem confronting political
ethics. This illustrates again that errors in ethics are not just unfortunate but often lethal.

There are other errors operating in politics. The concept of power
is basic to politics, and, by tendency, it is thought of in unimaginatively narrow ways. Lyndon Johnson illustrated this when he complained that he had more power than any man in history but that he
could not use it. He could only have been thinking of kill-power. But
kill-power is only part of the power of a nation. It is not the power
that comes out of the barrel of a gun that makes people willing to
die in what they deem a just war of revolution. Heroes are not heroes
because they are afraid of being shot. Other powers touch them, for
life is larger than fear, and so is power. Interpreting power in this
narrow way is politically and morally pernicious. Strategic thinking
that is unmoved by the moral dimension of its subject will miss this.

General Omar Bradley, Chief of Staff of the United States Army,
was alluding to all of this when he said in Boston on November 10,
1948:

> We have grasped the mystery of the atom and rejected the
> Sermon on the Mount. . . . Ours is a world of nuclear gi-
> ants and ethical infants. We know more about war than we
> know about peace, more about killing than we know about
> living.[51]

Politics abounds with other questions for moral discernment. On
the one hand it can be asked: Should civil disobedience be
punished? If history proves nothing, it proves that nations and the
majorities in them can err tragically. Nations are fallible. Consensus
is often a defective form of "group think."[52] Corrective dissent
would seem to be a constant need and a positive service which
should be institutionalized—not punished. Or is it that loyalty to established policy is the only thing that works and that this is the wisdom of traditional patriotism? But then what of the Nuremberg
trials and the patriotic, loyal men condemned there?

Are there political and moral problems involved in reverently freezing our governmental structures in their present constitutional form? The founding fathers considered a plural executive as an alternative to a single President. They rejected it as unsuited to their contemporary needs. Is it unsuited to ours?

Does the Nixon experience not illustrate a need to improve our structures? Contrary to the euphoric judgments that predominated at the time, the resignation of Nixon et al. did not prove the system worked. It only proved that a President who tapes discussions of his felonies and keeps the tapes will be detected in virtue of the tapes, not in virtue of the system.

Does the traditional ethics of truth-telling serve political ethics? Could successful diplomats, chiefs of state, or press secretaries always tell the truth as they know it? If a lie is, as I submit, the denial of truth to someone who has a right to it, is it always a lie to deceive? Could there be *moral* deceptions?

Part of the role of ethics is to question the unquestioned, to press the experts to check the ossified constructs and ideas with which we have bound ourselves. Habit can easily replace reflection and penetration. The process of humanization is deterred by this and ethics is the art-science which addresses the meaning of humanization. The power that operates in politics is in constant need of moral critique. If such critique is absent, self-serving interests will achieve their own kind of tyranny and the common good is victimized.

Questions that are important in private morality are more important in politics, because there is so much more power there. Bringing moral values to bear on the uses of power is the soul of the civilizing process and the goal of ethics.

It would be good to say in the face of the consternating problems illustratively listed in this chapter that ethical reflection is on the brink of a great renaissance. But let us, instead, be realistic. The prospects are mixed at best, and it is to the assessments of those prospects that we now attend.

NOTES—CHAPTER ONE

1. The source of this quotation is the Reverend Dr. Lyman P. Powell, who is quoted extensively in *Literary Digest* 103 (Nov. 23, 1929), pp. 23–24. The fragment cited is not identified and its authenticity

may be benignly doubted. The context of Dr. Powell's remarks is a stirring paeon of praise for New York City. Writes the doctor: "New York through its countless organizations, here financed and here directed, helps the entire world to peace and health, to love and happiness" (p. 24).

2. Karl Menninger, *Whatever Became of Sin?* (New York: Hawthorn Books, Inc., 1973), p. 671.

3. R. L. Bruckberger, *God and Politics* (Chicago: J. Philip O'Hara, Inc., 1972), p. 33.

4. Japan, of course, was not static during its two centuries of enclosure. Buddhism was losing its hold, and a secularization process of sorts was under way involving *Bushido*, "the way of the warrior," which gave a moral code in nonreligious form. Western ideas also managed to trickle in. See R. R. Palmer, *A History of the Modern World*, 2nd ed., revised with collaboration of Joel Colton (New York: Alfred A. Knopf, 1960), pp. 548–54. Similarly, the moral steadiness of the United States up to the 1950s could, upon analysis, be seen to have many cracks which readied it for the shifts of the 1960s.

5. Arthur Schopenhauer, *The Basis of Morality*, 2nd ed. (London: George Allen & Unwin, Ltd., 1915), p. 6.

6. No one book can address all of these issues with the fullness that they require. This book on method will not attempt to do so. I do plan in future books to apply my method to some of these problems in depth. Though I will use many illustrations to relieve the abstractness and keep my method honest, I am herein concerned to explain the method and theory of ethics.

7. "He is an immoral man" would carry a different load of connotation. Since in the vicious mythology from which we are slowly extricating ourselves, woman is identified with her genital sexuality and related functions, her "morality" is similarly confined. The male is allotted a broader scope as person according to the myths, and so his immorality, though possibly sexual, could be other things. Still even in the male culture, sexuality would certainly be included in the possibilities, whereas innumerable moral matters of great import would not be considered.

8. Albert Ellis, *The American Sexual Tragedy* (New York: Lyle Stuart, 1962), p. 94. He goes on to say that if the person only wants that kind of sex, we could say he is fixated, neurotic, or abnormal "psychologically speaking."

9. May Edel and Abraham Edel, *Anthropology and Ethics* (Springfield, Ill.: Charles C. Thomas, 1959), p. 81.

10. Reported in the Milwaukee *Journal*, Apr. 26, 1974.

11. Will McBride and Helga Fleischhauer-Hardt, *Show Me: A Picture Book of Sex for Children and Parents* (New York: St. Martin, 1975).
12. See John T. Noonan, Jr., *Contraception: A History of Its Treatment by the Catholic Theologians and Canonists* (Cambridge, Mass.: Harvard University Press, 1956), on intercourse during pregnancy, pp. 47, 77, 79, 80, 85, 203; on the man on top, pp. 238-39. On masturbation, see ibid., passim, and see E. H. Hare, "Masturbatory Insanity: The History of an Idea," *Journal of Mental Science* 108 (Jan. 1962), pp. 1-25.
13. Morton Hunt, *Sexual Behavior in the 1970's* (Chicago: Playboy Press, 1974), p. 150.
14. Eleanor Garst, "The A-Sexual Society," *Center Diary* 15 (Nov.–Dec. 1966), p. 43.
15. Nena O'Neill and George O'Neill, *Open Marriage: A New Life Style for Couples* (New York: M. Evans, 1972); Anna K. Francoeur and Robert T. Francoeur, *Hot and Cool Sex* (New York and London: Harcourt Brace Jovanovich, 1974).
16. Corliss Lamont, "How to be Happy—Though Married," *Humanist* 33, No. 3 (May–June 1973), p. 16.
17. *Ethics in Medical Progress* (Ciba Foundation Symposium), edited by G. E. W. Wolstenholme and Maeve O'Connor (Boston: Little, Brown & Co., 1966), p. 134. The quotation is from J. Rostand, *Pensées d'un Biologiste* (Paris: Stock, 1939).
18. Robert M. Veatch, "Does Ethics Have an Empirical Basis?" *Hastings Center Studies* 1, No. 1 (1973), p. 51.
19. Reported by Anthony Shaw, M.D., "Dilemmas of 'Informed Consent' in Children," *New England Journal of Medicine* 289 (1973), p. 885.
20. Ibid., p. 886.
21. The court, of course, could step in as it has in cases of Jehovah's Witnesses and not permit them to permit death. See *People* v. *Labrenz*, 411 Ill. 613, 104 N.E. 2d 769 (1952) where the court appointed a guardian for an eight-year-old child to effect lifesaving blood transfusions.
22. This procedure, of course, is illegal now in the United States. This raises the further moral question of taking the risk of legal recrimination in the hopes of legalizing the moral right to impose death in certain cases. It seems likely that the moral right to mercy death in certain cases can only be won in court, not in legislatures. It could be argued as an extension of the right to privacy as it emerged in the U. S. Supreme Court in *Roe* v. *Wade*, 410 U.S. 113 (1973). For a lower court nod in this direction, see Yetter, Alleged Incompetent,

41 Northampton, Pa. 67, 24 Fiduc Rep. 1 (1973). Not argued yet to my knowledge, but arguable, is the First Amendment right to mercy death on grounds of religious freedom. If one's moral openness to mercy death is in a substantial way a derivative of one's religious convictions, a First Amendment case could be made.

23. Amniocentesis involves taking a sample of amniotic fluid at around the fifteenth or sixteenth week of gestation. This is followed by two to three weeks of tissue culture. Not only sex but a variety of genetic disorders can be discovered by this method.

24. For ethical comment on this problem, see Marc Lappé and Peter Steinfels, "Choosing the Sex of Our Children," Hastings Center Report 4 (Feb. 1974), pp. 1–4.

25. Ibid., p. 3.

26. Roe v. Wade, 93 S. CT. 705, and Doe v. Bolton, 93 S. CT. 739 (1973).

27. H. Tristram Engelhardt, Jr., "The Ontology of Abortion," Ethics 84, No. 4 (Apr. 1974).

28. Rachel Conrad Wahlberg, "The Woman and the Fetus: 'One Flesh'?" New Theology 10, edited by Martin E. Marty and Dean G. Peerman (New York: Macmillan Co., 1973), pp. 130–39.

29. See Albert R. Jonsen, "The Totally Implantable Artificial Heart," Hastings Center Report 3 (Nov. 1973), pp. 1–4.

30. Ibid., p. 3.

31. For an example of a Bill of Rights for specially afflicted children, see Allen C. Crocker, M.D., "Present Status of Treatment of the Mucopolysaccharidoses," Clinical Cytogenetics and Genetics 10, No. 8 (1974), pp. 113–24. The style of Crocker's Rights is influenced by the formal declaration of rights for all mentally retarded persons, established by the International League of Societies for the Mentally Handicapped, October 24, 1948. Crocker is an example of the physician-scientist par excellence. He combines scientific skill with moral wisdom.

32. See Sissela Bok, "The Ethics of Giving Placebos," Scientific American 231, No. 5 (Nov. 1974), pp. 17–23; Robert M. Veatch and Sharmon Sollitto, "Human Experimentation—The Ethical Questions Persist," Hastings Center Report 3, No. 3 (June 1973), pp. 1–3. Veatch and Sollitto list cases of questionable experimentation which have been published in reputable medical journals or professional proceedings since 1966. They note that fewer than 25 per cent of the studies in their file claim that consent was obtained and none documented how the information was given to the subject to get consent. In E. Shils, N. St. John-Stevas, P. Ramsey, P. B. Medawar, H. K. Beecher, and A. Kaplan, Life or Death: Ethics and Options (Seattle and London: University of Washington Press, 1968), Dr.

Beecher lists a number of investigatory abuses. See also Richard M. Restak, *Premeditated Man: Bioethics and the Control of Future Human Life* (New York: Viking Press, 1975).

33. Edward O. Wilson, *Sociobiology: The New Synthesis* (Cambridge, Mass.: Harvard University Press, 1975).

34. For a report on the active response to Wilson's book, see Arthur Caplan, "Ethics, Evolution, and the Milk of Human Kindness," *Hastings Center Report* 6, No. 2 (Apr. 1976), pp. 20–25.

35. See Irenäus Eibl-Eibesfeldt, *Love and Hate: The Natural History of Behavior Patterns* (New York: Holt, Rinehart & Winston, 1970); Konrad Lorenz, *On Aggression* (New York: Harcourt, Brace & World, 1966); Desmond Morris, *The Naked Ape* (New York: McGraw Hill Book Co., 1967); Richard P. Michael, "Bisexuality and Ethics," in F. J. Ebling, ed., *Biology and Ethics* (London: Academic Press, 1969), pp. 67–72.

36. Gunther S. Stent, "The Poverty of Scientism and the Promise of Structuralist Ethics," *Hastings Center Report* 6, No. 6 (Dec. 1976), p. 33.

37. I am indebted for this term to my brother, Captain Connell J. Maguire, U.S.N. In his position as a Catholic chaplain in the United States Navy, he has been able to observe, from within, two redirectionings in the historical process.

38. Douglas Sturm, "Corporations, Constitutions, and Covenants: On Forms of Human Relation and the Problem of Legitimacy," *Journal of the American Academy of Religion* 41, No. 3 (Sept. 1973), p. 334. For a strong moral indictment of the operations of the MNCs, see Richard J. Barnet and Ronald E. Müller, *Global Reach* (New York: Simon & Schuster, 1974).

39. Sturm, "Corporations, Constitutions, and Covenants," p. 337.

40. I am not denying that metaphysical thought is part of human living, nor am I besmirching the legitimacy and inevitability of· metaphysics. I am merely saying that what can be metaphysically detached for intellectual examination may not be, as such, realizable in the concrete order. It is a fatal and common error to mistake our abstractions for concrete existents.

41. William G. Capitman, "Corporation Logic," *Center Magazine* 8, No. 3 (May–June 1975), p. 27.

42. Ibid., p. 26.

43. By limiting production to increase profits, the corporation also forces people onto government relief rolls, thus transferring the financial burden for these victims onto the taxpayer. Again, taxation without representation.

44. Capitman, "Corporation Logic," p. 26.

45. William O'Toole, "We the largest oil companies . . . ," *National Catholic Reporter* 11, No. 34 (July 4, 1975), p. 7.
46. Quoted by Robert W. Dietsch, "The One World of Multinationals," *New Republic* 171, No. 24 (Dec. 14, 1974), p. 8.
47. Ibid.
48. "The nationalism that, in the Atomic Age, is threatening to lead mankind to self-destruction is the Sumerian nationalism of the third millennium b.c., intensified and reproduced on a world-wide scale." Arnold J. Toynbee, *Change and Habit* (New York and London: Oxford University Press, 1966), p. 108. Responding creatively to the MNC crisis could fit into what Toynbee calls the "unifying movements in history." See ibid., pp. 54–87.
49. Reinhold Niebuhr, *Moral Man and Immoral Society: A Study in Ethics and Politics* (New York: Charles Scribner's Sons, 1932; renewal copyright, 1960), p. 4.
50. Arthur Schlesinger, Jr., "The Necessary Amorality of Foreign Affairs," *Harper's* 243, No. 1455 (Aug. 1971), p. 71. Schlesinger is said not to have chosen this title for his article, but he has no grounds for complaint. It expresses what he says in the article where he confuses moralism (the abstract, data-shy use of moral principles and ideals) with morality. The result is gross and unworthy of this usually wise writer.
51. Quoted in "Talk of the Town," *New Yorker* 9 (June 3, 1974), p. 28.
52. See Irving L. Janis, "Groupthink," *Psychology Today* 5, No. 6 (Nov. 1971), pp. 43–46, 74–76. For a fuller discussion, see Irving L. Janis, *Victims of Groupthink* (Boston: Houghton Mifflin Co., 1972).

CHAPTER TWO

ETHICS IN A CLIMATE OF NEGATION

The shadow of a weird, convulsive movement is discernible today in Western culture and is quite visible in the United States. In its negative, suicidal aspects, it is a block against ethical reflection, which is a work of hope. But in its positive implications, it may be clearing the decks for a new growth of moral consciousness.

The movement, known as Dada, came into being in Zurich in 1915 and eventually exported its people, "art," and outbursts to wherever an audience could be attacked. The name Dada is French baby talk for anything to do with horses, and like the movement, the name had no direct positive significance. Dada was in its outward form a nihilistic protest against everything. According to a Dada manifesto, its "position" was this:

> No more painters, no more writers, no more musicians, no more sculptors, no more religions, no more republicans, no more royalists, no more imperialists, no more anarchists, no more socialists, no more Bolsheviks, no more politicians, no more proletarians, no more democrats, no more armies, no more police, no more nations, no more of these idiocies, no more, no more, NOTHING, NOTHING, NOTHING.[1]

Dadaists adopted Mikhail Bakunin's slogan: "Destruction is also Creation!" "Suicide is a vocation," said one of their heroes, Jacques Rigaut. He did die that way as did many in the movement. Suicide was, in fact, the "logic" of the movement. Only negation made sense. All visible reality was a lie to be mocked with every force of macabre imagination.

The realm of art was of interest to the Dadaists, inasmuch as it was an avenue for the expression of destructiveness and contempt. They used actual rubbish and junk to make "art works" and pictures. Dadaist Arthur Cravan, described by A. Alvarez as "poet, art critic, and specialist in insult," was invited to lecture at the Exhibition of Independent Painters in New York in 1917.[2] He appeared drunk and proceeded to belch and swear at his audience. The address was concluded by the police when Cravan began to strip. Another Dadaist in attendance, Marcel Duchamp, remarked: "What a wonderful lecture!" Duchamp's own offering to the exhibition was a signed urinal. Among his other achievements was a Mona Lisa with a mustache. Other of his colleagues would paint trash or pictures of absurd machines that had no imaginable purpose, or they would sit around reciting nonsense poems to the deafening beat of a tom-tom. Some just drugged themselves to death.[8]

It is, of course, difficult for any movement to be purely negative. Even in Dada there were positive strands of hope in some of its protest which would later find expression in more positive forms of criticism of the reigning decadence. Much that Dada protested against was life-inhibiting, and therefore its protest was life-affirming. It is tragic that its prevailing shift was toward death and that it bore the painful suicidal mark of despair. For, in a certain way, Dada was a wild prophetic dance filled with symbolism. Did not Isaiah, the Hebrew prophet, walk around naked and barefoot for three years to make his point! (Dadaists would have cheered!)[4]

Dada was targeted on the sham and vacuousness of its contemporary society. It was saying, to use a major and forceful idiom of our day, "Bullshit" to the intellectual and artistic divinities of its day. It was an indecorous but needed call for catharsis. It was a spasmodic, disordered response to the perennial need of every society to be called back from its respectable deceptions to honesty—to be told who is and who really is not wearing clothes.

Dada was outrageous, but it may, prophet-style, have recognized that only outrage speaks to outrage. When outrageous fraudulencies wear the mantle of respectability in the academic, political, and artistic power centers, outrage might be in order.

It has been suggested that Dadaism died in 1929 with the suicide of Jacques Rigaut. Truer, it would seem, is the view of Georges Hugnet, a historian of Dada, who contended that Dada is "ageless."[5] Dada is, I would agree, a permanent type of human response, both in its positive and in its negative implications. It will, of course, not always appear in the salient caricature of Zurich's Cabaret Voltaire where it first emerged, but it is, I believe, a persistent presence.

Despair and Fear in American Dada . . .

At a superficial level, the signs of an American Dada are around us. We have seen empty Campbell soup cans painted or mounted in collage and we too have witnessed toilet art. We have Warhol, Polanski, and an assortment of last tangos on screen and canvas with bottoms bared to any value that anyone out there might esteem. But beyond the tin cans and urinals and the scatological epithets and imagery, we should be on guard for the deeper meanings of the Dada that is with us.

We should expect that contemporary Dada would be different from the Dada of Zurich, and it is. On the promising side, contemporary America has been tempered by some benign non-Dada influences and events: It has been touched by a long surge of idealism, by naïve but ebullient hopes for a "greening of America" which will come about in spite of the havoc wreaked on the spirit in our concrete wilderness. We have also shared in the advantages of being schooled in the specifics of justice by a growingly articulate "third world." The peace movement, the civil rights movement, and women's liberation have shown imaginative and powerful alternatives to the gyrations and confusions of Dada. All to the good, but not sufficiently to the good to exorcise entirely the negative demon of Dada. This demon is despair and fear, and a specifically American despair is now a reality. It is a reality that commands our attention because it conditions and shapes our thought. It looms as an enormous obstacle to the ethical enterprise. Reflection takes place in a context, and is influenced by that context whether those reflecting know it or not. Our context is embroiled by feelings of despair, loss, disenchantment, and fear. There are already copious signs of the toll being taken on our thought processes by these Dadaist poisons. It is unrealistic to ignore them. The most naïve of thinkers is he who will not check the contextual soil in which his thoughts are planted.

Despair is an unlikely American condition. It seems like a bad joke to impute it to us. Is not hope truly native American? Who could be more hopeful than this vibrant people who accosted and conquered the wilderness! So it would seem—but deeper than such seeming is what the existentialist philospher Gabriel Marcel writes of hope. Marcel, not speaking specifically of American society, notes the contrast between the "optimism of technical progress" and the "philosophy of despair which seems inevitably to emerge from it."[6] The reason why technical progress does not issue into hope, Marcel says, is the "metaphysical problem of pride-*hubris*" which was perceived by the ancients but has been all but ignored by modern philosophers.[7] Pride "consists in drawing one's strength solely from oneself." Hope, however, is "the will when it is made to bear on what does not depend on itself . . . the only genuine hope is hope in what does not depend on ourselves. . . ."[8]

The crisis of technological society, steeped as it is in impressive achievements, is that there is an ever-widening gap between vaulting technical intelligence on the one hand and human fragility and precariousness on the other. This precariousness has not been successfully routed by pretentious technological man, and he stands in terrible risk of despair when this fact breaks through his naïve belief that he has reality under his control.

Hope in what does not depend on ourselves is not part of the American story. The admission of limit is an un-American activity. But now limit reaches us and the *hubris* of a boyishly expanding "manifest destiny" is at an end. The news is that self-sufficient independence is a notion fit only for the archives; suddenly the end is in sight of our traditional energy resources; we have lost a war to a little nation; the dollar has paled; the governmental system sputters and putters; the melting pot does not melt citizens into predictable pawns; and, of all things, a sense of powerlessness becomes a new fact of American life. Arthur M. Schlesinger, Jr., writes:

> No social emotion . . . is more vital in America today than a sense of personal helplessness, uselessness and impotence. . . . everyone more or less has the sense of existing in the shadow of vast uncontrollable structures, impervious to human desire or need.[9]

As Rollo May says, "One age is dead and the other not yet born. . . ."[10] What that does is put us between spoiled optimism and hope. There is no alternative to learning how to depend, but we are dull students. Dada is therefore at the door. Understanding our incapacity for genuine hope may be more basic than anything else for an understanding of the contemporary American moralscape.

Let us move further into the phenomenon of despair. The feeling of despair, in individuals and in nations, is linked to a loss of self-respect and to the crippling emotion of fear. Both of these are present in today's America. They are also part of the cognitive context in which ethical reflection unfolds. This has been for us an image-shattering time. With a dreadful rush, our innocence is gone and our "good name" has been undermined. Given the egregiously high regard we had for ourselves in the past, this is an unsettling blow. A couple of examples will illustrate the traditionally naïve gall of America, the self-righteous.

We can recall President Wilson explaining why America need not go to war: "There is such a thing as a nation being so right that it does not need to convince others by force that it is right."[11] (We used force shortly thereafter.) And then there was preacher Nathaniel W. Taylor who declared in the Chapel of Yale College in 1828 to an audience that did not demur that this nation was the one "on which the Sun of Righteousness sheds his clearest, brightest day. . . ."[12] In the middle of the last century, George S. Philips, a Methodist preacher from Ohio, wrote that God had promised to found a nation fully complying with his will and that he had fulfilled that promise by establishing the United States. As he put it, with unmatchable chauvinism, ". . . the Government of the United States was set up by the God of Heaven."[13]

Most of our history has been marked by a most fervid self-esteem. This naïveté can no longer be maintained, and this adds to the darkness of the American psyche at this time. Now Americans suddenly find themselves remembering the comment of D. H. Lawrence after a visit to America: "The essential American soul is hard, isolated, stoic and a killer."[14] We may or may not be all of that, or only that, but we are clearly not a people confirmed in virtue. America has been bludgeoned by recent experience into some realization of its corruption and hardness of soul. To nations more conscious of their sins, the American loss of innocence must be welcome and wryly amusing. And indeed, such disenchantment is a necessary precondition for moral-cultural development. But it is also at this time a force for demoralization. False innocence is not lost without a price. With a nation (as with a young man or woman who identified virtue with virginity) the loss of innocence can lead to anomie and moral fecklessness, or, if you will, Dada. It could also, however, be a stimulus to ethical reflectiveness. Again, our thought processes are not immune to these cultural-emotional shifts, in their negative and positive implications.

Fear, too, is part of the negative emotional freight of contemporary Dada. Thomas Aquinas taught that only one to whom nothing or no one is superior is beyond fear.[15] The United States has, at times, been able to bask in the fear-free illusion of superiority. This indulgence also is now behind us. Our very prosperity has become a cause of fear. The geographical isolation of this country and its natural bounty allowed it to grow fat in relative peace. But now, others are watching us eat. Our alimentary processes are an international issue. The world food problem and the shrinkage of the planet brought about by communications and mobility have put us on the spot.

Daniel Shaughnessy in *War on Hunger* shows graphically the grounds for our nervousness. To help us visualize the billions of people who are watching us but who do not share our prosperity, he scales the world population down to a village of 1,000 people. Of these, 700 are nonwhite, 570 are Asian, 100 African, 50 South American, and only 60 are the United States. Five hundred of the villagers are chronically hungry, and half of these are suffering debilitating malnutrition. Eight hundred live in shacks or mud huts less commodious than those provided for animals in the United States. The 60 United States people receive half the total village income, use 30 per cent of the village's energy, and have obesity as a major health problem.[16]

In a similar vein, Robert Heilbroner writes in his pessimistic book *An Inquiry into the Human Prospect:* "Even the most corrupt governments of the underdeveloped world are aware of the ghastly resemblance of the world's present ecomomic condition to an immense train, in which a few passengers, mainly in the advanced capitalist world, ride in first-class coaches, in conditions of comfort unimaginable to the enormously greater numbers crammed into the cattle cars that make up the bulk of the train's carriages."[17]

The unnerving question is: Can we expect the hungry to observe all this and then shrug and die without a fuss? Can we be sure that cartels just like the oil cartel will not appear and then align themselves with other cartels to squeeze our multiple supply lines? One important reason why we are the rich few is that we have been able to buy natural resources cheaply from the poor and then manufacture them into goods which can be sold at high cost, even to the poor suppliers.

Violence might occur to these people as preferable to dying compliantly. Biological weapons have now been devised that could be developed by poor nations that cannot develop a nuclear striking force. The logic of détente, deterrence, and the balance of terror would be inappropriate in ensuing conflicts, since the desperate have nothing to lose.[18] Even if it did apply because these nations or groups used threat to force negotiations, the strategic picture would lack the clubby atmosphere of, for example, Strategic Arms Limitations Talks with the Soviets. And how many emergency "hot lines" could one White House have with angry poor nations and guerrilla groups who are armed with biological weapons? We might long for the good old halcyon days of the cold war with the more diplomatically astute and predictable Russians and Chinese.

Some have had the intestinal fortitude not to yield to fear in this situation. Garrett Hardin, a professor of human ecology at the University of California, argues manfully for the deliberate abandonment of the poor countries. *"Every life saved this year in a poor country diminishes the quality of life for subsequent generations,"* he says.[19] Were there an effective world government to control population and supplies, things would be different. But in the unfortunate absence of such, the hungry cannot look to us for food. He quotes approvingly the comment: "Cancerous growths demand food, but as far as I know, they have never been cured by getting it."[20]

Hardin's feisty aplomb, however, is not the spirit of contemporary America. Fear is.[21] Maybe it is American practicality, if not American idealism, that attunes people to the question of columnist and popular writer Jim Bishop:

> And what, may I ask, will happen if we are the last land able to feed itself? Will we live in a world of Americans only? Nonsense. Long before that day the starving of the world will come to take it from us. In a few years, three of every five faces in the world will be Oriental. Who knows? They may be the locusts of tomorrow.[22]

The thought seems not to have occurred to Bishop that we may be the locusts of today. The point, however, is fear, and he illustrates it.

Contemporary fear is accentuated by the spread of materials and technology for making nuclear and other weapons, by apocalyptic reports on creeping drought conditions and the shortening of the growing season due to cooling climatic trends.[23] Heilbroner compares our present state to that of the collapsing Roman Empire. "Certain analogues and correspondences are obvious. Then, as now, we find order giving way to disorder; self-confidence to self-doubt; moral certitude to moral disquiet. There are resemblances in the breakdowns of cumbersome economic systems, in the intransigence of privileged minorities."[24]

Our splendid and plentiful isolation is threatened, and the American psyche can only hide from this for a while. Then fear takes hold. Fear can be, as the Hebraic scriptures have it, the beginning of wisdom. Or it can be (especially when, at a late hour, it strikes the mighty) like the recoiling, retreating thing that moved from the Cabaret Voltaire to death.

If despair, disenchantment, and fear are operating in our psychosphere, moral reflection, in whatever form it takes place, will reflect that to some degree. It has already begun to do so. It appears in the thinking of Garrett Hardin when he convinces himself and others that it is feasible to sail merrily along in our affluent lifeboat and ignore the deaths in the boats and the water nearby. It appears in the thoughts of a distinguished professor of political economy at the University of London, who writes:

> Suppose that, as a result of using up all the world's resources, human life did come to an end. So what? What is so desirable about an indefinite continuation of the human species . . . ?[25]

It appears in the neo-hedonism that is among us, since hedonism is a classical form of escapism and a compensatory reaction to a loss of meaning. It appears in the glorification of data-heaping, computerizable knowledge, which is, for all its plumage, a positivisitic despair about the capacities of the mind.

So Dada in its negativity is with us. It is a pollutant in the intellectual air that we breathe in spite of ourselves. Ethical reflection should not commence as though it had no context. Ethics, a work of hope, confronts a context that is heavy with despair and fear. That is the bad news in contemporary Dada.

Dada as Prophet . . .

A prophet is someone (or some group) who stands at the piercing point of evolving moral consciousness. A prophet attacks what the Marxists call the "tissue of lies" that envelops every society, the mystifications and fictions that we fabricate as deceptive mantles for our real self-serving purposes. Nothing is more precious to a people than its lies, if those lies seem to ensure security and comfort. To assault those lies is a dangerous and almost hopeless task. In the prophetic view, however, it is not entirely hopeless. At stake are truth, justice, and the humanization of persons, and those stakes make it worth a try.

Dada is not a classical form of prophecy, since it seems to have no base for hope, and classical prophecy does. It also did not reflect the verbal eloquence of many of the historical prophets, but it was, perhaps, eloquent in its own wildly symbolic way. The problem with such prophecy is that it is hard to interpret. Its focus is not always manifest.

Contemporary Dadaist discontent is scattershot in its expression. Any effort to find its positive import will necessarily be interpretative. It would seem, however, that the current spirit of hopelessness is fixed upon "the Establishment" as that term has come to be used since 1955.[26] That includes a lot, but it clearly includes the intellectual and educational establishment. In Dadaist and also in more hopeful countercultural protests, there is deep distrust of the established intelligentsia and the way they explain life. To put it more mildly and more obviously, there is very little reverence for the tenured "wisdom." When we see what short shrift this shallow "wisdom" gives to moral values, and how jejune its assumptions are about our existence, there is no difficulty in seeing why it can elicit revulsion. So let us put contemporary wisdom on the dock to see how much it contributes to contemporary despair. In probing this potential cause of Dadaist unrest, we are paying tribute to the prophecy that Dada might contain.

Three areas in our intellectual situation claim immediate attention: first, the displacement of philosophy by science with the resultant shrinkage in the very meaning of knowledge; second, the cult of obscurity to which so many intellectuals are addicted and which they confuse with profundity; and, finally, the emasculation of ethics by those who have publicly pondered the meaning of the moral. Again, in citing these three areas, I am being freely interpretative, offering these as arguably operative stimuli of Dadaist malaise.

Philosophy in Exile . . .

The term "philosophy" covers a multitude of enterprises including some of what is called sociology, history, psychology, theology, and more. But, however loose its meaning, it always indicates an effort to probe beyond the immediacies of the empirical order around us into the deeper questions. If it is true that wonder is the beginning and source of philosophy, then only those who are utterly blasé, bored, and superficial are closed to the tasks of philosophy. In this sense, then, everyone with a mind is summoned to philosophize. Philosophy is based on a recognition that human life and its setting are mysterious. True philosophy is too modest to hope to dissipate the mystery; it only hopes to encounter it fruitfully.

In classical antiquity, philosophy was learning *par excellence*. Of course, philosophy was a term that covered virtually all knowledge including what we would call today the physical sciences.[27] The regal status of philosophy did not survive the development of the physical sciences in the past three hundred years. As the historian of philosophy Frederick Copleston puts it:

> . . . in the course of their development the various sciences have taken over one part after another of the field of exploration which was once attributed to philosophy. There has thus been a gradual substitution of scientific knowledge for philosophical speculation.[28]

All this was well and good, since the expansion of scientific learning required specialization and the creation of a number of empirical scientific disciplines. The end result, however, was not good. What came about was, in Copleston's words, "the conviction that the empirical sciences are the only reliable source of knowledge about the world." This view, he adds, "is obviously widespread."[29]

Philosophy began as king and ended as an exile. Or, where it is not positively exiled by the "hard-nosed" empirical scientists, it has been suggested that its state is like that of royalty in a constitutional monarchy. "The king reigns but does not govern."[30] Philosophy is allowed to piddle around with its ethereal speculation and maintain nominal honors as long as it does not meddle where the real action is and where science is *de facto* supreme.

What this deviate condition means is that knowledge has become a dwarf. Knowledge comes to be seen as that which fits within the arbitrarily and narrowly defined limits of today's science. Bertrand Russell booms out the message: "Whatever knowledge is attainable, must be attained by scientific methods; and what science cannot discover, mankind cannot know."[31] Russell's statement would make sense if science were understood more broadly, as it can be and sometimes is. But as sociologist Karl Mannheim observes:

> It is . . . well known how modern intellectual development reflects the dominant role of mathematics. Strictly speaking, from this point of view, only what is measurable should be regarded as scientific.[32]

To be limited to the measurable is to be intellectually strangled. Of course we cannot be contained within the measurable; living experience does not bow to such an absurd idea. Bertrand Russell himself illustrates that time and again. For example, he writes:

> There is a possibility in human minds of something mysterious as night-wind, deep as the sea, calm as the stars, and strong as Death, a mystic contemplation. . . . Those who have known it cannot *believe* in wars any longer. . . . If I could give to others what has come to me in this way, I could make them too feel the futility of fighting. But I do not know how to communicate it. . . .[33]

If what he experienced were measurable, it would be communicable. And yet, immeasurable though it be, it is clearly knowledge of a precious sort. (Significantly, he uses the word "know" in describing this experience. "Those who have known it . . .") To dismiss it because it cannot be shrunk to science size makes no sense, nor does Russell seem in the passage quoted to be about to do any such thing.

If Dada represents a reaction against this kind of science-monism, it is performing a prophetic function.

The Cult of the Obscure . . .

A second likely and worthy target of Dadaist protest is a perennial problem of intellectuals—obscurantism. Let it be said that when we encounter thoughts that seem unintelligible, the fault may be ours. Perhaps we are too dull or superficial to comprehend profundity, or we lack the energy or skill to decipher a reasonably useful technical jargon. There is another possibility. We may be in the presence of that kind of intellectual fraud which takes refuge in obscurity. Sometimes obscurity is really the best that can be achieved in an honest effort to express subtle and elusive truth. But sometimes obscurity is well-dressed gibberish. It is the latter kind of obscurity that demeans true intellectuality and true science and violates the human rights of those who believe they are in the presence of good faith communication.

An example drawn from the late highly esteemed German philosopher Martin Heidegger will put this culprit form of speech before us:

> What is to be investigated is being only and—nothing else; being alone and further—nothing. . . . What about this nothing? Does the Nothing exist only because the Not, i.e. the Negation, exists? Or is it the other way around? Does the Negation and the Not exist only because the Nothing exists? . . . We assert: the Nothing is prior to the Not and the Negation. Where do we seek the Nothing? How do we find the Nothing? . . . Anxiety reveals the Nothing. . . . That for which and because of which we were anxious, was "really"—nothing. Indeed: the Nothing itself—as such—was present. What about this Nothing?—The Nothing itself Nothings.[34]

Now, there are those who would argue that Heidegger is indeed saying something here, that the subtle tones of these words in his personalized vocabulary are rich with meaning for the initiated. Yet it would appear to be true beyond all quibble that whatever he was saying could have been said better and in such a way that his happy insight might be shared with many intelligent persons who find his statement, as it stands, nonsense.

The seductive attraction of obscurity is not limited to one culture. In any civilization, the most simple of insights can become its prey. Buddhism, in its origins, was a very simple doctrine. It sought to cope with sorrow by taking a middle course between self-indulgence and extreme asceticism and leading a moral and well-ordered life. However, as one student of Buddhism puts it: "This very simple doctrine was developed in various rather pedantic forms, most important of which was the 'Chain of Dependent Origination' . . . commented on again and again by ancient and modern scholars, and probably not fully understood by anybody."[35] It seems that, through some innate perversity, we will eschew clarity even when it is within reach.

My thesis here is quite concise: Obscurity and profundity are not identical. If our age is philosophically shallow, especially in value questions, and Dadaistically suspicious of the intellectual life, part of the blame is due to the thinkers among us who have not mastered the art of intelligible speech.

The nether side of my thesis is *not* that clarity is always profound or good. There is such a thing also as *clear* gibberish and *clear* inanity. As Immanuel Kant said, "There is really no art in being generally comprehensible if one thereby renounces all basic insight. . . ." The result of this can be "a disgusting jumble of patched-up observations and half-reasoned principles." He continues: "Shallowpates enjoy this, for it is very useful in everyday chitchat, while the more sensible feel confused and dissatisfied without being able to help themselves."[36]

Furthermore, the positivists, who led the modern attack on the legitimacy of ethics, were intent on clarity. And yet as one perceptive critic says of them, "The clarity which is today the ideal of positivistic and analytic philosophy seems to me nothing but thinness of content."[37]

Poetry (which is not confined to poems) is also hamstrung by an excessive insistence on clarity. As Jacques Maritain says in *Creative Intuition in Art and Poetry*: "The law of intelligible clarity imposed by the classical tradition has . . . been an occasion for innumerable mediocre poems. . . ."[38] Brilliance has flirtation rights when it comes to obscurity, as long as it does not sever all links with intelligibility.

Any effort to give voice to our deepest feelings and thought is liable to be unavoidably vague at times. Truth is greater than both our thoughts and our language. In our speech we are unprofitable servants who do the best we can to capture much that is truly ineffable. It is the beginning of wisdom to recognize that we cannot encapsulate the truth in our minds or our words. Truth is never contained by us; we can only be open to being touched by it. Our ability to articulate what we experience at the various levels of our consciousness should not be exaggerated. What we experience is always prior to, and more than, what we can say. Small wonder that we can be clumsy at times in the saying—and even obscure.

But there is a limit to obscurity beyond which one is no longer indulging in what can be called speech. No communication can be completely obscure or it fails the minimal requirements of language. It becomes mere noise, "signifying nothing." It represents intellectual autism. Why is it, then, that intellectuals are so susceptible to the lure of the obscure? Why, in particular, are ethicists prone, in Schopenhauer's words, to weaving "such a confused and wide-reaching tissue of phrases that they succeed in rendering unintelligible the clearest and simplest relations of life"?[39]

The causes are many and we can only cite a few: First there is the Gnostic syndrome. The Gnostics were elitist groups in the early Christian Church who claimed a special and esoteric knowledge. To keep this from the uninitiated, the Gnostics practiced their own zealous form of the so-called "discipline of the secret," and spoke a language that was unintelligible to the common man. Though the historical Gnostic movement is dead, the Gnostic syndrome still lives in the various professions and intellectual disciplines. George Bernard Shaw observed that every profession is a conspiracy against the laity. This shows up clearly in the barrier of jargon that is erected against the outsider. Complicated terms are concocted for the simplest of matters. Very often there is no defensible reason for resorting to arcane terminology. It does, however, serve the ignoble cause of elitism.

In the intellectual endeavors such as philosophy, which are not subject to laboratory testing, the Gnostic syndrome is complicated by the human ability to confuse language with reality. Thus, in the contemplation of a problem which is quite real, we can spin off into verbal and conceptual space and move and react in this detached universe of words and concepts. Then, when someone with his feet on the ground catches us saying (as we caught Heidegger) that "the Nothing itself Nothings," or that pure Being and pure Nothing are one and the same (as Hegel said), we are revealed for what we are—cut loose from the moorings of real experience.

There are stubborn attractions in obscurity: It is often taken for profundity and learning. This is true in the various sciences as well as in philosophy. The ability to know the mountain of terms in any science is impressive of itself, no matter what the bottom line might be in terms of truth. But the more abstract the exercise, the more likely we are to confuse vagueness with brilliance. We are disposed to put up with a lot from philosophically oriented writers. Our standards for their language and communications abilities are low. As John Henry Cardinal Newman wrote more than a century ago, "In a philosopher it is a merit even to be not utterly vague, inchoate, and obscure in his teaching, and if he fails even of this low standard of language, we remind ourselves that his obscurity perhaps is owing to his depth."[40] Obscurity, then, entails minimal risks and is a convenient shield for intellectual timidity, dishonesty, or confusion.

Obscurity is alluring also because it is a smoke screen which eases the pain of vulnerability. If it is not clear what one is saying, one can scarcely be faulted for it. (One can, of course, be faulted for not being clear about what is said, but since people are afraid they might be faulting profundity, obscurity is a safer path.)

Finally, obscurity can represent laziness and a failure of imagination. It is easier to wallow in jargon than it is to make language a creative force for bringing about communion at the level of thought. It, therefore, also implies a hostile pride and a lack of the sweet virtue of compassion. If the guns of contemporary Dada are targeted against obscurity, and not against intellectuality as such, they are engaged in a just war.

The Value Vacuum . . .

In a world where science becomes the reigning paradigm of knowledge, the results in the pursuit of ethics are peculiar and likely to provoke Dadaist critique. Let me illustrate this by adducing a representative number of influential witnesses who have conspicuously graced ethical inquiry with their speculations.

G. E. Moore was a professor in Cambridge, England, and his book *Principia Ethica*, published in 1903, is possibly the most discussed book on ethics in this century. Mary Warnock, commenting on the fact that Moore and his *Principia Ethica* loom so large in the moral philosophy of this century, says: "The reason is that the book is so good and so eccentric. Moore dominates us through its pages just as he dominated his contemporaries in Cambridge. There is no comparable book on ethics in this century."[41] It should be said immediately that there are favorable things that can be said about Moore. For one thing, his full work in ethics has not always been considered because of a remarkable fixation on the first two chapters of his *Principia*. Moore did not want to lock ethics into a narrow form of linguistic analysis. He also wanted to escape relativism and to maintain the autonomy of ethics. This makes him something of an ally to those who do not want ethics to be engulfed by hard or soft science. He recognized, chasteningly, against reductionistic rationalists, how proud and inane it is to feel that we can lock indefinable reality into our tidy definitions. He saw the limits of certitude in ethics and ap-

preciated that, in a sense, moral rules are predictions and thus intrinsically limited. He also was a hammer of vacuous idealism. In general
he was convinced that other philosophers were making things more
complicated than they are in fact, and he proposed to do something
about it. Unfortunately, he made things simpler than they are,
which is equally unhelpful. This shows through in a passage of his
book that has evoked obsessive-compulsive attention through the
years:

> If I am asked "What is good?" my answer is that good is
> good, and that is the end of the matter. Or if I am asked
> "How is good to be defined?" my answer is that it cannot
> be defined and that is all I have to say about it. . . . My
> point is that "good" is a simple notion, just as "yellow" is a
> simple notion; that, just as you cannot, by any manner of
> means, explain to anyone who does not already know it,
> what yellow is, so you cannot explain what good is.[42]

Moore's system is known as intuitionism because he says you cannot prove or define what good is, you must simply intuit it. Moore
rejects all systems that try to define moral good by identifying it with
well-being, pleasure, conformity to some divine law, or to human nature, or to some principle. That pretty much covers the field of all
other ethicists, leaving Moore alone with his intuition.[43]

Of course, he did not remain alone. There were other intuitionists
who followed somewhat different but contiguous tracks. As philosopher Henry Sidgwick describes them: "Writers who maintain that
we have 'intuitive knowledge' of the rightness of actions usually
mean that this rightness is ascertained by simply 'looking at' the actions themselves, without considering their ulterior consequences."[44]
If the reader finds any of these positions inane, then G. Warnock's
comment will be welcome. He described intuitionism as "a confession of bewilderment got up to look like an answer."[45]

Although he did not publish much, Moore had an extraordinary
influence on many other British and American philosophers. From
his professorial position at Cambridge, and as editor of the journal
Mind, he is credited with setting "the tone for what was or was not
to pass as philosophy at Cambridge and to a large extent Oxford between the two world wars."[46]

His legacy to modern ethics is a curious one. Moore's doctrine of
the good, which grounded his ethics, had, in the words of G. Warnock, a "surprisingly unnerving effect." Warnock continues:

> Now somehow—it would be a tricky business to work out just how—this obscure but potent doctrine of Moore's appears to have generated among analytic philosophers a prevalent sense that the moral philosopher must not try to say anything at all about the *grounds* of moral judgment, about the content of moral discourse, or its actual subject-matter. . . . It is in this sense that some recent general theories seem to me to deserve—and not, no doubt, for their own part to be at all ashamed of—the appellation "empty."[47]

With a refreshing directness, philosopher Girvetz sums up the remarkable matter of Moore and his *Principia*. He writes: "That a book as barren of results as Moore's *Principia* could be regarded as one of the important works of this century is perhaps a measure of the desperate state of contemporary moral philosophy."[48]

Professor Alfred Jules Ayer is, by academic standards, impressively pedigreed. He was educated at Eton and Oxford, and later was on the faculty at the University of London and at Oxford. He was also a member of a well-known group of scientists and philosophers known as the "Vienna Circle." These gentlemen were the source of what is known as logical positivism or neopositivism.[49] Their goal was to bring all knowledge into a single, unified system, while eliminating all unscientific speculation.

Now when one thinks about it, ethical questions such as those we discussed in Chapter One are really and truly distinct from the things treated in physics and chemistry. The statements we make about them are in a different category from purely scientific statements. "Lying is immoral" is different and not verifiable in the same way as "A body tends to expand when it is heated." This difference, however, can be acknowledged without reducing ethical statements to the status of an endangered species.

Rather than fruitfully exploring the differences between scientific and ethical statements, the positivists simply excommunicate ethical statements from the realm of meaningful expression. With them, ethical concepts are not concepts at all. They are, says Ayer, mere pseudo-concepts. They do not say anything!

> . . . sentences which simply express moral judgments do not say anything. They are pure expressions of feeling and as such do not come under the category of truth and falsehood. They are unverifiable for the same reason as a cry of pain or a word of command is unverifiable—because they do not express genuine propositions.[50]

Ayer is honest enough to give examples. If someone says, "Stealing money is wrong," he has uttered a statement "which has no factual meaning—that is, expresses no proposition which can be either true or false."[51] All it does is express a negative feeling, one which is beyond all truth claims. Someone else might feel differently. If so, there is no way of verifying who is right.

If Professor Ayer were a notorious thief, it would be easy to see what he is up to. Then we could say that if he is not wise, he is surely cunning. Since he is not a thief, his position is simply pathetic and possesses only burial rights. Intellectually he has painted himself into a corner where he cannot even say that Hitler was *truly* wrong to slaughter six million helpless Jewish people. He could be emotionally disturbed by what Hitler did, but he could not say he was *truly* wrong. He could not truly judge the morality of someone torturing a child. He could only emote, and whatever he said would be nothing more than an "ugh!" or a "boo!" It would be a nonstatement, neither true nor false.[52]

Ayer is not alone in his world of nonethics. Mary Warnock, for example, in her survey of contemporary ethics, says that Ayer's emotivist ethics "has great plausibility and appeal for any empiricist."[53] Nor are all of those who join him simply caught in the dogma of equating science and true knowledge. There is the form of existentialism which makes morality a matter of authentic personal decision. If you decide for something authentically, existentially, that is all that is required for morality. "Norms and values are in no sense valid in themselves; one creates one's own norms and values by one's act of espousal."[54] This is "doing one's own thing" elevated to the pretended level of philosophical statement. If one thinks of a rapist as creating his own norms and values, then in this extreme view, there are no theoretical grounds for arguing with him.

Strange as this view is, there are a number who hold something like it. Oxford University's R. M. Hare says that actions are right or wrong depending on whether they square with the kind of a life one has chosen. If a person accepts a particular way of life, "then we can proceed to justify the decisions that are based upon it; if he does not accept it, then let him accept some other, and try to live by it."[55] Those who take this position do add some conditions. They say that you should be willing to universalize your position—that is, you should be willing to see all others adopt your way of life and you should be willing to live with this. This might seem to civilize the position a bit, but it really does not. As philosopher William K. Frankena says, a person may take benevolence or social utility as his guiding principle. "But he must hold that anyone who adopts the opposite principle, as Nietzsche appears to do, may equally well have a morality, and . . . he cannot claim any validity for his principle which his opponent cannot also claim."[56]

Bertrand Russell is another witness to the modern assault on moral knowledge. He says that "if two men differ about values, there is not a disagreement as to any kind of truth, but a difference of taste. If one man says 'oysters are good' and another says 'I think they are bad,' we recognize that there is nothing to argue about."[57] So again the clear inference is: If someone enjoys getting innocent men convicted and someone else fights for their justification, "there is nothing to argue about." Russell did not live that way. When it came to issues of war and peace and freedom of speech, he felt there was plenty to argue about. Life often has a way of overruling the worst of our ideas.

There are some other despair-inspiring thoughts prestigiously ensconced in the intellectual Establishment. We can turn to the much-quoted thought of Ralph Barton Perry. Perry, a Harvard scholar, set out to explain value, including moral value, in terms of interest, which sounds harmless enough. He approved of Spinoza's statement that "we deem a thing to be good, because we strive for it, wish for it, long for it, or desire it."[58] Perry's "interest theory" of value came down to saying that something is a value because interest is taken in it. Interest in or liking something constitutes value. And there is the rub. In Perry and in other proponents of the "interest theory," there is "a more or less sharp cleavage between values and the cognitive processes associated with them."[59] In other words, interest, however linked it is to knowledge, is not knowledge.[60] As the grounding of moral value, this is slippery.[61] Perry is all the more slippery and unsettling since it is not clear even to the experts what he is saying. Philosopher Richard B. Brandt, after describing Perry as one of the most influential ethicists of this century, goes on to say: "Nevertheless it is not easy to say what exactly are the general outlines of his theory."[62] That is quite a commentary on the state of the discipline.

Before concluding this illustrative listing of the kinds of things purveyed in the academe that could make for intellectual despair, I must cite a figure who is very much in the forefront of modern thought, B. F. Skinner. Skinner can be seen as both a symbol and a symptom of the modern intellectual milieu.

Ethics and the Skinnerian Malady . . .

B. F. Skinner has won the attention that should be reserved for an intellectual event. He is no such event. Though he rushes boldly into philosophy, his work there is neither profound nor revolutionary. It is, rather, symptomatic. Skinner can be seen as the salient symbol of scientistic, intellectual vacuity. His thought provides for many in our age the image of their own mind. He articulates simplisms that are commonplace. For this reason, he merits special attention in a consideration of the contemporary Dadaist moralscape.

The story is told that Jonathan Swift once sat in a village square watching a fishmonger as she prattled and chatted through an afternoon of business. As he ended his bemused and reveried watch, he mystified her by commenting: "Would that I could be as sure of one thing as you are of everything!" After one reads *Beyond Freedom and Dignity* a similar remark could be made to its author, Burrhus Frederic Skinner. Skinner's world (like Moore's) is simpler than the world in which we actually dwell. All the mysteries and subtleties of humanhood that have taxed the best minds for centuries are found in Skinner tidily wrapped and scientifically boxed. And if you do not see things in Skinner's neat way, you are "prescientific," which, in Skinner's lexicon, is worse than being wrong. Skinner has, in effect, produced a caricature of what the despair of scientific reductionism can do to knowledge.

If Skinner had stuck to science, applause for his ingenuity might be in order, but Skinner philosophizes on, and applies to the human scene, what he has learned in his laboratory. He is not, however, really alert to the fact that there is a qualitative leap involved when you move from the behavior of pigeons to the behavior of people. He does allow that pigeons are not people, but the unwritten premise of his work is that people are pigeons. The result is a pigeon ethics.[63] Skinner's ability to draw a crowd to his ideas is not among the harbingers of hope.

Skinner's moral philosophy can be captured under four rubrics: all power to the environment; "psychology without a psyche"; ethics without morality; and life without mystery.

All power to the environment! The message is that people are

Charlie McCarthys and the environment is Edgar Bergen. Pre-scientific man used to personify Charlie, attributing his words and movements to what they thought to be his *self*. Scientific man has figured out that Edgar was doing it all the time. "A scientific analysis shifts the credit as well as the blame to the environment. . . ."[64] Prescientific folk thought "a person's behavior is at least to some extent his own achievement."[65] Scientific Skinner, however, knows us for the puppets we are.

"Psychology without a psyche."[66] For Skinner, all behavior is re-duced to interaction with the external environment. There is no in-ternal environment, no inner self, no mind, no personality. In a word, "we do not need to try to discover what personalities, states of mind, feelings, traits of character, plans, purposes, intentions, or the other perquisites of autonomous man really are in order to get on with a scientific analysis of behavior."[67]

Once upon a time, says Skinner, simple man tried to explain physi-cal events by attributing human qualities of will and emotion to things. For example, ancient physics taught that a falling body accel-erated because it grew more jubilant as it found itself nearer home. Good, scientific physics stopped attributing human qualities to inani-mate objects. Likewise psychology will advance if we stop attributing human motives to intentions, purposes, aims, and goals. As philoso-pher Peter Caws summarizes Skinner's psychology, scientific progress will follow in psychology "if we could stop attributing human char-acteristics to human beings."[68] So there it is: It was good physics to depersonalize inanimate things (we can only agree); it is good psy-chology to depersonalize persons (we can only gasp!).

Ethics without morality. Skinner's treatment of particular moral values is not so much a true ethics as it is a true mechanics. In fact he calls it "a technology of behavior."[69] It is also an exercise in ego-ism. The reason you should not steal or lie is that it will cause you trouble. " 'You ought not to steal,' . . . could be translated, 'If you tend to avoid punishment, avoid stealing.' "[70] If you treat others well and beneficently, it is not because of any "loyalty or respect" for them, but because "they have arranged effective social contin-gencies."[71] Love too is evacuated of personal meaning. ". . . we should not attribute behaving for the good of others to a love of others." Such behavior "depends upon the control exerted by the so-cial environment."[72] Likewise "a person does not support a religion because he is devout; he supports it because of the contingencies ar-

ranged by the religious agency." Neither does he "support his government because he is loyal but because the government has arranged special contingencies."[73] (One wonders where Skinner found
either governments or religious agencies organized enough to organize all those contingencies.)

Life without mystery. Skinner's world is, to transform a phrase of
Shakespeare, "sicklied o'er with the pale cast of technology." It is a
soulless vision he offers us. There is no room for generosity, nobility,
or mysticism, or for the marvelous unpredictable movements of the
human spirit. Admiration proceeds from ignorance—". . . we are
likely to admire behavior more as we understand it less."[74] A hero is
someone who is addicted to and controlled by the reinforcements of
praise and adulation. Thus reinforced, the hero "takes on more and
more dangerous assignments until he is killed."[75] (Implicit here is
the conception of hero as ass.) Heroic behavior is not unlike the
phototropic behavior of a moth whose proclivity for light "proves lethal when it leads into flame."[76] (The hero as moth.) Skinner cannot understand heroism because he has no room for the mysterious
fact that we can discover in the world of persons values so great that,
when they are at issue, we will die to all "reinforcements," including
life, to defend them—or at least we will admire those who have the
courage to do so.

There are other mysteries to which Skinner's theories blind him,
including the mystery of evil. Dietrich Bonhoeffer, the theologian
who was killed by the Nazis, lamented the inability of reasonable
people to comprehend the depths of evil. These and other depths
remain unplumbed in the unreal and mystery-free simplism of B. F.
Skinner. To the degree that Skinner illustrates contemporary penetration into ethics, we are in trouble.

The conclusion suggests itself that the primary despair in contemporary Dada (and maybe in any Dada) is not with the Warhols or
the bovine epitheters, but with those against whom these countercul-
turalists react. The real despair is in those who, under guise of learning, practice reductionism on human thought. Not all of those who
work in the field of philosophical or theological ethics do this. As
shall be seen throughout this book, there were strong thinkers in the
past, and are in the present, from whom all of us can learn. Geniuses
of the human spirit have been and are among us. It is a major task
of ethics to retrieve and to champion the brilliance that is out of
style in a superficial time. In looking for the fitting targets of Dadaist

protest, I have been stressing that all is not light and bright. Much has been done in the name of ethics that is tedious, trivial, and unhelpful. We have followed too many of the wrong drummers and been too slow to discover enlivening new cadences on our own. Ethics to a large degree has been busy at its own undoing.

My special concern has been to stress the reductionism practiced in the realm of values. And I do see this as despair, a classical despair rooted in disappointed pride. The University of Munich's Eric Voegelin refers to "the positivistic conceit that only propositions concerning facts of the phenomenal world [are] 'objective,' while judgments concerning the right order of soul and society [are] 'subjective.' "[77] It is significant that the term "value-free science" entered the philosophical vocabulary in the midde of the nineteenth century, when the prospects of technological genius were "in tiny leaf."[78] This was understandably an intoxicating moment when we began to catch glimmers of how much we could do within the more measurable realm of the sciences. Less precise modes of intellectual inquiry were left in the shadows before the thrilling advent of this great light. And ethics is, admittedly, not precise. It moves from muddied waters to cloud-covered peaks. It encounters paradox and imprecision and cases where contradictory answers seem equally defensible. All of this could be unattractive to the scientific mind of the nineteenth century, which was intellectually prepubic and as yet unacquainted with relativity and probability as the real facts of life. At any rate, the chimera of value-free objectivity was piously pursued.

Though this chimera has begun to be discredited somewhat today, the "positivistic conceit" is still very extant. It shows up, for example, not only in caricature form in Skinner, but in the penchant of many American and British ethicians for reducing ethics to logical and linguistic analysis. This type of analysis is patient of greater measure and precision, though it is also prone to becoming painfully tedious. The tedium is unrelieved by the nagging suspicion in reading these fellows that we are in the presence of an ingeniously played chess game that is not very relevant to the world which, right outside, is burning.[79]

If so many of the intelligentsia are really purveyors of despair, why are their works and their pomps tolerated, reprinted, anthologized, and enthroned? Part of the answer to that question is that there appears to be a lift-off point in the less than precise intellectual endeavors (and that includes many of the sciences and social sciences such as medicine, psychiatry, sociology, political science, etc.) after which a particular author or idea is in quasi-permanent orbit. This kind of orbit is more easily obtained, it would seem, if one's academic launching pad happens to be a sufficiently prestigious university. If there is a certain author whom people have heard of, read, seen quoted, taken examinations on, etc., he becomes simply part of the terrain. Even criticism does not banish him. It will still be a necessary ritual of sophistication to cite him as a reference point of one's own thought.

If something is being widely read and talked about, an urgent need develops to read it. Karl Marx once wrote to Engels: "I am also studying Comte now, as a sideline, because the English and French make such a fuss about the fellow." Marx, however, seduced as he may have been into reading Comte, did not lose his critical sense. He characterizes it as "this positivist rot."[80] Most people are not so judicious and are disposed to believe that the well known is good.

Timidity is also involved. It is a most common emotion, and, because of it, there are few, in any time, who are willing to proclaim the Emperor's nudity when all around them are treating him as magnificently clothed.

Albert Camus wrote that "even within the limits of nihilism it is possible to find the means to proceed beyond nihilism."[81] Nihilism and skepticism regarding inquiry into morality would seem at this time to hold sway. Dada is with us. It might be a mistake, however, to see this in terms of permanence rather than in terms of prelude. Sociologist Karl Mannheim looks back to "the first great surge of scepticism in the history of occidental thought" when Greek society faced a situation where "previous unambiguity of norms and interpretations had been shattered." This produced the Sophists, who appeared to be questioning everything and answering nothing. But maybe the Sophists were on to something and do not deserve their bad name. They may have divined, in Mannheim's words,

> that a satisfactory solution was to be found only in a thorough-going questioning and thinking through of the contradictions. This general uncertainty was by no means a symptom of a world doomed to general decay, but it was rather the beginning of a wholesome process which marked a crisis leading to recovery.[82]

There may be hope in our cultural and ethical disarray. It is in this hope that we can go on to test the foundation of moral experience and to see just what ethics is and what claim it has to be taken seriously by intelligent and sensitive persons.

NOTES—CHAPTER TWO

1. Manifesto by Louis Aragon at the second Dada manifestation, February 5, 1920, at the Salon des Independants, Paris. Quoted by A. Alvarez, *The Savage God* (New York: Random House, 1970), p. 226.
2. Ibid., pp. 229–30.
3. For more of the history of Dada, see Herbert Read, *A Concise History of Modern Painting* (New York: Praeger, 1959), and Robert Motherwell, ed., *The Dada Painters and Poets* (New York: Wittenborn, Schultz, 1951).
4. "Yahweh then said, 'As my servant Isaiah has been walking about naked and barefoot for the last three years—a sign and portent for Egypt and Cush—so will the king of Assyria lead away captives from Egypt and exiles from Cush, young and old, naked and barefoot, their buttocks bared, to the shame of Egypt." Isaiah 20:3–4. The Jerusalem Bible (Garden City, N.Y.: Doubleday & Co., Inc., 1966).
5. Quoted in Alvarez, *Savage God*, p. 233. "Dada is not a *mal de siècle*, but a *mal du monde*," said Hugnet (ibid., p. 234).
6. Gabriel Marcel, *The Philosophy of Existentialism*, 4th paperbound ed. (New York: Citadel Press, 1964; copyright © 1956, Philosophical Library), p. 32.
7. Ibid.
8. Ibid., pp. 32–33.
9. Arthur M. Schlesinger, Jr., *The Crisis of Confidence* (New York: Bantam Books, 1969), p. 183.
10. Rollo May, *Power and Innocence: A Search for the Sources of Violence* (New York: W. W. Norton & Co., Inc., 1972), p. 60. May reflects here the statement of Matthew Arnold: "Wandering between two worlds, one dead, / the other powerless to be born" ("Stanzas from the Grande Chartreuse").
11. Quoted by Charles A. Beard, *The Idea of National Interest: An Analytical Study in American Foreign Policy* (New York: Macmillan Co., 1934), p. 379.
12. Quoted in William A. Clebsch, *From Sacred to Profane America: The Role of Religion in American History* (New York, Evanston, and London: Harper & Row, 1968), p. 32.

13. George S. Philips, *The American Republic and Human Liberty Foreshadowed in Scripture* (Cincinnati: Poe and Hitchcock, for the author, 1864), pp. 130, 153. Quoted in Clebsch, *From Sacred to Profane America*, pp. 189–90.

14. Richard Hofstadter quotes this and says: "There seems to be more truth than we care to admit in the dictum of D. H. Lawrence." "Spontaneous, Sporadic and Disorganized," *New York Times Magazine*, Apr. 28, 1968. Also quoted by May, *Power and Innocence*, p. 52.

15. *Summa Theologica* II II, q. 19, a. 11, ad 2.

16. Quoted by TRB, *New Republic* 171, No. 19 (Nov. 9, 1974), p. 2.

17. Robert L. Heilbroner, *An Inquiry into the Human Prospect* (New York: W. W. Norton & Co., Inc., 1975), p. 39.

18. See Hannah Arendt, *On Violence* (New York: Harcourt, Brace & World, Inc., 1969), p. 10. See also Carl-Göran Heden, "The Infectious Dust Cloud," pp. 147–65; Nigel Calder, "The New Weapons," pp. 231–43 (particularly p. 239 on capacity of poor nations or groups to acquire and use biological weapons), in Nigel Calder, ed., *Unless Peace Comes* (New York: Viking Press, 1968). William G. Caitman, ibid., p. 27, writes of the reaction of the dispossessed to the unjust distribution of food and to the institutionalization of poverty that is insured by the policies of nations and multinational industries. He says: "An inevitable consequence of this will be increased violence as the poor and disconnected seek equitable distribution of the wealth of their nations and more rational use of their resources."

19. Garrett Hardin, "Living on a Lifeboat," *BioScience* 24, No. 10 (Oct. 1974), p. 565. The italics are his though they were quite unnecessary. The point of his article is inescapable.

20. Ibid. His quote is from A. Gregg, "A Medical Aspect of the Population Problem," *Science* 121 (1955), pp. 681–82.

21. I do not say that Hardin has none who would stand with him. Columnist and commentator Paul Harvey writes: "Americans have been compelled by scriptural injunction and by guilt-related compassion to share our food, but is it 'ethical' if our humanitarian effort to alleviate misery creates more misery? . . . Triage, in its battlefield hospital connotation, simply meant to make the most efficient use of scarce medical resources. Triage to this day is the unsentimental, morally uncomfortable, inescapable wartime formula. You don't waste limited resources on those who are inevitably doomed." Syndicated column, Apr. 1, 1975, quoted in *Worldview* 18, Nos. 7–8 (July–Aug. 1975), p. 8. The reliance on Hardin's thought and language is patent.

22. Jim Bishop, syndicated column, Apr. 13, 1975; quoted in *Worldview* 18, Nos. 7–8 (July–Aug. 1975), p. 8.
23. Heilbroner, *Inquiry into the Human Prospect*, pp. 166–67.
24. See Lester R. Brown with Erik P. Eckholm, *By Bread Alone* (New York and Washington, D.C.: Praeger Publishers, 1974), pp. 68–69, on the suggested causes of the global cooling trend in evidence since 1940, and pp. 10–11 on the desertification problem resulting from drought conditions. These theories have also been reported in the popular press.
25. Quoted in Robert L. Heilbroner, "What Has Posterity Ever Done for Me?" *New York Times Magazine* (Jan. 19, 1975), p. 14.
26. According to the new supplement of the Oxford English Dictionary the *locus classicus* for this new usage was provided by Henry Fairlie in 1955. See Henry Fairlie, "The Language of Politics," *Atlantic* (Jan. 1975), pp. 25–33.
27. Ancient Greek philosophy was divided into three parts: physics, ethics, and logic. Immanuel Kant says: "This division conforms perfectly to the nature of the subject, and one can improve on it perhaps only by supplying its principle in order both to insure its exhaustiveness and to define correctly the necessary subdivisions." *Foundations of the Metaphysics of Morals*, translated by Lewis White Beck (New York: Liberal Arts Press, 1959), p. 3.
28. Frederick Copleston, A *History of Philosophy*, Vol. 7, Part II (Garden City, N.Y.: Doubleday & Co., Inc., Image Books, 1965), p. 199.
29. Ibid., p. 200.
30. This is suggested by Karl Mannheim in his classic *Ideology and Utopia* (New York: Harcourt, Brace & World, Inc., A Harvest Book, 1936), p. 104.
31. Bertrand Russell, *Religion and Science* (London and New York: Oxford University Press, 1935), quoted in Richard B. Brandt, *Value and Obligation* (New York, Chicago, and Burlingame: Harcourt, Brace & World, Inc., 1961), p. 384.
32. Mannheim, *Ideology and Utopia*, p. 165.
33. Bertrand Russell, *The Autobiography of Bertrand Russell, 1914–1944* (Boston and Toronto: Little, Brown & Co., An Atlantic Monthly Press Book, 1967), p. 119.
34. Quoted from an article by Heidegger by Rudolf Carnap, "The Elimination of Metaphysics Through Logical Analysis of Language," in A. J. Ayer, ed., *Logical Positivism* (New York: Free Press, 1959), p. 69.
35. A. L. Basham, *The Wonder That Was India: A Survey of the Culture of the Indian Sub-Continent Before the Coming of the Muslims* (London: Sidgwick & Jackson, 1954), p. 269.

36. Immanuel Kant, *Foundations of the Metaphysics of Morals*, p. 26.
37. Eliseo Vivas, *The Moral Life and the Ethical Life* (Chicago: Henry Regnery Co., A Gateway Edition, 1963), p. viii.
38. Jacques Maritain, *Creative Intuition in Art and Poetry* (New York: Meridian Books, Inc., 1955), p. 192.
39. Arthur Schopenhauer, *The Basis of Morality*, 2nd ed. (London: George Allen & Unwin, Ltd., 1915), p. 18.
40. John Henry Cardinal Newman, *An Essay in Aid of a Grammar of Assent* (Garden City, N.Y.: Doubleday & Co., Inc., Image Books, 1955), p. 37.
41. Mary Warnock, *Ethics Since 1900* (London: Oxford University Press, 1960), p. 199.
42. G. E. Moore, *Principia Ethica* (Cambridge: Cambridge University Press, 1903), pp. 6–7.
43. As Vernon J. Bourke puts it after citing Moore's rejection of all these possible bases of ethics to which Moore gives the ambiguous title "naturalism": "Thus broadly understood, any ethics other than Moore's might be labeled 'naturalism.'" *History of Ethics* (Garden City, N.Y.: Doubleday & Co., Inc., Image Books, 1968), Vol. 2, p. 143.
44. Henry Sidgwick, *The Methods of Ethics* (New York: Dover, 1966), p. 96.
45. G. J. Warnock, *Contemporary Moral Philosophy* (London: Macmillan Co., 1967), p. 7. Moore was a utilitarian however much he parted from Mill and Bentham and thus consequences counted in his intuitionism.
46. James V. McGlynn and Jules J. Toner, *Modern Ethical Theories* (Milwaukee: Bruce Publishing Co., 1962), p. 81.
47. G. J. Warnock, *The Object of Morality* (London: Methuen & Co., 1971), pp. vii–viii.
48. Harry K. Girvetz, *Beyond Right and Wrong* (New York and London: Free Press, Collier Macmillan Publishers, 1973), p. 116.
49. Positivism was classically expressed by Auguste Comte (1798–1857) in the six volumes of his *Course of Positive Philosophy*. The empirical sciences are seen in positivism as the only reliable source of learning. All unscientific speculation is inane. As Copleston summarizes positivist and neopositivist thought: "Apart from the purely formal propositions of logic and pure mathematics, meaningful propositions were interpreted as empirical hypotheses, the meaning of which was coincident with the thinkable, though not necessarily practically realizable, mode of verification in sense-experience." *History of Philosophy*, Vol. 7, Part II, p. 201.
50. Alfred Jules Ayer, *Language, Truth and Logic* (New York: Dover Publications, Inc., 1952), pp. 108–9.

51. Ayer continues: "It is as if I had written 'Stealing money!'—where the shape and thickness of the exclamation marks show, by a suitable convention, that a special sort of moral disapproval is the feeling which is being expressed. It is clear that there is nothing said here which can be true or false. Another man may disagree with me about the wrongness of stealing, in the sense that he may not have the same feelings about stealing as I have, and he may quarrel with me on account of my moral sentiments But he cannot, strictly speaking, contradict me." Ibid., p. 107.

52. In the new introduction to the second edition of his book, Ayer made some nonsubstantive modifications of his position later making moral judgments expressions geared to influencing others and not just merely emotive outbursts. But he continued to stick stoutly to his position that ethical judgments are neither true nor false and not really statements at all.

53. M. Warnock, *Ethics Since 1900*, p. 91.

54. This is how William K. Frankena sums up radical existentialism, adding: "This Sartrian view transforms morality almost beyond recognition." "Recent Conceptions of Morality" in Hector-Neri Castaneda and George Nakhnikian, eds., *Morality and the Language of Conduct* (Detroit: Wayne State University Press, 1963), p. 3.

55. R. M. Hare, *The Language of Morals* (Oxford: Clarendon Press, 1952), p. 69. See also P. H. Nowell-Smith, *Ethics* (London: Penguin Books Ltd., 1954), pp. 319–20; C. L. Stevenson, "The Emotive Conception of Ethics and Its Cognitive Implications," *Philosophical Review* 59 (1950), pp. 291–304.

56. Frankena, "Recent Conceptions of Morality," p. 5. In the next chapter I shall elaborate further on this strange intellectual approach to the moral phenomenon. What is involved here is a decidedly unprofitable answer to the fundamental question: *What is morality?*

57. Russell, *Religion and Science*, quoted in Brandt, *Value and Obligation*, p. 382.

58. Spinoza, *Ethics*, Pt. III, Prop. IX, Note.

59. Harry K. Girvetz, *Beyond Right and Wrong*, p. 75. Girvetz' critique of noncognitivist and skeptical philosophical views of ethics is excellent.

60. As philosopher Girvetz says of Perry: "Thus, while he stressed the indispensability of cognitive processes to interested activity, Perry was equally emphatic about distinguishing between interest and cognition and assigning the locus of value exclusively to the former." Ibid., p. 78. However, Perry, in his *Realms of Value: A Critique of Human Civilization* (Cambridge, Mass.: Harvard University Press, 1954), does see morality as an endeavor to harmonize conflicting in-

terests, and it is difficult to do this without being cognitive and judicious. Also as a naturalist, he felt that his moral first principles are true by definition.

61. Perry can at times sound very cognitivist. He says duty consists in the enlightened recognition of the good. To rank values, Perry proposed four criteria: correctness, intensity, preference, and inclusiveness. However, as Vernon J. Bourke says of these: "Actually, the last three have to do with degrees of value, whereas the first is the test of whether something is a value or not." Bourke, *History of Ethics,* Vol. 2, p. 153.

62. Brandt, *Value and Obligation,* p. 263.

63. See Daniel C. Maguire, "Pigeon Ethics: The Moral Philosophy of B. F. Skinner," *Living Light* 9, No. 3 (1972), pp. 26–32.

64. B. F. Skinner, *Beyond Freedom and Dignity* (New York: Alfred A. Knopf, 1971), p. 21.

65. Ibid., p. 101.

66. The term is used by Peter Caws in a piercing review of *Beyond Freedom and Dignity* in *New Republic,* Oct. 16, 1971, pp. 32–34.

67. Skinner, *Beyond Freedom and Dignity,* p. 15.

68. Caws, *New Republic,* p. 33.

69. Skinner, *Beyond Freedom and Dignity,* p. 5.

70. Ibid., p. 114.

71. Ibid., p. 113.

72. Ibid., p. 110.

73. Ibid., p. 116.

74. Ibid., p. 53.

75. Ibid., p. 111.

76. Ibid.

77. Eric Voegelin, *The New Science of Politics* (Chicago and London: University of Chicago Press, 1952), p. 11.

78. Voegelin writes: ". . . it must first of all be realized that the terms 'value-judgment' and 'value-free science' were not part of the philosophical vocabulary before the second half of the nineteenth century." Ibid.

79. Harry K. Girvetz writes that "we must press beyond language to the experience of which our language is an expression if we are to understand the data of ethics—a reminder that might seem to be gratuitous were it not for the recent preoccupation of Anglo-American philosophy with logical and linguistic analysis and hence with what is *said* about conduct rather than conduct itself." *Beyond Right and Wrong,* p. 238. I am at a loss to know what Professor Frederick S. Carney might mean when he says that there is not "much doubt that the general approach to philosophy associated with Locke, Hume, J. S. Mill, Wittgenstein, and J. L. Austin, for examples, does

to some considerable extent articulate the thought processes of our 'man in the street.'" "On Frankena and Religious Ethics," *Journal of Religious Ethics* 3 (1975), pp. 8–9. I think the man in the street is wiser than all of that. As an example of something that I do not think would touch or tempt the man in the street, cf. Charles L. Stevenson, *Ethics and Language* (New Haven and London: Yale University Press, 1944).

80. Karl Marx, letter to Engels, July 7, 1866, *Selected Correspondence, 1846–1895* (London, 1934), quoted by Jacques Maritain, *Moral Philosophy* (New York: Charles Scribner's Sons, 1964), p. 267, note 1.

81. Albert Camus, *The Myth of Sisyphus* (New York: Random House, Vintage Books, 1955), p. v.

82. Karl Mannheim, *Ideology and Utopia*, p. 9.

CHAPTER THREE

THE MEANING OF MORALS

There is a strange and pathetic group of people who live in a desolate part of Africa. They are known as the Ik people. Once they were prosperous and aggressive hunters and a thriving people. But they were driven from their natural hunting grounds by the creation of a National Game Reserve with the expectation that they could somehow become farmers in the barren waste to which they were consigned. The result was a human debacle. The Ik became a desperate people, struggling to exist in a land where subsistence is hardly feasible.

The Ik people were visited by Colin Turnbull, an anthropologist, who tells the terrible story of their physical and cultural devastation in his book *The Mountain People*. He found the Ik a loveless, unfeeling people who sacrificed all values to the need for individual survival. They scorned any manifestation of generosity or concern and found cruelty and brutality amusing. Children were turned out by their parents at age three and would never be fed again even if they were to return begging and starving.

Turnbull has story after story to illustrate the remarkable state of the Ik. A nine-year old boy, for example, watched his six-year-old sister working for two days to make a little charcoal to sell to the nearby police for some food. (She was too young to sell herself sexually as she would in a few years, if she survived and was not by then too emaciated.) When she had the charcoal complete, she took her precious little package and headed across the field to the Police Post. At this point, her brother took off after her, slowly at first, to enjoy her panic, and then, as Turnbull tells it, "more swiftly, to give her time to begin to cry with the pain of hopelessness, and only then did he commit the physical violence of leaping on her, beating her savagely to the ground. . . ." He pummeled her further before even trying to get the charcoal. The little girl was clutching the charcoal to her stomach trying to save it. That presented an opportunity to her brother. "When he could not tug it away he just stood up suddenly and jumped on [her] back, forcing the bag of charcoal into her belly so that she screamed with pain and rolled over, clutching her injured stomach." With this amusement at an end, the boy casually picked up the charcoal and proceeded to the Police Post to sell it.[1]

Such behavior was normal for the Ik and no eyebrows would be raised by it. A person could sit quietly eating while starving parents or siblings watched with voiceless despair. Stealing food from the mouths of old people was literally child's play. It was thought foolishness not to grab whatever the weak or the dying could not protect. Sexuality showed the same predatory qualities. What sexual interest was there was usually adulterous and seemed motivated by a desire to gain at another's expense.

What did confuse the Ik and stir them to disapproval was any display of tenderness and affection. One little girl, named Adupa, simply did not accept the harsh ethic of her people. She insisted on being kind and hopeful. She wanted love from her parents and wanted to be with them; she would even bring them food when she could. Everyone, including her parents, considered her to be mad. Finally, since she kept insisting on being taken back, her parents did take her into their compound, to the child's delight. As Turnbull relates it:

> . . . Adupa was happy and stopped crying. She stopped crying forever, because her parents went away and closed the *asak* tight behind them, so tight that weak little Adupa could never have moved it if she had tried. But I doubt that she even thought of trying. She waited for them to come back with the food they promised her. When they came back she was still waiting for them. It was a week to ten days later, and her body was already almost too far gone to bury.[2]

The Ik People vs. Adupa . . .

There are good reasons for looking at the Ik. For one thing, as Turnbull is at pains to stress in his book, there is possibly a bit of the

Ik in the best of us. But, more specifically to our purposes here, the Ik present some real questions to us. To most of us who read about these sad people, little Adupa is a redeeming presence, a beautiful flower growing in an arid wilderness. The Ik, however, thought her insane and quite unable to comprehend reality. Who, pray tell, is correct? Maybe the Ik are. Maybe in such desperate circumstances there is no realistic room for compassion, gentleness, decency, or hope. But then, how do you judge the gentle Adupa? She and the others cannot both be right.

The debate, of course, extends beyond Adupa and her people. It touches on the basis of all moral discourse. Why admit into our vocabulary such terms as "right" and "wrong," "good" and "bad?" If we find no basis for such terms, why should they trouble our consciousness? If the results are more convenient than inconvenient, why not cheat, deceive, break promises? Why not go where the power and the advantage are and take for our models those German scientists who, as Abraham Maslow commented, "could work with equal zeal for Nazis, for Communists, or for Americans"?[8] Are not all mores a matter of cultural conditioning? Anthropology seems to support the idea that, when it comes to morals, one man's meat is another man's poison, that variation in moral norms is the rule and not the exception. Could we not then have done with the lingering and troubling pieties that attach to the terms *right* and *wrong?*

Underlying all of these questions and underlying our initial question as to whether Adupa or the rest of the Ik were right are the most fundamental and most neglected questions in ethical inquiry: *What is morality?* and *What is the foundation of moral experience?* If we cannot answer those two related questions with any satisfaction, then all moral categories are evacuated. The idea of moral obligation is meaningless, and narrow considerations of utility, advantage, and security will do nicely. Before offering my response to those correlative and foundational moral questions, I believe it is instructive to see how these questions are treated and evaded by many who ply the art-science of ethics or who step into the question of moral values while doing the work of the social sciences. There are four groups that merit attention in this regard: *the relativists, the survivalists, the analytical evaders,* and *the presumers.* The number of those who fit into these four categories is legion, and I shall submit that they miss or do no justice to the foundational concerns of ethics, as represented in the questions: *What is morality?* and *What is the foundation of moral experience?*

The Relativists: The Reduction of Morality to Custom . . .

In an article published in the *Journal of General Psychology* in 1934, anthropologist Ruth Benedict articulated a rather blunt form of cultural and ethical relativism. As she put it, normal and good behavior "is that which society has approved. A normal action is one which falls well within the limits of expected behavior for a particular society."[4]

Normality, as Professor Benedict says it, is culturally defined.

> We do not any longer make the mistake of deriving the morality of our own locality and decade directly from the inevitable constitution of human nature. We do not elevate it to the dignity of a first principle. We recognize that morality differs in every society, and is a convenient term for socially approved habits. Mankind has always preferred to say, "It is morally good," rather than "It is habitual," and the fact of this preference is enough for a critical science of ethics. But historically the two phrases are synonymous.[5]

Her point then is not lacking in clarity. The morally good and the habitual are synonymous. Ethics is thereby reduced to an analysis of the habitual, which we opt to call the good.[6]

If we take this thinking and apply it to Adupa, she fares poorly. Those of us who would be disposed to admire what we see as her gentle goodness are simply misjudging the moral fabric of that society and applying alien criteria. Cruelty was habitual for the Ik and socially approved. Thus, by Benedict's criterion, it was "morally good." Adupa was out of joint with the morality of her group, a heretic against the dominant orthodoxy, and, hence, evil. The boy who stomped on his hungry sister to steal her charcoal was good, as were the children who plucked food from the mouths of the aged, for such had become utterly habitual and socially acceptable with the Ik.

Whoever chokes on the notion of calling poor Adupa evil and her torturers good has choked on "cultural and ethical relativism" and properly so. Such relativism has enjoyed some brief scholarly favor, especially at the beginning of this century when we began to discover the vast variety in mores from culture to culture. The simplistic idea of one human nature interpreted univocally as to right and wrong perished as we encountered other societies with radically variant moral outlooks. The notion of a pan-human moral blueprint became passé. Relativism overreacted to this discovery, saying: "Whatever they are accustomed to do is good for them; whatever we are accustomed to do is good for us." Most thoughtful people have taken a second look at this superficiality and rejected it, recognizing that there are no grounds for equating custom with virtue, since vice can easily become customary in a person or in a people.

Relativism has not, of course, perished from human consciousness just because it has lost status among most scholars. Neither is it likely to disappear, since it is a convenient alternative to the strain of doing ethics in a confusing world. Relativism will continue to seduce as long as people prefer ease to effort. It finds residence today among those who see "doing your own thing" as an inalienable right. Relativism, however, has trouble being consistent. (Many a do-your-own-thinger roared to the attack when President Nixon was discovered doing his own thing, without noting their logical embarrassment.) Even Ruth Benedict in the article quoted above, after stressing that all local conventions of moral behavior are without absolute validity, still concluded that ". . . it is quite possible that a modicum of what is considered right and what wrong could be disentangled that is shared by the whole human race."[7] If cultural customs are *always* a variable and if even a "modicum" of morality is transculturally *invariable*, then morality and custom are not the same.

If it can be said that ethical relativism will remain a permanently seductive force in our mental world, it is also true that common sense will always be its major adversary. It is common sense that makes people morally prefer the gentle Adupa to her torturers. Ethical relativism cannot explain that preference. Those who so prefer and judge have to explain to the ethical relativists why that preference is serious and supportable and not a matter of caprice, whim, or cultural conditioning. This explanation is not easy and many who must explain it fail to do so.

As to our questions regarding what morality is and what its foundations are, relativism replies that the moral is reducible to approved custom. Its foundations are found in the mutable conditions of the society. This leaves no room for ethics as a normative enterprise which would seek out what *ought to be*, regardless of what socially approved habits might obtain. Complete relativism would leave no grounding for criticism or for moral creativity. It amounts to saying that *what is, ought to be* . . . depending on where the *is* happens to be. Up may be down or down up, depending on where you are. As ethical theory, such a position is vacuous.

It is, of course, true, as I shall subsequently discuss, that morality is *relational*. What is moral for one person may be immoral for another because of the diversity of circumstances. The moral quality of behavior depends on circumstances and how those circumstances relate to one another. This, however, does not open the door to the mush of a complete relativism. What it does do is make the art-science of ethics a permanently questing process. It also makes ethics humble and firm in its resistance to the human penchant for unfurling false absolutes.

Morality as the Condition of Survival . . .

The error of ethical relativism is crude. The survivalists, those who see the moral, not as the habitual and socially approved, but as that which is required to survive, would seem to have more going for them. For a rather pure example of survivalism we can turn to philosopher Ayn Rand. She has no time for a relativism which would reduce "good" to "habitual." She knows that if torture became habitual, it would not thereby become good. Rand wants to make some definite statements about right and wrong. She has no time for those whom I shall call in my fourth category the "presumers." Rand states that most of the philosophers simply took it for granted that ethics existed and did not concern themselves with discovering its objective validation.[8] She sees Aristotle as the greatest of the philosophers and yet, she notes, his ethics was based on what the good and wise men of his day chose to do without attending to the question of why they chose to do what they did or why he decided that they were good and wise in the first place.[9]

So what, then, is the ethical tool that can, with objectivity, make the incision between right and wrong? For Rand the tool is survival. The very life of that organism constitutes its standards of value. That which promotes and enhances that life is good and that which destroys or threatens that life is evil.[10] Thus, for Rand, good and evil are not whatever we decide they will be: the requirements of survival are dictated by one's nature. Our job is to discover what those requirements are, and this is precisely what the "science" of ethics is all about. A code of ethics lays out the right goals to pursue for survival.[11]

Rand may seem to have found some solid ground here. Anthropologists have pointed out that there is a remarkable amount of agreement among all peoples about those moral values that aid survival.[12] We might then be touching the deepest roots of ethics here. The good is that which promotes survival and the bad is that which impedes it. And, indeed, is this refreshingly simple idea not operating in a great deal of ethical reflection? A war is said to be just if it is necessary for survival, evil if it is not. An abortion is called good if it is necessary for the physical or psychological survival of the mother. (Of course, the fetus does not survive!) A divorce is good if the marriage cannot meet the needs of the parties. There are survivalist elements in all of these judgments.

It is sad to dismiss that which has the joyous merit of simplicity, but this must be done for survivalism. A survivalist base for ethics is not deep, solid, or broad enough. First of all it presumes that survival is an absolute good, and it is not. People readily and fervently admire someone who heroically gives his life in "the supreme sacrifice." Such a person is sacrificing survival to higher values. Also, terminal patients in unbearable, unrelievable pain might reasonably decide that death is preferable to survival. Survival is only a relative good. It can become undesirable or even ignoble in certain circumstances.

Also, survival is a free-floating concept. Its ambiguity calls out for adjectives. Just how much health, education, and welfare (and what quality of welfare) is required before one could say he is really "surviving"? The Ik were doing what they were doing to survive. Hitler felt that the elimination of the Jewish people was most conducive to the survival of his *Reich*. Survival is a good, but it is not an absolute good upon which all ethics can be built. It is also a potentially troublesome good since the survival needs of various people might compete. Some standard beyond survival would then be needed to settle the ensuing debate. Survivalism could also slip into a crude utilitarianism where the survival of the group, however conceived, would become the absolute, and the survival of the individual would be subordinated. The thrust of this would be totalitarian. Survivalism could also provide a cover for a raw and hostile egoism, whether of the individualistic or collective sort. The hollowness of the survival concept allows for some crude content.

Ayn Rand recognizes that survival at any price is not a good. She speaks of man's surviving qua man. Thus he should not survive after the fashion of a mere animal or a thug or an insensitive playboy.[18] Like Aristotle, Rand has her own presuppositions about what the good life is and about what befits man qua man, but she cannot establish these views as correct simply by asserting them. Some whom she sees as playboys or thugs would say she is wrong. Rationality is Rand's supreme hope. But those in various forms of thuggery, whether of the socially respectable or socially unrespectable sort, might argue that their behavior is very reasonable and very conducive to survival, given the hard realities of social existence. Rand could then only retreat—as she sees Aristotle doing—to her presumptions about what the good life is. She criticizes Aristotle for basing his ethical system on what the noble and wise men of his time decided upon as good, without asking why they chose to do it or why he evaluated them as noble and wise. Rand has her own wise men, and it is their conception of what kind of survival befits man as man that she takes as self-evident. She therefore commits the error that she condemns.

The merit of Ayn Rand from our perspective here is that she does try to answer the two fundamental questions about what morality is and what its foundations are. Her fixation on the rubric of survival, however, leaves her in debt on both questions. She does not get to the foundations of moral meaning. She does properly look for that form of survival which befits man qua man, but she presumes, like an intuitionist, that this should be obvious. As a matter of fact, her system of elaborated selfishness is not self-evidently correct and is to many rather evidently wrong. Her announced desire not to take the existence of ethics for granted and her quest for the objective validation of ethics are laudable and on target. Stopping at survival, however, was stopping short.

Rand has not cornered the market on survivalism. Ethological approaches to ethics are naturally drawn to a survivalist ethics. Anyone studying the evolution of species will naturally be taken by the master theme of survival that characterizes that drama. This can lead to the invalid transference of the laws of physical nature to the laws of ethics. Such things as altruism will be explained simply in terms of the survival needs of the species. This error is not limited to those who bring ethology to bear on moral values. Science in general is led to see survival as the rudimentary value. When this is transferred to ethics, where survival cannot be shown to have foundational status, problems occur.

The Linguistic Bypass . . .

Ludwig Wittgenstein proposed the idea that philosophy "does not result in 'philosophical propositions,' but rather in the clarification of propositions."[14] Wittgenstein was convinced that "our philosophical problems arise when language goes on holiday."[15] Remarkably, this stress on the linguistic dimension of understanding took hold. As Harry K. Girvetz comments:

> In amazing numbers the ablest philosophers of the English-speaking world have abandoned the historic interpretation of philosophy's role as the pursuit of wisdom, and, rejecting Plato's definition of the philosopher as the "spectator of all time and all existence," have obeyed Wittgenstein's injunction and gone out to do battle against the "bewitchment of our intelligence by . . . language." Almost in concert they have turned their attention to the analysis of language, convinced that if the philosopher cannot give us wisdom or truth, he can at least teach us to be clear.[16]

This grand philosophical defection has not left ethics untouched. There are many in ethics who confuse busyness about moral language with the business of doing ethics. We would not expect from such philosophers of language much help in exploring the foundations of ethics. Yet in their own special way, it is precisely the question of *what morality is* that consumes these thinkers. Professor William K. Frankena, of the University of Michigan, has suggested that the primary concern of contemporary moral philosophy is with the question *What is morality?* The editors of the volume in which his work appeared, Professors Castaneda and Nakhnikian, call his effort a "searching evaluation of the most important contemporary views of what morality is."

Here is the way Frankena puts it: "Contemporary moral philosophy may . . . be represented as primarily an attempt to understand what morality is, meaning by 'morality' not the quality of conduct which is opposed to immorality but what Butler so nicely refers to as 'the moral institution of life.' The current endeavor is . . . to grasp the nature of morality itself. . . . In this endeavor both Continental and English-speaking philosophers are engaged, though to different degrees, in different ways, and with different equipment."[17]

Now, at first blush, that sounds exactly like what I have been calling for. This surely sounds like these philosophers are intent on exploring the foundations of moral experience. Disappointment, however, awaits us. When they set out to understand "what morality is," they do not, of course, mean to tell us what is right or wrong. But neither do they want to discuss the basis of rightness or wrongness or why it is that moral statements have any meaning that should be of concern to us at all. They do not get to the foundations of moral experience. Suppose, for example, someone, impressed by the story of the unsentimental Ik, were to say: "Parents *should* abandon their children at age three." The philosophers discussed by Frankena are not speaking to the question of whether or not it is wrong to abandon one's children. They are absorbed in showing whether this is a statement in the realm of morality or in some other realm such as science, or sports, or the culinary arts.[18]

In Frankena's helpful summary of this not very helpful contemporary moral philosophy, we find three groups distinguished: the first two groups, with various subtleties interposed, say that a statement is *moral*, not because of any content it may have about right or wrong, but because of the *form* of that statement. The third group insists that for a statement to be moral, it must contain reference to the welfare of others.

In its fullest form, the first group informs us "that one has a morality if and only if one has principles which, in the light of full knowledge, one takes as supreme and is ready to see anyone else take as supreme; and that such principles are moral simply because they meet these formal conditions, regardless of their content and acceptability to others."[19] The second group is almost the same as the first group, but they add that there must be some kind of consensus to constitute one's judgment as *moral*.[20]

The third group feels that a statement is not *moral* unless it implies the welfare of society. As third group philosopher K. Baier puts it, "Moral rules should also have a certain sort of content. Observation of these rules should be for *the good of everyone alike*."[21] If someone does not believe that he should work "for the good of everyone alike," his statements on the subject are not within the realm of morality. "The man has simply put himself outside of morality altogether, and can be reasoned with only in non-moral terms, or not at all."[22] Thus, the Ik people explaining their view of life, or even someone like Garrett Hardin, who does not propose solutions to the human crisis that are "for the good of everyone alike," are not talking ethics at all. Their statements, according to this last group, are not morally adjudicable at all, since they do not include the requisite concern for all others. What confuses this group is that they are using *moral* as the opposite of immoral . . . not as the opposite of amoral or nonmoral. Lack of concern for others is arguably immoral, but it is still a *moral* matter in the sense that it can be evaluated ethically.

This sorry enterprise (to which I alluded in suggesting sources of Dadaist reaction) does not tell us what morality is, nor does it lead us to the foundations of moral experience. It would not be surprising or unwelcome if all of the discussion just summarized struck the astute reader as unreal. An air of unreality regularly attends the missing of the main point or main question. These philosophers err, not in stepping back from particular issues of normative ethics (abortion, war, sexual ethics, etc.) to see what morality is. This is what should be done, as a prelude, to know what one is about in doing ethics. Their mistake is in attempting to say what morality is by noting the external shape of moral language rather than by showing what moral statements *mean*. When they have told us that a statement is moral and not geological, they have neglected the fair question: So what? Form without content will not tell us what morality is any more than a man's shadow will tell us what a person is. (And because shadows are deceiving, it may not even tell us if it is a man.) Rather than telling us what morality is, as they purport to do, these philosophers merely note that whatever it is, it has to do with universalizable values. That could be the prelude to an answer; an answer it is not. Since these philosophers miss the main question, the absence of an answer could not be surprising. What they are doing is tracing the shadows that morality casts on language. Their analysis could only appear wan to whoever senses that morality is heavy with mystery, that it spans humanness from its linguistic surface to its mystical, often paradoxical, and ineffable depths. Its meaning and its mystery is the meaning and the mystery of personhood.[23]

Fortunately, not all of modern moral thought has been hamstrung by narrowly linguistic fixations and even those who have been significantly limited in this fashion have not, blessedly, been consistently so. Also, many of the more recent preoccupations of philosophers have had the effect of drawing them to the foundations. However, unless we come to grips with why it is that moral statements have meaning and whence that meaning derives, and unless we dare to tangle with such things as the role of affectivity in moral knowledge and with the supreme moral enigma of self-sacrifice perceived as noble, we have remained unprofitable and timid servants. To this I shall return. But, next, we can look to those who eschew the foundations by issue-hopping in the field of ethics. These are the presumers.

The Presumers . . .

The philosophers whom we have just considered do at least ask what morality is, thus evincing some concern for the foundations of ethics. Unfortunately, they are locked into the linguistic pocket and so afford us only minimal light. The presumers, on the other hand, just take the foundations for granted. They presume that it is obvious what morality is and why moral discourse should be taken seriously. The presumers are foundational intuitionists. They act as though we all intuit what morality is and why it is a sufficiently grounded activity to merit our serious attention. The presuming ethicists whom I have in mind are those who ply their trade only at the level of normative ethics, addressing specific issues. They energetically go about the business of doing practical ethics, discussing and debating matters like abortion, medical problems, business and political practices, war, peace, capital punishment, and sexuality without unpacking their presuppositional baggage and telling us why all of this is a legitimate and special field of inquiry.

Such issue-oriented moralists are apparently unaware of the lacuna in their theoretical foundations. If they would speak to ethical issues, they must let us know whence they come. *One's arguments and one's conclusions are often controlled by one's presuppositions and are always influenced by them.* The presumers presume too much, especially in a positivistic age in which the art-science of ethics is either subjected to scientistic reductionism or considered a pariah in the intellectual order.

Not all the presumers ignore the question of foundations entirely. There are two kinds of presumers who have at least an implied position on the foundations. They still, however, presume too much. I refer to the religious and the legalistic presumers.

The religious presumers are those who feel that they have said enough when they have said that God's will explains morality. Not all religious persons do this, of course, but those who do are open to two perils. First of all, they are bearers of certain historically conditioned presumptions about the nature of the good life which they then are inclined to attribute to God. We are all instinctively and dangerously disposed to seek numinous auspices for our moral opinions. Religious people throughout history have attributed many a horror to the will of God. Those who embarked on the slaughterous Crusades did so under the motivation of a *"Deus vult!"* (God will it!). Soon they were sending back reports like this: ". . . in the portico of Solomon, men rode in blood up to their knees and the bridle reins. Indeed, it was a just and splendid judgment of God, that this place should be filled with the blood of the unbelievers, when it had suffered so long from their blasphemies."[24] On the other hand, there are believers who claim that God wills no violence whatever. Where does this leave us? Modern debate abounds with dogmatic assumptions about precisely what God wants in debated issues such as abortion, divorce, family planning, the work ethic, and much more. It is a dangerous and presumptuous game.

The second problem of the religious presumers is a logical one. They presume that religious experience is logically prior to moral experience, and it is not. Belief in God is an inference from other experience, including moral experience; it is not primary. Primary experience is within the world that we can see and touch. Theistic or atheistic conclusions are possible conclusions from that experience. Moral experience originates in the tangible visible world. It is prior to religious judgments.[25]

Those who see law as the foundation of the moral life are also presumers. This is the heresy of the common man, at least in Anglo-Saxon cultures with their native and optimistic reverence for legality. This error sees "good" and "legal" as synonymous. If something is wrong but not illegal, the legalist concludes: "There ought to be a law!" What else—if the legal circumscribes the good!

Such legalists are great presumers. They presume, first of all, that legality and morality are the same thing. They forget that there can be such a thing as bad laws. Slavery, remember, was once legal in these United States. And organized crime often manages to work within the legal. Also, there are many areas in private life which are rich in moral meaning and into which the law should not intrude at all. On the positive side, heroic acts are not prescribed by law, and yet they are moral. The presumption of the legalist is completely upside down. He misses the fact that something is not good because it is legal; rather good laws are good only if they are moral. Laws have to conform to something more basic, and that is morality. When they do not conform, those laws have to be resisted—in the name of morality. If law were the basis of the good life, there would be no reason for conscientious objection, legal reform, or revolution. Legality is based on morality, not vice versa.

The error of such legalism is crude, but it is not rare. It is, for example kneaded into American culture, so much so that most Americans would not countenance the American Revolution of 1776 today, although they celebrate it annually, having forgotten what it was. It was a strike against legality in the name of morality. It was an act of corporate dissent against established "law and order" perceived as unjust.[26]

The presumers, then, are those who go about doing ethics in the form of trying to answer particular ethical questions without pausing to validate the whole enterprise by seeking to discern its foundations. Religious and legalistic presumers are slightly less presumptuous since they feel that either the will of God or the law is all the grounding they need. They still, however, merit their place among the presuming moralists, since their supposed foundations are neither adequate nor ultimate.

Ethical Realism . . .

At this point, I am obviously on the spot. I have dismissed four groups of thinkers who stand before the twin questions of what morality is and what are its foundations and either ignore those questions or answer them erroneously. It is my turn and I propose what I am calling ethical realism as the answer.[27]

First of all, one can explain what morality is by addressing the word *moral*. Moral as the opposite of amoral or nonmoral refers to all judgments of *what befits or does not befit persons as persons*. Certain things may befit (be valuable to) persons from narrower perspectives. To a seeker of wealth, the acquisition of wealth is befitting, but *as a person*, not just any kind of acquisition is befitting. We agree that there are some ways that persons ought not to get wealth and we bring on "moral" language, such as "thievery" or "fraud," to describe it.

The word *moral* as the opposite of immoral is a second order term which means that a judgment has been made that something is not

just morally adjudicable (moral as the opposite of amoral), but that
it has already been judged and judged favorably. Thus the Ik people
defending their way of life, or Garrett Hardin recommending the
neglect of starving peoples, or Adolf Hitler describing the need to
make his Third Reich "free of Jews," are all involved in ethics. They
are pronouncing on what befits persons as persons in their judgment.
As such they are involved in moral discourse. We may do battle with
them on whether what they are defending is morally defensible, but
we will at least recognize that what they are doing in their own way
is ethics. We may argue that what they are doing in their ethics is a
radical perversion of moral experience, but we need not be unclear
on what it is they are about. They are discussing or at least assuming
in a controlling way what befits persons qua persons and to that extent they are engaged in the work of ethics. In a word, morality
refers to that which is fitting vis-à-vis persons; ethics is a systematic
discussion of morality.

To say this, however, is not enough. The conjoining question
remains: What are the foundations of morality? Why are we concerned about what befits persons qua persons? Is it because of convention or enlightened self-interest, or because of the command of
society or of God? What is the experience that gives us that kind of
awareness that we call *moral*—that gives moral judgments their basis
in reality? In stating my answer to this, I am impelled to register an
immediate plea that you not be put off by its apparently excessive
simplicity. It is the simplest and most basic of truths that we are
often most prone to ignore. And it is often the simplest truths that
invite us to the deepest penetration.

The foundation of morality is *the experience of the value of persons and their environment*. This experience is *the* distinctively
human and humanizing experience and the gateway to personhood.
It is this experience that sets us apart from beast and barbarian. It is
the seed of civilization, the root of culture, and the badge of distinctively human consciousness. Without an in-depth participation in
this experience, morality would seem a meaningless intrusion on our
whim and fancy, and moral language would be non-sense. If human
activities, institutions, and religions do not enhance this experience,
they are negligible and indeed objectionable, for they are failing at
the constitutional level of human existence.

Every discussion of every moral issue, from mercy death to abortion, from nonmarital sex to the rights of citizens—whether we

speak of medicine, politics, or business—is an attempt to apply the meaning of this foundational moral experience to concrete and specific cases. Moral debate takes place because persons are perceived as valuable in such an exquisite way that a world of awe and oughts is born in response to them. Ethics exists as an effort to see what does and does not befit persons in all of their marvelous and compelling valuableness and sacredness. Where this valuableness is not perceived, or where it is perceived as applying only to a few, distinctively human living is cut short. Obviously, this experience is not to be presumed or bypassed by any who study the mysterious chemistry of human personhood. In exploring this experience, we touch not just on what morality is and means, but on what a person is and what the human power which we call love is. Morality and love are contiguous notions rooted in the experience of the value of persons. Thus we are simultaneously exploring the meaning of morality, love, and personhood.

Up to this point, I have simply asserted that the foundational moral experience is the experience of the sacredness and valuableness of persons and their environment. I have not proved it. Neither do I intend to "prove" it now, for it does not fall within the simpler zone of the provable. Like all of our deeper experiences, it can only be illustrated. What we can do is open ourselves to its impact, see it emerging in certain manifestations of human life, listen to those who speak of it, and show that moral meaning evaporates if the experience is not appreciated for what it is. Finally, we can attempt humbly to describe it. In other words, it can be shown that we cannot think or speak morally or understand ourselves if this experience is not accepted as foundational. All of ethics is organically linked to the sacred value of persons. We have no choice but to look at it closely and see that this is so.

The notion of sacredness is more basic than the notion of God. Even those who dispense with the idea of God must deal with the sacred. (Those who infer to the existence of a deity will explain sacredness in the light of that belief.) It is a functioning category of human existence without which the human animal cannot be understood. If nothing is sacred, human life becomes absurd, and ethical discourse is rendered inane.[28]

Philosopher Eliseo Vivas has said that "experience is the plasma of relevant, meaningful thinking."[29] It is thus also the plasma of ethics if it is to be relevent and meaningful. To illustrate what we mean when we say that the perception of the sacredness of persons is the foundation of ethics, we should look first to the most striking and salient manifestation of it in our experience—the so-called supreme sacrifice. The foundational moral experience of the value of persons exists in quiet ways throughout the whole of moral experience and gives that experience its meaning. The reason promises are to be kept and debts paid, and the reason we should seek to bring justice and harmony to human affairs, is that persons are valuable. If we had not been struck to some degree by the perception of that value, we would experience no force in those obligations. If we think of the foundational moral experience as a continuum, these obligations are at the undramatic, day-to-day end of that continuum. They are, of course, utterly basic and foundational, and human society would not endure were these person-related values not to some degree experienced and enshrined.

The foundational moral experience, however, is most discernible and its mysterious depths are most clearly revealed at the dramatic end of the continuum to which I will first attend. I refer to that outstanding phenomenon which is visible with great consistency in the plasma of human experience. My reference is to our mysterious tendency to esteem certain person-related values so highly that when they are at issue, we will die for them. Or, if we do not have the courage or the opportunity to do so, we will admire those who do and will call them heroes.

What makes this sentiment so mystifying is that the one incontrovertible thing that we all know is that this physical life of ours is the matrix for all the good things we experience. When we become a cadaver, that matrix is gone. Many people believe that when we become a cadaver, that matrix perdures in another form and our personal life continues in a new mode. However, those who affirm this *believe* it. They do not *know* it with the immediacy and certainty with which they know their lived experience.[30] Therefore, believers and nonbelievers in an afterlife are at one in this: The one thing they know with direct immediacy is that this life in the body is good and is the precondition of all the goods we have experienced. Still, we live with the anomaly that we are drawn to admire those who give this life up in certain value situations with no guarantee of any sequel and with the distinct possibility that they are giving up existence for nonexistence. No one who does ethics can ignore this outstanding paradox in human experience. I am focusing on it here because I believe that it shows in the most dramatic and outstanding form the depths of the experience of the sacredness of persons that grounds all of ethics. The boldest manifestations of any experience reveal more of what that experience is even when it comes to us in subtler pose.

My argument here is not based on a claim of the universality of this experience. No one lacking universal knowledge could make such a claim. I will point out the extraordinary prominence of this experience, which is enough, I believe, to show that it is not the yield of one specific culture and that it is not a freakish element in human experience. Obviously, there are persons and cultures where heroic self-sacrifice is not esteemed. Something need not be universal to be considered genuinely and normatively human. No virtue that we would defend as enhancing our humanity will be found to be universally prized or practiced.[31] The poor Ik, for example, would see self-sacrifice as madness. Even closer to home we find those who, while not ignoring this experience, try to evacuate it of all significance. We saw how Skinner makes a moth or a dupe out of someone who would die for others.

Ayn Rand is a bit more contorted in explaining this. She is, of course, utterly consistent with her apology for selfishness. In her wizened view, love is a personal and selfish value and a reaction to one's own value discovered in another person. The goal and yield of love is one's own selfish well-being and happiness.[32] From such soil, self-sacrifice will not grow.

Applied to a situation of risking your life for another, she says that to do so for a stranger would be immoral unless it involved minimal risk. It could be moral and rational to risk all to save someone you love dearly for the simply selfish reason that you could not bear to live without this person.[33] Sacrifice is not sacrifice for Rand. It is just another investment of the ego in itself.

Ayn Rand is overreacting to those philosophers and theologians who say that all self-love is morally bad. They are, of course, in error, as is she in overreacting to them. Some of the classical systems of morality teach that you should love your neighbor *as* you love yourself, so that self-love is seen, not as a deviation, but as the paradigm for neighbor-love. In fact, the legitimacy and inevitability of self-love heightens the point about which we are speaking. Because we do and must love ourselves, the fact that we admire and perhaps feel drawn to imitate the supreme sacrifice of one's life in certain cases becomes all the more of a mystery.

The Supreme Sacrifice in Religion, History, and Literature . . .

This mystery is a fact which shows up with great persistence in various and unconnected human experiences. Our folklore, literature, and religious history are likely to include many examples of heroic self-sacrifice. There is a saying in Buddhist literature which is accepted by all Buddhists, however varied they may be in other teachings. "As a mother even at the risk of her own life watches over her own child, so let everyone cultivate a boundless love toward all beings."[34] Of "the good man" Aristotle says "that he does many acts for the sake of his friends and his country, and if necessary dies for them; for he will throw away both wealth and honours and in general the goods that are objects of competition, gaining for himself nobility. . . . Now those who die for others doubtless attain this result; it is therefore a great prize that they choose for themselves."[35] Hindu literature does not give notable prominence to acts of positive benevolence, and yet in their sacred writings we still find a recognition of the value of loving self-sacrifice: "Men without love think only of self, but the loving strip themselves to the bone for others."[36] And in Christianity, the idea of dying for others as the supremely moral action attains classical expression: "A man can have no greater love than to lay down his life for his friends.[37]

Some modern Jewish scholars argue that laying down one's life for one's friends is actually a Jewish ideal and thus does not separate Judaism from Christianity. Others disagree but allow that it could be looked upon as an act of special piety and thus esteemed as a high act of virtue. Also, in Jewish thought it could be mandatory to lay down one's life for the nation.[38]

Adam Smith, in his *The Theory of Moral Sentiments*, written in 1759, said: "A brave man ought to die rather than make a promise which he can neither keep without folly nor violate without ignominy."[39] Person-related values, in other words, might be such that death is preferable to their violation. The psychologist Abraham H. Maslow laments "the widespread 'valuelessness' in our society, i.e., people having nothing to admire, to sacrifice themselves for, to surrender to, to die for," and sociologist Richard L. Means, condemning the vacuity of dying for abstractions or for material things, observes: "Only dying for human beings . . . is moral."[40] The experience of moral values and readiness to die when these values are at issue is healthy for Maslow, notwithstanding his stress on self-actualization. And sociologist Means sees self-sacrifice as noble only when it relates to the value of persons. He observes that even Socrates said he was dying for the youth of Athens.

This remarkable paradox of self-sacrifice perceived as heroically noble also emerges regularly in history and in literature. Concrete examples can make the mystery more present to our consciousness.

J. Glenn Gray, in his thoughtful and absorbing book *The Warriors*, tells some poignant stories about persons who risked death in the face of values they thought more important than living. During World War II in the Netherlands, there was a German soldier who was a member of an execution squad ordered to shoot innocent hostages. When the hostages arrived, he suddenly stepped out of line and refused to shoot them. What could be anticipated, happened. He was charged on the spot with treason, lined up with the hostages, and promptly executed by his erstwhile comrades. Gray calls the incident an "episode [which] cannot fail to be inspiriting" and a "revelation of nobility in mankind."[41] The incident had become fabled among the Dutch who related it to Gray.

Notice in this story that the hostages still died in spite of the soldier's dissent; the result of his refusal was that there was more death, not less. His action, therefore, had a certain futility about it, and yet, I submit, it remains admirable. If someone did this whom we had always thought of negatively as ruthless, egoistic, and self-serving, we would have to change our estimate of his character. The soldier's action is not a manifestation of meanness of spirit, but of its opposite. Is it not true to our deepest experience to say that we would hope that in a similar situation we or our children would have the courage not to stand there like the other soldiers and obediently blast lead into the quivering flesh of innocent and desperate hostages? If we were among those hostages and knew that we would die anyhow, would we not still have experienced something in this soldier that was beautiful and good, even if not useful to us? If we were a friend of the soldier and would miss him sorely, would not the incident have confirmed the good qualities that caused us to love him as a friend? Would not his sacrifice seem to represent the fullest flowering of his goodness?

Gray tells another story of another German soldier who was ordered on a reprisal raid on a French village. The orders were to burn the village and allow no man, woman, or child to escape alive. He obeyed and joined the others in shooting down the villagers as they fled screaming from their burning homes. When Gray met this soldier, he was fighting with the French underground against his own people. Shortly after the slaughter, he had abandoned the German cause. When the soldier recounted the incident to Gray, his "face was contorted in painful fashion and he was nearly unable to breathe."[42] His whole being shuddered anew at his offense of the sacred. If he had refused to shoot the people, he would have been shot. He would not have saved the people. Refusal would not have been a "useful" action. Yet we recognize that it would have been moral—supremely so. And we can identify with his guilt for not having refused, even at the risk of his life. Again the paradox is with us and cannot be facilely explained away. We are the only animal who knows and understands death and its devastation. And yet we are the only animal that knows it should prefer death to the violation of certain person-related values. The mystery of this should not be missed. It shows the depths of the apparently simple experience of the value of persons.

The mystery intrudes itself again in the prison rebellion in Attica, New York. Prison conditions were utterly dehumanizing. The spirit of the rebellion was expressed by one of the older inmates: "If we cannot live as people, we will at least try to die as men." The opportunity to "die as men" was given a few days later. These men were in prison because at some time they had not lived as men. Yet, history records that some of the prisoners died redemptively using their bodies to protect their hostage prison guards from the shots.[43] To the person who could find no nobility or beauty in this, very little could be said. A true reaction would seem to be that these prisoners died "as men" because the mode of their death showed a profound and humanizing—albeit belated—awareness of the sacred value of human life, value that is so precious that it makes inexplicable but exquisite sense even to die for it when the circumstances so invite. The life-saving deaths of these men illustrated in climactic form the foundational moral experience of which I speak.

The French theologian R. L. Bruckberger speaks of the inherent sense in political martyrdom. There are times when death is preferable to continued living, when the voice of conscience and integrity outweighs the urgency of self-preservation. Is it not true, he asks, that we can say "that the individual conscience transcends political obligation, that there is something in man which dominates society; that this something which dominates society also transcends life and death, since men are willing to die in order to preserve that integrity and refuse to live if life is to be preserved at the expense of it? Yes, these are indeed the essential features of martyrdom: death, to bear witness to what exceeds life, to place its seal on what death cannot touch."[44]

In illustration of this, Bruckberger recalls the execution of seven young Communists who were shot at Clairvaux prison in 1942. Even in the face of the firing squad, they sang the "Marseillaise" and the "Internationale." Bruckberger allows that it is no easy thing to explain what this "something" was that had them singing rather than bowing to save their lives. What he does affirm relates directly to my effort here to look into experience and sense anew our native admiration for heroic death.

> . . . if one had to choose between the victims who die and the executioners who survive, who would not be on the victims' side? . . . The fact is that I can never think back to that execution without the image which I retain of those seven young men being haloed by victory. There can be no doubt that this execution, like so many others, and this blood that was spilled, were an affirmation in death of a reality which transcends both life and death but which would have been destroyed if those young men had denied it and betrayed it by going over to the enemy.[45]

Literature turns to this experience also in its dramatic form of self-sacrifice. Charles Dickens' novel A Tale of Two Cities ends with the story of Sydney Carton's death. Carton substituted himself for Charles Darnay and went to the guillotine in his stead. Carton's appraisal of his deed on the way to his death was that "it is a far, far better thing that I do than I have ever done. . . ." The novel endorses Carton's act in terms of high heroism.

We find a similar use of this kind of heroic ending in Arthur Miller's play Incident at Vichy. The German Von Berg explains to the Jewish LeDuc that "there are people who would find it easier to die than stain one finger with this murder." Thereupon he presses his exit pass upon LeDuc, allowing him to escape, while he himself assumes the risk of death as the play ends.[46]

In approaching the foundational moral experience, I have begun at its enigmatic depths where the supreme sacrifice for persons is felt as noble and not foolhardy. I am not, of course, implying that self-sacrifice is an absolute value, admirable under all circumstances. Indeed it could be irresponsible and immoral in certain circumstances. Also, in most day-to-day moral situations, the supreme sacrifice simply has no direct relevance. I make special note of this phenomenon because it represents a dramatic response to the perceived value of persons. It witnesses to the enigmatic depths of the foundational moral experience and shows what that experience can command. Although such sacrificial behavior is a rarity, it is broadly and transculturally admired and storied. All of this speaks to what persons are perceived to be worth and thus to the roots of ethics.

Less dramatic manifestations of the foundational moral experience are with us in the normal unfolding of human life and consciousness. The experience emerges in the perception of what we owe to persons, and, correspondingly, in the moral shock or sense of profanation we feel when persons are denied their due. Here again we are not moving at the level of scientific proof. Ethics, like much of important human reality, is beyond the proofs and measures of scientific method. This could only be offensive to one who has given science a monarchical status. As Aristotle says: "It is a mark of the educated man and a proof of his culture that in every subject he looks for only so much precision as its nature permits."[47] He must also be prepared to let truth emerge in a way suited to the matter in question and not try to corral all truth by the methods suitable to some other area of knowledge.

With that understood, we can seek to discern the foundational moral experience in our more normal appreciation of moral oughts and moral shock. Sir William David Ross, the British ethicist, said: "To me it seems as self-evident as anything could be, that to make a promise, for instance, is to create a moral claim on us in someone else."[48] He called this a "prima facie duty," and he considered among other such duties the obligation to tell the truth, to make reparation for wrongful acts, to give to each his own, etc. Ross said that he could not prove these oughts to anyone who would deny them. All he could do is to try to open them to the experience.

Ross, of course, goes too far in saying that these duties are self-evident, since they are not evident to everyone at every level of moral development. Life would be more lovely if indeed they were. These duties could, however, be called primal moral experiences which are available to mature persons. These experiences, however, only make sense if we see them as manifestations of the foundational moral experience of the value of persons. Every moral ought derives from such experience. Because persons are so valuable, we owe them fidelity and truth and justice. A moral ought is basically a specified utterance of awe before the phenomenon of personhood. Because persons are persons, they may not be bought and sold like cattle, plucked like weeds, set aside and segregated like mere objects, misled, etc. To know this to some degree is to be civilized, moral, and human to that degree.

Immanuel Kant also speaks to this. He says: "For the commonest observation shows that if we imagine an act of honesty performed with a steadfast soul and sundered from all view to any advantage in this or another world . . . it elevates the soul and arouses the wish to be able to act in this way."[49] For Kant, acting honorably and honestly even when it causes you pain or inconvenience is so admirable and noble that "even moderately young children" would perceive it so.[50] Being more general, Kant puts it this way: ". . . every rational being exists as an end in himself and not merely as a means to be arbitrarily used by this or that will . . . rational beings are designated 'persons' because their nature indicates that they are ends in themselves, i.e., things which may not be used merely as means."[51] Again, what this says is that moral experience is experience of the value of persons. Anyone who has this experience knows that persons are too valuable to be reduced to exploitable means. They have a certain primacy of value that does not permit that.

In another way, Albert Camus witnesses to the same experience when, during the French-Algerian crisis in 1958, reprisal raids against civilian populations were being used, and torture had become established policy. He wrote at that time that "it is better to suffer certain injustices than to commit them even to win wars. . . ."[52]

Better to be killed than to kill unjustly. Better, in other words, to be tortured than to torture! Long before Camus, Socrates reached this same conclusion: "It is better for a man to suffer injustice than to commit it."[53] The reason for this could only be traceable to what could be called a mystical perception of the inviolable sanctity of human life. This mystical perception undergirds every moral ought and those who are alien to it are alien to moral consciousness. Camus's remarks show us how moral shock gives a kind of negative entree to the experience of the value of persons. Violation often serves to show the value of the violated. Such moral experience finds expression as a *Thou shalt not*. It was torture and slaughter that stimulated Camus's profound expression of the value of persons.

That same value and the sense of profanation is evoked by way of shock when, for example, we hear of the medical experiments done on retarded children in Willowbrook on Staten Island in New York. In a 1956 study sponsored by the Armed Forces Epidemiologic Board and endorsed by the executive faculty of New York University School of Medicine, live hepatitis virus was administered to a number of the retarded children at Willowbrook. Conditions at Willowbrook were a horror and hepatitis was rampant. Richard Restak, M.D., gives us a summation of how the justification for the experiment went:

> Most of the children were going to contract hepatitis at some point in their stay at Willowbrook anyway. Many of these would not be diagnosed if the case were mild, even if it resulted in severe liver damage. By deliberately giving the hepatitis virus, an extremely mild form of the infection would be induced, followed by immunity. In the event that hepatitis developed, the children would be under care in a special, well-equipped, optimally staffed unit.[54]

Given the fact that the accepted treatments for hepatitis were not generally in use at Willowbrook, that effective steps to improve conditions were not taken, and the fact that hepatitis cannot always be controlled, even within the best medical context, the exploitation of these children was gross. In Kant's terms, they were treated as means, not as ends. They were treated as objects, not as persons. Important scientific discoveries came from the experiments and were published in prestigious journals such as the *Journal of the American Medical Association* and the *New England Journal of Medicine*. Yet few are they today who would not admit that the affair was morally outrageous. Our sense of profanation tells us that the foundational moral experience was in abeyance as far as these children were concerned. For that precise reason, the term *immoral* applies.

The Willowbrook atrocity also serves as an argument against a simplistic intuitionism. The misuse of these already offended persons was not self-evidently immoral to many who were thoroughly acquainted with the facts. Intuitionism underestimates the volitional, affective elements in moral understanding. It underestimates, too, the impediments due to lower stages of psychological moral development. Many, in the presence of profanation, feel no sense of profanation.

Similarly, our indignant objections to torture, biological or nuclear warfare, the neglect of starving peoples, rape, racism, or sexism would be stripped of meaning were it not for this experience whereby the term "moral" comes to life.

The Sanctity of Life . . .

In much of Western and also of Eastern culture, it is the principle of "the sanctity of life" that is employed to express the foundational moral experience. As Daniel Callahan says: "On the basis of this principle, moral rules have been framed; human rights claimed and defended; and cultural, political and social priorities established."[55] Some dislike the term because it might imply an exaltation of life regardless of its quality. The idea of "sanctity" offends some nonreligious persons. Still, in Callahan's thought, there seems to be "no other widely affirmed principle which presently serves so well."[56] Whatever the value of the term, it is clear that much of what discussion does go on regarding the foundational moral experience takes place under the symbol of "the sanctity of life." Most importantly, those who discuss this matter admit that there is an experience of the value of persons that is the grounding of moral consciousness. Sociologist Edward Shils, in an essay entitled "The Sanctity of Life," asks: "Is human life really sacred? I answer that it is, self-evidently. Its sacredness is the most primordial of experiences."[57] P. B. Medawar says that the defense of the sanctity of life rests upon "a certain natural sense of the fitness of things, a feeling that is shared by most kind and reasonable people even if we cannot define it in philosophically defensible or legally accountable terms."[58] Daniel Callahan, after asking what the ultimate justifications are for the normative principles embodying a valuation of the sanctity of life, replies: "The 'ultimate justifications,' I believe, have to be human experience; that is where we all start and therein we have a common standard of reference."[59]

The underlying question in all of these statements is How do we justify our ultimate justifications? Shils says the experience is self-evident—which leaves him vulnerable to examples of people who do not appear to see it. Medawar enters the condition that "kind and reasonable people" will see it. Others argue that life is unlivable if you do not see it and that all values and rights are undermined by the denial of the sanctity of life. All are struggling with a justification of that which is seen as ultimate and foundational. Normally we refer to something more generic or more ultimate when we define or attempt to prove something. We cannot do that in speaking of so basic an experience as the sanctity of life. What one can do is say that *moral experience cannot be explained nor can we be true to our own experience if we do not accept the foundational role of our perception of the value of persons and their environment*. To negate the foundational status of this perception is to undermine the conditions for moral discourse. If, as Teilhard de Chardin says, coherence and fruitfulness are the marks of truth, then we have reached to truth here. Incoherence and chaos would be the yield of a denial of the value of persons and the sanctity of life.

However, it is not too helpful if we simply stop here. We must look into the experience as best we can and try to say more about its character. This could make its reality somewhat more apparent and lend a more secure status to what we see as basic. I shall attempt to show that the foundational moral experience is an *affective, faith* experience which must be understood in terms of *process*.

Affectivity, Faith, Process . . .

Affectivity. It is in the heart that morality has its birth. Ethics moves on to confirmatory reason and theory, to demonstrations of the coherence and fruitfulness and truthfulness of one's positions; but it is in feeling that its roots are found and nourished. The foundational moral experience is an affective reaction to value. It is not a metaphysical or a religious experience primordially. It is not a conclusion to a syllogism, though it may subsequently be supported by syllogisms and reasoning. The value of persons cannot be taught, subjected to proof, reasoned to, or computerized. It can only be affectively appreciated.

The foundational moral experience is marked by the discovery that all life, whether it be in leaf, flower, bird, or beast, is awe-inspiring, a kind of miracle of energy and organization. Personal life is discovered to be even more marvelous. Here are beings who transcend everything. Not only can they perceive what is and react to that, but they can also imagine what is not but could be, and bring it about. They can find and create beauty. They can speak and sing and laugh and be merciful. They can and sometimes do transcend everything, even their own lives, in the phenomenon of benevolent love that is called the supreme sacrifice. In the face of all this, anyone with any sensitivity should be impelled to the affirmation that this life is outstandingly valuable. Superlatives like "sacred" are needed to give voice to one's awe and appreciation. But the experience means more than our superlatives can convey. It springs from the depths of affectivity. And it is in this affective response that we locate the birthing of morality. foundational moral experience

In locating this experience in the affections, I am, of course, not thereby lapsing into the stupidity of emotivist ethicists who say that subsequent moral judgments about particular issues are only emotional noises, not statements that could be true or false. Obviously, even two persons who have profound affective experiences of the value of human life could enter into intellectual disagreement about what does and does not befit that life. What is born in the heart is to some degree expressible in the language of the mind. Ethics, which starts in awe, proceeds to reason. There is no effort here, then, to say that morality and ethics are just a matter of feeling.

Intelligent discourse on moral matters is indispensably necessary for a humane society. Persons will not always agree on what does or does not befit valuable human life. The problem of the Persian Emperor Darius I is a symbol of the perennial human problem. He found that some of his Indian subjects ate their fathers' corpses while the Greek subjects burned them. The pollution of holy fire was as shocking to the Indians as cannibalism was to the Greeks. And so, we Greeks and Indians today, though united in reverence for life, are forever diverging on what does or does not befit that life. Intelligent, sensitive ethical debate is the human response to this divergence. Ethics is not just a matter of emotive preference. It seeks after truth by argument, comparison, analysis, and by all of the evaluational modes that I shall submit as pertaining to ethical method. To the mode of this essential, intellectual, ethical discourse we shall return. My purpose here is to urge that the origins of moral experience are in the affections.

Anthropologist Loren Eiseley, starting from the existence of the

one-armed skeletal remains of a Neanderthal man, offers an imaginative reflection that is relevant:

> Forty thousand years ago in the bleak uplands of south-
> western Asia, a man, a Neanderthal man, once labeled by
> the Darwinian proponents of struggle as a ferocious ances-
> tral beast—a man whose face might cause you some slight
> uneasiness if he sat beside you—a man of this sort existed
> with a fearful body handicap in that ice-age world. He had
> lost an arm. But still he lived and was cared for. Somebody,
> some group of human things, in a hard, violent and stony
> world, loved this maimed creature enough to cherish him.[60]

Somewhere back there in the period of harsh beginnings, there appeared, in Eiseley's words, loving, caring, and cherishing. Concern
was born, and with it, morality. Eiseley compares its emergence to "a
faint light, like a patch of sunlight moving over the dark shadows on
a forest floor."[61] What it was was the light of a distinctively human
consciousness, animated by the unique energy that we have come to
call love. This capacity for love, this ability to appreciate and respond to the value of personal life in all its forms, is the foundation
of moral consciousness. The appearance of this capacity was an event
more significant for human existence than the first appearances of
technology or of art, although these latter events are more easily
chronicled and have won more attention. Yet somewhere back there,
the signs of moral-value-consciousness appear. It might be visible, for
example, in the ceremonial burying of the dead which began before
the extinction of Neanderthal man.[62] Along with ever-present superstition, the liturgies of burial could be a sign of grief, and thus of
concern and love. More to the point is Arnold Toynbee's observation
that "the distinction between good and evil seems to have been
drawn by all human beings at all times and places. The drawing of it
seems, in fact, to be one of the intrinsic and universal characteristics
of our common nature."[63]

Distinguishing between good and evil, however, points to the discovery of the value of human life which leads to the concern for
what befits it (good) and what does not (evil). The encounter with
such life in one's self and in others engenders an affective response of
reverence and wonder, and yields the "moral" desire to react to this
life and its terrestrial setting in a fitting way. With this does consciousness enter the moral realm.

Faith. The foundational moral experience is a faith experience.

Like much that pertains to morality, faith has a bad name among many intellectuals. It has reprobate status because it reeks of association with superstition and with antiscientific and anti-intellectual bias. This is an ultimately ungrounded prejudice since faith in a true sense makes the intellectual world go around. To be re-enfranchised, it must be clearly defined.

Faith is a normal and basic way of knowing. Contrary to the common wisdom, seeing is not believing. Believing is *knowing* what you cannot see or prove, but what you still accept and hold with firmness. Life is full of faith-knowledge, a kind of knowledge that has its source in affectivity. Every lover knows this. The lover cannot explain or justify with reasons the insights of his heart. And yet he calmly believes that these make consummate sense. He knows this believingly and is surer of it than of many things he sees or can prove.

Thomas Aquinas says that faith lends a kind of certitude that is "in the genre of affection." It is knowledge, but it is knowledge that comes from the will and is best described in terms of affectivity.[64] This is the kind of knowing that characterizes the foundational moral experience.

All this fits into a full understanding of how we know. The mind cannot stand a vacuum of meaning. In some areas where it cannot intellectually see meaning or claw its way to it with reason, it is equipped to find it in affective belief. In a sense, our affections can be a divining power that goes further into reality than our reasoning minds can take us. We feel and sense more than we can see or explain, and feeling can be a way of knowing. Knowledge is basically sensitive awareness. In affective experience we become aware of and sensitized to many things that escape the cold light of unfeeling intellectuality. Faith is a species of this kind of knowing.

As Professor Wilfred Sellars has written: "Recent psychological studies make clear what has always, in a sense, been known, that the ability to love others for their own sakes is as essential to a full life as the need to feel ourselves loved and appreciated for our own sakes, unconditionally, and not as something turned on or off depending on what we do."[65] Sellars is here stating that *unconditional love*, not calculating love based on advantage and hope of gain, is not just a luxury but is essential to human fulfillment. Indeed, it can be said that the only force that slowly nudges us from cold barbarity into humanness is benevolent love, love that is not awarded on merit but bestowed from largesse. We would all be more beastly than we are were we not at times the recipients of such an undeserved gift. But this is obviously the stuff of faith. How could anyone see or prove that love of such a sort makes sense! It can only be taken on faith. Proving that persons are worth loving beyond their deserts is as much a futility as trying to prove that life is worth living. Both are conclusions of faith. Proving further that persons are worth dying for or worth limiting our own egoism for is impossible. You cannot prove that persons are worth doing ethics about or that ruthlessly calculating self-interest should not be your only guide. Yet you can know it believingly.

Love and morality are works of faith. Never has there been genuine love that was not an adventure in faith. And love is the fulfillment of morality.

As Blaise Pascal put it: "We know truth, not only by the reason, but also by the heart. . . . The heart has reasons which reason does not know."[66] Bergson said we have a "genius of the will" as well as a genius of the intellect.[67] And as John Macquarrie puts it, "All affective and conative experience has its own understanding."[68] But if these witnesses seem too ponderous, consult again the lover in you who knows that love knows more than it can say. And that is the point precisely. The experience of the value of persons and their environment, then, is an affective faith experience.

It is well to note here that faith has nothing immediately or exclusively to do with religion. Every man is a believer. It is one of the human ways of knowing and being sensitive to reality. The man who infers believingly to the existence of God will interpret his other beliefs in this light. But theist and atheist have this in common; they are believers. Faith is their natural human lot.

Faith, then, is an interpretive, affective, knowing act. It is not knowledge of the sort that basks in self-evidence. What we accept on faith might even seem on its face absurd. And yet it appears even more absurd not to believe. We "hang in there" with what we believe because the alternative is unbearable and we could make no sense of it. The British writer Gilbert Keith Chesterton said that he could not be an atheist because it would take too much faith. Belief in religious and other matters is often like that. We believe because we could not not believe. The foundational moral experience of the value of persons is belief. We cannot see or prove that persons are sacred in their worth. We cannot prove that the Jewish philosopher Martin Buber is right when he says that a human being "is *Thou* and fills the heavens."[69] But we believe it, and so morality is born.

The experience that I describe here admits the weakness of reason. This does not mean that knowledge fails, but that primal moral knowledge unfolds in a mystical and contemplative form. At its core, ethics is believing and contemplative. Its bases lie in what Thomas Carlyle called those "quiet mysterious depths" which exist in the center of personality "underneath the region of argument and conscious discourse."[70] It is at these depths that we are opened to the inexhaustible mystery of value in personal form. It is here that the impact of personhood is felt, and caring begins.

The centrality of faith in human cognitive experience is not something that can be affirmed only by philosophers and theologians. Scientist John Rader Platt, for example, speaks of the capacity for self-sacrifice, which I have noted, as the most outstanding manifestation of the foundational moral experience. He observes that the self-sacrificial behavior "of the mother for the child or the soldier for his buddy is so instinctive and irresistible in moments of crisis that it proves we have grown up in families and tribes and have survived only by being willing to dare for each other."[71] From that statement alone it could appear that Platt is going to practice reductionism on the mystery of self-sacrifice, treating it as a phylogenetic, instinctive reflex geared to the survival of the species. Platt, however, moves on to speak of faith, saying that we are capable of self-sacrifice because "we have faith in the ultimate value of acts of love and mercy even when all the consequences are not foreseeable." Platt concludes that "science can add nothing to these moralities of faith."[72] Sensing the link between morality and faith is the beginning of moral wisdom and realism.

Notice that this is not a collapse into intuitionism which would overestimate what can be self-evidently *seen*. Neither is it a naturalism which would reduce the good to the scientifically examinable. The experience of the moral that I am presenting here admits the incapacity of reason in constituting the foundations of morality, but not the impossibility of knowledge.

Process. The foundational moral experience is a matter of more or less. It is difficult to imagine someone identifiably human being utterly untouched by it. But to be touched by it is to start a process

that admits of growth. (It can also decline.) As we grow in it we civilize and become more human. One senses that this process is precarious and slow. Moral concern is a tender shoot.

Historically it would seem that, thus far, the gentle forays of moral
awareness have been limited by private egoism and tribalism (collective egoism). Concern spread slowly, spilling out first only on those
who were near and thus somewhat dear. As anthropologist Ralph
Linton writes: "At the primitive level the individual's tribe represents for him the limits of humanity and the same individual who
will exert himself to any lengths in behalf of a fellow tribesman may
regard the non-tribesman as fair game to be exploited by any possible
means, or even as a legitimate source of meat. . . ."[73] Economically,
it might be said that we are still eating non-tribesmen. Our cannibalism is indirect now, operating through such things as "the terms
of trade" and the widening structured gaps between rich and poor.
But, in our newly efficient fashion, we are still at it.

Thus the value of persons and their environment has historically
meant the value of certain persons. Racism, anti-Semitism, nationalism (modern tribalism), slavery, the subjugation of women, etc.,
all witness to the primitive state of the process. Some observers of
the human scene have pronounced dismal judgments on our lagging
moral development. Adam Smith is one of these. In 1759 he wrote:

> Let us suppose that the great empire of China, with all its
> myriads of inhabitants, was suddenly swallowed up by an
> earthquake, and let us consider how a man of humanity in
> Europe, who had no sort of connection with that part of
> the world, would be affected upon receiving intelligence of
> this dreadful calamity. He would, I imagine, first of all ex-
> press very strongly his sorrow for the misfortune of that
> unhappy people, he would make many melancholy reflec-
> tions upon the precariousness of human life, and the vanity
> of all the labours of man, which could thus be annihilated
> in a moment. He would, too, perhaps, if he was a man of
> speculation, enter into many reasonings concerning the
> effects which this disaster might produce upon the com-
> merce of Europe, and the trade and business of the world
> in general. And when all this fine philosophy was over,
> when all these humane sentiments had been once fairly ex-
> pressed, he would pursue his business or his pleasure, take
> his repose or his diversion, with the same ease and tran-
> quillity as if no such accident had happened.[74]

Smith did not let his imaginings rest here. He went on to wonder what would happen if his supposedly typical "man of humanity" were to face a comparatively very slight misfortune himself. Would his benevolence come to be seen as a veneer?

> . . . The most frivolous disaster which could befall himself would occasion a more real disturbance. If he was to lose his little finger tomorrow, he would not sleep tonight; but, provided he never saw them, he will snore with the most profound security over the ruin of a hundred millions of his brethren, and the destruction of that immense multitude seems plainly an object less interesting to him than this paltry misfortune of his own.[75]

In concluding his reflection, however, Smith does pull up short of judging his "man of humanity" as totally depraved. He poses the question of what this man would do if he were in a position to prevent "this paltry misfortune of his own" in exchange for consigning a hundred million unseen Chinese to their death. Says Smith: "Human nature startles with horror at the thought, and the world, in its greatest depravity and corruption, never produced such a villain as could be capable of entertaining it."[76] Perhaps! But when we view the contemporary fact that close to a billion persons on planet earth are malnourished—many to the point of starvation—while others are overfed, the thought occurs that Smith may have been overly kind.

In a singularly dismal tone, the Russian philosopher Vladimir Solovyev, writing in 1895, asserted the enduring ascendancy of egoism in the human species. "Egoism is a force not only real but fundamental, rooted in the deepest centre of our being, and from thence permeating and embracing the whole of our activity—a force, functioning uninterruptedly in all departments and particulars of our existence."[77] And Solovyev can be grimmer yet. He sees love, the specific antidote to egoism, as still undeveloped in our species. His one sanguine allowance is that love *could* develop among us; the dire truth is that it has not.

> It would be entirely wrong to deny the possibility of realizing love merely on the ground that hitherto it never has been realized: you must know that many another thing was once found in the same position, for instance, all science and art, the civic community, our control of the forces of Nature. Even the rational consciousness itself, before be-

coming a fact in man, was only a perplexed and unsuccess-
ful aspiration in the world of animals. . . . Love is as yet
for man the same as reason was for the animal world: it exists in its beginnings, or as an earnest of what it will be, but
not as yet in actual fact.[78]

Solovyev may have gotten a bit carried away. It is hard to believe
that our achievements in science, art, and the civic community have
issued forth without at least some rudimentary emergence of the
power of love. Heroic influences have been with us urging the process
on, pushing us more deeply into the foundational moral experience.
"Pioneers in morality," as philosopher Henri Bergson calls them,
have warmed us with a vision of human moral possibility. We have
heard the Buddha, Lao-tse, Confucius, Jesus, Mohammed, Marx,
and Gandhi, and to a slight degree we recognized, again in Bergson's
terms, that "life holds for them unsuspected tones of feeling like
those of some new symphony, and they draw us after them into this
music that we may express it in action."[79] Solovyev is right, however,
in his main thrust. We do overestimate our civility. Barbaric apathy
is still a fact of life.

The signs of retarded moral sensitivity are visible also in our response to physical nature. The foundational moral experience is not
limited to persons, but reaches into the material context from which
we evolved and to which we are kith and kin. Like relatives who became rich, we have trampled on our familial earth-roots with little
sign of reverence or affection. As Loren Eiseley writes:

> It is with the coming of man that a vast hole seems to open
> in nature, a vast black whirlpool spinning faster and faster,
> consuming flesh, stones, soil, minerals, sucking down the
> lightning, wrenching power from the atom, until the an-
> cient sounds of nature are drowned in the cacophony of
> something which is no longer nature, something instead
> which is loose and knocking at the world's heart, something
> demonic and no longer planned—escaped, it may be—
> spewed out of nature, contending in a final giant's game
> against its master.[80]

The foundational moral experience is only at its beginnings. The
process is young and precariously tender.

The foundational moral experience then is rooted in *affectivity*
and *faith,* and it is subject to the ebbs and flows of a still young

and precarious *process*. The object of this experience is the value of persons and their environment. It includes an awareness of the value of others (all others), and of the connection between one's own value and that of others. The experience is aborted if one of these elements is lacking. In other words, we cannot just value self or just value others and be integral. We must see the link between these loves.

The Propriety of Self-love . . .

Strangely, some philosophers and theologians have had a hard time justifying self-love, the loving response to one's own value. Schopenhauer, for example, said that moral worth can be ascribed only to behavior that has no "self-interested motives." "The absence of all egoistic motives is thus the criterion of an action of moral value."[81] In theology, Martin Luther is an example of those who assaulted the legitimacy of self-love. Reacting against Catholic Christianity, which found love of self compatible with love of God, Luther claimed that self-love had to be plucked out by the roots. Citing the apostle Paul's statement "Love seeks not its own," Luther called self-love "crooked" and it "is not made straight unless it ceases to seek what is its own, and seeks what is its neighbour's."[82] Luther confronts the obvious difficulty in the scriptural text that says you should love your neighbor as you love yourself by saying that this means self-love should be diverted and transferred to the neighbor and thus be set straight.

Both Schopenhauer's and Luther's attacks on self-love are scattershot. The enemy they fail to target is egoistic self-love that gives self a hierarchical and inherently hostile prominence above all other values. The recognition of one's own value as a person is not only not at odds with love of others but is the only feasible base for such love. The need to love ourselves and feel ourselves loved is essential to mental health and normal socialization. It is a rule of nature, in Goethe's phrase, that "love begets love." Only the gift of love and the experience of our own lovability can release us from a cringing self-centeredness, and empower us to love.

The personal life that makes my neighbor valuable is a life in which I also share. It is a participated glory. And it is no less valuable for being mine. Out of love I may sacrifice myself for another person as that person might also for me. Such sacrifice is not caused by low esteem for self but is rather a mysterious response to the person-related values which can at times merit such an absolute gift.

Because life is sacred does not mean that continued existence in life is an absolute obligation. Life is more than any single embodiment of it and sometimes death serves that *more* better than continued living. There is a perplexing and enduring paradox here, but the truth is not served either by negating the experienced authenticity of noble sacrifice or by denying the validity of one's own value. The paradox is heightened by the fact that it is from persons who have achieved a high degree of self-actualization and confidence, born of proper self-love, that heroic self-sacrifice could be anticipated. (A morbid self-sacrifice is possible from a number of psychiatric causes. These, however, would not be perceived as heroic when understood.)

Self-love is legitimate and unavoidable also because of the very nature of moral values. Moral values, as philosopher John Dewey says, determine "what one will *be*, instead of merely what one will *have*."[83] If we are clumsy, poor at mathematics, nonaffluent, or ugly by common standards, it is unfortunate. We lack certain values. It does not, however, make us bad people. The values we lack are not moral values. Such nonmoral values grace us; they do not make us.

Moral values make us what we are as persons. Moral values make us human. Failure here is drastic, not just unfortunate.

To be moral then by being benevolent, fair, and just to others is also good for the self and is, in a good sense, self-serving. Even Schopenhauer in his attack on self-love had to admit that "conduct having real moral worth . . . leaves behind a certain self-satisfaction which is called the approval of conscience. . . ."[84] This is understandable since it is humanly normal to be moral and hence it has its own built-in satisfactions and sense of self-fulfillment.[85] By the very nature of moral value, being moral is self-love as well as love of the other. How you love yourself in relation to others is where the ethical questions rise.[86]

Justice as the Minimal Shape of Other-love . . .

In our foundational moral experience, then, life is loved wherever it is found, in self or in others, and no hostile partitioning is compatible with the experience. Thus far, however, I have spoken only of the love of self since its legitimacy has been challenged. Self-love, however, does not occur in a social vacuum nor is it unrelated or even feasible outside of relationships with others. As I have said, the foundational moral experience includes a positive response to the value of self and the value of others, and an appreciation of the link between the two.

To explain our basic response to the value of others, I turn to the generic concept of justice, arguing that justice is the minimal manifestation of the foundational moral experience and the minimal manifestation of other-love. Justice is the least that we can do in response to the value of persons. It is love in embryonic form. When love matures, justice, with its concerns for rights and obligations, is transformed in the superior dynamism of love. Since, however, love is not all in all, justice presents itself as the minimal expression of moral sentiment.

Before explaining this, however, I pause to note that in discussing the legitimacy of self-love and in presenting justice as a specification of the foundational moral experience, I have moved beyond the description of the affective faith experience that grounds moral consciousness. What I have begun here is the philosophical spelling out of the implications of that experience. This is a never-ending process in which all of our faculties conspire to determine, in more specific ways, what does or does not befit the dignity and value of persons and their environment. The whole of my method exposed in the following pages will be doing this in the variety of ways that is required. Here my specific suggestion is that justice is the minimal shape of effective morality. In so saying, I am not just indulging in an affective impulse even though such impulses may, as I have said, have a high content of wisdom. In citing justice as the basic and minimal expression of the foundational moral experience, I am drawing on many cultural and intellectual and personal resources. This use of justice, though it cannot pretend to be infallible, is not arbitrary. I believe it can be seen to be the only coherent and fruitful basis for a moral and viable society.

In Montesquieu's letter on justice, he wrote: "If, my dear Rhedi, there is a God, he must necessarily be just. For if he were not, he would be the worst and most imperfect of beings. . . . Thus, were there no God, it would still be our duty to love justice, that is to say, to do our best to be like that being of whom we have such a wonderful idea and who, if he did exist, would necessarily be just."[87] Montesquieu is allied here with that general view of justice as the foundation of the good life. Justice is variously and sometimes more narrowly defined. But in its broadest meaning, justice is as Aristotle says "not part of virtue but virtue entire, nor is the contrary injustice a part of vice but vice entire."[88] In this same sense Pierre Joseph Proudhon said: "Justice is that which is most primitive in the human soul, most fundamental in society, most sacred among ideas, and what the masses demand today with most ardour. It is the essence of religions and at the same time the form of reason, the secret object of faith, and the beginning, middle and end of knowledge. What can be imagined more universal, more strong, more complete than Justice?"[89]

Justice, in my view, is the first fruit of the foundational moral experience or of the "sanctity of life." It is said of the sanctity of life that it is so basic a notion that life is unlivable if it is not allowed. The same can be said of justice.

The absence of justice would subject human existence to unbearable chaos. Philosophers Peter Bertocci and Richard Millard begin their book *Personality and the Good* with the assertion: "A human being will not accept chaos. Nor can he long tolerate chaos. When he can no longer cope with it, he begins to get sick, both physically and mentally. When chaos has won out, he is dead. But as long as he is alive, he is seeking to reduce chaos in some way or other."[90] Justice can be seen as the essential line of defense against human chaos. Without some achievement of justice, human society as such disintegrates.

Justice is conceptually subsequent to the sanctity of life since it is a virtue *because of* the sacredness of life. Thus it is not foundational in the same sense as the experience of the value of persons is. It seems true, however, to say with Cicero that men are called good chiefly from their justice. So what then is justice and why do I see it as the primordial and minimal expression of our perception of the value of persons?

Basically it can be said that there are three kinds of justice: *commutative justice, distributive justice,* and *legal justice.*[91] All three forms involve rendering to others what is their due. Justice is the first shaping of our response to the value of persons. It recognizes that their value is such that they may lay claims on us. Justice is the first of many virtues telling us how we should react to persons in view of what they are. In its relationship to other virtues, however, I do not see justice as simply the first among equals. It provides us, rather, with the first lineaments of an anthropology. All of ethics is based upon some *anthropology*, that is, some conception of what these sacredly valuable persons are so that we can judge what befits them. One's anthropology (or conception of personhood) first shines through in the explanation one offers of justice. The definition of the three forms of justice will show this to be so.

Commutative justice renders what is due in relationships between individual persons, or between discernibly individual social entities such as nation-states or corporations. *Distributive justice* directs the fair distribution of goods and burdens to the citizens by those who are the representative officials of the state. It moves from the social whole to the individual. *Legal justice* represents the debts of the individual citizen to the social whole or the common good. Justice, therefore, either moves between individuals (commutative), from society to the individual (distributive), or from the private individual to the society (legal). In each case persons are rendering what is due to others. We pay what we owe to other individuals (commutative); or the society through its official representatives distributes what is due to individuals (distributive); or we give what is due to society in the form of such things as taxes, military service, or social action for the common good (legal).

No one form of justice can be stressed to the point of repressing another form. All three serve in concert to create the basis for moral existence and to establish one's anthropology. If one were to succumb, for example, to a radically individualistic anthropology (and this is an indigenous American temptation), justice would be limited to commutative, interindividual justice. Of course, the complete individualist is a freakish and rare bird since most people, even those of a highly individualistic bent, admit some manifestation of legal justice, such as the payment of taxes and fines or admitting the rights of eminent domain. However, the underlying bias of an individualistic anthropology is so jealous of individual rights and freedoms that it sees legal justice as something akin to a necessary evil.

On the other hand, a radically collectivist anthropology would downplay commutative justice by submerging the individual more or less into the collectivity. In a completely collectivist view, as Josef Pieper says, "Man's life has a totally public character because the individual is adequately defined only through his membership in the social whole, which is the only reality."[92] Collectivism, like individualism, will not exist in all of its conceptually potential purity. Some private relations between individuals will exist and be recognized, but the bias in a collectivist situation will be against individual considerations and fixated more upon the social whole. When one alleges, as I do, that there should be an even stress on all three forms of justice, one is establishing this as his basic anthropology upon which his system of ethics will be based. I submit that if there is excessive emphasis upon the individual or upon the social whole, our view of what persons are is distorted.

We are individuals, but we are individuals in society, social individuals. The just person in this view must not only pay his debts and make due reparation to those he has wronged or with whom he has contracted (commutative justice); he must also pay his debts to the social whole so as to fulfill his human duty to create a society marked by equity and harmony. We are social beings not by contract or convenience but by our very nature, and both legal and distributive justice reflect that. Our basic ethical anthropology may not prescind from that or limit discussion of our debts to the interindividual level, as the spirit of individualism would have us do. To do so distorts our nature and constitutes an ethical heresy of a foundational sort, since it defines persons atomistically and nonsocially. It is similarly simplistic to so stress our sociality as to downgrade our individuality, as is done in a collectivist anthropology. The balancing tension between the one and the many is real and must be maintained in one's fundamental view of personhood. A stress on all three forms of justice does maintain this balance and does present us with just such a fundamental view of what personhood entails. A denial of this is an invitation to chaos.

Notice here that we have moved a reflective step beyond the foundational moral experience. I said that this experience involves (1) a respect for one's self; (2) a respect for others; and (3) a recognition of the link between the two. Justice, as explained, gives theoretical formulation to all of this, and stresses that respect for others unfolds in a social context, not in a context of atomistic individualism. Justice, of course, is not enough. It is only the minimal expression of what respect for persons entails. Justice, in fact, should be superseded by friendship as our regard for others matures. As Aristotle says, "when men are friends they have no need of justice. . . ."[93] Justice is consummated in friendship. But justice does set the stage upon which friendship in society may grow. It also serves to give us the earliest intimations of the least we should do in response to the value of persons—the discovery of which is the beginning of ethics.[94]

Summary: My position is that the foundation of moral experience is not the will of God, custom, convention, contract, or caprice. Moral experience begins in the mystery-laden discovery of the value of persons and their environment. This is an affective faith experience and is processual in form. It can increase or recede. The supreme sacrifice is the most dramatic and revealing expression of this experience. Justice is the first and minimal expression of what this experience means in our relationship to other persons. Justice is the first, not the last, thing to be said about what the foundational moral experience entails. But everything that follows will trace back to these beginnings.

NOTES—CHAPTER THREE

1. Colin M. Turnbull, *The Mountain People* (New York: Simon & Schuster, 1972), pp. 261–62.
2. Ibid., p. 132.
3. Abraham H. Maslow, *Religions, Values, and Peak-Experiences* (New York: Viking Press, 1970), p. 16.
4. Ruth Fulton Benedict, "Anthropology and the Abnormal," *Journal of General Psychology* 10 (1934), p. 73.
5. Ibid.
6. Ibid. See also William Graham Sumner, *Folkways* (Boston: Ginn & Co., 1906). For Sumner, to say that something was "right" meant that it conformed to the established folkways of the group. Sumner did, however, use some utilitarian criteria to adjudicate the values of varying folkways, and thus his ethical relativism was tempered to this extent. One of the more notable recent exponents of the relativist thesis is Melville Herkovits, *Man and His Works* (New York: Alfred A. Knopf, 1965).
7. Benedict, "Anthropology and the Abnormal," p. 79.
8. Ayn Rand, *The Virtue of Selfishness: A New Concept of Egoism* (New York: New American Library, Signet Books; copyright © 1961, 1964 by Ayn Rand; 1962, 1963, 1964 by the Objectivist Newsletter, Inc.), p. 15. In the original manuscript of this book I quoted Ms. Rand's writings seven times. Since this came to a total of some 320 words quoted in all, the standard request for permission was made. Ms. Rand, through her secretary, denied permission and

relayed the word that she resented such excerpting and quotation of her material. In response to this unusual situation I had to paraphrase Ms. Rand's relevant remarks, although I would have preferred to afford my readers the experience of direct quotation. In each case I refer to the appropriate place in Ms. Rand's writing where her thought may be found in its pristine originality.

9. Ibid. She is imprecise here. Aristotle's eudaemonism did not neglect this question. Whether he faced it adequately is another matter.
10. Ibid., p. 17.
11. Ibid., p. 22.
12. See Ralph Linton, "The Problem of Universal Values," in Robert F. Spencer, ed., *Method and Perspective in Anthropology: Papers in Honor of Wilson D. Wallis* (Minneapolis: University of Minnesota Press, 1954), pp. 145–68.
13. Ibid., pp. 24–25.
14. Ludwig Wittgenstein, *Tractatus Logico-philosophicus* (London: Rutledge & Kegan Paul, 1961), 4, 112.
15. Ludwig Wittgenstein, *Philosophical Investigations* (New York: Macmillan, 1958), p. 38.
16. Harry K. Girvetz, *Beyond Right and Wrong* (New York and London: Free Press, Collier Macmillan Publishers, 1973), p. 87. Vernon J. Bourke says that Wittgenstein "convinced many English philosophers that the main work of philosophy is simply to get things straight in regard to the use of language. From logical positivism he brought the theory that propositions can be verified only if they are tautologous or if they accord with the direct evidence of sense perception. This makes nonsense of metaphysics, of religion as a creedal institution, and of theoretical ethics." Vernon J. Bourke, *History of Ethics* (Garden City, N.Y.: Doubleday & Co., Inc., Image Books, 1968), Vol. 2, pp. 175–76.
17. William F. Frankena, "Recent Conceptions of Morality," in Hector-Neri Castaneda and George Nakhnikian, eds., *Morality and the Language of Conduct* (Detroit: Wayne State University Press, 1963), pp. 1–2.
18. If this sounds somewhat detached and unhelpful, it will be easy to understand the practical lament of Frank R. Harrison: "A great deal of contemporary professional philosophy in America, growing out of the influences of positivism and various forms of language analysis, simply has not addressed itself to practical moral issues. . . . Their study is one of language not of morally correct action. . . . To expect much guidance in the practical area of action from these philosophers is to expect too much. Moral problems revolving around, say, a particular case of abortion are not satisfactorily handled by remind-

ing us of how we use the word 'abortion.'" Frank R. Harrison, "Dilemmas and Solutions," *Journal of the American Medical Association* 230, No. 3, p. 402. Harrison indicts only half the problem. Not only is it true that these philosophers will offer slight guidance "in the practical area of action," but it is also true that they cannot offer as an excuse that they are importantly engaged at the foundations. They ask what morality is, but they do not answer the question.

19. Frankena, "Recent Conceptions of Morality," p. 4.

20. Notice here that the term "moral" is used as the opposite of amoral or nonmoral, not as the opposite of immoral. Moral here means adjudicable in moral terms. Regarding the second group, Frankena says: "In the weaker form it says simply that one's judgment, whatever words one uses, is not a *moral* one unless one claims some such consensus or intersubjective validity. In the stronger form it adds that the status of one's judgment is affected if the consensus claimed does not obtain." Ibid., p. 6.

21. K. Baier, *The Moral Point of View* (Ithaca: Cornell University Press, 1958), p. 200; quoted in Frankena, "Recent Conceptions of Morality," p. 11.

22. Frankena, "Recent Conceptions of Morality," p. 11.

23. Among those whom Frankena lists in the first group of philosophers are: R. M. Hare, P. H. Nowell-Smith, J. A. Brunton, John Ladd, and Bernard Mayo. In the second group are: H. L. A. Hart, Margaret MacDonald, H. D. Aiken, John Rawls, and Roderick Firth. In the third group: W. Kneale, H. D. Aiken, K. Baier, and S. E. Toulmin. Mary Warnock's comment is to the point: "One of the consequences of treating ethics as the analysis of ethical language is . . . that it leads to the increasing triviality of the subject. . . . Thus the concentration upon the most general kind of evaluative language, combined with the fear of committing the naturalistic fallacy, has led too often to discussions of grading fruit, or choosing fictitious games equipment, and ethics as a serious subject has been left further and further behind." Mary Warnock, *Ethics Since 1900* (London: Oxford University Press, 1960), pp. 202, 204. All classifications, even Frankena's, limp. These authors do not remain captives of a narrowly linguistic perspective and address the question "What is morality?" implicitly and in divers ways, often with great profit to foundational ethics.

24. Raymond of Agiles in *Historia Francorum,* translated by Frederick Duncalf and August C. Krey, *Parallel Source Problems in Medieval History* (New York: Harper & Brothers, 1912). Quoted in Roland H. Bainton, *Christian Attitudes Toward War and Peace* (New York and Nashville: Abingdon Press, 1960), pp. 112–13.

25. The first problem for the "will of God" people is in normative ethics, the second, in foundational ethics. If we believe we have oracular access to God's mind, then normative ethics can be neglected. (There are voluntarist and nominalist implications here too.) The foundational problem of not seeing the derivative, inferential nature of belief in God also errs by mislocating theistic experience. However, I am not denying—indeed, I affirm—that religious experience and other experiences can reinforce the primary, foundational moral experience.

26. The legalists are also reductively relativists, since laws are institutionally and societally sanctioned customs.

27. Calling one's own position "realism" may seem arrogant. It is almost like saying to an adversary: "My position is truth; what's yours?" I object to the use of the term by the self-styled "political realists" in the field of political theory, since I do not think they are realistic in their understanding of the moral dimension of political life. Yet I use the term here for my position and I am sticking with it. I see the term as a bulwark against abstractionism, nominalism, voluntarism, rationalism, and other "isms" that imagine us out of our real and *de facto* earthly existence. Only the way I use the term could vindicate my selection of it. Let the reader judge.

28. Sociologist Robert Nisbet writes: "The Typology of the sacred-secular has the same methodological significance that we find in community-society, status-class, and authority-power. It is a conceptual framework of analysis by which not only the nature of religion but the nature of society, economy, and state is illuminated in fresh ways. The religio-sacred, far from being more superstructure or illusion, is ingrained in society. . . ." Robert Nisbet, *The Sociological Tradition* (New York: Basic Books, Inc., 1966), p. 222.

29. Eliseo Vivas, *The Moral Life and the Ethical Life* (Chicago: Henry Regnery Co., A Gateway Edition, 1963), p. vii.

30. As I shall shortly argue, belief is a kind of knowledge. My point here is that belief does not come near the certainty of direct, immediate knowledge such as we have of our embodied existence.

31. Obviously, we can argue that for the well-being of humankind, this or that value ought to be universally esteemed. I would submit that the capacity for heroic self-sacrifice is broadly enough esteemed to be highly suggestive, and even that it ought to be universally esteemed. I do not pretend that it is.

32. Rand, *Virtue of Selfishness*, p. 44.

33. Ibid., pp. 45–46.

34. Sutta Nipata I, 8, quoted in Kenneth W. Morgan, ed., *The Path of the Buddha* (New York: Ronald Press Co., 1956), p. 386.

35. Aristotle, *Nichomachean Ethics*, Bk. 9, Chap. 8, 1169a, 20–26. Un-

less otherwise noted, all references to Aristotle are from *The Basic Works of Aristotle*, edited by Richard McKeon (New York: Random House, 1941). Aristotle presents this noble option in a eudaemonistic context in which the good man out of proper love of self chooses nobility as "the greater share." One might part from him in his philosophical explanation here and still accept him as a witness to the perceived nobility of self-sacrifice.

36. A. L. Basham, *The Wonder That Was India: A Survey of the Culture of the Indian Sub-Continent Before the Coming of the Muslims* (London: Sidgwick & Jackson, 1954), p. 339. The quotation is from the maxims of the early *Tirukkural*.
37. John 15:8.
38. For a discussion of Jewish attitudes toward self-sacrifice, see Jakob J. Petuchowski, "The Limits of Self-Sacrifice," in *Modern Jewish Ethics*, edited by Marvin Fox (Columbus: Ohio State University Press, 1975), pp. 103–18. Although Ahad Haam taught that "your own life comes before the life of your brother," and notes that this has strong support in the Jewish tradition, the issue is not as simple as such a strong expression might suggest. As Raphael Loewe observes, Halacha was "governed by a common-sense appreciation of what may, and what may not, be realistically expected of the average Jewish man and woman and this has preserved it from utopian idealism when framing its requirements, recommendations, or encouragements as to how to meet a given situation." Quoted ibid., p. 110. Thus the supreme sacrifice of self could be appreciated as ideal in certain circumstances without becoming enshrined within the stipulations of Halacha.
39. Adam Smith, *The Theory of Moral Sentiments* (New York: Augustus M. Kelley, 1966), p. 489.
40. *Religions, Values, and Peak-Experiences*, Maslow, p. 42. Richard L. Means. *The Ethical Imperative* (Garden City, N.Y.: Doubleday & Co., Inc., Anchor Books, 1970), p. 84. The views of psychologist Thomas A. Harris in his popular book *I'm OK—You're OK* are relevant. Under a subtitle "The Worth of Persons," he writes: "I would like to suggest that a reasonable approximation of this objective moral order, or of ultimate truth, is that *persons are important* in that they are all bound together in a universal relatedness which transcends their own personal existence. . . . The idea that persons are important is a *moral idea* without which any system of understanding man is futile. . . . We cannot prove they are important. We have only the faith to believe they are, because of the greater difficulty of believing they are not." *I'm OK—You're OK* (New York: Avon Books, 1969), p. 254.
41. J. Glenn Gray, *The Warriors: Reflections on Men in Battle* (New

York, Evanston, and London: Harper & Row, Harper Torchbook, 1959), pp. 185–86.

42. Ibid., p. 185.

43. This is reported and discussed in Rollo May, *Power and Innocence* (New York: W. W. Norton & Co., Inc., 1972), p. 32.

44. R. L. Bruckberger, *God and Politics* (Chicago: J. Philip O'Hara, Inc., 1972), p. 46.

45. Ibid., p. 47.

46. It is interesting that *philopsychia* (literally "love of life"), which would seem to have a promising denotation, came to signify cowardice and slavishness in classical Greek literature. See Hannah Arendt, *The Human Condition* (Garden City, N.Y.: Doubleday & Co., Inc., Anchor Books, 1959), p. 311, note 30; see also p. 33 and p. 166.

47. Aristotle, *Nichomachean Ethics*, Bk. 1, Chap. 3, 1904b, 25. Translation of I. A. K. Thomson, *The Ethics of Aristotle* (Baltimore: Penguin Books, 1955).

48. W. D. Ross, *The Right and the Good* (Oxford: Clarendon Press, 1930), pp. 20–21, note 1.

49. Immanuel Kant, *Foundations of the Metaphysics of Morals*, translated by Louis White Beck (New York: Liberal Arts Press, 1959), p. 27, note 2.

50. Ibid.

51. Ibid., p. 46. Kant's formulation can be confusing, since it is possible to "use" persons legitimately and not exploitatively in moral human relations. Kant's reference clearly is to exploitative, depersonalizing use.

52. Albert Camus, *Resistance, Rebellion and Death* (New York: Alfred A. Knopf, 1969), p. 114.

53. See the dialogue *Gorgias* (469c) and also the first two books of *The Republic*. For a discussion of the Socratic statement, see Dietrich Von Hildebrand, *Christian Ethics* (New York: David McKay Co., Inc., 1953), pp. 54–63 and pp. 175–76.

54. Richard M. Restak, *Pre-meditated Man: Bioethics and the Control of Future Human Life* (New York: Viking Press, 1975), pp. 114–17.

55. Daniel Callahan, *Abortion: Law, Choice and Morality* (New York: Macmillan, 1970), p. 308.

56. Ibid.

57. Edward Shils, "The Sanctity of Life," in *Life or Death: Ethics and Options* (Seattle: University of Washington Press, 1968), p. 18. See pp. 12, 14–15.

58. P. B. Medawar, "Genetic Options: An Examination of Current Fallacies," in *Life or Death*, p. 98.

59. Callahan, *Abortion*, p. 316.

60. Loren Eiseley, *The Firmament of Time* (New York: Atheneum Publishers, 1960), pp. 144–45.

61. Ibid., p. 145.

62. See Arnold Toynbee, *Change and Habit* (New York and London: Oxford University Press, 1966), pp. 20–22.

63. Ibid., p. 13.

64. Thomas says: ". . . faith has certitude of the sort that exists outside the genus of knowledge in the genus of affection" (*extra genus cognitionis in genere affectionis existens*). *Commentum in Quatuor Libros Sententiarum Magistri Petri Lombardi*, Dist. 23, q. 2, a. 3. While distinguishing faith from knowledge here, Thomas does consider faith to be a kind of knowledge as when he writes: ". . . the knowledge of faith proceeds from the will." Ibid., Dist. 23, q. 2, a. 1. See also *Summa Theologica* II II q. 45, a. 2.

65. Wilfred Sellars, "Imperatives, Intentions, and Ought," in Castaneda and Nakhnikian, *Morality and the Language of Conduct*, p. 212.

66. Blaise Pascal, *Pensées* (New York: Washington Square Press, 1965), Nos. 282 and 277. Pascal relates faith to affectivity. "This then is faith: God felt by the heart, not by reason." (No. 278.)

67. Henri Bergson, *The Two Sources of Morality and Religion* (Garden City, N.Y.: Doubleday & Co., Inc., Anchor Books, 1956), p. 58.

68. John Macquarrie, *Principles of Christian Theology* (New York: Charles Scribner's Sons, 1966), p. 88.

69. Martin Buber, *I and Thou*, 2nd ed. (New York: Charles Scribner's Sons, 1958), p. 8.

70. Thomas Carlyle, "Characteristics," in *Essays* (Boston: Brown & Taggard, 1860), Vol. 3, p. 9.

71. John Rader Platt, *The Excitement of Science* (Boston: Houghton Mifflin Co., 1962), p. 169.

72. Ibid.

73. Ralph Linton, "The Problem of Universal Values," in Robert F. Spencer, ed., *Method and Perspective in Anthropology: Papers in Honor of Wilson D. Wallis* (Minneapolis: University of Minnesota Press, 1954), p. 157.

74. Smith, *Theory of Moral Sentiments*, pp. 192–93.

75. Ibid., p. 193.

76. Ibid.

77. Vladimir Solovyev, *The Meaning of Love* (London: Geoffrey Bles, Centenary Press, 1945), p. 25.

78. Ibid., pp. 32–33.

79. Bergson, *Sources of Morality and Religion*, p. 40.

80. Loren Eiseley, *Firmament of Time*, pp. 123–24.

81. Arthur Schopenhauer, *The Basis of Morality*, 2nd ed. (London: George Allen & Unwin, Ltd., 1915), p. 163. He goes on to say that

if one acts with an eye to his own weal and woe, he is acting egoistically and not morally. Ibid., pp. 166–68.

82. Martin Luther, *Weimar Auflage* I, 654, 14–26, 6–30. *Ad Dialogum S. Prieratis de Potestate Papae Responsio* (1518).

83. John Dewey and James H. Tufts, *Ethics*, rev. ed. (New York: Henry Holt & Co., 1932), p. 302. See also Von Hildebrand, *Christian Ethics*, Chapter 15, "The Nature of Moral Values." Von Hildebrand says moral values are marked by the fact that one is held responsible for them, they presuppose freedom, their violation causes guilt, they are indispensable, not optional, and they relate to punishment and reward.

84. Schopenhauer, *Basis of Morality*, p. 163.

85. I use the term "normal" here in the normative sense, not in the sense that it is statistically normal.

86. The experience of guilt shows how unloving to self immoral activity is. Guilt is a tearing and disintegrating experience. Bernard Häring writes of it: "*C'est la conscience mauvaise, qui ronge. C'est d'abord un sentiment sombre, rétrécissant, la douleur non rachetée, provenant du déchirement intérieur.*" Bernard Häring, *Le Sacre et le Bien* (Paris: Éditions Fleurus, 1963), p. 72. To want to avoid this experience is in a proper sense self-loving. For an excellent and lucid exposition of the nature of self-love and other-love, see Robert B. Ashmore, Jr., "Friendship and the Problem of Egoism," *The Thomist* 41 (January 1977), pp. 105–30.

87. Montesquieu, *Lettres Persanes*, letter 83.

88. Aristotle, *Nichomachean Ethics*, Bk. 5, Chap. 1, 1130a, 10.

89. Pierre Joseph Proudhon, *De la Justice dans la Révolution et dans l'Église*, new ed. (Brussels, 1868), p. 44; quoted in Ch. Perelman, *The Idea of Justice and the Problem of Argument* (New York: Humanities Press, 1963), pp. 5–6.

90. Peter A. Bertocci and Richard M. Millard, *Personality and the Good* (New York: David McKay Co., 1963), p. 3.

91. It is my position that it is not only in its generic formulation that justice is the first expression of the foundational moral experience. It is this also when it is spelled out in terms of commutative, distributive, and legal, since without all three of these forms of justice, there is no justice.

92. Josef Pieper, *The Four Cardinal Virtues* (New York: Harcourt, Brace & World, 1965), p. 74.

93. Aristotle, *Nichomachean Ethics*, Bk. 8, Chap. 1, 1155a, 25.

94. Having said that justice is the minimal expression of livable human and moral existence, it may not be inferred that all will agree on what is just. Views on justice often take the form of discussion of *rights*. Rights cover the three forms of justice and so provide a

catchall category for stating the implications of justice. Consensus
on just what human rights are is something reserved for an age so futuristic as to be unimaginable. For the present, rights talk will always
find itself in the crucible of debate. Does everyone, for example,
have a right to complete health care from cradle to deathbed or is
health care the right of those enterprising or lucky enough to be able
to afford it? Underlying this discussion is a theory of justice reflecting a particular view of the nature of man . . . a particular anthropology. Such is always the way with rights. *Rights* is a late-order
term reflecting several layers of presupposition, ideals, and theory.

The dependence on rights language is such in our moral discourse
that there was considerable surprise some years ago when Chung
Sho Lo, a professor of philosophy and member of the Unesco Commission, pointed out that there is no precise equivalent in Chinese
for our word "right." There is, of course, a notion of justice! This
would have to baffle American individualism which trades in the
currency of ruggedly conceived individual rights. For an example
of old-time American individualism bedecked in intricate arguments
from economics and the theory of choice, see Robert Nozick, *An-
archy, State, and Utopia* (New York: Basic Books, Inc., 1974). In
a book now in process I plan to address the gratuitous faith posture
of individualism and the reductionism it practices on the concept of
justice. For a view of the deeper implications of justice and love as
they relate to the foundational moral experience, see Marjorie Reiley
Maguire, "The Ultimate Value Question," forthcoming at this writing in the spring 1978 issue of *Counseling and Values*, and "Immortality and Ethics," to be published in the proceedings of the
American Society of Christian Ethics, 1978.

CHAPTER FOUR

LOVE'S STRATEGY

When moralist Robert M. Cooper wrote that "love without strategy is little more than a fleeting feeling," he was touching on the fundamental question of method in ethics.[1] Every ethicist is a strategist about the ways of love since moral living is the flowering of love. Every ethicist, therefore, should offer a method which shows the way that moral evaluation should proceed. Ethics is indispensable because anyone who is even slightly alert knows that moral and immoral mean something really different. Morality is a meaningful category of our existence. We have to have a way of judging it.

Clearly, there is a real, not an imaginary, difference between Adolf Hitler and Francis of Assisi, between Attila the Hun and Albert Schweitzer, between a sycophant and a prophet, a hero and a conniving coward. We know we are saying something real when we describe certain conduct as contemptible, disgusting, demeaning, or when we call someone a thief or a liar. In such speech, we are describing what persons ought or ought not to be. If we did not agree that persons ought to be truth-tellers, there would be nothing wrong with being a liar. If human life ought not to be respected, murder would be as innocent as cribbage. But there are these *oughts* and so there is the realm of morals and the need for ethics to refine our moral consciousness.

Now at first look it might seem that ethics is simple. If we agree that killing and thieving and lying are immoral, then let us simply cease and desist from them and persuade or constrain others to do likewise. Why need we tax the mind with ethical inquiry? Fortunately or unfortunately, ethics is a necessary exercise of the human mind. The reasons for this will emerge more fully as I expose my over-all method for doing ethics. For the moment, however, let us note that there are easily perceptible problems that bind us to the ethical task. The first obvious problem is that there is increasingly less agreement on what is or is not moral and on what our obligations are. And secondly, even if we become clear about what our obligations are, those obligations collide.

The more that history and communications spread our horizons regarding past and present ethical views, the more divergence we discover. The range of moral beliefs is enormous. There was surprise some years ago to learn that Eskimos viewed marital fidelity differently from us. In their hospitality, Eskimo men would lend both bed and wife to a visitor. Also, their elders would perform suicide to ease food pressures. Some societies have considered it grossly immoral to eat anything from one's own crops or any game that one may have caught. Some societies look on cheating as a sign of admirable prowess. Others have standards of honesty that would make our society look criminal. Some societies view premarital and even extramarital sex as matters involving only the preferences of the persons involved. As Abraham and May Edel have said, looking at the data of anthropology: "We know that such contravention of our attitudes—to adultery, or truth-telling or killing or toward virtually any rule we accept—are extremely common among the peoples of different cultures of the world."[2] The fair question arises, therefore, as to whether we or they are right.

In our own society, consensus on morals is evaporating. We can find a businessman explaining to his incredulous sons and daughters that the money his company pays secretly to foreign officials to do business there is not a bribe, as they naïvely think. It is rather like a toll or a surcharge one has to pay to gain access to an important market. Everyone does it. And then the sons and daughters try to explain to the businessman father that the sex they have and the marijuana they smoke do not import licentiousness and moral decay, but are rather the currently acceptable liturgies of social exchange. Everyone does it.

However, even when we happily achieve agreement on standards, our standards clash with one another. We may agree that we should save innocent life when it is within our power to do so, and that we should tell the truth. But what do you do if a man intent on murder asks you where his intended victim is—and you know? If you give him misinformation to save a life, you have failed to tell the truth. If you tell him, you have facilitated a murder. Someone who always told the truth, of course, would be a source of chaos and could never be confided in. And that illustrates the problem of ethics. After discovering what we think are real moral values, it is often a delicate task to see how they apply or which of them applies when two or more compete. To be moral is to love well. How to love well amid conflicting value claims is the problem. Love needs a strategy and that strategy is ethics.

From Morality to Ethics . . .

Ethics, that bruised discipline, is misunderstood to mean everything from etiquette to the study of customs. The first thing, therefore, that it ought to do is define itself. Ethics is *the art-science which seeks to bring sensitivity and method to the discernment of moral values*. It is the way we do our systematic thinking about moral values. It is neither pure art nor pure science and is best, though imperfectly, described as art-science.

Art. Ethics is like art in one sense of that term as defined by Webster's Third New International Dictionary: Art is "the conscious use of skill, taste, and creative imagination in the practical definition or production of beauty." The focus of ethics is not on aesthetic values but on moral values. But it too involves imagination, intuition, and taste. Just as sensitivity to beauty cannot be really taught, just as a sense of the exquisite cannot be diagrammed, so too the good or the moral cannot be spelled out or efficiently captured in the jejune processes of "reason." Ethics, like art, is not just a work of uninvolved intellectuality but is rather immersed by its nature in feeling, in a sense of fittingness, of contrast, and even in a sense of the macabre. It involves an intuitive sense of correspondence that can be cultivated only in lived experience. At times it will body forth appreciations which have been stirring inarticulately in group consciousness. At times it will resonate from the unrepeatable uniqueness of a heroic soul. Always, ethical evaluation will involve us at many levels of our psyche and in ways that are only partially chartable.

When we discuss things such as the idea of group sex, or of having special places for the performance of mercy death, of an abortion late in pregnancy, or of chemical or psychosurgical manipulation of

personality, or even less bizarre matters, evaluation will have many
psychic dimensions and will not be simply a syllogism unfolding
tidily.

The comparison of ethics to art is important and redemptive since
ethics has been done too rationalistically in the main. Ethics is comparable to art because art that is really worthwhile is to some degree
unexplainable. There is no way of giving an account of all that
makes art genuine or great. Even what the artist says about his own
work is not all that important. If he is successful as an artist, he has
achieved more than he can say or even conceptualize. If the art is
good, its value verges on the inexhaustible. And, in a sense, moral insight is an inexhaustible work of art. No principle or no ethicist can
exhaust it or enflesh it. This is a caution to the overly wise which
should be built into the very definition of ethics.

There is another contact point between ethics and art. As John
Dewey writes: "One of the earliest discoveries of morals was the similarity of judgment of good and bad in conduct with the recognition
of beauty and ugliness in conduct. Feelings of the repulsiveness of
vice and the attractiveness of virtuous acts root in esthetic sentiment."[3] Dewey ties the native emotions of disgust and admiration
to the appreciation of moral value and disvalue. Herein lies, according to Dewey, whatever truth there is in the "moral sense" theory of
ethics. In support of his contention, Dewey notes the double meaning of "fair." Also, the Greek *sophrosyne*, imperfectly translated as
"temperance," represented a harmonious blending of affections into
a beautiful whole. This, says Dewey, was essentially an artistic idea.
Justice also can be seen as closely allied to the sense of symmetry and
proportion. And the Greek identification of virtue with the proportionate mean is an indication of "an acute estimate of grace, rhythm,
and harmony as dominant traits of good conduct." Dewey concludes: "The modern mind has been much less sensitive to esthetic
values in general and to these values in conduct in particular. Much
has been lost in direct responsiveness to right. The bleakness and
harshness often associated with morals is a sign of this loss."[4]

To be sensitive to the beauty of the moral, however, should not
push us to conflate the two categories. Some of the Nazi planners
had a high sense of the aesthetic, and Tolstoy speaks of the women
who wept at the beauty of the symphony but had no care for their
coachmen who were freezing outside. A sense of beauty and a sense

of morality are not as one. This, however, need not impede our recognizing with Dewey that the good has its own loveliness and that moral awareness evokes our aesthetic sense. This is why Leibniz could speak of the beauty of virtue. And this too is the import of Schopenhauer's statement: "The metaphysics of nature, the metaphysics of morals, and the metaphysics of the beautiful mutually presuppose each other, and only when taken as connected together do they complete the explanation of things as they really are, and of existence in general."[5]

Science. In comparing ethics to art (and it is a comparison, not an identification) there is no effort to consign ethics to a normless subjectivity. (The theory of art would accept no such consignment for art either.) To stress this, I hyphenate art to science. Like science, ethics weighs, assesses, analyzes, and studies relationships of empirical data. Ultimately, moral values, whether conceptualized or real, have radical reference to the empirical order where persons dwell. Like a scientist bent on hunting, gathering, and analyzing amid that data, the ethicist has an inductive fact-gathering and analytical task. His goal is completeness and objectivity. He has of course no illusions about what objectivity means. As philosopher Eugene Fontinell writes: "It is now being suggested that even scientific knowledge is symbolic in that we no longer have a one-to-one correspondence between mind and reality but rather a continuing transaction in which man's knowledge is a pathway to a more adequate relationship with reality."[6] Similarly, Hannah Arendt notes that "the allegedly absolute objectivity and precision of the natural scientists, is today a thing of the past."[7] The "impartial spectator" or the "ideal observer" theories of ethical knowledge are inadequate when they represent an outmoded hunger for absolute objectivity. They also represent a false passion for clean, intellectually pure knowledge, thus bypassing the illumination that comes from affective and existential immersion in the realities of the moral order. (If the role of "sympathy" is adequately stressed, the perils of the "ideal observer" stratagem are mitigated and some conceptual gains may be achieved.)

In the ethicist, there is not just something of the scientist at work; there is also the artist, the believer, and the mystic, as we have seen in looking at the foundational experience that grounds the ethicist's quest.

Sensitivity. Our definition of ethics says that it seeks to bring "sensitivity and method to the discernment of moral values." Stress on sensitivity is needed because insensitivity to the moral dimension of all human affairs is a baneful commonplace. The moral dimension is easily submerged by other preoccupations. Then we hear that something is "a political, not a moral matter," or "an economic, not a moral matter," or even "a practical, not a moral matter." There is pernicious mischief afoot here, since the onus of moral responsibility is being effectively avoided. Part of the role of ethics is to reassert the moral dimension of *all* deliberate human behavior, whether private or collective, so that the civilizing presence of conscience will not anywhere be lost.

Method. My definition of ethics speaks of method for discerning moral values. Ethics is like breathing in the sense that everyone is already doing it. Unlike breathing, we do not all do it the same way; neither is our doing it blessed with the same instinctive efficiency. We can make a mess of it and that is serious, since ethical errors can be cruel or even fatal.

There are two general obstacles to effective ethical discernment: One is at the level of personality development, and the other comes from a lack of theoretical clarity regarding the nature of ethical inquiry. Sophisticated studies in developmental psychology have shown that we may grow from one way of doing ethics to another. At early stages of development we may antisocially conclude that good is whatever we want it to be. We are likely to be impulse-ridden, opportunistic in evaluating, with little ability to distance ourselves from our own interests or to relate properly to moral authorities. Some people may grow old and die at these early levels. Others go on to develop an ability for more sensitive judgment and can respond to principles and ideals in a way that shows a maturely integrated awareness of the value of self and others. If a person is impeded in personality development, he may "learn" but could not appreciate what ethics is about.[8]

The obstacle to ethical discernment that concerns us here is the general lack of clarity about how we should go about judging and discerning moral values. This is the problem of method. Every person is a valuing animal and is willy-nilly involved in his own method of making ethical judgments. It would be quite possible to have an extended interview with anyone, to discuss moral matters and cases, and then to show in broad outline the ethical method this person is operating with. Probably the person has never clarified in his own mind this important aspect of his personal existence. Probably, too, he is tied to a number of opinions, which, if he became critically reflective about it, he would alter. But he just lumbers along, thinking and evaluating in the way he has fallen into through a number of unco-ordinated and untested influences.

In a sense the person we are suggesting as typical does not really have a true and reflective method for approaching moral issues. Rather he has been programmed into certain set ridges of thought, and in the face of moral issues he reacts predictably. In a sense he is morally trained, not morally educated. He has been efficiently patterned like a watch but he does not enjoy the freedom of personal judgment. He is doing ethics, but he is not doing it freely. He is in a box and does not even see the horizons that are open to the free. He is likely to feel threatened by those who are being freed through critical reflection, even if they are not abusing their freedom. His box is normalcy and they are obviously not in it.

Some persons will have an unrealistic confidence in authority or tradition, whereas others will rely on an almost vertical intuition into the immediate facts and will lack breadth of vision or any sense of continuity or history. Others will trust firmly in principles and group expectations and be unequipped to handle exceptional cases or to trust their intuitions. In all these cases the problem is a limited grasp of the epistemological dimensions of moral evaluation. What concerns us here is that this limit is found not just in practice but also in theory. Those who think and write about ethics often lend authority to limited ethical approaches. Our effort here will be to offer a more complete ethical method that tries not to bypass any of the personal or cultural processes of evaluation.

Moral. A final and brief word on my definition of ethics relates to the key category *moral* of which I have spoken in the previous chapter. Moral cannot be defined in the sense that it could if it were a species of some more generic reality. Morality is a basic concept and hence can only be described. Moral in my definition means human in the *ought* or normative sense. In other words, the word "human" can be used normatively (what humanity ought to be) or descriptively (what it is observed to be). Thus, you can say descriptively that *it is human to lie* (meaning that people do) and you can say normatively that *it is not human to lie* (meaning that people should not). It is in this latter, normative sense that I use human as the synonym of moral. When we say that rape is immoral, we are saying that it is inhuman activity; that it is not what humans ought to do in expressing their sexuality. Some cultures will express moral disapproval by saying: "That's acting like a dog." It is not what humans ought to do. It is immoral. (Whether the poor dog would act that way is not the point.)

A Model for Ethical Method . . .

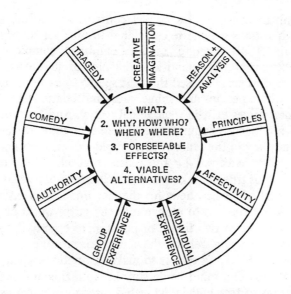

What the wheel model represents is the two phases in ethics: the expository and the evaluational. Pursuing the questions at the hub of the model is the expository phase . . . something akin to the assembling of the facts in the processes of law which precedes the actual legal argumentation. The spokes of the model represent the nine evaluational processes and resources available to us personally and socially. As should be observed and conceded from the outset, every intellectual model limps. It justifies itself only if it gives significant form and consistency to thought. In reality, as would be clear, evaluation does not stay obediently in abeyance while we run through the expository phase. What the model does do, as I shall attempt to show, is call attention to the pluriform possibilities of evaluation that are available to man, the valuing animal. I hope through this method to provide a systematic framework for moral inquiry whether in private and interpersonal matters or in collective or political situations.[9] In this chapter, I shall discuss the presuppositions and limits that affect my discussion and any discussion of ethical method. Then in subsequent chapters, I will try to defend the realism of my proposed method.

The Quest for Realism . . .

The hub or center of the model contains a schedule of reality-revealing questions which are calculated to uncover the moral situation in all of its concrete, unique, empirical complexity. Moral significance is not just found in principles or in theory, although much moral insight is housed there. It speaks to us from the existential order where persons and things meet and relate. Here, in fact, is where moral values exist in their actual reality. And here too is where all moral intelligence commences. "There is nothing in the intellect that was not first in the senses," says an old axiom, meaning that it is from the data perceived by the senses that all intellectualization takes off. This is true of all knowledge including moral knowledge.

This fact of life is bad news for the lazy mind. It is easier to bask in generalities than it is to plunge into the gritty world of empirical experience where no two things or persons are exactly the same and where meaning-giving relationships are crisscrossing and shifting. This taxes the mind and calls it to make distinctions where there are real differences. The mind easily shrinks from this and prefers false generalization to true and individuated discernment. An example of thinking in false generalities might be helpful.

I have polled different groups on whether they approved of homosexual couples adopting children. The response was uniformly low, running between 6 to 8 per cent approval. I then told them the story of two homosexual women known to me. When I first met them, they were completing their studies in special education which was training them to teach handicapped children. They considered themselves married and had even solemnized their union in a private religious ceremony with friends. When they completed their studies, it was their intention to move to another part of the country where their homosexuality would not be known to anyone and where they would presumptively be two single women sharing a home. They would settle where it would be legal and feasible for single persons to adopt children. It was their desire to adopt one or two children whose disabilities made them unlikely candidates for adoption and whose lives would probably be lived mostly in institutions. With the strength of their mutual relationship and with the skills they had in special education, these two women felt they could bring more happiness and development to these children than could be found even in a good institution. As far as their homosexual relationship was concerned, they felt this could either be kept from the children permanently or revealed to them if they reached the possibility of mature understanding.

After telling this story, I have asked how many would approve of this particular case of adoption by homosexual persons. Approval went as high as 80 per cent. The change in approval rates indicates that when first asked the question, the respondents were thinking of homosexuals stereotypically and mythically . . . in other words in a falsely generalized, unindividuated fashion.

However the reader might judge the morality of this case does not concern us here. It is a point of method that has to be made. The proper answer to the original question should have been: *it depends*; or *generally yes*; or *generally no*. It is possible to think of actions as generally good or bad.

It is fair to say that both killing and using heroin are generally bad. But this limited generalization allows for individuated differences. Using heroin for pain relief for a terminal cancer patient may be quite moral. Likewise killing in self-defense may be morally good.

The point of ethics we are making here is that "human actions are good or bad according to the circumstances,"[10] and the center of the wheel model represents that inductive phase of ethics in which we search for the relevant circumstances. I have mentioned that persons often eschew this phase of ethics, preferring the ease of false generalities and inherited impressions of what is good or bad. There is another reason why this process is avoided in practice and slighted in theory. If it is true, as I have quoted above, that "human actions are good or bad according to the circumstances," then it would seem that we have opened the door to complete ethical relativism and to a rather flaccid and normless "situation ethics." If it all depends on the circumstances, then there is no solid ground in ethics, for circumstances are always changing.

The quote about the circumstances is from Thomas Aquinas, and it would help to know what he meant by it. Thomas recognized that certain circumstances do not affect the morality of an action. Thus it might be immaterial to the morality of an action if the circumstances of time or place were changed. (If you are robbed on a Tuesday or a Wednesday, it would probably make no moral difference.) Such circumstances may be quite incidental and have little or no effect on the moral status of the behavior in question. Not all circumstances, however, are such. In fact, notes Thomas, there are circumstances that constitute the "principal condition" of the conduct to be judged and establish the moral status and species of that conduct. Thus to the question whether the moral judgment is circumstantial, Thomas' answer is affirmative.

This did not make Thomas an ethical relativist. It did make him a realist who recognized (in theory, at least; he did not always stay with his insight in judging certain issues) that you cannot make a moral judgment if you do not know the circumstances that specify an action and give it its moral meaning. Killing as the only alternative in self-defense is not the same morally as killing while robbing. The circumstances are different; therefore, the morality of the actions is different, which is to say that "human actions are right or wrong according to the circumstances."[11]

Actually, this insight is the fruit of common sense, and most people recognize it and live and judge accordingly. It is an insight, however, which is hostile to a taboo mind-set. The moral tabooist, while granting that most things are right or wrong according to their circumstances, holds that certain actions are wrong regardless of the circumstances. People, for example, have considered as wrong *regardless of the circumstances* gambling, contraceptive intercourse, remarriage after divorce, interracial marriage, conscientious objection to civil authority, and a thousand other things. If they judged that all of these things were likely to be bad precisely because of the circumstances that attend them, then we might agree or disagree with their assessment of the circumstances, but we could not fault their ethical method. The error in method arises from proclaiming certain activity wrong with no perceived need to consult the circumstances that undergird and constitute its moral meaning.[12]

This tendency to judge preter-circumstantially is typical of children, as it is of many primitive peoples. Psychologist Jean Piaget has pointed out that young children do not evaluate intentions and other circumstances in their value judgments. A type of action has a fixed meaning *regardless of the circumstances*, to use the language of taboo. Thus a child will not see any moral difference in breaking a cup accidentally or out of spite. The cup got broken; that is all that really counts. As the child matures, or, we might better say, if the child matures, he sees the essential difference circumstances make.[13]

Human Nature and the Illusion of Self-evidence . . .

It is easier to stereotype than to make distinctions where there are differences. This is why the inductive, expository process in ethics is regularly short-circuited with resultant errors in moral judgment. The problem is heightened by the fact that we are born into a moral universe where pat answers to most moral questions are solidly ensconced in the culture. Seemingly, they are as fixed and eternal as the starry skies above . . . and as self-evident. What is self-evident, of course, need not be investigated and is immune to challenge. In the atmosphere of illusory self-evidence, questions will go unasked, problems will be unsuspected, and growth into the unfolding mystery of humanness will be impeded.

This is the reason the reality-revealing questions in the hub of the wheel-model are really and graphically central. Without a fundamental devotion to questioning, ethics settles for figments and loses contact with the real. Jean-Paul Sartre, with his existentialist's aversion both to false generalization and to the lack of specific awareness, can be instructive here. Sartre has said that the greatest evil of which man is capable is to treat as abstract that which is concrete. This is exactly what we do if we blur unique persons and situations into ill-fitting, abstract categories and if we do not seek out the empirical specifics of every person and every case. Sartre's press for specific acuity even leads him to say that there is no such thing as "human nature." The "human nature" he denies is one which is "abstract, an essence independent of man or anterior to his existence" or in any way "superior to him" in his concrete reality.[14] In fact, Sartre says that "there is no such thing as a human condition in general," so concerned is he to avoid losing concrete and individual reality in the fog of abstract conceptualization.[15]

One need not buy all of Sartre's interpretations or run with all his metaphors to share in what is true of his insight here. In fact, one can keep a concept of human nature and still profit from his insight into the moral significance of concrete situations and actual persons. If human nature is conceived of as a blueprint from which every manner of moral conclusion can be deduced, then the likelihood is that the notion of human nature is being used as a depository for a number of untested assumptions that are abroad in the culture about what does or does not befit persons. For example, it has been argued that a number of categories of human behavior are absolutely and always wrong because they are incompatible with human nature. Theoretically it might be true that all of these things are wrong in every imaginable case. However, if this were so, it would not be because an intuitive insight into human nature revealed these things to be beyond the human pale. There is no such revelatory grace which dispenses you from the task of searching out and assessing the meaning-giving circumstances of any moral problem. As ethicist John Giles Milhaven says, ". . . it is empirical evidence, not direct insight into what something is, but the observation, correlation, and weighing out of numerous facts, which reveal the value of most human acts. . . ."[16] Milhaven should have said *all* human acts. No human behavior can be judged uncontextually or outside of its actual relationships.

It is, of course, possible to say that certain things are generally wrong. Indeed, when fully described, they may be seen as so negative, disruptive, and neglectful of creative alternatives that no circumstance could be imagined in which they might be justified. I have argued elsewhere that capital punishment is in this category.[17] I did not so argue, however, on the grounds that an intuitive perception of the moral implications of human nature issues inexorably into a judgment of the moral infeasibility of penal killing. Rather it is because there are alternatives to it and because an analysis of what this kind of killing is when viewed in all of its historical and foreseeable circumstances supports the conclusion that it cannot be justified. I establish it as wrong by argument, not by edict or purported intuition.

The point of method here is that capital punishment (or anything else) cannot be proved wrong by direct intuition into its radical incompatibility with human nature. It can only be shown wrong, to return to Milhaven's words, by "the observation, correlation, and weighing out" of the alternatives, foreseeable consequences, and all other morally meaningful circumstances.[18]

Indeed it should be clear that the "observation, correlation, and weighing out of numerous facts" of which Milhaven speaks is not of the sort that marks an empirical science. The moral is unique, and so too is the approach to it. Neither is the ultimate conclusion here that ethics is purely inductive and empirical. There are valid and indispensable generalizations, replete with moral experience and wisdom, from which valuable directives can be deduced. And, indeed, ethics cannot be rationalistically reduced merely to induction plus deduction. Of its essence it involves us in creative imagination, affective appreciations, faith, insights mediated through tragedy and comedy, and full recognition of the social roots of knowing. This is illustrated by the spokes of my wheel model. All of this, however (and the foundational moral experience itself), has its beginnings in the empirical order where persons, animals, and things dwell in uneasy community. It is the questioning mind in its fullness that achieves discernment here.

The goal of ethics is moral insight. The original sin of erroneous ethics is incompleteness at the level of empirical inquiry. Morality is based on reality, and if we have not probed the real with zealous questions, our conclusions will be realistic only by accident. Describing the meaning of "insight" in his monumental study on the subject, Bernard Lonergan writes:

> In the ideal detective story the reader is given all the clues yet fails to spot the criminal. He may advert to each clue as it arises. He needs no further clues to solve the mystery. Yet he can remain in the dark for the simple reason that reaching the solution is not the mere apprehension of any clue, nor the mere memory of all, but a quite distinct activity of organizing intelligence that places the full set of clues in a unique explanatory perspective.[19]

Someone seeking moral understanding is comparable to a detective. He seeks the "explanatory perspective" that can be found amid the complexities of the case. The reality-revealing questions are geared to make sure that he will have "the full set of clues" without which moral intelligence is crippled.

Of Modesty and Paradox . . .

In stressing the need for energetic questioning in the pursuit of moral truth, there is no suggestion here that the quest will lead to the perfect possession of the quarry. Simplicity will often enough elude us and limpid clearness will be rare. The effort of the ethical persuasion known ineptly as "naturalism," which attempts to answer moral questions by scientific observation and method, is symptomatic and symbolic of Western myopia. Morality too should be wrapped up with scientific tidiness according to the dominant intellectual belief in the West. As Joseph M. Kitagawa writes, "By and large, the Westerner's mindset has been conditioned by strong emphases on reason, judgment and discrimination." He agrees that the profound gulf between East and West is provided by the word "system," which denotes the task of getting things together in a rational order. This is the keynote of the West. The Easterner is more contemplative, more receptive, more modest in taking the measure of things.[20]

Modesty is especially important in ethics. Whoever would think ethically must reacquaint himself with the alien notion of paradox. The Western passion to get everything squared away is a hazard in ethics. Often we are left with perceptions which seem separately true but contradictory. Our sense of hope and our sense of tragedy might point convincingly in opposite directions, but we cannot negate either appreciation to achieve a superficial complacency for the mind. Often too, in practical cases of ethics, we will find contradictory answers to the same question defensible and well braced by reason. We cannot rest easily with such a situation, but sometimes we can do no more. Ethics does not enjoy the simplicity of what has been hopefully called "precise science." Sometimes it can only lighten the darkness slightly but not dispel it, leaving us with an only partially guided leap in the dark. This is disconcerting to those who look to ethics for a neat code of do's and don'ts. The desire for this, of course, is understandable. It is a desire to escape from the disturbing responsibility of having to decide when wracked by unbanishable doubt. This, however, is part of the burden and challenge of being both free and finite.

The undergirding epistemology of ethics must be humble, since arrogance is a blinding force. And it would be arrogance to feel that we can achieve perfect light in ethics. Surprisingly for those who do not know him, Thomas Aquinas supplies an epistemological approach that is marked by this humility. One might conclude inaccurately that one who wrote a massive *Summa* provides a prime example of getting it all together into a closed system. Thomas, however,

believed, as one of his commentators summed it up, that "truth cannot be exhausted by any [human] knowledge; it remains therefore always open to new formulation."[21] Thomas had some very negative
things to say about our capacity to understand. He said, for example,
that "the essential grounds of things are unknown to us."[22] He also
says we do not know the "essential differences" or the "substantial
forms" of things as they are in themselves.[23] And Thomas, the theologian, says that the highest form of knowledge of God is the knowledge of God "as the Unknown."[24] Thomas did not see human
knowledge as ever complete, but always imperfect and struggling to
contain a light that exceeded our capacity. As knowers, we are always
unprofitable servants of truth. In fact, Thomas himself illustrated
the experience of this by giving up the writing of his *magnum opus*
with the announced conviction that all that he had ever written was
"nothing but straw." His reminder of the straw quality of our best
understanding is a chastening valedictory. Given the excessive certitudes that abound in moral discourse, we need the message.

NOTES—CHAPTER FOUR

1. Robert M. Cooper, "Faith, Hope, and Love: Three Books," *Cross Currents* 23 (Fall 1974), p. 337.
2. May Edel and Abraham Edel, *Anthropology and Ethics* (Springfield, Ill.: Charles C. Thomas, Publisher, 1959), p. 19.
3. John Dewey and James H. Tufts, *Ethics*, rev. ed. (New York: Henry Holt & Co., 1932), p. 298.
4. Ibid., p. 299.
5. Arthur Schopenhauer, *The Basis of Morality*, 2nd ed. (London: George Allen & Unwin, Ltd., 1915), p. 8. One may compare ethics to art without adopting the position of John Stuart Mill to the effect that ethics is not a science but an art. Mill saw science as a descrip- tion of things as they are and ethics as a normative discipline con- cerned with things as they ought to be. He saw science as moving from the particular to the general and ethics as going from the gen- eral to the particular. It is not all that simple, as will be seen in this elaboration of ethical method. See John Stuart Mill, *Utilitarianism, I Utilitarianism, Liberty and Representative Government* (New York: E. P. Dutton & Co., Everyman Edition, 1910), pp. 1–2.
6. Eugene Fontinell, "Reflections on Faith and Metaphysics," *Cross Currents* 16 (1966), p. 36.

7. Hannah Arendt, *Between Past and Future* (New York: Meridian Books, 1963), p. 48.
8. The work of Jean Piaget, Lawrence Kohlberg, and Jane Loevinger on the developmental patterns of moral evaluation have been most illuminating. They are especially helpful for work in moral and pastoral counseling as well as for warning ethicists away from the presumption that moral maturity is statistically normal. By calling attention to the way people actually do ethics, these psychologists can help the ethicists in their study of how they *ought* to do. It is a mistake, however, to think of these scientists as ethicists. Theirs is an effort to show psychometrically how persons do and may do moral evaluation. While some normative implications are unavoidable in this, these people are not plying the theoretical-practical and normative discipline of ethics.
9. There are enormous differences in the way morality is assessed for individuals and for collectivities. The model, however, may be accommodated as a methodical framework for evaluation in both kinds of situations.
10. Thomas Aquinas, *Summa Theologica* I II q. 18, a. 3. "*Ergo actiones humanae secundum circumstantias sunt bonae vel malae.*" In ethics, the terms "good" and "bad," "right" and "wrong" are equivalent. The efforts of some, such as H. A. Prichard, to say that right refers to the action aside from motive and good relates solely to the motive, are misplaced, since motive is essential to moral meaning and we cannot speak of what is right or good while prescinding from motive. This leads to saying that a right action might be bad, because of motive, and a wrong action might be good, also because of motive. Prichard wrote this in an essay in which he wondered why there was so much dissatisfaction with moral philosophy. "Does Moral Philosophy Rest on a Mistake?" *Mind* 21 (1912); reprinted in W. T. Jones, F. Sontag, M. O. Beckner, and R. J. Fogelin, *Approaches to Ethics*, 2nd ed. (New York: McGraw-Hill Book Co., 1969), pp. 469–80.
11. The I II q. 18 of Thomas' *Summa* is a pivotal part of his ethical theory. All the articles of this *Quaestio* are important. Thomas says that "everything has as much of good as it has of being. . . . But God alone has the whole fullness of his being in a manner which is one and simple [*secundum aliquid unum et simplex*], whereas every other thing has its proper fullness of being according to diverse things [*secundum diversa*]" (a. l; my translation). Facing the objection that circumstances are mere "accidents" and thus could not determine the moral species of the action, Thomas says that some cir-

cumstances are *"per se accidentia,"* not *"accidentia per accidens"* (a. 3), which means that some accidents enter into the principal condition of the object in such wise that they determine the moral species. "... *circumstantia . . . in quantum mutatur in principalem conditionem obiecti, secundum hoc dat speciem"* (a. 10). See also *Summa Theologica* I II q. 64, a. 1, ad 2, where Thomas says that the means of the virtues is established "according to the diverse circumstances." Thomas' imprecision in the use of the term "object" has allowed his theory to be distorted by "Thomists" plying the idea of intrinsically evil actions. Thomas does not clarify the relationship of the object, which includes some circumstances, to other specifying circumstances. For example, in I II q. 18, a. 2, Thomas says that an action is specified by its object getting its primary goodness therefrom. Thus using one's own goods is *ex obiecto* good and accepting the goods of someone else is *ex obiecto* bad. It would have helped if Thomas had noted that receiving or taking the goods of others, e.g. food when one is starving, is good because different circumstances have entered into the "principal condition of the object," to use his words from I II q. 18, a. 10. Also, using one's own goods in a way that damages the environment is bad. Thus his examples in a. 2 can be misleading, since they imply something like intrinsically good or intrinsically evil, although this is not what his over-all theory imports. For an example of the misuse of Thomas in the Catholic manuals of moral theology, see A. Tanquerey, *Theologia Moralis Fundamentalis,* Tomus Secundus, (Parisiis, Tornaci, Romae, 1955), pp. 130–37.

12. The term "situation ethics" is almost useless to describe what we are speaking about, since it has been stretched to cover so many things. Any ethics that is not sensitive to the situation it is judging is not ethics at all. And any ethics that is controlled by the situation is closed to creativity. Pope Pius XII condemned what he called "situation ethics" in very vigorous terms, but since he did not say whose work he was attacking, it is not easy to say what he attacked. See *Acta Apostolicae Sedis* (AAS) 48 (1956), pp. 144–45, for a condemnation of "situation ethics" by the Holy Office which forbade "this doctrine of 'Situation ethics,' by whatever name it is designated, to be taught or approved in Universities, Academies, Seminaries and Houses of Formation of Religious, or to be propagated and defended in books, dissertations, assemblies, or, as they are called, conferences, or in any other manner whatsoever." For the Pope's statements, see *AAS* 44 (1952), pp. 270–78, and *AAS* 44 (1952), pp. 413–19. Yet we read Louis Monden, S.J., saying, after citing the

limits within which he uses the term, that "we must clearly affirm with the great classical authors that Catholic morality is, in fact, a *situation ethics." Sin, Liberty and Law* (New York: Sheed & Ward, 1965), p. 104.

13. Jean Piaget, *Six Psychological Studies* (New York: Vintage Books, 1968), pp. 54–58 and p. 37. See also Piaget's *The Moral Judgment of the Child* (New York: Harcourt-Brace, 1932).

14. Sartre is targeted here particularly against the eighteenth-century philosophical conception of human nature. Of the individual, he says, "*Il n'y a pas une nature humaine supérieure à lui, mais une existence spécifique lui est donnée à un moment donné." L'existentialisme Est un Humanisme* (Paris: Éditions Nagel, 1959), p. 111. See also pp. 22ff. where he asserts that there is no such thing as a human nature because there is no God to conceive of it. In this sense, he could conceive of no nature or essence for anything natural, but only for artifacts. For a commentary on this and a comparison with Aquinas, see Josef Pieper, *The Silence of Saint Thomas* (Chicago: Henry Regnery Co., Logos Book, 1965), pp. 50–53.

15. Ibid., p. 116. ". . . *il est certain aussi qu'il n'y a pas une condition humaine en général.* . . ."

16. John G. Milhaven, "Towards an Epistemology of Ethics," *Theological Studies* 27 (1966), p. 235.

17. Daniel C. Maguire, *Death by Choice* (Garden City, N.Y.: Doubleday & Co., Inc., 1974; New York: Schocken Books, 1975), Chap. 8.

18. In the literature of ethics, two terms arise here which I have not heretofore employed in the text. The terms "teleological" and "deontological" are used to describe theories of ethics. Teleological theories tend to hold that actions are right or wrong depending on whether they produce consequences which are good or bad. Teleology asks: "What is the end or good man seeks?" Deontological theories hold that certain kinds of actions are right or wrong regardless of the consequences. These terms, though unavoidable, have some problems attached. First of all, it may be impossible to find a pure type of either kind of theorist. Kant is seen as a deontologist, and yet, for example, in defending his view of truth-telling, he argues by reference to consequences. Furthermore, ethics is by its nature both deontological and teleological, concerned with the ought and not merely in consequentialist terms. Ethics does not prescind from consequences, which would be theoretically irresponsible and practically disastrous. Ethics is concerned with the right as well as the good, with the ought as well as the end. For a discussion of the typical uses of deontology and teleology, see C. D. Broad, *Five*

Types of Ethical Theory (London: Routledge & Kegan Paul, 1930), pp. 206ff.

19. Bernard J. F. Lonergan, S.J., *Insight: A Study of Human Understanding* (New York: Longmans, Philosophical Library, 1957), p. ix.

20. Joseph M. Kitagawa, "The Asian Mind Today," *Worldview* 16 (Jan. 1973), pp. 8–9.

21. Pieper, *Silence of Saint Thomas*, p. 103.

22. *Commentary on Aristotle, De Anima, I, 1, 15.* Pieper comments that "it would be easy to set alongside of it a dozen similar passages (from the *Summa Theologica*, the *Summa Contra Gentiles*, the *De Veritate*, and the other *Quaestiones Disputatae*)." *Silence of Saint Thomas*, p. 65.

23. *Quaestio Disputata de Spiritualibus Creaturis*, 11, ad 3, and *Quaestiones Disputatae de Veritate*, 4, 1, ad 8.

24. *Quaestion Disputata de Spiritualibus Creaturis*, 11, ad 3.

CHAPTER FIVE

THE ROUTES TO REALISM

1. WHAT?
2. WHY? HOW? WHO? WHEN? WHERE?
3. FORESEEABLE EFFECTS?
4. VIABLE ALTERNATIVES?

The Reality-revealing Questions . . .

Good ethics is characterized by a passion for knowing what one is talking about. Asking the right questions is the way to move toward this ideal. The hub of the wheel model represents the expository phase of ethics, the phase in which, hopefully, all of the reality-revealing questions get asked. The enemy here is the unasked question; the goal is the greatest achievable completeness. The questions in the hub of the model might appear as simple and obvious. The annals of human moral discourse, however, would indicate that, here again, the obvious is easily missed.

What will also emerge in discussing the expository or questioning phase of ethics is that the deep question at issue is *How do we know?* In moving through these apparently simple questions, we will find ourselves engrossed in ways of viewing reality known by such ungracious terms as deontology, teleology, utilitarianism, and proportionalism. We will be enmeshed in the troubled relationship between means and ends where innumerable confusions are engendered in the processes of human thought. We will also see the relationship between ethics and the social sciences. We will, in a word, be led to face how it is that we know in general and how it is that we know moral truth in particular. I will intersperse this fundamental chapter with a variety of examples. This I will do because the examples will illustrate the probative power of this line of questioning. With that said, on to the reality-revealing questions.

What? and the First Cognitive Contact . . .

Ethics begins with the question *what?*, a question that may seem unduly simple but is disastrously neglected or bypassed in much moral debate. In asking the question *what?* our target is the *prima facie* facts that lie beneath the figments and arbitrarily imposed meanings with which we drape things.

The word *what* may seem too large and ungainly, since it could be stretched to cover all of the answers to all the other questions in the center of the wheel model. In a sense, since it is a kind of umbrella question, we will be filling out the answer to it as we answer the other questions. Here, however, *what* fixes attention on the primary data (physical, psychological, systemic) by which we make our first cognitive contact with a subject or case. All knowledge is a process, but the process does not begin until we have some discernible first-stage impression of our cognitional target. After attaining this first cognitive contact, we have to move on to seek to know the object in greater depth and breadth, but, at least, if we have been initially successful, we will know *what* we are talking about as we set out and will not be sidetracked from the beginning.

My contention here is that, properly understood, the *is* is parent to the *ought*. Or, put in another way, the moral judgment is about what befits or does not befit the personal situation as it really is. Knowing what really *is*, therefore, is the goal of ethical inquiry. If our judgment of the *prima facie* facts is skewed, the brilliance of subsequent discussion and analysis will be victimized by this original sin. What we say may be impressive, but we will not know *what* we are talking about. The first step toward prescribing what ought to be is describing what is. Description is the beginning of prescription.[1] Description, of course, is not the end of prescription. True ethics is creative and is as concerned with what might be as it is with what is. However, we will never know what might be if we are unaware of what is. The possible emerges from the actual. The creative mind is always well informed.

Many, if not most, ethical debates result from ignorance of *what* is being discussed. Some examples will help to make the point.

A good deal of discussion of capitalism and socialism is lamed from the start by a failure to identify *what* it is that is meant by capitalism and socialism. Professor Robert L. Heilbroner points out that in much that is said about capitalism, the explicit assumption is that the United States is the most typical capitalist nation. Thus Paul Sweezy, the American Marxian critic, says that "the United States is a capitalist society, the purest capitalist society that ever existed. . . ."[2] And French Marxist Roger Garaudy sees the United States as the capitalist system in its most typical expression.[3]

Important results flow from deciding that this is *what* capitalism prototypically is. The definition of the *what* here contains what Heilbroner calls "the assumption that certain contemporary attributes of the United States (racism, militarism, imperialism, social neglect) are endemic to all capitalist nations. . . ."[4] Could it not be better argued that the United States is not a pure realization of capitalism but rather "a deformed variant, the product of special influences of continental isolation, vast wealth, an eighteenth-century structure of government, and the terrible presence of its inheritance of slavery—the last certainly not a 'capitalist institution' "? "Indeed," Heilbroner continues, "could we not argue that 'pure' capitalism would be best exemplified by the economic, political, and social institutions of nations such as Denmark or Norway or New Zealand?"[5] Obviously, the latter assumption would affect all subsequent analysis of the political, economic, or moral dimensions of capitalism. We would start with a different *what*.

Heilbroner's important caution applies equally to the conservative who would single out the Soviet Union as the incarnation of socialism, whereas the argument might be made that Russia, strapped as it was with some tragic historic legacies, just happened to be the wrong place for the ideal of socialism to flourish.

Clearly many critics of capitalism and socialism have functioned under a dominant assumption that prejudiced them from the start in their fundamental assessment of *what* they were talking about. Good moral evaluation (or any other kind of evaluation) would not follow easily from such an initial intellectual misdemeanor. Not all conclusions thereafter would necessarily be wrong. As the scholastic saying put it: *Ex falso sequitur quidlibet* (from false premises, anything can follow). Still, the odds are poor.

This particular example from Heilbroner is something that probably affects most of us. It is a failing that is still with us. An example of a *what* error of the sort that is largely committed to history can also be illustrative of this first and basic phase of ethical inquiry. In an article in the *Journal of Mental Science* entitled "Masturbatory Insanity: The History of an Idea," E. H. Hare points out that only a hundred years ago, it was the established belief in the medical profession that masturbation was a frequent cause of mental disorder. Today almost no one believes that this is part of the *what* of masturbation. In explaining *what* masturbation was, these medical experts said it was an activity that caused an increased flow of blood to the brain and thus was enervating in its effects. As the first textbook on psychiatry published in the United States put it, masturbation, excessive or not, "produces seminal weakness, impotence, dysury, tabes dorsalis, pulmonary consumption, dyspepsia, dimness of sight, vertigo, epilepsy, hypochondriasis, loss of memory, manalgia, fatuity and death."[6] Other experts added that masturbation caused senility, stupidity, melancholy, homosexuality, suicide, hysteria, mania, religious delusions, auditory hallucinations, conceit, defective offspring, and eventually racial decay. The masturbator, according to one expert, was incapable "of any generous impulse or act of loyalty; he is dead to the call of his family, his country, or of humanity."[7] This is obviously a dim view of *what* masturbation is. Drastic conclusions followed from it. At the medical level, in order to discourage the masturbator from indulging his catastrophic penchant, there followed clitoridectomy, the insertion of a silver ring through the prepuce of the penis, castration, ovariotomy, and severing of the pudendal nerves.[8] Morally, of course, there was a crescendo of condemnation. Masturbation was seen as a heinous moral crime. This is understandable. With such chaotic perceptual errors as to *what* masturbation was and thus as to what effects it could have, rational moral discourse on the subject was not possible.[9]

A significant fact about the long-tenured masturbatory hypothesis was that the data to refute it had always been available. As Hare says: "Its fall was not brought about by fresh discoveries or new techniques . . . the evidence had always been there for the taking."[10] What happened was that the misconception became orthodoxy. Even the most astute observers were timid about criticizing the established view. Thus the error reigned from the early eighteenth century into the twentieth. There were various elements that culturally supported the long stand of this view, but its firm survival in the face of contradictory facts illustrates our capacity to accept error as truth, when the error enjoys prestigious auspices, and to go on our way confidently while not knowing *what* we are talking about.

It would be comfortable, but not convincing, to say that this error was freakish and unique, the product of an almost unrepeatable confluence of circumstances, a lonely exception to the standard ability of observant persons to see what is. Rather, this history illustrates the ability of the mind to turn from evidence in preference for socially blessed and widely esteemed misconceptions. The beginning of wisdom would be to see that this seemingly peculiar incident represents a stubborn, native inclination to sidestep the *prima facie* facts, and, succumbing to prevalent social forces, to explain the reality in question. A major task of good ethics is to be on the lookout for other cases where the evidence is in Hare's words "there for the taking" but no one is ready to challenge the false orthodoxy and take it. Enlightened "heresy" is a task of ethics, and one way the task is carried out is to accost the false dogmas that block our access to the *what's* that are the objects of moral investigation.

To illustrate with a further example how the initial definition of a reality can be controlling, the Fellows of the Drug Abuse Council have expressed concern about the consequences in the criminal justice systems of defining drug addiction as sickness: ". . . drug addiction is defined as a sickness and through the use of criminal sanctions drug users are channeled involuntarily into treatment where the label 'rehabilitation' masks the danger of controlling behavior."[11] The social danger here is even broader than that realized in the penal system. Chemical dependencies of various sorts represent a broad genus and proceed from a variety of causes. If they are simplistically defined at the outset as "sickness" and all responses to them are seen as "medicine," "cure," or "rehabilitation," then we are starting out in a blur. The *prima facie* facts are distorted from the first. Similarly there is a broad range of possible responses to the problem meriting very different evaluations. Some involve involuntary behavioral modification of the sort that seems not to distinguish between persons and animals. In ethics, the question *what* presses us to make distinctions where there are differences and to do this from the beginning of the inquiry. Otherwise subsequent distinctions may be ineffectual.

On the subject of death, there are definitional problems at the level of *what*. Medically, the situation has been complicated by the discovery that death is not a moment but a process. Some organs may die while others live. At what point in the process do we declare that death has come to this person?

Beyond these more mechanical questions of death detection, there are deeper questions about what death is. Is it an anomaly to be resisted and fought at all costs. Or is it something natural, like birth, to be accepted on its own terms? As Carl Jung observed: "We grant goal and purpose to the ascent of life, why not to the descent? The birth of a human being is pregnant with meaning, why not death?"[12] Elisabeth Kübler-Ross is functioning out of a particular answer to the question *What is death?* when she says: "It might be helpful if more people would talk about death and dying as an intrinsic part of life just as they do not hesitate to mention when someone is expecting a new baby."[13] Obviously, *what* we think death basically is will condition our judgments of how to approach it.

In the area of sexuality, it obviously will be telling if one immediately defines sexual intercourse as "the marital act." The case has already been set against the possible morality of sexual exchange outside of marriage. In this vein, the widely respected moralist Richard McCormick writes: "Since sexual intercourse and its proximate antecedents represent *total personal* exchange, they can be separated from total personal relationship (marriage) only by undermining their truly human, their expressive character—in short their significance."[14] McCormick says further of nonmarital sexual exchange: "Regardless of the emotional concomitants, the high purpose, the repeated protestation of love, this cannot be an act of love toward that person, but must remain objectively even if not consciously, an act of manipulation."[15]

McCormick is here answering the *what* question regarding sexual intercourse. His answer is that it is either marital or it is objectively wrong. He wants to show that "human sexual intercourse has a sense and meaning prior to the individual purposes of those who engage in it." One might agree with that and still query McCormick about how he knows that sexual exchange always means this kind of totality in every culture and in every circumstance. That is an enormous assumption. McCormick explains the meaning of sexual exchange in terms of language, and that is a useful simile, but is even natural symbolic language ever so transculturally and preter-circumstantially unambiguous? Is it not that in answering the *what* question, McCormick has set up all the subsequent answers in a sexual ethics? Further inquiry would seem unnecessary except to drive home the point already made. That is how important the *what* question can be.

To be brief about further examples, the primal understanding of *what* one decides war is will be ethically critical. Is war merely another act of statecraft, an extension of politics into armed conflict, and a policy option that stands on equal footing with peaceful alternatives? Or is war really the collapse of human statecraft, a resort to primitive bludgeoning when distinctively human modes of communication and problem-resolution fail? How or whether one justifies war will relate intimately to how one has initially answered those questions about *what* war is. Here as in the other issues, *what* performs exploratory surgery on one's influential presuppositions.

This critical use of the interrogative *what* would obviously be useful in a moral examination of such things as racism, sexism, national security, national interest, etc. In every case we would encounter primal and established misconceptions of *what* we would be talking about, and those would be the target of our ethical inquiry.

It should be noted that sometimes the *what* will reveal more that is morally suggestive than at other times. Without checking on *all* the circumstances we cannot know whether infanticide or the consumption of poisons is right or wrong, but both certainly do alert moral consciousness more than, say, eating or whistling. At any rate, having answered *what*? we do not know the final moral verdict (unless we have answered it in such a way as to prejudge the case). However morally suggestive the first-stage answers are, the true moral meaning will only emerge when all the questions are asked and all the circumstances accounted for, as far as that is possible. It is not, of course, completely possible. We will never know exhaustively and comprehensively *what* we are talking about. The process of human knowing is never terminated in total fulfillment. Modesty, even when we have done our best, is always in order. Universally applicable and absolute practical principles are not to be anticipated.[16]

Why? and How? and Ends and Means . . .

To ask *why* we are doing something and *how* we are doing it may seem innocent and obvious aspects of moral inquiry, since, as every devotee of detective stories or romantic fiction knows, your motive, the means you use, and the manner in which you go about things are all quite significant in human affairs. However, *why* and *how* are the gateway to the enormous amount of confusion that obtains in human thought regarding ends and means.

For example, it is a prevalent popular error among nations, institutions, and private persons that if your end (motive, intention, purpose) is good, the means to that end are thereby blessed and good. Anyone who has experienced the harm done by well-intentioned people should wince at this idea. Still motivation is so important that it is seductively easy to think that a good end (motive) does bless whatever means you use to achieve it. In fact an axiom from moral philosophy seems to say just that: "The end sanctifies the means" (*Finis sanctificat media*), and in theology some have defended the thesis: "When the end is licit, the means are licit."[17] The danger in these words is that lofty ends can be a heady wine. Indeed, they have a maniacal potential to cover over many sordid means that are deemed necessary along the road to the glorious end. The widespread, documented stories of torture in a number of nations of the world are all set against a backdrop of unimpeachably noble goals that these nations are pursuing. Whether one's end is "to remain profitable," or "to promote the revolution of the proletariat," or "to make the world safe for democracy," or "to make love"—all laudable ends—the means used and the manner of proceeding in the pursuit of those ends are often unambiguously outrageous. In effect, an end conceived as noble and good can even obscure one's vision of *what* he is really about. If the end is seen also as having a sacred dimension (as is regularly the case in nationalistic matters or with religious groups) it can be completely intoxicating.

The other side of the coin is forthrightly stated by the Russian philosopher Nicolas Berdyaev:

Man's moral dignity and freedom are determined not by
the purpose to which he subordinates his life but by the
source from which his moral life and activity spring. It may
actually be said that in a sense "the means" which a man
uses are far more important than "the ends" which he pur-
sues, for they express more truly what his spirit is. If a man
strives for freedom by means of tyranny, for love by means
of hatred, for brotherhood by means of dissension, for truth
by means of falsity, his lofty aim is not likely to make our
judgment of him more lenient.[18]

Beyond the question of whether ends or means are more important, there is the tendency to confuse ends and means. That which is
a means easily slips over into the status of end. A government is intended to promote the common good, but the preservation of that
government can easily come to be seen as more important and the
common good will be unhesitatingly sacrificed to it. This, in fact, is a
pattern, not an exception, in the behavior of governments whether
socialist or capitalist.

Another example: A job is a means to survival and, hopefully, to
personal fulfillment. It can become the end of one's existence, so
that family, health, and creative leisure and simple fun can be utterly subordinated. Even life can be sacrificed to the job as many premature deaths would seem to show. Absorption in the means can
make you forget your true end and install the means into the primatial position. The popular term "workaholic" describes someone who
has become addicted to means-made-end.

Wealth is another means that often becomes an end in itself.
Wealth is a means to happiness and well-being, but when it becomes
an end, persons under its sway will sacrifice both happiness and well-
being and even their lives for wealth. A sure sign of wealth's shift
from means to end is the inability to know when enough is enough.
If wealth is treated as a means, it would be less avidly pursued when
the end has been satisfactorily achieved. If the wealth has become an
end in itself, then there is no inner logic for saying *enough*. There is
a fundamental irrationality in transmuting means into ends, and
therefore it is not surprising that means-become-ends are removed
from chastening comparison with other values and are demonically
absolutized.

Means can so commandeer our attentions and affections that the
originally desired ends are lost and not even missed. For example,

the avowed purpose for development and the accumulation of armaments is to bring security and power. Czar Nicholas II of Russia in his proposal for the first Hague Conference in 1898 spotted the fatal flaw in equating arms and safety.

> In proportion as the armaments of each power increase, so do they less and less fulfill the objects which the Governments have set before themselves. . . . It appears evident that if this state of things were prolonged, it would inevitably lead to the very cataclysm which it is designed to avert, and the horrors of which make every thinking man shudder in advance.[19]

If armaments debilitate the economy and distract from necessary expenditures for research on energy, water supply, etc.; if it is true "that military technology is a Hydra: for each weapon that seems familiar and containable, others rise up threatening to defy containment";[20] if arms breed fear and thus more conflict and then more arms and more fear, then armaments are means run wild, cut loose from the desired ends. In the words of Nicholas II, "They less and less fulfill the objects" for which they were intended. By consuming and distracting expenditures, they take away from the over-all power of the nation. By reaching genocidal proportions, they cannot even be rationally used, since they could not do more good than harm. The arms race, therefore, makes its participants less powerful and less secure. The ends are lost; the means go roaring on to ever bigger budgets.

The key to a solution is found in the words of Jawaharlal Nehru of India who said that "perhaps ends and means are not really separable and form together one organic whole."[21] Berdyaev too sees the direction of the answer when he writes: "One of the main problems of ethics is to overcome the dualism between means and ends, and make the means more and more conformable to ends."[22] To overcome any antagonistic dualism between means and ends, between *why* and *how*, some conceptual clarification is needed.

In a sense, *why?* is the most obviously important ethical question. As we have said, it is so important that it overshadows other important aspects of the real moral situation. The common temptation for collectivities and persons is to believe that if their *why* is good, all is well. The importance of the *why* question is seen also when, for example, that which seems to be a gift at the *what* level becomes a bribe when the *why* is answered. That which sounds and looks like love at the *what* level might be seen as exploitation when the *why* is known. At the same time, that which may seem awkward and unpromising at the *what* level may be appreciated as delicately and exquisitely human when the motives and intentions are known. Again, what looks like a mercy death might be a murder when we know *why* it was done. No ethics can be done without an appreciation of the human meaning of motive, the reason *why* someone acts.

What Is Motive?

Motive is as subtle and complex as it is influential. First of all, it is numerically complex. There is never one reason *why* anyone does anything. Nor does anyone know in a conscious way all the motivational forces that move him to act. Thus the problem of understanding motive is the problem of understanding freedom. An older and long regnant view of man's freedom saw it, in Louis Monden's words, as "a perfectly *autonomous power of decision*, hindered in the exercise of its sovereignty only accidentally, by factors which although possibly often at work, remain by their nature exceptional."[23] Now, with the developments in psychology in this century, it is recognized that we are shot through with determinisms and even with contradictory motivational elements. Egoistic and primitively instinctive motives can be found operating in tandem with generous and highly idealistic ones. Any notion of "purity of intention" in the older simplistic sense is passé. The older psychology of freedom felt that freedom was normal, though it might at times be battered and even reduced to nothing by storms of fear or passion. When the storm passed, freedom returned with the fullness that was thought normal. Now we know that a panoply of motivational elements unites, conspires, or accommodates in the production of behavior. *Why* we are acting then is a pluralistic and not an entirely penetrable mystery.

However, assessment of motive is not a hopeless task if we can escape the simplism of a Skinnerian behaviorism which would reduce freedom to nothing, and the other extreme of the old psychology which exaggerated the extent of our psychological freedom. A healthy psyche, for all of its mystery and complexity, has a power for ordering and for fusing its intentional powers into deliberate action

which has willed direction and sense. Dominant motives can operate
and give form to our intentionality. Here is where moral assessment
is possible as long as it is chastened by an awareness of the complexity it addresses. A person who steals, or murders, or the businessman
engaged in "crime in the suites," may be so controlled by neurotic,
unfree factors as to merit psychiatric judgment. Or he may be discernibly free to the extent where moral consideration of his motives
is in order.

Motive obviously refers to an internal psychological reality and yet
it has impact on the external world. Sometimes this impact is obvious; sometimes it is more subtle and drawn out. If one is doing helpful things for people from some concealed and markedly egoistic motive, it might appear that the hidden meanness is a purely internal
matter, since good is being done, whatever the intentional reasons
behind it may be. Motive, however, is not like a motor. It is more
than an efficient, prodding cause that gets actions going. It is a formal cause that gives behavior shape and distinctively human consistency. The action is taking place, not among interacting objects but
among interacting and interrelating persons. The effects of human
action are personal and not just physical. They are geared to building
or disrupting community among persons. As persons grow and
develop in what I have called the foundational moral experience,
community, something qualitatively better than coexistence develops. This developing unity and harmony of human life are kneaded
through and knit together by respect, justice, and improving modali-
ties of friendship. Actions which are only externally good, though
less disruptive and not without helpful effect, will not humanize persons into communitarian life. The poison will out. Defects at the
foundational level of caring could only be temporarily concealed and
only temporarily constructive. The assessment of motive is not just
of introspective importance. Why something is done is partially but
essentially constitutive of what is done.[24]

I have alluded to the link between motive and the foundational
moral experience. The link is one of blossom to root. Morally good
motivation could only grow from some successful development of that
fundamental grounding of moral experience. In this sense, motive
is not just numerically but also qualitatively complex. Motives
which seem the same when we classify them will always be a unique
manifestation of the person in his distinct moral process. Sameness
is thus theoretically infeasible.

Furthermore, motive, like the foundational experience, is processual, not static. The motives that move a couple in a young marriage
while they are still under the exuberant spell of early romance will
not be the same as the motives that may move them in their
cherishing in old age. In a true sense it can be said that no couple
stays married for the reason they get married. This need not be interpreted cynically. There may be better reasons (motives) for staying
married than there were for getting married. Some of the same
things may be done later on in a process but done from motives that
tap deeper and better wellsprings of affection. The external sameness
is only apparent. Process, of course, can also go in reverse. It is not
only true, as Augustine said, that that which is begun in fear may
come to be perfected in love. That which is begun in love might
come to be maintained only by fear.[25] Love's lively beginnings might
wither and be atrophied in routine. Many of the same things might
be done, but the change in the relationship would be substantial.

Moral motives can range in their moral quality from the
superficial to the heroic. Motivation and its roots would not be the
same. This too serves to illustrate the signal importance of motive in
determining the moral meaning of behavior. Significant moral reality
is revealed in responding to the question *why?*

Sincerity in Motivation . . .

He who wills the end wills the means necessary to that end.

Good motives and intentions are often the mask of hypocrisy. The
old saw has it that the road to hell is paved with good intentions.
There is a lot to that. Superficially good motives are like playful flir-
tations. They lack the strength needed for follow-through. Yet they
can serve a devious purpose by making us feel that our heart is in the
right place. For example, it is encouraging if someone says he is in
favor of racial integration. It is suspicious if he then opposes all the
means necessary to that end such as a certain amount of busing, the
use of quota systems where other avenues to fairness are closed,
reallocation of funds to address the problem vigorously, etc. He who
opposes the means necessary to an end opposes the end.[26]

The same applies to the will to have children. If one is not ready
for the enormous follow-through, then the desire for children is not
real. Likewise, the avowed desire of business management to be eco-

logically responsible when there is no readiness to spend what is needed in money and imagination represents a motivational failure. If you do not will the necessary means, you do not will the end. All protestations about one's commitment to good ends are hollow, if there is no corresponding commitment to the means necessary to achieve those ends.

In Latin, there is a distinction made between *volitio* and *velleitas* (which can be inelegantly Englished as "volition" and "velleity"). Volition comes from *volo*, meaning "I will"; *velleitas*, from *vellem*, meaning "I would like." Velleity moves willing from the forthright indicative to the hedged subjunctive. Applied here, this means that many apparent volitions are merely velleities. Volition refers to what you really will; velleity, to what you would will, were things more to your liking. Many apparent volitions, from "I love you" to "Our corporation is committed to improving the environment," are but pale velleities underneath their fervid exteriors.

Does the End Justify the Means?

Some questions are best answered by saying that they are bad questions. This is one of them. It is bad because misconceived. An end does not justify a means any more than a means justifies an end. Ends and means must be judged in relational tension to one another and to all the other essential circumstances. When we have completed all the questions that are within the wheel model, we will have shown all the dimensions of any situation that have to be considered to know what that situation means morally. The ends and means will only be two of the many elements that constitute the moral significance of the case to be judged. To ask if the end justifies the means makes no more sense than to ask if the end justifies the effects. Like the detective who achieves insight when he sees how *all* the clues before him relate to one another, so in matters moral, insight is achieved when we see how *all* the circumstances relate to one another. The answer, then, to the bad question that heads this paragraph is *no*.

That said, what can we say in conclusion about the troubled marriage between ends and means? At the least, we could be attuned to the ethical insight of Augustine when he wrote in a letter to a certain Darius that it was better to maintain peace by peace rather than

to maintain peace by war. This was the same Augustine who had
helped to baptize the theory of just war and thus give justified war a
respectability in Christendom that it had not previously enjoyed. And
yet he sensed the anomaly of justifying such a slaughterous means to
so gentle an end as peace.

It is not always possible to have a happy harmony between our
ends and our means. We may have to be harsh or, in an extreme situation, violent, in defense of justice, integrity, and peace. But the
goal is that quoted above from Berdyaev, to "make the means more
and more conformable to ends." Disharmony between ends and
means is violent and a sign of our moral primitivity. Comfort with it
is deadly and inhibits moral development. A simple term for such
comfort is moral decadence.

If, to return to Augustine's example, we must maintain peace by
war, then the situation must be faced in Augustine's "mournful
mood" and this tragic necessity must summon us imperiously to
create the conditions that require less drastic remedies. Normalizing
means that are discordant with our ends, treating them as part of the
nature of things (as is regularly done in politics and business), is a
surrender to the anomalous and is morally deviate. It also represents
an implicit faith that good ends do justify any means . . . a position
which is, as we have seen, ethically untenable.

The Moral Meaning of Style . . .

The questions *why* and *how* are introduced as two of the multiple
reality-revealing questions that mark the beginning of ethical analysis. *Why* points us to motive (intention, purpose, end) and *how*
points us to means and also to style. Of style, we have not yet
spoken.

In presenting this schedule of questions, we are searching out the
essential circumstances that make up the moral meaning of a human
situation. Our concern is not for those extraneous circumstances
which do not specify the moral status, but merely modify in a secondary and accidental sense. Thus, for example, robbing a poor man
on a Tuesday may introduce an essential specifying circumstance,
since he may not have access to money until the end of the week. If
a rich man were robbed on Tuesday, the day would probably not
enter in as an essential circumstance in the ethical analysis.

Style might at first seem nonessential in the category of trimmings, and not something that would make behavior moral or immoral. This is due partly to the fact that concern with style is often associated with superficiality. The superficiality, of course, comes not from the concern with style, but from the concern with little else. This is seen in persons who stress external image and "public relations" to the neglect of substantial performance. The sham of this approach gives style a bad name.

In the terms of our questioning process here, what you do may be morally promising. Why you are doing it may be heroically noble. But the style may make the action decisively immoral. The Irish story of the man who undertook to inform a woman of her husband's death provides a blunt illustration. "Are you the widow Murphy?" he asked. "No," she replied. "You are now!" he said and departed. It would be hard to criticize *what* he was doing and *why*, but the *how* was an epic of insensitivity. The way you break news (your style) may, like the way you make love, be of the essence. The way you disagree or correct may make your behavior humanizing (moral) or atrocious. Style is often the soul of diplomacy. A good diplomat is one who knows that being right is not enough, that having military and economic power is not always enough, since how you communicate and deal often gives the definitive tilt to negotiations.

The reason for the importance of style is that it bodies forth the inclinations of the heart. A nation that goes about doing good violently will not be perceived as peaceful in its intent whatever its ideological protestations. Help given arrogantly will produce adverse reactions, however needed the help given may be. Aid that insults will disrupt. This is so because the *how* is intimately related to the *why*. How you do something tells much of *why* you are doing it. The *how* can strip away the avowed motive and show the real one because *how* reflects the foundational moral experience and serves as an index of the development of that experience. The insensitive may only see *what* you are doing and only hear your expressed motivation. The sensitive will detect your deepest spirit in the *how* (manner, mode, style, and means) of what you do.

The importance of *how* thus relates to the above-mentioned fact that interaction among persons is not merely physical but is rather a community-building (or community-disrupting) activity. The sensitivity that specifies our style of acting will easily have greater impact on community than what we do.

Who? The Question of Person

The question *who?* enters into the calculus of ethics to make us address the following realities:

What is right for one person may be wrong for another.

What is right for a person now may be wrong for the same person at another time.

Some persons are, in ethical calculation, worth more than others.

No two persons are the same.

Persons are social by nature, not by choice.

To miss the truth of any of these propositions (and the missing is commonplace) is to be liable to ethical confusion. To put it more briefly, persons are relational, social, historical, and unique. Only if we know this can we do the work of ethics, which is a work of knowing what befits persons as they really are.

What we say at this point relates to what we will say later about moral principles. We will then be speaking about the validity of universalizing and generalizing in regard to persons. Here we are stressing the special claims of persons as they are found in their unrepeatable concreteness. As will be seen, this does not mean that principles are invalid but only that the validity of moral principles depends on clear perception of what is and what is not generalizable.

It is all well and good to generalize about the states and practices that befit persons morally. Thus, if I were to defend the idea of marriage as the ultimate form of friendship achievable between sexually attracted persons, I would be up to my neck in generalization. However, I would not and could not be saying that I had found the universal grid for moral sexual relating or that I know that marriage is the only moral mode of sexual interaction. I would, in fact, say that the surpreme moral achievement of friendship finds unique expression in marriage. Having said that, however, one must face the concrete reality of the various *who's* in any moral equation. Some of these persons will fit into the category of the premarriageable. Marriage in a complex society shares that complexity and is not entered into as easily as it once was. Marriage in a monolithic and simple cultural setting was supported by the structures of that society. With established supports and fewer challenges, it was more manageable and almost uni-form. Today that is often not the case, and there also may be a prolonged period where a person may not yet have the maturity needed for the marital enterprise.

Also, there are persons who are not married because of a simple lack of opportunity. They have not met someone whom they want to marry and who simultaneously wants to marry them. Not everyone gets asked and not everyone gets asked by someone whom they would love enough to marry. There are also those older persons who live together because marriage would reduce their retirement benefits below the subsistence level. In discussing the sexual ethics of these persons, one would have to do more than laud the humanizing possibilities of marital friendship. Such an approach would ignore the person (the *who*) to whom marriage is not available in his or her concrete situation. If one has enormous confidence in the generalizable value of marriage, he might say that whoever does fit into the precincts of this generalization has no moral alternatives save celibacy. What this *assumes* is that the generalization regarding the value of marriage is applicable to all persons in such wise that they must fit themselves into it or not function sexually at all.

The theoretical error here is in the presumption that the generalizations that serve us within limits actually exhaust the possibilities of the real. Rather than modifying the scheme that does not meet the moral needs of persons, persons in their contradicting concreteness are sacrificed to the theory. The perversion is elementary and the arrogance is extreme.

It is not, of course, true that there are no generalizations relevant to the sexual lives of unmarried persons. Sexual exchange has a power to involve persons at many psychic levels, and in approaching it, ethical discernment is the alternative to personal chaos. However, to draw a line called marriage and say that everything to one side of that line is immoral is abstract and simplistic. It does not address the personal and sexual reality of those who have no access to marriage. The concrete value implications of the individual person are shunted aside in preference for the tidiness and seeming security of generality. Such generalizers might seem to know what they are talking about, but they really do not since they are not sensitive to the reality of *who* it is that they are judging morally.[27] Their reality-contact is thus impaired at the important level of sensitivity to the person in his existential reality. It is to this personal reality that the *who* question directs us. For this reason, we have to attend to the difficult question of what that reality is that we dignify with the title *person*.

In ethics, a person is not just an element among elements or a circumstance among circumstances. The centrality of person (to which the question *who?* directs us) comes from the fact that ethics proceeds from the foundational experience of the value of persons and their environment. Ethics, then, is centered on persons. Persons, however, come under the survey of essential circumstances in ethical evaluation, because they do not exist as detached essences. They are existentially realized and particularized in the shaping influences of social and historical reality.

Unlike a physical *datum* or an artifact, a person is constituted by his relationships unfolded in his personal history and in the cultural history to which he is a natural heir. A person is shaped in history as an infant's body is shaped in a womb. Personal life, like all life, is a process, a *personing* process. I am not suggesting here that existence precedes essence for persons as Sartre does. A person is not free to become a tomato plant. But also, a human being is not born with personhood in the way it can be said he is born with a heart and limbs, etc. These physical elements can grow in size, but in essence they can only be what they are from the beginning. With the person, it is not so. Persons can become more fully what they are. Human life is personal life in process. By analogy with physical growth, a person can grow, but the change implied by growth is not quantitative, but is rather a fulfillment along the lines of one's essence. Existence does not precede essence. We get essence and existence together, but it can be said that what we are precedes what we may become. Essence is not a static quality but rather a kind of expanding life potential. When a tomato plant grows, it is not any more a tomato plant than it was in its early days. But to grow as a person is to be more of a person. It is growth in essence. (Growth can also be reversed and personal life can become less personal and human than it was.)

There are two ways in which personhood can be said to grow: psychologically and morally. Personal psychological growth refers to the gradual development of those capacities that we associate with persons and not with mere animals.[28] Persons are distinguished by such things as their capacity to imagine, create, be amused, and love benevolently. A fetus cannot do these things yet, since it is only at the faint beginnings of personal consciousness. Persons at the other end of the life span who have lost all power of recognition through profound senile dementia may display no signs of distinctively personal life. Between the fetal beginning and the dementated end, personal psychological life flowers, and grows, and eventually declines into death.

Moral personal growth presupposes some psychological growth. Concerning moral growth we could say with Sartre, given the distinctions we have made above, that "man is nothing other than that which he makes himself to be." And, again, "man is responsible for what he is."[29] With moral decisions we flesh out our possibilities and carve the shape of our personhood. Moral decisions make us frauds, villains, and ruthless exploiters, or saints, prophets, and heroes, or a little bit of each. In the exercise of responsible freedom, we become a certain kind of person. This is not, of course, to say that personal value is confined to full personal flowering. It is generally conceded that value attaches even to the cadaverous remains of persons. How that value will count against other values in ethical evaluation is another question. Value is not a univocal or an unrelational term.

Both psychological and moral growth occur in a context of interaction with persons. Persons unfold in sociality. As Martin Buber puts it: "I become through my relation to the *Thou*; as I become *I*, I say *Thou*. All real living is meeting."[30] This is an idea that has found expression in various lines of reflection including social psychology. George Herbert Mead, for example, says that the self is essentially a social structure, and it arises in social experience . . . it is impossible to conceive of a self arising outside of social experience."[31]

And as ethicist, H. Richard Niebuhr writes:

> To say the self is social is not to say that it finds itself in need of fellow men in order to achieve its purposes, but that it is born in the womb of society as a sentient, thinking, needful being with certain definitions of its needs and with the possibility of experience of a common world. It is born in society as mind and as moral being, but above all it is born in society as self.[32]

The person becomes a person and grows in personhood interpersonally. The self is the counterpart of other selves. Thinking, choosing, and growing cannot take place or be understood apart from our sociality. The social ambience in which we are formed as persons, however, will differ according to culture and will affect different individuals differently. No two social matrices will be the same. There is something unique in every culture and in the impact that culture has on every individual. Every social matrix will have its own history and geography and its own symbols of self-understanding. It will be differently tuned to possibility and to fact. It will have dominant gender and particular accentuations. There will be special sensitivities and concerns. Some faculties of perception will be emphasized, others repressed. And every cultural situation is in a state of reaction to unique and unrepeatable challenges. It will think and feel in a web of relationships and reactions never found before or afterward. If the wombs are not the same, neither will persons who develop there be marked by sameness. Persons will vary too because of differing abilities to transcend their cultural environment creatively.

Thus, it is easy to see the reasons for the propositions with which we opened this section on the ethically diagnostic question *who?* That is moral which befits and enhances the humanization of persons as they are. Persons are in some ways unique and importantly different. Therefore what befits one may not be right for another, and what befits a person now may not be good for that same person later. No two persons are the same nor is any one person the same forever. Thus a doctor who has a hard-nosed policy about "laying it on the line" immediately with all patients who have terminal illnesses will make mistakes. Every *who* will vary. No uniform policy will meet the needs of each patient. No sensitive ethics will bunch disparate persons under one rubric.

In the political sphere there is a strong tendency not to perceive the reality of other *whos* and deal with them accordingly. For example, as Ross Terrill writes: "It is widely believed, in the West, that 'modernization' and 'westernization' mean the same thing."[33] It has been very difficult to shake the dogmatic faith of the United States that capitalistic democracy and salvation are one and the same thing. Accepting other peoples as they are with sensitivity to their distinctive spirit and élan has not been the genius of our foreign policy. Too often, we have not known *who* it was we were dealing with. Fundamental policy failures are the natural sequel of this. Not knowing *who* it is you are dealing with is neither good politics nor good morals.

Finally, sensitivity to the *who* leads to the conclusion that persons are not of univocal value in ethical calculation. Clearly, such a statement has an undemocratic, not to say, immoral ring to it. The statement, however, is based on the fact that persons are not just physical entities but are constituted by their relationships. This shows up clearly in the pressures of a situation of *triage* where there is not enough medical aid for all the claimants and some must be selected while others are left to die. In this case, decisions may be made about who is worth more in that social context. Thus, for example, a wounded physician may be treated even though the selection of him means that the unselected will die. Similarly, in a case where inadequate medicine cannot save both mother and child in a problem delivery, it is arguably moral to save the mother by procedures that are fatal to the child. In such cases it might be possible to remove the child intact through interventions that would kill the mother. But a decision is made about which of the two is more deserving of life.

This does not contradict the fundamental equality of persons in the sense that all persons are alike in having fundamental human rights. What it means is that persons are judged in the context of their sociality. In neither the triage nor the childbirth examples is there an egoistic, individualistic competition going on about who tops whom in worth. The assessment is social. Given the relationship of the mother to other children, etc., she is judged more deserving of life in this either-or crisis.

Comparative evaluation of this sort may emerge in less dramatic situations. For example, it may be medically feasible to keep an irreversibly comatose patient alive for two years at enormous expense by the use of a respirator. The error here is in judging the value of this person's life individualistically, and not socially. If there were no other needs for the money or facilities used to preserve this person's physical life, it might somehow be morally defensible. (I doubt it.) As it is, however, there are other needs in the society and this patient's claim cannot be judged as though it were absolute and unrelated to those other needs. This is not utilitarianism where the individual is sacrificed to the good of the group. This is rather a recognition that no human rights can be conceived outside of reference to other human rights. To do so would be a denial of our intrinsically social nature. The child who is sacrificed to save the mother is not morally violated, for it did not come into the world with rights

that were individualistically compacted and unrelated to others. To
say that such was the case would be to deny the child's humanity.

When? and Where? . . .

When? and *where?* are also reality-revealing questions that may
turn up essential and specifying circumstances. An abortion might be
defensible at the level of *what, why,* and *who,* but if it is being done
in an ill-equipped abortion mill, the *where* becomes decisive. Making
love in public is significant at the level of *where,* given the intimacy
and privacy that most persons in most cultures associate with sexual
exchange. In other cases, *where* something occurs may have little or
no moral import.

When something is done may be important if the timing shows
an awareness or unawareness of process. The desire to impose democratic forms on countries that are not prepared for them shows an
inability to assess the dimension of time. Of course, an alleged concern for the proper and due time might represent a refusal to meet
the moral demands of a situation. In this sense, justice delayed
might be justice denied, as when, in the United States, two hundred
years after the founding of our constitutional government, some are
still saying that the implications of that constitution are not yet applicable to black persons or to women.[34]

The Link with the Future:
The Question of Foreseeable Effects . . .

David Ben-Gurion sagely said that there are no experts on the future. Both theory and history confirm his observation. There can
only be experts on what has happened, not on what has not yet happened, and thus, may not happen. This points to a problem in ethics. The future is unavoidably present in moral action. Our decisions
reverberate out into space and forward into time. Sometimes the
effects of particular decisions are explicitly felt for centuries. But in
subtle ways all actions reach out beyond the present and enter into
the fabric of the future. The future will always be the product of
what was once the present.

And so, when we say that human actions are right or wrong according to the circumstances, we face the fact that some of those circumstances that determine the moral kind of our behavior are in the

future. Morality is based on reality, and the reality of our conduct
has future implications. Moral responsibility requires that our knowledge follow the impact of our behavior as far as is possible. Of
course, our influence on the future goes further than our knowledge
can go, but our knowledge must strain to go as far as it can. Personal
responsibility must extend to the full reality of what we are about; to
limit it to the present is abortive and immoral.

It is for this reason that consequences, or foreseeable effects, loom
prominently in ethics. So intrinsic are effects to moral meaning that
there is even a strain called *consequentialism* in ethical theory which
would make consequences all important. In this view, actions are
right or wrong primarily or exclusively according to their consequences.[35] This, of course, is excessive, since there are other circumstances to which the other reality-revealing questions refer us. But
the consequences are a focal point of essential moral meaning. Sometimes this is obvious, as when we irresponsibly allow a very drunk
person to get into his car to drive home. Augustine and Aquinas
stressed consequences when they concluded that it was moral to legalize prostitution because of the disruptive consequences of banning
it.[36] Sometimes it is only by hindsight that we know the morally
critical meaning of effects. Germany, after World War I, was stung
not only by the final suddenness of defeat but also by the harsh stipulations of the Versailles Treaty. As John L. Snell writes: "The German nation after 1919 lived in psychic rebellion against the loss of
the war and the Treaty of Versailles. Hitler was first a by-product of
this rebellion, then its catalyst. . . ."[37] With knowledge of this,
Winston Churchill in 1940 called Hitler a "monstrous product of
former wrongs and shame."

Sometimes an analysis of effects will cause a major shift in one's
moral stance. Bernard N. Nathanson, M.D., in 1969, was one of the
founders of a political action unit organized to legalize abortion.
Among other things, he picketed a New York hospital that had refused to perform abortions. His wife was on the picket line with him
as was his three-year-old son, who carried a placard urging the
legalization of abortion. Nathanson's activities were a major stimulus
for the passing of the New York State Abortion Statute of 1970. He
became director of an abortion clinic which performed 60,000 abortions with no maternal death.

Then suddenly Nathanson resigned and explained why in the *New
England Journal of Medicine.* While still believing that abortion

should be unregulated by law, he became uneasy over the fact that he "had in fact presided over 60,000 deaths." The first thing that is clear is that Nathanson did not, in my usage of the term, know *what* he had been doing. "We must courageously face the fact—finally— that human life of a special order is being taken." Adverting to the Harvard Criteria for the detection of death, he observes that "the fetus does respond to pain, makes respiratory efforts, moves sponta- neously, and has electroencephalographic activity." The fetus is alive. The long-term effects of ending so many of these lives so easily worries him. He fears that our society will lose the "pervasive sense of loss that should accompany abortion and its most unfortunate in- terruption of life." He fears that we will "coarsen our sensitivities through common practice and brute denial." This is so especially since "there are seldom any purely medical indications for abortion." He also fears that a mindless rush to abortion in a society might lead to "a debased level of utilitarian semiconsciousness" marked by the absence of "moral tension" in the face of widely imposed death.[88]

Nathanson's mainly consequentialist assessment does not lead him to the conclusion that all abortion is wrong. He properly deplores such a polarized position. But because many persons do not know *what* they are doing when they abort, and because of *how* our soci- ety has rushed into this practice, the better part of wisdom might be to bring to this issue "the reverent stillness and ineffably grave thought appropriate to it."[89] Otherwise the effects may be dehuman- izing in ways that we cannot predict but which Nathanson senses.

Nathanson's thinking here is an example of keen sensitivity to the moral significance of effects. It exemplifies a seriousness that is needed in ethical method broadly, and not just in the particular case of abortion. When we act (by deliberate commission or omission), we commit our initiative to the future. We can, of course, act again to repair harm or enhance good, but the danger is that when choices become a practice (for an individual or for a society) there arises a momentum that is potentially immune to reflection and evaluation. Choices grown into practices can run away with us. That is why eth- ics must pause for the "reverent stillness" of contemplation. In one way, the effects of our actions are out of our control as soon as we act. We can go after those effects with other actions, but the effects are not subject to recall. Human action, therefore, is an amalgam of power and impotence; the power to touch and shape the future through the consequences of our acts, and, simultaneously, the impotence to control those consequences. Hence the centrality of concern for consequences in ethics.

Our sense of the future is undergoing a qualitative change in modern times. In the past, as professor Hans Jonas writes, "The good and evil about which action had to care lay close to the act, either in the praxis itself or in its immediate reach, and were not a matter for remote planning. . . . The long run of consequences beyond was left to chance, fate or providence. Ethics accordingly was of the here and now. . . ."[40] Jonas notes that the maxims that came to us from the ethical systems of the past involved others who were "sharers of a common present." Thus: "Love thy neighbor as thyself"; "Do unto others as you would wish them to do unto you"; "Treat others as ends, never as means." In all of these, the ethical universe is composed of contemporaries and the horizon of the future is constricted. Now, with nature no longer immune in its immensity as it was for primitive man, our technology can destroy the ingredients for future life. Suddenly, posterity is the neighbor whom we must love as ourselves if the future is to have a chance. Interpersonal responsibility has swollen to planetary size and reaches billions of years into the future. Never before has the present tense had the ability to preclude the future, and never before, therefore, has moral responsibility for consequences been of such proportions. Never before have not-yet-existing persons featured so prominently in our ethics. This is an extension of our natural sociality. Action is interaction; agency is influence. This is the core of ethical concern for consequences.

The effects of our gargantuan technology touch not only on the physical possibilities of life. Technology can insinuate itself into the heart of man and change the way he values himself and others. For example, the improving technology of prenatal diagnosis would seem an innocent and welcome advance. Yet Marc Lappé notes the ingrained tendency of Western society to deprecate the "less-than-optimal" and the genetically unfit and to deprive them of full human community and rights. From the Greeks, who were ready in Aristotle's words "to let no child be brought up flawed," through the long tradition of neglecting and disparaging "defectives," the West has born peculiar witness to a vicious instinct of exclusivism. The depths of this passion for normality should not be underestimated. At one time, as Lappé writes, "Even common barnyard animals whose behavior or appearance transgressed God's laws (a 'cock' laying an egg as a result of normal senile sex reversal in hens, for example) were actually tried in *human* courts of law."[41] The ferocious prosecution of homosexuals is an enduring manifestation of our intolerance of variation from what we think ideal.

The process of genetic purification must go on, but it will go on humanly only if we are sensitive to the effects it will have on our abstemious sense of acceptable normality. How will we feel, in a genetically purer world, about those who slip through our clinical dragnet? How will less dramatic imperfections to which science has no access be coped with? How much wiser will we be in coping with tragedy and inevitable limit, and especially the ultimate limit of death? Science must go forward with moral sensitivity to the expanding range of effects. And, at times, again with sensitivity to foreseeable effects, science must hold back, brake its momentum, and accept a reflective moratorium. A can-do-must-do assumption must be seen as what it is: mindless. We are more responsible for more effects than we used to be, and that new moral fact of life must be faced.

The Limits of Consequentialism . . .

Not of consequences alone is reality or ethics made. An exclusively consequentialist analysis, for all the breadth of consequences, will be too narrow and too precarious. For one thing, since consequences stretch into the future, consequentialism rests on the frailty of our capacity to predict. The prominence of the physical sciences which work largely within the repetitive and cyclic regularity of nature and its events has given undue hopes to futurism and foretelling. A knowledge of what is and what has happened in the physical order enables scientists to predict with great accuracy what will happen in the future. The developing science of earthquake prediction illustrates the traditional and well-founded hope of science that when all is known, all is predictable. "By contrast," as Arnold Toynbee writes, "in the field of human affairs, experience enables us merely to guess. In this field, what has occurred in the past may, of course, recur, but it is not bound to recur and, indeed, it was not bound to occur in the first instance."[42] The past is, of course, illuminating, and a knowledge of human history is a basic ingredient of mature moral judgment. Without a sense of history, we are, like the amnesiac, unsure of our identity. But it must be remembered that inferences from history are limited. There are two factors that militate against certitude about what will happen in the human future: freedom and imagination. Persons can choose, and the choices do not emerge with the predictability of natural processes in physics or chemistry. The evidence is that persons have some freedom, enough freedom to make unpredictability an inexorable trait of human life. Also, persons are perceivers of possibility. They can get new ideas about how to do things. They can sometimes, when challenged, create and set events on a new direction. The power of the creative spirit makes prediction in human affairs, at its best, a learned guess. Surprise is a constant in history.

Adam Smith was remarkable in his insight into the processes of economics, but he could not foresee the power of monopolies to prosper in the laissez-faire world he recommended. Karl Marx's insights were extraordinary, and yet he completely missed the versatility of capitalism and so failed in some of his crucial predictions. And on a more folksy level, Futurama at the 1939 World's Fair predicted that by 1960 automobiles would sell for two hundred dollars, that Americans would be bored with possessions by then and be seeking satisfaction in other ways. And factories by that time would be admirable for their cleanliness.[48]

There is, however, an even more serious danger in a narrowly consequentialistic approach to moral issues. It is one that combines two great errors: first, the error of saying that the end justifies the means, and second, the error of a utilitarianism that insensitively sacrifices the good of individuals to the good of the group without even being very clear about what the good of the group is.

Consequentialism and the Glorification of Ends . .

Our minds are too open to seduction by abstractions. The effects on which we base our ethical calculations are to some extent abstract and in the future. Their reality is not as yet proved. They may in fact never exist. And yet they can, in a consequentialist approach, assume the demonic power of romanticized ends. In the name of desired effects which hopefully are to be realized, realities of the present tense may be sacrificed. Enamored of what might be, we can ride roughshod over what is. Thus a professional or businessman could try to justify consequentially the neglect of his family in view of the good things that his success will someday mean to them. And

indeed the affluence he hopes for might assure them first-class education and future security. In the process, however, the family well-being that might be could undermine the family well-being that is.
Russian tanks could roll into Budapest in 1956 to crush a revolution
by the proletariat in the name of the revolution of the proletariat.
Present-tense proletariat were sacrificed to projected successes of proletariat yet to be.

Present-tense realities have a *prima facie* priority over the future.
They may at times have to be sacrificed to make way for future possibilities, but now without due process in the court of conscience. To
ensure due process, the other present-tense ethical questions must be
asked: *What? Why? Who? When? Where?* and *What are the alternatives?* It will also be necessary to use a full ethical method such as
I am elaborating in these pages. Principles, which are the deposi-
tories of wisdom gained by experience in the past, will have to be
tested against the facts. Affectivity, imagination, authority sources,
and all the evaluative resources suggested in the spokes of my wheel
model will have to be brought to bear on the case. All of this is necessary to prevent projected glorified effects from acquiring a kind of
diabolic possession of our moral decision process. The agent who is
mesmerized by possible consequences can ignore all of this. The results range from unfortunate to lethal. An example will illustrate this
crucial point.

During the early debate on nuclear deterrence, the question of the
moral significance of consequences was keenly felt. Nothing but the
good result (effect) of peace-through-deterrence could justify turning
the world into a lethal arsenal where the superabundant capacity to
end all life is prepared and readied for instant delivery. The thinking
that prevailed in justifying nuclear deterrence was consequentialist. It
was justified because the effects were good and no one could think of
any other practical way of getting those good results. This meant
that the tense peace resulting from deterrence was enough to bring
calm to conscience. Consequentialism, purely and simply.

In the discussions surrounding this, the limits of a morality of consequences were sensed by some. It was, for example, suggested that if
a practice could be devised which the projections showed would cut
down on traffic fatalities by 80 to 90 per cent, this practice would, by
consequentialist analysis, be moral. The practice suggested (for the
sake of illustrative argument) was that the law would require us to
install seating on the front bumper of our automobiles for our chil-

dren and everyone would have to drive with their children up front in that fashion. While granting that this would indeed revolutionize driving patterns in the direction of caution, almost anyone would balk at this suggestion if it were made seriously. Why? It makes good consequentialist and good utilitarian sense, and a consistent consequentialist or utilitarian would be hard pressed to marshal a case against it, since both of these strains of thinking are theoretically tilted toward the crassly pragmatic popular insight: *If it works, don't knock it.*

But why do we shrink from the babies-on-the-bumper concept even though it would save many lives and possibly even our own? Is it not because it evokes a sense of profanation in us—a firm impression that such a policy violates human life in a way that goes beyond moral tolerance, regardless of the happy results it promises? The prospects of dramatically improved traffic data and the saving of numerous lives do not justify putting the babies on the bumpers. To explain this we must enter into an old debate between deontological and teleological ethical theories. Some things about this debate are unfortunate; first, its nomenclature is cumbersome and easily misunderstood, and second, it suggests a false dichotomy. However, in the cause of clear thinking in matters moral, the main issue of the debate cannot be avoided.

Teleology vs. Deontology: Another Misplaced Debate . . .

Certain ways of thinking about what is right are classified as teleological . . . from the Greek *telos*, meaning "end" or "goal." Actions are right or wrong according to the end or goal to which they lead. Consequentialism and utilitarianism (which seeks the greatest happiness of the greatest number) are obviously teleological theories. Opposed to teleologists are the deontologists . . . from Greek *deo* meaning "I ought." The deontologist says that certain things are wrong regardless of the consequences. (Rarely, if ever, are persons who are classified as one or the other of these purely and consistently so. Still the terminology is commonplace.) For example, promise-keeping might be consequentially defended as moral on the grounds of the disruptive effects on society if reliance on promises perished. Promise-keeping, in this kind of thinking, is good because it promotes a general confidence. W. D. Ross presents a case which illustrates the deontologist's view of the moral ought. He speaks of the case of a promise made to a dying man. After the death of the promisee, if no one knows about the promise, why must it be kept? It is hard to see how the general well-being or other social consequences would be impinged if this secret promise were deliberately ignored. Ross asks if we would really think that the duty to fulfill the promise "would be extinguished by the fact that neither act would have any effect on the general confidence." The effects on the general confidence, of course, would be the basis for a teleological argument for promise-keeping. But Ross is certainly correct in saying: "We need not doubt that a system by which promises are made and kept is one that has great advantages for the general well-being. *But that is not the whole truth. . . .*"[44]

In the words of William Frankena, the deontologists "assert that there are, at least, other considerations which may make an action or rule right or obligatory beside the goodness or badness of its consequences. . . ."[45] He continues: ". . . a deontologist contends that it is possible for an action or rule of action to be the morally right or obligatory one even if it does not promote the greatest possible balance of good over evil for self, society, or universe."[46] The consequences are significant, but, in W. D. Ross's phrase, "that is not the whole truth."

In other words, there is something within the nature of a promise between persons which establishes a binding obligation that exists aside from all consideration of consequences. The example of a promise between two dying persons is helpful. It seems to entail a moral bond and obligation, even though the failure to keep it would presumably have no social consequences, since after the death of the promiser, no one but the promisee even knows of the promise.

Some deontologists feel that this is true of truth-telling and all other basic moral obligations. Similarly, on the negative side, torture is seen deontologically as wrong regardless of the supremely valuable consequences it might produce. Just as any morally sensitive person knows that promise-keeping and truth-telling befit persons, so too it is said to be clear that torture is incompatible with the minimal regard for personal life needed to embark on ethics in any meaningful way.

The difficulty that people have had in fitting into one or the other of these classifications is because teleology and deontology are both integral to moral experience. Consequences and results, though not all, are part of the reality that we judge when we make a moral judgment. Not to assess them and be sensitive to them is ethically irresponsible. Indeed the effect tells much about the cause. Predictably ill effects are often a clue to something amiss in the causal act. So let us all be teleologists . . . but not to the extent of ignoring the rest of what is real.

What the deontologist is on to is that there can be important appreciations in the present moment that cannot be sacrificed to all the felicitous consequences imaginable (the baby on the bumper). The appreciation, like all of ethics, is rooted in the foundational moral experience of the value of persons. One expression of the foundational moral experience is a sense of profanation which recoils from certain options as incompatible with even minimal respect for persons. The German soldier who refused to shoot the hostages and so had himself shot with them was not busily calculating possible consequences when he withdrew from the firing squad to certain death. Furthermore, he was certainly not thinking that his action would be conducive to the greatest good of the greatest number, or, hedonistically, that it was a pleasure to do what he was doing. If we could corner him in another life and grace him with a consequentialist vindication of what he did, he might be impressed but would probably feel that we had not touched the heart of his experience. If he could articulate it at all, he would probably say that, from his perspective, the *consequences* he could foresee were awful. The most impressive consequence was that he was about to be shot for disobeying orders. This foreseen consequence, if anything, tempted him to stand with his comrades and commit murder. He did not do that because he could not violate the persons who stood before him. He may have killed other equally scared persons in battle, even in face-to-face combat. There he was protected by the rationale for the war or at least by some ambiguity and group *esprit*. Here moral shock replaced ambiguity, and the sense of profanation was overwhelming. Had the soldier been given the time for reflection, he might have said that to kill in this instance would have struck at the foundations of his moral consciousness and of his own identity. It would be a kind of moral suicide that would undercut the grounds for respecting not only others but also himself. In that case, his *doing* would violate his *being*, opening the painful fissure that we call guilt. The empirical details of the case were such that human value was here at issue, and felt to be at issue in the depths of personality where faith and affectivity touch at the meaning of morality and thus of life. Acting in any other way than he did became almost impossible since it would have been an act of violent self-contradiction.

Intuitionists' ideas about self-evidence would give only a pallid explanation of what happened here as would any simplistic "moral sense" theory of ethical cognition. What happened was, however, more deontological than teleological. Of course, there were good effects from his action. Witness was born to justice and integrity amid the decay that is war. Such witness keeps the human spirit from flickering out entirely, and that is a service which could be accurately, if unhappily, called teleological. But, again in the words of W. D. Ross, "that is not the whole truth." The analysis of the whole truth is as difficult as the analysis of the foundations of moral experience itself. To say as an intuitionist would that such a felt obligation (like the obligations of promise-keeping, truth-telling, etc.) is self-evident is simplistic and reductionistic. Intuitionist H. A. Prichard, for example, would say that the apprehension of an obligation "is immediate, in precisely the sense in which a mathematical apprehension is immediate, e.g., the apprehension that this three-sided figure, in virtue of its being three-sided, must have three angles. Both apprehensions are immediate in the sense that in both insight into the nature of the subject directly leads us to recognize its possession of the predicate; and it is only stating this fact from the other side to say that in both cases the fact apprehended is self-evident."[47]

Such confusion of moral experience with mathematics is another example of the intrusion of scientific method into ethics. What actually happens in the appreciation of the moral ought is not merely or not primarily intellectual but springs from our affective faith reaction to the value of persons. Ought experience is not automatic, and it can be misguided. It is the work of ethics to check, compare, and verify. Yet the roots of the moral ought are in the precordial depths of personal consciousness where personal moral awareness originates.

To return to our examples, the scheme to put the babies on the bumpers is another example of fundamental contradictoriness (forgive the term). Ethics is an attempt to apply the foundational moral experience to life in its concrete complexity. Any action that seems per se to negate that foundational experience by exploiting persons by treating them as things and not as persons is precluded by the nature of the enterprise. Therefore, buying and selling persons as in slavery, or assigning them rights according to their color, or putting them on bumpers to prevent accidents, or setting up a nuclear capacity to incinerate hundreds of millions of them is beyond the pale of justification. All of these are elementary sins that radically offend moral meaning. The offense is not appreciated by all. History shows that the evil of slavery, for example, has not been intuitively obvious to human consciousness. Debate was needed to dissipate moral obtuseness. And that debate had to include both deontological and teleological strains.

In this category too is the case offered by several moralists to show the limits of consequentialism and utilitarianism. As moralist Charles Curran puts it: "Can one innocent person be directly killed or framed to save the lives of 10, or 20 or 200 or 2000?"[48] Only a negative answer would appear justified, and for arguments that are both teleological and deontological. Teleologically, with regard to foreseeable effects, framing a man and sending him to his death to prevent an imminent riot or to satisfy extortioners who will kill a large number of persons if denied is a public, verifiable fact. The actually guilty man lives on and the guilt is publicly knowable. The officers of justice who allowed such a cruel stratagem to be used for short-term gains will have succeeded, in a longer view, in discrediting the system of justice and engendering bitterness among those associated by class, race, or other tie with the innocent victim. Practically speaking, and with an eye to teleology, ultilitarianism, and consequentialism, this does not make moral sense. But, again, "that is not the whole truth." The predictably bad effects are not the only reason why the act is wrong.

Framing a man and sending him to death is considerably worse than just murdering him. What happens before the death is even crueler than the death itself. It strips the man publicly of the respect that is our deepest need, reducing him to a hideous Kafkaesque despair. Aside from whatever good may come from this, this is in itself unconscionable because it clearly seems to contradict the foundational moral experience itself and so could not be a work of ethics which seeks to apply that foundational experience to life. The offense here is felt at the level of that core affective faith experience.

This is not a matter of taboo where something is seen as wrong regardless of its circumstances. Rather, this is perceived as wrong *precisely because of its circumstances*. Among those circumstances are the effects. But the action is not wrong only because of them. In fact the action is wrong even if all the projected effects seemed favorable.

It would be analytically tidier if we could limit our attention to effects, and perhaps that is the allure of merely teleological theories since their approach is more quantitative and measurable, and thus more congenial to the scientific proclivities of modernity. Of course, if it is true, as I submit it is, that teleology and deontology are both to be accounted for in realistic ethics, the adverse effects predictable from this kind of action are symptomatic of trouble at the core. The trouble is, too, that adverse effects are not always foreseeable, and this is another reason for the inadequacy of consequentialism in any of its forms. It might in fact be possible to avoid most or all of the adverse effects. This, however, would not make the action right. In this case, circumstances are such that it becomes impossible to *think* or to *feel* that this type of project is at all compatible with the minimal conditions of person-valuing that initiates moral discourse.

Since moral judgment is intrinsically reliant on circumstances, is it possible that some circumstance is eluding our cognitive grasp that would justify the framing of an innocent man? Could there ever be a case where an innocent man could be framed morally? Theoretically we cannot deny the possibility without pretending to a knowledge of all possible circumstances, but we can say with firmness that we do not see or believe that there could be, since the framing of an innocent man would appear to depart irrevocably from the very experience that ethics is trying to apply. At the least we could say here that we are in the presence of *the unimaginable exception*.

Rape too is something like this, and one would have to go to a bizarre point of imagining that a despotic individual, angry at a particular woman who had spurned his advances, ordered her to be raped at the price of saving the lives of a large number of persons. Outside of such weirdly imaginative circumstance, rape has so many negative and counterpersonal implications in the circumstances of the act itself that a lengthy consequentialist argument is not needed to understand its immorality.

A case that is very much with us is capital punishment, where an unarmed prisoner is killed mainly to deter other criminals who are at large, even though there is no hard evidence that they are deterred by an occasional execution. The sense of the macabre and of profanation that attends an execution points to the degrading nature of this kind of act. Hopefully, as we grow in civility, we will recognize that this ritualistic slaughter is an unacceptable means to any human end. Capital punishment for reasons of deterrence is an example of utilitarian consequentialism at its nadir. Here the *one* is completely sacrificed for the *many;* someone is killed for the common good. The death is justified not in terms of self-defense, since the person being killed is unarmed and in custody, but because of the benefits the death itself promises to society.[49] The end justifies the means.

Nuclear deterrence, the example with which we began, is perhaps the clearest example of something that is immoral by both teleological and deontological reasoning. For nuclear weaponry to deter, we must be ready to use it. As soon as an enemy knows that we are bluffing and would not use it, it loses all deterrent influence. Therefore being prepared to kill a huge segment of humanity and perhaps to render nugatory the possibilities for human life on this planet by a massive nuclear exchange is the core reality of a nuclear deterrence policy. Since there are no good effects that could outweigh this evil, no teleological case can be made for this policy. But even prescinding from effects, the readiness to obliterate much or all of human life could not be sanctioned by any ethics based on reverence for human life. Thus even aside from the dangerous side effects of nuclear weaponry (proliferation with political destabilization, accidents, excessive expense, etc.) the nuclear policy itself is immoral because of the readiness to destroy human life that it requires to do its deterring. Such readiness could not proceed from the perception of the value of persons, and no ethics grounded in that experience could treat such a posture as moral. The only moral reaction to the nuclear deterrence policy that we are laced to at this time (the babies have already been mounted on the bumpers) is to move out of it by negotiations and initiatives seriously and urgently directed toward nuclear disarmament. *Whether* we should move toward nuclear disarmament is not morally in doubt. This clarity should be reflected in the expeditiousness and imagination that are brought to the enormously difficult problem of how to neutralize the international monster we have created as a prop for "peace." A piddling, ineffectual approach to disarmament indicates that the moral barbarity of our current posture is not appreciated and that the respectability that accrues to the familiar has sedated the sting of guilt.[50]

The Problem of Unwanted Effects . . .

The effects that flow from our activity are many and varied and not all desirable. Some, in fact, may be positively disturbing and unwanted. The decision to remove a cancerous uterus early in a planned and desired pregnancy is an example of wanted and un-wanted effects flowing from the same action. The decision to give a strong painkiller to a patient is another example of mixed effects presenting a moral dilemma. The physician might know that the painkiller will shorten life as it eases the pain. A business that is planning some new system of automation looks ahead to the good effects of improved productivity and better competitive standing, but also faces the undesirable effect of laying off a large number of workers.

The question that arises is whether we have moral responsibility for the bad effects of our actions. The answer, of course, flows from what has been said. Foreseeable effects are within the precincts of our moral responsibility. Human actions are good or bad according to the circumstances, and effects are among those circumstances. They have to be weighed in relationship to all the other circumstances.

This illustrates something further about the nature of ethics. Ethics is the art of weighing and balancing. Human behavior finds itself amid values and disvalues. The morally good choice is the one that is the most humanly valuable. In doing this, we face the delicate challenge of balancing goods and bads, and when the bads are considerable, we have to judge whether the goods are proportionately greater. If so they may justify the unwanted elements that are unavoidably entailed in our behavior. What operates here is what has been called the principle of proportionality. In a sense it may be said to be the master principle in ethics. Since there are likely to be disvalues in the foreseeable effects of all human choices, a judgment that value proportionately outweighs disvalue is implied in all moral choice, even though, as I have been saying, a high quota of good effects does not justify *any* kind of causal action. Still there is a need to weigh the values and disvalues in moral discourse. The whole of ethics is involved in this. All of the essential circumstances, not just the effects, are weighed and balanced in a comparative judgment. The alternatives (which we have not discussed as yet) are especially important when some considerable disvalue is involved.

A quota system, used to establish racial balance in a society, is a case where a comparative judgment must be made between value and disvalue. For example, when a school of medicine is required by law to admit a certain percentage of blacks, it is done with specific desirable effects in mind. The socially important symbols of injustice as well as the fact of injustice are being removed in this attempt to correct an ingrained pattern of discrimination. However, there is a marked *disvalue* involved. As a result of the quota system, some nonblacks who would have gotten into that school will not get in. A quota system seriously modifies the system of admission by "merit"; it is a system that imposes a temporary inequality to correct past inequalities. That modification will affect some who would have gained entrance to that school under a different system. Because of this system, they may lose their opportunity to enter that school and they might lose their opportunity to enter the medical profession. The disvalue here even has the *prima facie* appearance of injustice in the light of Professor John Rawls's statement:

> All social values—liberty and opportunity, income and wealth, and the bases of self-respect—are to be distributed equally unless an unequal distribution of any, or all, of these values is to everyone's advantage. Injustice, then, is simply inequalities that are not to the benefit of all.[51]

The student who is refused admission into the medical school but would have been accepted in the absence of preferential affirmative action is not going to say that this temporary and strategic inequality is "to the benefit of all."

The essential moral question, then, is this: Is the good done by this program proportionate to the harm it does? Again, one would have to summon one's whole system of ethics to answer this question. It would not be a matter of weighing the good and the harmful effects. Illustratively, not exhaustively, the argument would proceed like this: At the foundational level of ethics it could be pointed out that we are social by essence, not by convenience or contract. The foundational moral experience of (1) the value of self, (2) the value of all others, and (3) the connection between 1 and 2 sets the stage for such a discussion. Justice (commutative, legal, and distributive) fills out the minimal implications of the foundational moral experience. We are not atomistically segregated individuals who only owe interpersonal (commutative justice) debts. We also owe debts to the social whole (legal justice) and may have to sacrifice equality temporarily to bring social fairness. We are constitutionally, not conventionally or contractually, committed to the common good. That commitment may have to be expressed in the sacrifice of one's life, as in the case of collective self-defense, or in the surrender of one's property in eminent domain, or in the quota system. To this there seems no alternative outside of a rugged, brutish, and inhuman individualism.

Social justice may require inequalities that are not to the benefit of all. If there can be such a thing as a just war, it would be judged fair though unequal to draft some and not others to fight and die in it. It is only in the social nature of persons, not in the individualistic computation of benefits, that this can be understood.

As to circumstantial analysis, it would have to be seen first *what* antiblack discrimination is to the United States. It is not excessive to say that whites and blacks exist as two nations in this country or as one nation and one distinct diaspora. It is in fact easier to slip across a border than to pass with full rights from the black nation to the white nation. Color is an efficient sensoring device, and a distinctively American apartheid is the result. The evasive possibilities within a supposed merit system would predictably be used as they have always been used. So this is *what* we are dealing with when we discuss antiblack discrimination in the United States. All of the other reality-revealing questions and evaluative processes would point up aspects of the case. Special attention would be due to the foreseeable effects of allowing things to go on without change, leaving intact the entrenched inequities. Also, the alternatives would be enormously important. Whenever there are undesirable effects such as temporary corrective inequality, imagination must strain to find alternatives. If imagination has access to the treasury and to political power, a holy trinity is formed which could minimize significant inequalities. An increase in the number of medical schools along with the quota system would expand opportunity generally. Morality would seem to point policy in this direction, but until this is brought about, the temporary inequalities used to correct antiblack discrimination would appear to be morally justifiable. This is not because the one can be sacrificed for the many, utilitarian-style, but because intrinsically social persons may, in the absence of alternatives, have to yield some of their goods and even their lives to maintain the basic conditions for human society. Alternatives should be pursued to make this unnecessary, but in the interim, it could be justified as a policy grounded in justice . . . all three kinds of justice—commutative, legal, and distributive. To show that a quota policy is morally justifiable, a fully systematic treatment would seek to show that, in the verified absence of alternatives, there is proportionate reason to impose temporary inequalities to achieve racial balance. In this way it can be seen whether the unwanted effects are morally tolerable.[52]

Effects and the Utilitarian Temptation . . .

I said above that excessive fixation on effects can lead to the glorification of ends. This is corrected by seeing the teleological *and* the deontological aspects of morality. I also said that the glorification of ends can lead to a utilitarianism that insensitively sacrifices the good of individuals to the good of the group without being very clear about what the good of the group is.

Utilitarianism is a term that covers a number of somewhat differing theories. There is, however, a common thrust to utilitarian theories. Philosopher William Frankena identifies what the term usually means. Utilitarianism, or "ethical universalism" as he calls it, holds "that an act or rule of action is right if . . . conducive to at least as great a balance of good over evil in the universe as a whole as any alternative would be, wrong if it is not. . . ."[53] Or as John Rawls puts it: "The appropriate terms of social cooperation are settled by whatever in the circumstances will achieve the greatest sum of satisfaction of the rational desires of individuals."[54]

Utilitarianism is a teleological theory that holds that actions are good if they promote the greatest sum of happiness and well-being. That may sound harmless, but it is not. Utilitarianism is an intellectual temptation to be resisted. In utilitarianism, foreseeable effects acquire an unquestioned hegemony. Utilitarianism contains, among other things, the ingredients of totalitarianism. In the natural tension that should exist between the one and the many, between the individual and the common good, utilitarianism comes down on the side of the many and the common good. And that is dangerous because abstract. No one ever met the common good or "the greatest sum of satisfaction of the rational desires." That greatest sum cannot be touched or embraced. It cannot bleed. The individual can. Any system which becomes obsessed with commonality to the neglect of individuality stands in need of the existentialist insight that a person is more important than justice . . . meaning that what you mean by justice may be so abstract and detached that it may overlook the good of concrete persons. This, of course, is not meant to deny that the notion of the common good is an indispensable intellectual tool which focuses the individual on the social implications of his humanity.

The critical weakness of utilitarianism comes out in the term which Frankena uses to describe it: "ethical universalism." It seeks ethical salvation in the good of *the many*. In its universalist fervor, individual persons can be overlooked and sacrificed to "the cause."

Utilitarianism can wear many political uniforms. It can appear as a revolution of the proletariat where the pursuit of the good of the many can crush individual rights and basic liberties. It can also present itself in the American ideology of freedom, where freedom is identified as the greatest sum of happiness and many things—including justice—may be sacrificed to it. Utilitarianism is fixated on the generic to the neglect of the particular wherever it appears. As John Rawls says, "The striking feature of the utilitarian view of justice is that it does not matter, except indirectly, how this sum of satisfactions is distributed among individuals. . . ."[55]

One of the overlooked aspects of utilitarian thinking is that it is a convenient disguise for elitism. The supposed "ethical universalism" is often quite particularistic. Utilitarianism in patriotic dress can be a cloak for the operations of a dominant minority. What could be more endearing to a self-aggrandizing minority than a philosophy that conceals narrow interests in an unspecified commitment to the sum of happiness and goodness and simultaneously blunts the claims of very specific individuals? Under the appearances of universal good the nuisance of concrete individual claims can be dismissed. Utilitarianism opens the door to exploitation, while stressing, with seeming generosity, the good of the nation or the good of the corporation or the goals of the movement. Beware, then, of those who are committed to the greatest sum of goodness (however defined) until you test their commitment to persons.

Another generally overlooked aspect of utilitarianism is its linkage to the principle of proportionality. This principle I have described as a master principle in ethics, since we must always test, proportionwise, the relationship of value to disvalue in our decisions. But this principle, central as it is, is also abstract, and as such must be checked against concrete reality. Judgments of proportionality especially in social ethics could easily yield to the quantitative bias of utilitarianism and become a judgment of the greatest good of the greatest number. It could become more interested in the sum of good effects and advantages that proceed from a policy and become insensitive to the collateral damage wreaked upon many persons by that same policy. Proportional thinking by its very nature could usher in a mathematical preoccupation with net gain. In mathematics, if the final sum is plus, minus quantities along the way have no further significance. Ethics has no such right to ignore negative factors affecting persons, and rest in the final affirmative sum. In ethics the minus quantities will be losses to actual persons and their environment. Sometimes these losses will be justifiable but not by the easy utilitarian calculus of being out of debt morally and in the black in view of the impressive sum of happy results on the bottom line.

Applied to the question of quota policy to correct injustices against blacks, a liberal utilitarian calculus could write off too easily the disadvantages of nonblacks who lose opportunities because of this policy. Proportionately, it would seem, we are way ahead. Thus, utilitarianism, obsessed with the results on "the bottom line," could feel too little urgency to seek for alternatives of the sort that redress wrongs while minimizing inequalities in the process.

The principle of proportionality is a prominent part of the classical just war theory. In the context of war, which by its nature almost commands utilitarian thinking, the idea of proportionate reason has been sorely bent. In war, victory easily becomes the sum of greatest happiness and satisfaction, and, in decisions made with regard to war, this assumption normally becomes dominant. For both the French and the Americans in Vietnam, victory in the war ceased to mean existentially the greatest sum of happiness and so both war efforts collapsed, illustrating that it is difficult to wage a war without crude utilitarian simplisms in command.

In a war it becomes too easy for the principle of discrimination (which seeks to minimize scattershot warfare and ensure noncombatant immunity) to yield to a utilitarian usage of the principle of proportionality. Victory in war becomes the dominant utilitarian principle, and thus an alarming readiness to sacrifice almost anything to achieve that sum of goodness becomes normal. The atomic bombings of Hiroshima and Nagasaki are examples of utilitarian insensitivity. "To save American lives" was the sum of happiness that made us unaware of what we were doing and blind to the alternatives then available and suggested to save lives and end the war. Pope Paul VI, on the twentieth anniversary of the Hiroshima bombing, in uncharacteristically blunt language, called that bombing an "outrage

against civilization" and a "butchery of human lives." The weapons
we used he saw as "nefarious and dishonorable," the day of their use
"disgraceful."[56]

Given the proximity of Japan to defeat and the presence of viable
alternatives, there are few who would justify our atomic assaults on
those two population centers. However, few of the utilitarians who
danced in the streets on V-J Day were touched by the signal immorality of what we did without cause to so many persons.

The incident illustrates the errors that go with utilitarianism. The
end justified the means. Many *ones* were sacrificed for the greater
good of the *many*. Proportionate reasoning was used mathematically
and impersonally; the "bottom line" was all that counted. (In fact,
if one keeps the principle of proportionality in a moral analysis of
war and strips it of utilitarian presuppositions, it becomes extremely
difficult to justify a war.) Alternatives were ignored and a narrow
consequentialism ruled the day. What is more, my reference to the
dancers serves to show that utilitarianism is not limited to the scholarly devotees of Jeremy Bentham and John Stuart Mill. Utilitarianism has a virulently infectious quality in it to which minds
within and without the academe are susceptible. It represents a self-
serving escape from *complete* moral responsibility.

A final word: Having said all of this, it must be reasserted that the
principle of proportionality remains a basic intellectual tool. It calls
attention to the balancing that must be done to assess the humanizing behavioral possibilities. Awareness of its potential for abuse clears
the way for its fruitful use.

What Are the Viable Alternatives?

Sloth is most at home in the human imagination. It is to this
problem that the last of the reality-revealing questions is addressed:
What are the viable alternatives? In situations where many alternatives are open to us, it is a mournful fact that our tendency is to see
but a few of them and then feel that these few circumscribe reality.
Accordingly our decision will be based on that segment of reality
that our semi-atrophied imaginations allow us to envision. Many realistic possibilities will be missed, to our resultant moral detriment.
A rule-of-thumb estimate would be that in a situation where there
are a hundred existent viable alternatives, we normally would perceive about ten of them.

This might seem a harsh indictment in view of the impressive technology that has issued from creative human imagination in recent years. However, it is necessary to take a longer view of our history to get a full picture of our inventiveness. For most of his two-million-year existence, man survived as a hunter and as a gatherer of fruits, nuts, and berries. Life was lived under the constant threat of starvation, and the growth in human numbers was slow and precarious. Nevertheless, necessity was not the mother of invention, for it was not until ten thousand years ago that it occurred to man to start domesticating plants rather than just wait for them to appear. With his discovery we moved from hunter to tiller.

The food crisis did not disappear with this belated leap forward. It took another four thousand years for a distinctly irrigated agriculture to appear. Again, one would think that *Homo sapiens* would have come upon this a bit sooner, just as one would think that it would not have taken man maybe as much as another thousand years to think of harnessing animals to add to his own muscle power! The picture of the animals resting in the shade and watching as *Homo sapiens* pulled the plows should give us pause. It was only when it finally struck us that animals could be harnessed to help with the work that the earliest cities emerged. Before then, there was no time for social organization, since we were busy plowing as the animals watched.[57]

A cynical footnote can be added to this unflattering picture of most of our history. One cannot help but imagine the reactions that the first persons got who came up with the new ideas. Can you imagine the scorn heaped by the established wisdom upon the first fellow who rolled in what was to be known as the wheel! And probably the first one to think of harnessing an animal to pull the plow was put off by an impressive lecture on the theme of: Who ever heard of such a thing?! These are irreverent thoughts, but not unlikely.

In modern times, the same slowness to seize upon a discovery appears. For seventy-five years after the discovery that vaccination could be used no one thought of extending the idea to other diseases until Louis Pasteur did, in 1879. In like fashion, Einstein discovered the principle of relativity without the help of any observation that had not been available for at least fifty years. As Arthur Koestler says: "The plum was overripe, yet for half a century nobody came to pluck it."[58] Good ethics should press us to realize that there must be plums galore out there waiting to be plucked.

This little vignette of history should be that backdrop for technological man as he stands to sing lauds to his own creative genius. The
momentum of technological invention has certainly grown, and one
thing has been leading to another at an accelerating pace. Small
wonder we are so impressed with ourselves.

In spite of this, three wet blankets of suspicion ought to be
dropped on the glow of our contentment. (a) It would be foolish to
think, given our long-haul track record, that we are now seeing more
than a small percentage of the alternatives and possibilities open to
us. A current example is at hand. Just as we scorned the fellow who
brought in the first wheel and the first sail, we have been until
recently laughing at the fellow who brought in the sun and the wind
as potential sources of energy. These energy sources have been
resisted not just because of the vested interest of the companies that
process the fuels that are now in early obsolescence. The slowness to
move has been more broadly based, in spite of the glaring fact that
sun and wind are nonpolluting and superabundantly present. If the
Arabs had not slowed the pumps and inconvenienced us grossly, it is
likely we would still not be stirring . . . and stirring is about all that
we are doing as yet.

The likelihood is strong if not obvious that there are many wheels
not yet invented and many animals not yet harnessed. Intoxication
with what we have done works against what we might be able to do
now.

(b) Insensitivity to systemic alternatives is a weakness that is with
us and is being increasingly felt. What we have done is invent some
wheels but no steering apparatus. Our inventions have poured out
but have not been co-ordinated. The new world that springs from
our inventiveness requires alternate modes of management. Systems
of national government and international co-operative action suited
for another time are still ensconced. In many ways, the global community is like a promising new city under the divided governance of
a number of old patriarchs in their dotage whose schemes and plans
reflect the state of things in an antiquity that is no more. A substantial change has occurred in the social and material conditions of the
earth that is not reflected in creative managerial and governmental
response.

As *The Second Report to the Club of Rome* puts it:

> In the past the world community was merely a collection of
> fundamentally independent parts. Under such conditions

each of the parts could grow—for better or worse—as it pleased. In the new conditions, exemplified by the global crises-syndrome, the world community has been transformed into a world system, i.e., a collection of functionally interdependent parts.[59]

In spite of these changes, the interdependent parts are still behaving as independent parts. The resistance to progress that appeared during our first two million years is still in evidence. It was Heraclitus who said that it is not possible to step into the same river twice. The waters are always changing. At times they change with a rush, as they have done in our century. And yet those in a position to direct social forces step down into the river and bathe, confident that all is essentially as all was. Thus it is not surprising, in the words of the same report, that "many recent analyses of the long-term prospects for mankind have produced gloomy conclusions."[60] The grounds for the gloomy conclusions are not limited to the realm of prognostication. The signs are present right now. As the Brown-Eckholm study on hunger says: "The silent crisis of malnutrition may be denying close to a billion human beings the basic right to realize their full genetic potential, their full humanity."[61] Hunger affecting a quarter of the human race to that extent is, at the least, a sign of inefficiency and neglected alternatives. The retarded reaction to our energy needs has already been mentioned. Beyond that, captured by the pull of a sightless momentum, national economies are still absorbed in developing and deploying kill-power. With children and others dying of hunger, we still spend fortunes on catapults and crossbows, acting out the worst in our barbaric past. Swollen military budgets are also a symbol of despair implying as they do that security ultimately will come from killing people, not from nourishing them.

Therefore, it would be myopic to be taken in by the glitter of disparate technological miracles or to believe that our imaginations have at all shown themselves ready for the systemic needs of a situation that is rapidly becoming a plight.

(c) Whatever our skills at the level of tools and toys, it is gloomily possible that at the level of morals, we are still hunting and gathering. Morals, of course, involve more than skill; they involve caring and appreciation. This, however, redounds to the area of creative technological skills. If there is a defect at the level of caring, if what we hopefully call "modern man" is more advanced in handiwork than in the humanizing sentiments of the heart, then the stimulus to create will be lacking. Barbaric thinking is egoistic and nonsocial. The soul of barbarism is not so much manifested in active cruelty as it is in apathy, in the absence of caring. If the moral barbarian is comfortable himself, he has little felt need to address in a creative fashion the needs of others. If technocracy is in the hands of the morally barbaric, then all hopes that human imagination will uncover the alternatives needed to defeat the causes of our gloom must be guarded.

The Nature of Alternatives . . .

The beginning of wisdom is in knowing how we know. Human knowledge is distinguished by its capacity to know not just what is, but what could be. The human mind does not just reflect the actual; it also perceives the possible. This capacity to perceive the possible is the root of both freedom and creativity. We are free basically because we are not locked in under the regimen of the current state of the real. We are natively aware that reality does not drop off into nothing at the horizon of the currently given. What *is* cannot be absolutized; it is relativized by what might be. Knowing this is the foundation of freedom. It is also the foundation of creativity, that human talent for bringing the actual out of the possible.

It has been waggishly said that when you have no alternatives, you have no problem. If there were only one choice open to you, that would indeed simplify life. Probably, however, you got into that apparent crunch by neglecting alternatives along the way. And more probably, the alternatives are there and you just do not see them.

The fact is that we live in a process of expanding alternatives. The subsistence level hunter-and-gatherer did have few choices. He was bound by necessity to scratch out an existence in a way that left him room for little else. Even he, of course, had alternatives which he only gradually appreciated, but at that stage of the process, possibilities were limited. Now complexification and diversification have become the outstanding traits of human existence. Just as the effects of our behavior reach further and further into the future, so too the horizons of present possibilities are receding, leaving us less and less confined. Not only is the world unfolding in its material possibilities, but our consciousness of what it is and what it can be is unfolding with it. Reality is broader for us and steadily broadening. This is so not just in view of the technological expansion though technology has had a significant symbolic role. It has become normal to see the undoable done. This provides the symbolic matrix in which our culture unfolds. Its impact is felt in morality, art, religion, in the social sciences, and wherever human reflection transpires. If the undoable can be done, the unthinkable can be thought. Living and moving and having our being in a world where the impossible is proved possible creates an atmosphere of daring. Little is deemed beyond challenge. In this sense the atmosphere is favorable to the discovery of alternatives at every level of existence and thought.

The conservative reaction is to resist this. This is understandable. First of all there is danger in dare-all times of recklessness and unreflective adventurism throughout the gamut of human experience. But beyond that, the conservative instinct is to shrink from the risk of the new. New alternatives involve a risk and a departure from the security-centered allure of habituation. The conservative preference is for the tried and the true over the untried, even though the tried and the true may only be an example of the familiar being mistaken for the good.

The problem and the glory is that in choosing we normally face a number of alternatives . . . the problem being that we do not see many or most of them . . . the glory being that we might. Since morality is based on reality, ignoring realistic alternatives makes for bad ethics. (Ignoring alternatives is destructive of any analysis, but I am treating here the process of moral analysis.) Preoccupation with our creative potential is a characteristic of good ethics. Only a cultivated habit of creativity intent upon the discovery of alternatives can drive sloth and inertia from their tenured positions in the imagination.

Some examples can illustrate the result of sensitivity to alternatives, or the lack of it. In the political arena, the Bay of Pigs invasion has been called "a perfect failure" and a classical fiasco. As social psychologist Irving L. Janis says of it:

> The Kennedy administration's Bay of Pigs decision ranks among the worst fiascoes ever perpetrated by a responsible government. . . . all the major assumptions supporting the plan were so completely wrong that the venture began to founder at the outset and failed in its earliest stages.[62]

It was generally agreed that the men who took part in the Bay of Pigs decision were among the brightest ever to participate in the councils of government. Yet Theodore Sorensen reports the minimal concern for alternatives that characterized this decision-making process. He says in fact that no realistic alternatives were presented. Arthur Schlesinger, Jr., supports him in this, saying that had one senior adviser proposed an alternative to the misadventure, it is his judgment that President Kennedy would have accepted it. No one did. The only basic alternatives seriously considered were to go ahead with the invasion or to do nothing.[63] The reality-revealing question —*What are the existent viable alternatives?*—was not asked. The results were both morally and strategically disastrous.[64]

President Johnson's Vietnam War decisions were most thoroughly studied in the Department of Defense's analysis known as the Pentagon Papers. This analysis shows the consistent failure to canvass the full scale of alternatives in the military recommendations of 1964 and 1965. In fact, the Defense Department's study concludes that the hopeless decision to break Hanoi's will by bombing "seems to have resulted as much from the lack of alternative proposals as from any compelling logic in their favor."[65]

This comment is especially noteworthy. In bypassing alternatives, the state of the question is actually redefined, or, better, artificially defined. We do not deal with what is; we deal with what we have decided to deal with. Within this artificially defined state of the question, brilliant minds can operate, but they operate in self-inflicted darkness. The felt gain here is obvious. Returning to the adage: *When you have no alternatives, you have no problem,* the mind, as rascal, can easily blind itself to alternatives in order to have "no problem." Our conclusions then are not based on "any compelling logic in their favor" but on "the lack of alternate proposals."

There is another element about alternative-shy thinking. It is related to insensitivity to effects. A remark by William Moyers, who had been a member of President Johnson's "in-group," is illuminating: "With rare exceptions we always seemed to be calculating the short-term consequences of each alternative at every step of the process, but not the long-term consequences. And with each succeeding short-range consequence we became more deeply a prisoner of the process."[66]

Effects and alternatives relate in two principal ways: first, sensitivity to the broad scale of foreseeable effects and sensitivity to alternatives are both horizon experiences. They stretch our vision toward a fuller understanding of the reality in question. They represent

depth and breadth perception and they run counter to the desire of
the mind for a quick fix. The mind's natural hunger to make sense of
things makes us susceptible to premature judgment. We are easy
prey to the facile answer and to immediacy—the thinking which bars
the door to the possibilities and broader ramifications of the situation. We easily become, in Moyer's terms, "a prisoner of the process." In the manner of an addict, the mind's craving to know can become a prisoner of illusory, short-lived satisfactions. Good ethical
analysis works against this indigenous weakness by stressing long- as
well as short-term effects and by urging us to pry open our angle of
vision so as to be aware of more of the alternatives actually available
to us. The desired result is improved reality-contact and better ethics.

Second, effects and alternatives are dynamically related because a
pattern of thinking within the arbitrary limits of short-term effects
slackens our need to think of alternatives. Seduced by the simplicities of short-term thinking, the need for the alternatives that are out
there vanishes. Similarly, blindness to alternatives works against the
perception of effects. When we become aware of other viable alternatives, a process of comparison must begin which will inevitably involve a study of foreseeable short- and long-term effects. If we are
blinded to alternate energy sources, we are less likely to be aware of
the effects of the currently dominant forms of energy. If we exclude
the possible, the actual takes on a certain inevitability and is thus
likely to evade critical judgment. Therefore, in the knowing act, foreseeable effects and existent alternatives are linked even though
effects refer to the future and alternatives refer mainly to the possibilities of the present.

This linkage is illustrative of what can be said of all the elements
to which the reality-revealing questions direct us. By the necessity of
analysis, we will have to dwell on the various factors of reality separately, but in moral insight and judgment all of the factors will inter-
sect and relate, just as all clues come together and link in the conclusion of the detective. Solving the case occurs when the mind can
relate all of the clues meaningfully. The same is true in ethical judgment.[67]

Moral judgment is not identical with the judging process of the detective. The comparison, like every comparison, falters. In its distinct
way, ethics involves affectivity and imagination as well as analytical
reasoning. Yet it is a judgment of how all that we can learn about

what we are judging comes together in meaningful coalescence. The
reality-revealing questions point us toward all the empirical data.
The moral judgment expresses the humanizing (moral) or dehumanizing (immoral) implications of how those data relate in the value
equation. Before going on to the distinctive way in which ethics
moves to judgment (represented by the spokes of the wheel model),
it should be noted that at this expository level of hunting and gathering the essential circumstances, the kinship of ethics to the disciplines of science and social science, should be observed.

From Value Vacuum to Value Source . . .

The illusion that science could function outside the purview of
morality is in a process of slow demise. Marquette University Professor of Electrical Engineering James D. Horgan writes:

> Today there is a "circle of action" in which changes in
> technology bring on changes in human values and therefore
> changes in technology. The engineer, intimately involved in
> this circle of action, has the special responsibility to ponder
> consequences and to disseminate information concerning
> the possible effects of his innovations on the human value
> system. To do this he must develop a much closer working
> relationship with the humanist. He must come to under-
> stand the interrelationships of technology and human
> values and, indeed, what consitutes the good life.[68]

What Horgan is calling for here is a relationship with ethics and
the end of a bad divorce. Technology is achieved by men and shapes
men's lives. That it proceed humanly, i.e., morally, i.e., in a way that
befits persons and their dignity should have been obvious. It has not
been so. Science tended to unfold as though it were immune to
value questions. This is happily beginning to change. Efforts to separate science from ethics are as futile as efforts to equate the two. The
scientific and the ethical enterprises are distinct but related experiences.

Sciences relate to ethics in two ways depending on whether they
are "hard" sciences or social sciences . . . a distinction that is made
without necessary implications of intellectual softness in the latter.
In a fundamental way, all science relates to morality by the fact that
it is a work of men whose moral reality is prior to their scientific

goals. Thus, moral responsibility, except where it is evaded by stratagem, is coextensive with humanity.

In the hard sciences, however, the relationship to morals is more causal and indirect. This is the sense of Horgan's "circle of action." By working in what would appear to be purely neutral research, science changes the state of man, thus affecting the matrix of moral values. This is particularly obvious when it introduces new issues of moral responsibility, giving us massive power over the conditions of life and thus making us newly responsible to the future. Science develops the atom bomb, and amniocentesis, and acquires the ability to prolong life when death would have been welcomed and now speaks of changing life through genetic intervention. Modern ethics faces problems which older ethics never dreamed of. In this clear basic sense there is a moral dimension to science which is becoming more visible.

The relationship of the social sciences to morality is more direct and intrinsic. The social scientist has attempted to attain the supposed "value-free" objectivity of the natural sciences. However, as Robert Heilbroner observes, "this ambition fails to take into account that the position of the social investigator differs sharply from that of the observer of the natural world." The natural scientist, he continues, may study the stars, "but he is not himself morally embedded in the field he scrutinizes." The social scientist, on the other hand, "is inextricably bound up with the objects of his scrutiny . . . not only his material position but his moral position . . . is implicated in and often jeopardized by the act of investigation. . . ."[69]

What Heilbroner is on to here is that, morally speaking, there is no presuppositionless social science. As professor Lewis Lipsitz writes in the *American Political Science Review:* "Despite our proclamations of value 'neutrality' it is increasingly clear that many of the analytical frameworks and conclusions of behavioral political scientists have normative roots and branches."[70] Social sciences that believed themselves value-free and morally neutral did not realize that they functioned out of some foundational conception of man and that thus moral oughts about what befit or did not befit man as they conceived him would of necessity abound in their analytical frameworks and conclusions. The new enlightenment in this regard must be welcomed, since it urges social scientists to drop the façade of neutrality and show what hidden and untested gospels they carry.

Eric Voegelin notes that the terms "value-judgment" and "value-free" science became part of philosophical vocabulary only in the second half of the nineteenth century.

> . . . this situation was created through the positivistic con-
> ceit that only propositions concerning facts of the phenom-
> enal world were "objective," while judgments concerning
> the right order of soul and society were "subjective." Only
> propositions of the first type could be considered
> "scientific," while propositions of the second type expressed
> personal preferences and decisions, incapable of critical
> verification and therefore devoid of objective validity.[71]

The pretense of moral neutrality is, in fact, the most unneutral stance imaginable. If one admits the morally normative side of his research, his presuppositions are thereby laid out for inspection. The pseudoneutralist, however, presents his views as if they were coincident with reality portrayed with limpid and unalloyed objectivity. His presuppositional baggage is not open to inspection. In fact, he claims he is traveling with no such baggage at all. If he gets away with this, he has succeeded in smuggling into academic discussion his own implicit moral structure and method and his concealed philosophical and even theological assumptions about the nature and meaning of the human material he addresses.[72]

To put this directly, the social scientist is involved with ethics because he is exploring the phenomenon of the *humanum* through the method of his distinct social science. He is supplying theoretical and practical answers to some of the reality-revealing questions that are the grist of ethical inquiry. Without the social scientist, those questions cannot be answered. So integral is the work of social science to ethics that it is impossible for ethics to function independently of the social sciences. In simpler times, the ethicist could pose as something of the universal man who could learn enough of the other disciplines to purvey value judgments on all. Such grandness is now outdated.

In the past, for example, the moralist felt that he could know enough about international politics to provide an adequate political ethics. Now the study of world politics has swollen to multidisciplinary size. No one could master it in all of its dimensions. The result is that the critical moral questions raised by politics cannot be answered from the sidelines by ethicists. The answers can only come now from the shared insights of ethicists and the various students of political reality. The ethicist can clarify the nature of moral value, delineate the moral dimensions of political life, and suggest a method of moral evaluation. The political theorist can operate through the distinctive method of his specialization. Conversation must blend the contributions of each. There is no pope in this dialogue; neither can any participant be excommunicated from the ecumenical endeavor of morally evaluating the complexities of our political existence. The social scientist must acknowledge that his work has morally normative implications. He is to some degree doing ethics and thus is in no position to ignore evaluative ethical theory. Similarly the ethicist cannot pretend that his art-science is independent of the sciences that explore our social reality, or that, because morality is a universal quality of conscious human behavior, he has *ex officio* wisdom of a universal sort. Without reliance on the social scientists, he will not know *what* he is talking about.

Ethics is not just a discipline among other disciplines. I do not say this as a prelude to proclaiming it the queen of all disciplines. Rather, it is less circumscribable than other disciplines since it views the whole of human conscious behavior. Thus, to do its work, it needs dialogical communion with all the other disciplines which study the human phenomenon.

In a university, ethics ideally would be done in what could be called a Center for the Study of Moral Values. This center would relate formally to the other departments of the university so that moral evaluation would proceed in an interdisciplinary way. The ethicists in the center would learn to establish lines of communication with the experts in other areas and so further the multidisciplinary study of moral values. From this contact the ethicists could return to correct and expand their theoretical framework in ethics. Realistically it must be allowed that formidable vested interests in the academe stand against the hopes for any such creative structuring.

With this said, the center of the wheel model is completed. This has been the questioning and gathering phase, where ethics begins by learning what it is to judge in all of its empirical complexity. Abstractly speaking, we have thus far been gathering, not evaluating. Actually we have been doing a lot of evaluating as we moved through various cases. In the face of a moral issue, the mind instinctively begins to evaluate. The wheel model is therefore, like any model, imperfect and abstract, implying as it does that we could unfold reality with our questions and then, as if by signal, commence evaluation.

The problem, however, is that the initial evaluative reaction to a moral situation will be impulsive, partial, and impatient. In a sense ethics is a systematic defense against intellectual impatience in value issues. By stressing and stretching all of the reality-revealing questions, we attack myopia and our reliance on figments and surface impressions. We reach for the glory of knowing what it is that we presume to judge. The spokes of the wheel model represent systematic concern for the shape of our evaluative response to what our questions have gathered. If response can instinctively and easily be partial and biased, ethics seeks to make it more sensitive and complete. If we do not conceptualize the possibilities of our personal and social resources (the spokes of the wheel model), we will miss out on ways that we can experience truth. We are shortsighted enough without enduring unnecessary blindness.

Theoretically, then, the "spokes" focus upon the highly complex way in which persons can approach moral truth. By systematically exploring our evaluative capacities, we may be able better to avoid "top-of-the-head" or "top-of-the-culture" responses to moral questions. Hopefully, such consideration will sensitize us to the manifold ways in which moral truth emerges. Knowing how we know can never be complete, but concern for knowing how we know is the beginning of wisdom in any subject.

There is, of course, no implication here that persons (including myself) when faced with a sudden moral decision will withdraw, sketch out the wheel model of ethics, and plod from point to point. Such immediate decisions are made by conscience, i.e., by the morally sensitive self which is attuned to values as they emerge in the concrete situation. The reaction of conscience is often "on the spot" when there may be virtually no time for reflection. The nature of conscience will be subsequently discussed, but here it is mentioned to note its distinction from detached ethical reflection. Reflection always requires leisure as its matrix, whereas conscience must normally respond to the urgency of action. Conscience, however, is nourished in reflection. Ethics is one of its parents.

NOTES—CHAPTER FIVE

1. The point here, of course, is not that a simple observation of the *is* will yield appropriate *oughts* in the same sense that observation of

heating water will yield legitimate conclusions about a boiling point. Ethics is not a science or even a social science and its methods are distinct.

2. Paul M. Sweezy, "The American Ruling Class," in *The Present as History* (New York: Monthly Review Press, 1953), p. 126.

3. Rod Roger Garaudy, *Marxism in the Twentieth Century* (New York: Scribner, 1970), p .13.

4. Robert L. Heilbroner, *An Inquiry into the Human Prospect* (New York: W. W. Norton & Co., 1975), p. 64.

5. Ibid., p. 65.

6. From Benjamin Rush, *Medical Inquiries upon Diseases of the Mind* (Philadelphia, 1812), p. 347; quoted in E. H. Hare, "Masturbatory Insanity: The History of an Idea," *Journal of Mental Science* 108 (Jan. 1962), p. 4.

7. From C. F. Lallemand, *Des Pertes Seminales Involontaires* (Paris, 1842), p. 133; quoted in Hare, "Masturbatory Insanity," p. 8.

8. Hare, "Masturbatory Insanity," pp. 10–11.

9. There was some reciprocal causality between moralists and scientists in the condemnation of masturbation. It has been viewed negatively in a number of moral traditions, and indeed the initial stimulus for the psychiatric condemnation may have been given by an influential book early in the eighteenth century written by an anonymous author who was apparently a "clergyman turned quack." See Hare, "Masturbatory Insanity," p. 2.

10. Ibid., p. 15.

11. Quoted in *Hastings Center Report* 4 (June 1974), p. 16.

12. Carl Jung, "The Soul and Death," in Herman Feifel, ed., *The Meaning of Death* (New York, London, Sydney, and Toronto: McGraw-Hill Book Co., 1959), p. 7.

13. Elisabeth Kubler-Ross, M.D., *On Death and Dying* (London and New York: Macmillan, 1970), p. 141.

14. Richard A. McCormick, "Human Significance and Christian Significance," in Gene H. Outka and Paul Ramsey, eds., *Norm and Context in Christian Ethics* (New York: Charles Scribner's Sons, 1968), p. 254.

15. Ibid., p. 253.

16. I have criticized Thomas Aquinas for an insufficiently specified use of the term "object" in I II q. 18 of his *Summa*. My use of what as a tool of inquiry insists that this is the beginning, not the end, of the expository ethical process, and that no fixed moral meaning can be established until all other circumstances have been judged in their relationship to one another. This should avoid the misunderstandings that have accrued to Thomas' description of "object," especially in I II q. 18, a. 2. See Chapter Seven below for my treatment of principles and universalizability.

17. The only acceptable meaning of this would be that if your end is good and your means are harmoniously suited to that end, then they will be similarly good and licit. See Bernard Häring, *The Law of Christ* (Westminster, Md.: Newman Press, 1961), p. 292.

18. Nicolas Berdyaev, *The Destiny of Man* (New York and Evanston: Harper & Row, Harper Torchbook, 1960), p. 80.

19. Quoted by Philip Noel-Baker, "We Have Been Here Before," in Nigel Calder, ed., *Unless Peace Comes* (New York, Viking Press, 1968), p. 215.

20. Calder, "The New Weapons," ibid., p. 231.

21. Jawaharlal Nehru, *The Discovery of India* (New York: John Day Co., 1946), excerpted in Paul E. Sigmund, Jr., ed., *The Ideologies of the Developing Nations* (New York and London: Frederick A. Praeger, 1963), p. 88.

22. Berdyaev, *Destiny of Man*, p. 164.

23. Louis Monden, *Sin, Liberty and Law* (New York: Sheed & Ward, 1965), p. 20.

24. Here I am speaking of "what" in a generic sense, not in the more narrowly defined sense of first-stage cognition.

25. Augustine said: *"Pietas timore inchoatur, cartate perficitur"* (*De Vera Religione*, cap. XVII).

26. This does not say that all good men must agree on what means are necessary for what end. The absolutizing of certain means to an end often signals the death of imagination in the face of a problem.

27. This example from sexual ethics obviously leaves many questions unasked and unanswered. A fuller discussion of the ethics of sex would be needed to exemplify in detail the method being developed here.

28. What is found in persons can be appreciated in an incipient way in animals, and in comparing persons to mere animals, one would deprive the animal of all the spirit that is in man. That spirit is adumbrated in animals sometimes in ways that are instructive.

29. Jean-Paul Sartre, *L'Existentialisme Est un Humanisme* (Paris: Éditions Nagel, 1959), pp. 22, 24.

30. Martin Buber, *I and Thou*, 2nd ed. (New York: Charles Scribner's Sons, 1966), p. 11.

31. George Herbert Mead, in A. Strauss, ed., *The Social Psychology of George Herbert Mead* (Chicago: University of Chicago Press, 1956), p. 217.

32. H. Richard Niebuhr, *The Responsible Self* (New York, Evanston, and London: Harper & Row, 1963), p. 73.

33. Ross Terrill, "Pax Americana and the Future of Asia," *Cross Currents* 18 (1968), p. 483.

34. Obviously, *where?* and *when?* overlap with other questions such as

what? and *who?* The separate listing of these questions, however, is helpful, since they point the way to circumstances that could easily be missed in the rush of the mind to moral judgment.

35. This is the thrust of teleological ethics. As Harry K. Girvetz writes: "Plato, who sought in *Republic* to prove that the just man is happier than the unjust man, Butler, Paley, Bentham, Mill, all sought to justify moral conduct by a reference to consequences." *Beyond Right and Wrong* (New York and London: Free Press, Collier Macmillan Publishers, 1973), p. 107.

36. Thomas Aquinas, *Summa Theologica* II II q. 10, a. 11, in corp.

37. John L. Snell, *Illusion and Necessity: The Diplomacy of Global War, 1939–1945* (Boston: Houghton Mifflin Co., 1963), p. 5.

38. Bernard N. Nathanson, M.D., "Deeper into Abortion," *New England Journal of Medicine* 291, No. 22 (Nov. 28, 1974), pp. 1189–90.

39. Ibid., p. 1190.

40. Hans Jonas, "Technology and Responsibility: Reflections on the New Talks of Ethics," *Social Research* 40, No. 1 (1973), pp. 35–36.

41. Marc Lappé, "How Much Do We Want to Know About the Unborn?" *Hastings Center Report* 3, No. 1 (Feb. 1973), pp. 8–9.

42. Arnold J. Toynbee, *Change and Habit* (New York and London: Oxford University Press, 1966), p. 5.

43. See William Manchester, *The Glory and the Dream* (Boston: Little, Brown & Co., 1974), p. 199.

44. W. D. Ross, *The Right and the Good* (Oxford: Clarendon Press, 1930), p. 39. Emphasis added.

45. William K. Frankena, *Ethics* (Englewood Cliffs, N.J.: Prentice-Hall, Inc., 1963), p. 14.

46. Ibid.

47. H. A. Prichard, "Does Moral Philosophy Rest on a Mistake?" *Mind* 21 (1912); reprinted in W. T. Jones, F. Sontag, M. O. Beckner, and R. J. Fogelin, *Approaches to Ethics*, 2nd ed. (New York: McGraw-Hill Book Co., 1969), p. 474.

48. Charles E. Curran, *Ongoing Prevision: Studies in Moral Theology* (Notre Dame, Ind.: Fides Publishers, Inc., 1975), p. 199. For a similar discussion, see H. J. McCloskey, "An Examination of Restricted Utilitarianism," in Thomas K. Hearn, Jr., ed., *Studies in Utilitarianism* (New York: Appleton-Century-Crofts, 1971). See also Philippa Foot, "The Problem of Abortion and the Doctrine of the Double Effect," in James Rachels, ed., *Moral Problems* (New York: Harper & Row, 1971). This essay appeared originally in *Oxford Review* 5 (1967), pp. 5–15.

49. There are, of course, a number of primitive forces behind the enthu-

siasm for capital punishment. No practice in society is ever the simple product of a theory. See my *Death by Choice* (Garden City, N.Y.: Doubleday & Co., Inc., 1974), pp. 203–9.

50. The possibility of limited or tactical use of nuclear weapons is not entirely credible given the symbolic impact of totality that nuclear weapons have acquired, the difficulty in defining or establishing the limits of tactical weapons, the *quid pro quo* effect which would evoke other forms of now forbidden weaponry, etc.

51. John Rawls, *A Theory of Justice* (Cambridge, Mass.: Belknap Press of Harvard University Press, 1971), p. 62.

52. For a fuller discussion of the morality of quotas, see Daniel C. Maguire, "Unequal but Fair: The Morality of Justice by Quota," in *Commonweal* 104, No. 21 (Oct. 14, 1977). The so-called principle of double effect was an attempt to deal with cases of one desirable and one undesirable effect. It was an imperfect tool and could not substitute for a wholistic ethical approach to the presence or absence of proportionate reason to tolerate undesired effects. Four conditions were stated for the double effect approach: (1) The causal action must not be intrinsically evil; (2) the disruptive or "bad" effect must not be desired; (3) the "bad" effect must not causally precede the good effect or it would be desired and intended; (4) there must be a proportionately grave reason to permit the "bad" effect. There are problems with this structure: In 1 it is implied that an action could be intrinsically evil without reference to the circumstances such as, for example, the end which is contained in 2. The use of the term "bad" or "evil" confuses moral evil with nonmoral evil. This shows up in 3, which is therefore a confusing statement that is gratuitously made.

53. Frankena, *Ethics*, p. 14.

54. Rawls, *Theory of Justice*, pp. 25–26.

55. Ibid., p. 26.

56. Paul VI, "Remarks before recitation of the Angelus, August 8, 1965," *The Pope Speaks* 10 (1965), pp. 358, 406.

57. Lester R. Brown with Erik P. Eckholm, *By Bread Alone* (New York and Washington, D.C.: Praeger Publishers, 1974), pp. 19–20. Arnold Toynbee, *Change and Habit*, p. 21, notes on a table of technological advances that it was five thousand years ago that man thought of harnessing wind power for driving ships, two thousand years ago that water power was harnessed for driving mills, and that the age of harnessing of nonmuscular power, other than wind power and water power, was just two hundred years ago.

58. Arthur Koestler, *The Act of Creation* (New York: Dell Publishing Co., Laurel Edition, 1967), p. 111. On Pasteur's discovery, Koestler notes the special ripeness of Pasteur himself to make this discovery.

We shall discuss the relationship of preparation to discovery in the subsequent chapter.

59. Mihajlo Mesarovic and Eduard Pestel, *Mankind at the Turning Point: The Second Report to the Club of Rome* (New York: New American Library, A Signet Book, 1976), p. 5.

60. Ibid., p. vii.

61. Brown with Eckholm, *By Bread Alone*, p. 12.

62. Irving L. Janis, *Victims of Groupthink* (Boston: Houghton Mifflin Co., 1972), p. 14.

63. Ibid., p. 34. After citing a possible surreptitious infiltration plan which would allow small groups of guerrillas to join guerrillas in the mountains, Janis says: "Evidently this solution to the disposal problem, which would have had less damaging political repercussions than the all-out versus all-off alternatives that were considered, was never seriously examined."

64. To say that the results were "morally and strategically disastrous" does not, of course, suggest that morality and strategy are parallel concepts. Political and military strategy is a manifestation of human activity. Thus there is always a moral dimension to that activity. Also, something may be strategically advantageous in the short run, and yet be morally wrong. I would submit, however, that short-term strategic success that operates without conscience will ultimately be undone even as strategy.

65. Quoted in Janis, *Victims of Groupthink*, p. 102.

66. Quoted ibid., p. 103.

67. In presenting the reality-revealing questions, I am drawing on a long history of ethical inquiry traced back to Aristotle (*Nichomachean Ethics*, Bk. 2, Chap. 3, 1104b 26) and Thomas Aquinas (*Summa Theologica* I II q. 18, a. 3, *Sed Contra*). Some of these questions become staples of the Catholic manuals of moral theology. Significantly, however, these manuals do not stress and usually ignore the question of alternatives. Since these manuals represented a close vision of morality and a classicalist mentality largely unchastened by the facts of historicity and process, it is not surprising that they would have shown avoidance of alternative-consciousness, since this of its nature is unsettling and broadening and is thus a hazard to the closed mind.

68. J. D. Horgan, "Technology and Human Values: 'The Circle of Action,'" *Mechanical Engineering*, Aug. 1973, p. 19.

69. Robert L. Heilbroner, *An Inquiry into the Human Prospect* (New York: W. W. Norton & Co., Inc., 1975), pp. 22–23.

70. Lewis Lipsitz, "If, as Verba Says, the State Functions as a Religion, What Are We to Do Then to Save Our Souls?" *American Political Science Review* 62 (1968), p. 534.

71. Eric Voegelin, *The New Science of Politics* (Chicago and London: University of Chicago Press, Phoenix Books, 1952), p. 11.
72. One worthy object of study would be to analyze certain pseudo-neutralists in social science and to show that they have assumed definite, albeit veiled, positions in many of the classical ethical debates and also that they are up to their necks in theology. As unlikely as it would seem to them in their "value-free" posture, they have willy-nilly taken stands on such theological discussions as realized vs. futurist eschatology, redemption, grace, and personal, collective, and original sin.

CHAPTER SIX

ETHICS AND CREATIVITY

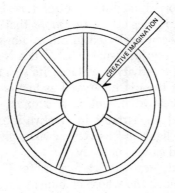

Creative Imagination

No one has a right to be as small as his own past. . . .
Clyde A. Holbrook

Creative imagination is the supreme faculty of moral man. Through
it he breaks out of the bondage of the current state of things.
Through it he perceives the possible that is latent in the actual but
which would be unseen by any less exalted consciousness. Like God's
spirit in the Book of Genesis, creative imagination can find the possibilities of order in the "formless void" and begin the rout of chaos.

Ethics and the process of moral judgment is not just a matter of
sitting in state and passing judgment on the passing goods and bads.
Moral thinking at its best perceives goods that have not as yet existed

and brings them into being in the creative act. Creative imagination, obviously, will be most concerned with the reality-revealing question about alternatives and with the enlargement of reality and advancement of moral evolution that new alternatives may provide.

Creativity has not had the attention that is its due in ethical reflection. Partly, this is related to the tendency of cultures to shy from the creative spirit. As the Brazilian philosopher Rubem Alves says, creativity "is a forbidden act. The Organization of our world is essentially sterile and hates anything that could be the seed of regeneration. . . . Remembering Revelation, 'The dragon stands in front of the woman who is about to give birth, so that when her child is born he may devour it.' "[1] Creativity upsets the timid little order we have achieved, and makes the uncourageous cringe. Reflecting this, much ethical theory through the centuries has been content to direct thought to what is, neglecting the *more* that might be. Creativity might also have been neglected in ethics, however, because it is no simple matter to say just what it is. Order is more easily analyzed than ecstasy, and creativity is ecstatic. Its sources are in the preconceptual depths of the psyche as well as in the configurations of the social setting. Creative insight is a surprise. There is something unpredictable and unchartable in creative intelligence. It is a leap into unsuspected light and its very newness gives it some immunity to the accustomed canons of study.

With all of that, creativity is a fact of life. There are blessed examples of it throughout the whole of human life. By looking at them and with a studied modesty in the face of this mysterious, vaulting power that is among us, we can and should inquire into the meaning and nature of creative imagination. "Fortune favors the prepared mind," as Louis Pasteur said. Perhaps we can see something of what creativity is and from this learn what conditions set the stage for its break-through. First then to creativity in general; then to the place and the preconditions of creativity for ethics.

What Is the Creative Act? . . .

Professor J. Bronowski, a person in whom science and philosophy are happily wed, has given attention to the nature of the creative mind. Bronowski turns to the famous creative incident of young Newton, who saw an apple fall while he was sitting in the garden of his widowed mother. What came to Newton was not the thought that the apple must be drawn to the earth by gravity, since that thought was older than Newton. "What struck him was the conjecture that the same force of gravity, which reaches to the top of the tree, might go on reaching out beyond the earth and its air, endlessly into space. Gravity might reach the moon: this was Newton's new thought; and it might be gravity which holds the moon in her orbit."[2] What Bronowski draws from this is that Newton had discovered a previously hidden likeness . . . "seized a likeness between two unlike appearances; for the apple in the summer garden and the grave moon overhead are surely as unlike in their movements as two things can be. Newton traced in them two expressions of a single concept, gravitation: and the concept (and the unity) are in that sense his free creation."[3] The general conclusion that Bronowski offers is that "the progress of science is the discovery at each step of a new order which gives unity to what had long seemed unlike."[4] Thus Faraday saw the link between electricity and magnetism and Einstein linked time with space and mass with energy. Creation is an act of fusion; creative science is a "search for unity in hidden likenesses."[5]

In the creative act then, according to Bronowski, "the scientist or the artist takes two facts or experiences which are separate; he finds in them a likeness which had not been seen before; and he creates a unity by showing the likeness."[6] Creation can be seen as "a hand reaching straight into experience and arranging it with new meaning."[7]

Bronowski's theory seems correct as far as he goes, but even as given, it is enlightening for ethics. There is an experience of previously missed likenesses and of the achievement of a new unity in moral discovery. Take, for example, the belated discovery that women are not essentially domestic and sexual functionaries, but are persons with an infinity of possible meaning beyond their historical roles. This discovery is taking longer to establish itself than the discovery of relativity, electricity, or nuclear physics for reasons that make moral discovery distinctive. After all, a woman is more like a man than an apple is like the moon. It should have been easier to make connections here than between time and space, or mass and energy. We shall return to the peculiar problems of moral discovery in treating the hazards of moral discourse which to some degree incapacitates the mind for ethical penetration. Still, the nature of this discovery can be partially illuminated by Bronowski's theory. In the discovery of the genuine and fully fledged personhood of woman there is a hand reaching into human experience and arranging it with new meaning. There is basically here a new realization of the fundamental similarity of persons that is more profound than any historically assigned system of roles or social arrangement. Like the scientist, the feminist is moving beyond an unfruitful separateness and is creating a new and promising unity. Something similar happened in the abolition of slavery and is now happening in the incipient discovery of likeness between persons who are heterosexual and persons who happen to be homosexual in their affectional orientation. In each case creative moral imagination is at work. Obviously, likeness says something, but not all. It remains too pale and incomplete an explanation of what happens in creative moral movements.

Arthur Koestler has also produced an insightful study of the act of creation. Like Bronowski, he stresses the discovery of hidden likenesses, but Koestler introduces a number of other aspects of the phenomenon of creativity. He writes: "The creative act, by connecting previously unrelated dimensions of experience, enables [man] to attain to a higher level of mental evolution. It is an act of liberation —the defeat of habit by originality."[8] He distinguishes various kinds of creative activity, humor, art, and "objective analogy" and says that the creative process is the same in all three: "it consists in the discovery of hidden similarities."[9] Thus, Gutenberg's discovery of the printing press came from watching a wine press crushing the grapes. "At this moment it occurs to him that the same, steady pressure might be applied by a seal or coin—preferably of lead, which is easy to cast —on paper, and that owing to the pressure, the lead would leave a trace on the paper—Eureka!"[10] Thus far, then, Koestler is at one with Bronowski. But Koestler probes more deeply into the mystery of the creative act.

Koestler stresses that the creative event is not unrelated to work and preparation. Again, in the words of Louis Pasteur: "Fortune favors the prepared mind." This was certainly the case when Pasteur hit on what should have been an obvious idea—extending the idea of vaccination for smallpox to inoculation for other diseases. This involved blending two elements, and Pasteur was especially ready to see their possible linkage. First there was the technique of vaccination, and then there was independent research on microorganisms. This gave Pasteur the prepared mind which fortune favored.

Still, Koestler rejects a behaviorist conception of "ripeness" in which, when the conditions reach a peak of preparedness, the creation happens. If that were so, says Koestler "the role of genius in history would be reduced from hero to midwife, who assists the inevitable birth; and the act of creation would be merely a consummation of the preordained."[11] Still, as is illustrated by the spate of scientific discoveries in our age, inventions do trigger one another, and genius does depend on genius. One genius waters and another reaps, as can be seen in the work of Charles Darwin, who profited from the preceding work of Buffon, Erasmus Darwin, and Lamarck.[12] Still there is a solitary leap taken by the creative mind in spite of all that he owes to others. It comes from depths of the mind that are not easily visited with inspection. "In the creative act there is an *upward* surge from some unknown, fertile, underground layers of the mind. . . ."[13] The frequent experience of sudden solutions to problems, or the solution of problems during dreams—even the creation of art during dreams as when Tartini composed the Devil's Trill Sonata while asleep—show that there is in the unconscious "a breeding ground of novelties."[14] No matter how hard one labors, the creative moment comes only after a period of incubation, the length of which is not in our control. One must work and then wait, with the waiting as important as the working.

Koestler's ideas are helpful for understanding break-throughs in moral imagination. We can apply them to an example of moral creativity given by the philosopher Henri Bergson. Bergson credits the Hebrew prophets and Christianity with revolutionary creative changes in the modern Western notion of justice. In spite of the tribalistic limits of most of Hebraic prophecy, they introduced a new urgency to all issues of justice. The prophets imparted to justice, in Bergson's view, "the violently imperative character" which has marked it ever since. This was followed by another creative breakthrough in Christian experience. "Humanity had to wait till Christianity for the idea of universal brotherhood, with its implication of equality of rights and the sanctity of the person, to become operative."[15] These ideas were adumbrated among the philosophers of old. Plato included the idea of man among the transcendent ideas, which implied that men were of the same essence. Stoic philosophers claimed that all men were brothers and that the wise man was a citizen of the world. The Chinese produced a noble moral theory, but it, in fact, was focused only upon the Chinese community and not upon the whole of humanity. But the break that Christianity made

was not made by others. To follow through on it would have meant
condemning slavery and giving up the idea that foreigners were not
fully enfranchised in humanness. This did not happen. As Bergson
allows, Christianity did not live out the creative implications of its
thought on justice for a remarkably long time: ". . . eighteen centuries elapsed before the rights of man were proclaimed by the
Puritans of America, soon followed by the men of the French
Revolution. It began, nevertheless, with the teachings of the
Gospels. . . ."[16]

Bergson's example is supported by what Hannah Arendt writes
about the discovery that life is the highest good. Against the ancient
idea that only the world was permanent and immortal, the Hebrews
brought on the relativizing contention of the potential immortality
of their people, and Christianity went so far as to stress the immortality of individual persons. Only at this point, "only with the rise of
Christianity, did life on earth also become the highest good of
man."[17] This represented a creative turn-around in history.

> . . . the modern age continued to operate under the as-
> sumption that life, and not the world, is the highest good
> of man; in its boldest and most radical revisions and criti-
> cisms of traditional beliefs and concepts, it never even
> thought of challenging this fundamental reversal which
> Christianity had brought into the dying ancient world.[18]

This creative achievement in human moral history illustrates those
elements of creativity which we cited from Koestler. There was the
defeat by originality of well-entrenched habits of understanding. The
Christian break-through was not unrelated to other break-throughs
such as that of the prophetic justice of the Hebrews and their exaltation of the Jewish people against the divinity of the world. Plato and
the Greek philosophers had influence on Jewish and early Christian
thought and had further influence on much of the world in which
Christian thought would take hold. Incubation had been going on a
long time when the ideas of the Gospels were put together. Christianity drew from the work that had been going on and yet it took a
strikingly original turn. The shock of the world around it at what it
said, the vigorous attempts to eliminate it, show it to be "a forbidden act" of creativity.

And yet this example illustrates the distinctions that must be
made when we speak of moral creativity. In a true sense, the discov-

ery of the fundamental equality of persons, including persons of
other tribes, was a discovery not entirely unlike the discoveries of
Newton, Gutenberg, and Pasteur. It was not entirely like them either. The law of gravity is one thing. The value and rights of persons
is another, and one should suspect that the approach of creativity to
the latter discovery would be as distinctive as the discovery itself.

Creative Ethics . . .

Creative imagination, in any forum, is the power to perceive the
possible within the actual, and creative action is the ability to invite
and bring the possible into the realm of the actual. As mentioned in
our discussion of alternatives, our historical record of inventiveness is
charry and leads us to suspect that self-laudation in this regard is premature. Still, creativity remains a promising power that is native to
us, and our times are not without good portents regarding the unfolding of this capacity.

For one thing, although we may withdraw from creative movements that disturb or challenge our security, we cannot but admire
creative talent and esteem the inventor. As Sir Cyril Burt writes:

> From time immemorial the gift of creativity has been
> venerated almost as if it were divine. There is more than a
> grain of truth in the romance of old Euhemerus, which
> relates how the gods and demigods of the ancient myths
> were really "men of preeminent accomplishments deified
> out of flattery or gratitude." Prometheus, the discoverer of
> fire, Vulcan, the first of the smiths, Hermes, the inventor of
> writing, Aesculanius, the founder of the most ancient
> school of medicine—each was welcomed into the classical
> Pantheon, much as today an outstanding scientist is elected
> to the Royal Society.[19]

Furthermore, it is important for ethical method to note that there
is a creative fire that burns in every man, a thirsting for the new and
the not yet. Professor John Platt says there is an absolute necessity

> throughout our waking life for a continuous novelty and va-
> riety of external stimulation of our eyes, ears, sense organs
> and all our nervous network. . . . Our brains organize, and
> exist to organize, a great variety of incoming sensory mes-
> sages every waking second, and can become not only emo-
> tionally upset but seriously deranged if these messages cease

or even if they cease to be new. New experience is not merely a childish want; it is something we cannot do without.[20]

Experiments on the eyes have shown that the unconscious movements of the eyes are a necessary condition for vision. If a subject's eyes were mechanically fixed on a stationary object, the object seemed to disintegrate. The experiments seem to show that at the level of physical vision, we cannot see without exploring.[21]

Beyond this, there is a deeper spiritual restlessness to our minds. As Berdyaev writes: "The soul is afraid of emptiness. When there is no positive, valuable, divine content in it, it is filled with the negative, false, diabolical content."[22] Like water, persons or cultures that are unstirred become stagnant. Sloth is a vice that lowers our expectations and blunts our searching instincts. But the nemesis of sloth is boredom. Boredom is the throbbing pain that comes when we are denied newness. It sends us back on the search. We can dull that pain with superficial newness, but that leaves us still unrequited in the deeper regions of the personality, as when we satisfy hunger by eating only candy.

Our intellectual and volitional hunger is such that even fulfilling experiences have a bitter edge to their sweetness. As Loren Eiseley says of the yearning of our minds, "so restless is man's intellect that were he to penetrate to the secret of the universe tomorrow, the likelihood is that he would grow bored on the day after."[23] This restlessness is the wellspring of creativity. Its radical insatiability is our hope that the power of creativity will not disappear. Indeed there is a possibility that we are only at the budding state of man's creative intelligence. Studies have shown that man's brain has increased in size rapidly since he began using tools and fire so that it is now three times as large as before. This may have happened in a much shorter space of time than had been long supposed . . . perhaps in "only a few hundred thousand years."[24]

Also, human brains are marked by their capacity to learn. Insects apparently do not learn. As soon as an insect emerges from its pupa, it knows how to search for its particular kind of food and build its special habitat. The nervous system here is closed and fixed. In us, it is open and geared to expand throughout life in response to external stimulation and challenge. As Platt writes:

The network may finally be able to play Bach and to pilot planes, responding quickly and accurately to experiences that never happened to any ancestor. . . . It is a tremendous evolutionary step for the individual to be able to go so far beyond the instructions contained in the egg; and we may be only at the beginning of this development.[25]

We have spoken of creativity primarily in terms of intellect, and in using examples outside of ethics this is understandable. Though creativity is indeed an intellectual flowering, the one-sided stress here could overshadow the fact that its roots are in affectivity. I believe that this is true for all creativity, but it is saliently true in moral experience. Bergson puts it directly: "There are emotions which beget thought; and invention, though it belongs to the category of the intellect, may partake of sensibility in its substance."[26]

It is a weakness of the mind to distinguish tidily things which are not tidily discrete. This happens when we distinguish too confidently intellect and will, knowledge and desire. It is the person, after all, who knows and desires. Both kinds of activity are present within one conscious vitality. Perhaps it is in the creative act that we can know how intimately conjoined knowing and wanting may be. In works of rote, we might think of the will as a kind of prodding, disciplinary force that presses the intellect and reason to get the job done. The relationship of will to intellect then seems more extrinsic. Not so in the creative act. Bergson seems correct when he says: "A work of genius is in most cases the outcome of an emotion, unique of its kind, which seemed to baffle expression, and yet which *had* to express itself."[27] Bergson thinks this is true of all work into which there enters some degree of inventiveness. There is an emotion which not only precedes the final result, but "which virtually contains it, and is to a certain extent its cause."[28] To illustrate this, he turns to the experience of any writer who has felt the difference between "an intelligence left to itself and that which burns with the fire of an original and unique emotion." In the first instance, the mind "coldhammers" the materials. "In the second, it would seem that the solid materials supplied by intelligence first melt and mix, then solidify again into fresh ideas now shaped by the creative mind itself."[29]

In the creative moment, the writer is buoyed and carried by this emotion. There is an element of eruption and excitement in the work. The emotion is central, not peripheral to the experience. We probably experience no closer collaboration of emotion and intellect, for the act is one of understanding in a thoroughly intellectual way. Yet it is also an ecstatic, excited act, and an explosion of joy. André

Marie Ampère, for whom the unit of electrical current is named, describes a moment of mathematical discovery with the words: "I gave a shout of joy."[30] We see Archimedes running from his bath and shouting: "Eureka!" Koestler, I believe inaccurately, sees this explosion as a release of energies that have now become redundant since the problem to which they were directed is solved. "The Eureka cry is the explosion of energies which must find an outlet since the purpose for which they have been mobilized no longer exists. . . ."[31] This seems as inaccurate as describing sexual orgasm as the release of energies that have become redundant at the end of love-making. The orgasm and the love play are a continuum. Similarly the emotions from which creativity issues relate uninterruptedly to the joy of discovery. As soon as intellection assumes a creative tack, emotion and intellect are blended and the joy of completion is the organically related sequel to the desire that animated and sustained the creative process. This is present in all creative work. Creativity is imaginative insight born of the emotions of love and desire.

In instances of moral creativity, this relates to the foundational moral experience. This experience of the value of persons and their environment, in creative moments, reaches more deeply into the mystery of the human and finds what was hitherto missed. The English Quakers in 1802 won exemption from military service on the grounds of the rights of conscience. The passage of time obscures the splendor of their creative achievement. What they convinced the English state to do was to grant civil status to a position of conscience that was deemed wrong by that same state. Previous ethical thinking had taught that the person may have a right to feel this way but the state has a right to coerce. The fact that the state was made to yield to the contradicting conscience of individuals in this instance was a major leap forward and an important relativization of the tendentially divine pretensions of all states. The Quakers' success here was a creative application of the foundational moral experience. Their discovery that persons merit this was not simply comparable to the discovery of Newton or Archimedes. The knowledge advanced in this case was more formally affective. No sterile syllogisms or dry analyses yielded this revolutionary conclusion. It was the fruit of awareness and intelligence working through feeling and was a typical example of creative imagination at work in the civilizing, moral process.

Every such advance in the application of the foundational moral experience to human life is creation. And it is to be noted that the affective foundations of creation in the moral life are more obvious than they usually are in other discoveries. They are distinguished too because of their grounding in that affective faith process that is the basis of moral consciousness.

The Conditions for Moral Creativity . . .

Excitement is the precondition for all success; it is also the first condition for moral creativity. Without it there will be no creative stirrings. Some years ago, Ronald A. Knox wrote a book about various forms of religious enthusiasm, many of which fell into deviant excess. He called the book *Enthusiasm*. As if to redeem the virtue that was his title, he concluded his book with a quotation from *La Princesse Lointaine*, which said that when all is said, there is really only one vice, indolence or inertia. Likewise there is really only one virtue, and that is enthusiasm![32]

Creativity has fiery roots. In morality, only those who are alive with humanizing love and care will lead us across new thresholds or expand the horizons of moral consciousness. The apathetic are constitutionally disqualified, and even if they are "decent" by the accepted mores, they will never do any more than dicker within fixed and morally imprisoning limits.

The moral creator comes within the realm of what is called the "daimonic." "The Daimonic," as Rollo May explains, *"is any natural function which has the power to take over the whole person.* Sex and eros, anger and rage, and the craving for power are examples." The "daimon," for the Greeks,

> included the creativity of the poet and artist as well as that of the ethical and religious leader, and is the contagious power which the lover has. Plato argued that ecstasy, a "divine madness," seizes the creative person. This is an early form of the puzzling and never-solved problem of the intimate relationship between the genius and the madman. . . .[33]

The daimonic will be seen in morally creative times as well as in morally creative persons, and the daimonic is excited, enthusiastic, and often unsettling. Morally progressive times and persons are usually disturbing and the forces of moral conservatism react violently.

Moral innovators are forced to drink hemlock or are crucified in one fashion or another. Take, for example, the period of the 1960s in the United States (and in other parts of the world) which was looked on as the worst of times and yet was in some important ways the best of times. These were excited times and the excitement was not without meaning. The most creative moral movement in the American society was probably the civil rights movement. This enthusiastic assault on racism encouraged and helped shape the woman's movement and the struggle for rights among other minorities. Also, in the exciting charisma of that period, oracles too long unchallenged in Church and State were re-evaluated. Dissident resistance to war-making as policy acquired a new legitimacy. Dust-covered assumptions about the meaning of success, authority, power, the sacred, and peace were freshly scrutinized in the melee. In the enthusiasm of the period, it was thought that more was done than could be done, and the greening of the society was naïvely and prematurely announced. Likewise, the awful power of retrenchment was underestimated. Still there was slight but significant turning of the enormous worm, and some of the effects of that turning have perdured into the graying period of retrenchment in the 1970s.

The period of the sixties illustrates some aspects of the social excitement that marks creative moral shifts. First, the development is to a large degree inarticulate. What is going on is a massive shift of affect. Persons begin caring about different things, or caring in a different way. Much of the rhetoric and much of the theory that arises from the movement is likely to be amiss. There will be an abundance of apocrypha, and the true gospels of the movement, if they emerge, will only come later.

Second, the creative period is likely to be highly romantic, not to say confused in its manifestation. This is the price of enthusiasm.

Third, the creative moment can be easily lost. Excitement is not easily sustained; neither is the creativity it heralds and marks easily translated into attitudes and social forms that give it the grace of survival. The high moment can pass because moral creativity clashes with the reigning canons of meaning. As Bergson says,

> Most great reforms appeared at first sight impracticable, as in fact they were. They could be carried out only in a society whose state of mind was already such as their realization was bound to bring about; and you had a circle from which there would have been no escape, if one or several

privileged beings, having expanded the social ego within themselves, had not broken the circle and drawn the society after them.[34]

Bergson notes how this happens in art also.

A work of genius which is at first disconcerting may create, little by little, by the simple fact of its presence, a conception of art and an artistic atmosphere which bring it within our comprehension; it will then become in retrospect a work of genius; otherwise it would have remained what it was at the beginning, merely disconcerting.[35]

Obviously, then, there is an element of risk in creativity. Not every artistic masterpiece, we may assume, revolutionizes the aesthetic atmosphere creating a context receptive to its genius. Neither does every great moral movement produce the "privileged beings" who can draw the whole of society after them. Insight of the most creative sort is pathetically perishable.

In apparent contradiction to the first condition of creativity, excitement, the second is quiet and passivity. The contradiction is only apparent. Excitement is not the exclusive property of action. Moments of high receptivity may be exquisitely exciting, and receptivity is a factor in creativity. It may be, as George Bernard Shaw felt, that creation is 90 per cent perspiration and 10 per cent inspiration, but no one who thinks about creativity will entirely slight the muse. The sense of receiving is strong, as in Picasso's "I do not seek—I find!" What Jacques Maritain says of artistic experience meshes well with creativity in general. There is motion in artistic creation, says Maritain . . . the motion that puts notes on scores or color on canvas but the experience "is of itself a sort of natural contemplation, obscure and affective, and implies a moment of silence and alert receptivity."[36] In a similar vein is Robert Henri:

The object, which is back of every true work of art, is the attainment of a state of being, a state of high functioning, a more than ordinary moment of existence. In such moments activity is inevitable, and whether this activity is with brush, pen, chisel, or tongue, its result is but a byproduct of the state, a trace, the footprint of the state.[37]

Notice that the passivity is not inertness. Henri paradoxically calls creative receptivity a "state of being" and "a state of high functioning." Maritain speaks of "alert receptivity." The stillness of creativity

is one of the ecstatic intensity of life. It has nothing in common with
the leaden stillness of death.

There is an important word here for ethics. Ethics could deafen itself with the noise of its own work. If we think that knowing is
something that we *do*, then pragmatic pressure is the route to wisdom. Josef Pieper attacks the influential Immanuel Kant on precisely this point. For Kant, knowledge is discursive, not intuitive.
"The reason cannot intuit anything."[38] This has been seen as "the
most momentous dogmatic assumption of Kantian epistemology."[39]
Because of this assumption, knowing and philosophizing for Kant
are *work*. Knowledge is realized by comparing, examining, relating,
distinguishing, abstracting, deducing, and demonstrating—that is,
by active intellectual effort. Kant had scorn for those who felt
romantically that they need only listen to the oracle within one's
breast. For Kant, reason acquires its possessions through work. Thus
he could admire Aristotle, whose philosophy was work. The weight
of this view is heavy upon modern ethics. Pieper parts with Kant and
looks back to a fuller wisdom.

> The Greeks—Aristotle no less than Plato—as well as the
> great medieval thinkers, held that not only physical, sensu-
> ous perception, but equally man's spiritual and intellectual
> knowledge, included an element of pure, receptive contem-
> plation, or as Heraclitus says, of "listening to the essence of
> things."[40]

In medieval philosophy, a distinction was drawn between understanding as *ratio* and understanding as *intellectus*. *Ratio* does the
work that Kant admired. It searches, defines, examines, and draws
conclusions. Intellectus, however, is intuitive, offering "that simple
vision to which truth offers itself like a landscape to the eye."[41] It
was *intellectus* that was considered divine by the philosophers of antiquity and the Middle Ages just as divinity was attached to creative
power in antiquity. And it is clear that for this highest intellectual
power to be actualized, there must be some repose from the tumult
of the worker-mind.

This relates to what Aristotle alluded to when he said that the
highest forms of knowledge were discovered "first in the places
where men first began to have leisure. This is why the mathematical
arts were founded in Egypt; for there the priestly caste was allowed
to be at leisure."[42] The historical recognition of this is illustrated by

the history of the Greek word for leisure—*skole,* from which derives the English word "school." In Latin, too, the word for leisure was *otium;* for work, one term was *negotium*—the denial of leisure. For Aristotle, it was obvious that leisure was a primary value. It stands above work. Work is not our highest achievement; rather, "we are occupied that we may have leisure."[43]

This leisure, of course, is not just idleness. In his *Leisure: The Basis of Culture,* Pieper describes it as a kind of inner calm that lets things happen.

> Leisure is a form of silence, of that silence which is the prerequisite of the apprehension of reality: Only the silent hear and those who do not remain silent do not hear. Silence, as it is used in this context, does not mean "dumbness" or "noiselessness"; it means more nearly that the soul's power to "answer" to the reality of the world is left undisturbed.[44]

There is a message here for us who live and do ethics in a society which glorifies work. We have inverted the priorities between work and leisure, between *pragma* and *skole.* Aristotle saw work as something that prepared the way for leisure; we see it as restorative for work. Leisure is not our forte. The "leisure" we have is more busy than work and as noisy.

This shows up in much of our academe where cultural values are mirrored. The humanities are on the defensive. The pragmatic arts and sciences, which Aristotle said developed understandably before men had leisure since they responded to necessities, enjoy a primacy. These are the work-arts in a work-society. The arts of contemplation, for which in the view of Aristotle the work-arts should clear the way, are suspect. Similarly, the minuscule budget of the National Endowment of the Humanities illustrates that on the federal scene too we put our treasure where our heart is, and withhold it where the heart is not. All of this is symbolic of a cultural setting in which the intellectual need for silence, receptivity, and contemplation is not a felt need. It signals a culture of *ratio,* not of *intellectus.* One would look to such a culture for achievements, rather than for wisdom. Moral knowledge is wisdom. It comes within the province of the contemplative arts.

With all this said, however, it must be insisted that the next condition for creativity is nothing other than *work.* If fortune favors the prepared mind, it is work that gives much of the preparation. If creativity involves, among other things, the discovery of latent connections, then the more you know about what are connected, the more qualified you are to discover *that* they connect. Creativity is a power to discern the possible within the actual, and so the more attuned you are to what is—as long as you do not conclude that nothing else could be—the more readied you are to see what might be.

To make creative break-throughs regarding more humane modes of modern government, for example, we have a terrible dependency on those who study government and know it well. The dependency is terrible because those who study in any field tend to huddle into clubs and into eyebrow-arching orthodoxies. Also, expertise tends to cause reverse-telescopic vision, by fixating attention on the immediate target of the expertise and bypassing other essential dimensions of the problem. Of such stuff, creativity is not made. In fact, it constitutes a major hazard to the liberation of the creative spirit.

When Darwin's theory of evolution was first read to a group of his peers, they yawned. And at the end of that year the president of the Linnean Society, for which the paper was presented, wrote in his annual report that "the year which has passed . . . has not, indeed, been marked by any of those striking discoveries which at once revolutionize, so to speak, the department of science on which they bear."[45] Darwin persisted and turned their world upside down.

David Hume, who eventually was to be recognized as a major philosophical critic, says that his *Treatise of Human Nature* when published in 1738 "fell dead-born from the press, without reaching such distinction as even to excite a murmur among the zealots." And when he recast and published in 1752 what he considered to be his most important work on morals, "it came unnoticed and unobserved into the world."[46]

Yet, for any creative moral advance, those who are expert in the realities of the situation are at the edge where the cutting could occur. Again the humanization of governmental structures cannot proceed apart from those who know those structures. It can also not be achieved by them alone. Government is a vast human enterprise which now has unavoidably international dimensions. No serious reform should be expected by those in the "club" of governmental expertise operating alone. There would be too many paralyzing vested interests and too much fixated vision. Much as it would gall the experts, other voices must be heard who would be sensitive to human aspects of the subject to which the experts have long been inured.

A still fledgling development in medical ethics illustrates the way of creative improvement. In recent years, medicine has recognized that the ramifications of its work go well beyond what could be called medical science. Interdisciplinary centers for the study of medical value questions have been founded such as the Society for Health and Human Values and the Institute of Society, Ethics and the Life Sciences. Broad-ranged publications on moral issues have begun to appear. The principal journals of the medical field have been opening their pages more and more to ethical discussions. And, more importantly, many medical schools have moved away from a purely technical training of physicians by including ethics and other humanities in their regular curriculum.

So far, the concern in all of this has been more with the tantalizing aspects of medico-moral conundrums rather than with a creative rethinking of what medical care should be in a humane society. Still, value-consciousness is returning to medicine, and the climate is less congenial to narrowly technical treatments of medical questions. Scientific expertise and broader philosophical theory are coming tentatively closer there than in many of the areas of the sciences and social sciences. The conditions for moral creativity are "in tiny leaf."

Among the conditions conducive to creativity, I have thus far listed *excitement, quiet,* and *work.* A fourth condition is *malleability.* The term is used to apply both to individual personality and to cultural setting. A closed, classical culture in which it is thought that the answers are all in is geared to produce only more of the same. A culture healthfully subverted by questions and unsettled by value collisions is fertile ground for creative thought. In other words, for creativity, agitation is preferable to inert serenity.

Arnold Toynbee has an intriguing theory that is relevant here. In studying the origin of "higher religions" (those that do not direct worship to nature or society), he observes that "when we mark down the birthplaces of the higher religions on a map, we find them clustering in and around two relatively small patches of the total landsurface of the Old World—on the one hand the Oxus-Jaxartes Basin and on the other hand Syria. . . ."[47]

Toynbee did not let this pass as a coincidence, creative historian that he was. He searched for something that the two small regions would have in common that would make them so spiritually fruitful.

His conclusion: "This prominent common feature of Syria and the Oxus-Jaxartes Basin is the capacity, with which each of them had been endowed by nature, for serving as a 'roundabout' where traffic coming in from any point of the compass could be switched to any other point of the compass in any number of alternative combinations and permutations."[48] This geographic fact resulted in "exceptionally active intercourse between civilizations in these two areas."[49] Toynbee concluded from this that the law for the development of higher religions was that there must be a setting in which cultural experiences and diverse world views were in collision. Only then could deeper answers be sought or found.

And not only were these two "numeniferous" regions fruitful in the development of religious thought; they were also politically fecund in that each of them was included in a series of universal states, or in other empires performing similar social functions, that had been thrown up by those colliding civilizations in the course of their histories."[50] Political life developed there as well as religious life.

A placid cultural setting where no major questions are outstanding, where agreement on the main values of life have gelled, will stimulate no creative movement in personal or social moral consciousness. The native tendency of the mind to take its ease when ease is offered will be acted out. Only in the presence of serious dissent can we expect to be pressed to break camp and move to higher terrain. If contemporary America is ill-suited to creative moral thought by reason of the absence of quiet and genuine leisure, it is outstandingly prepared by reason of the presence of radical questioning. The Oxus-Jaxartes valley is our home. What brittle consensus on values we achieved in the past is shattered. The caravans of new ideas are coming at us from every direction. This could lead to a situation in which one could become, in the contemporary idiom, "unglued"; or one might profit from the cultural malleability and be moved to look for the answers that lie just beyond the melee. What the Oxus-Jaxartes mood does is to remove any premature notion of completeness or any sloth-serving impressions that reality is a *fait accompli* rather than an incipient process to be tackled creatively. Serious dissent modifies the "already" with the "not yet." It enables us to believe, with John of Patmos, that "it has not yet appeared what we will be."[51]

Those who believe that what we will be or can be has already appeared will view creative moral thinking as a heresy against the established sense of the status quo. Persons or cultures in which a sense of the "not yet" is lacking are disenfranchised from creativeness.

Moving on from *excitement, quiet, work,* and *malleability,* a fifth condition for creativity is what we can call, with hedged apology, *kairos.* The hedged apology is evinced because every departure from the enormous richness of the English language must be on the defensive to show that it is not a failure of imagination, a pedantic flourish, or a sin of obscurantism. I submit that *kairos* is rich enough to be brought in from the Greek intact and naturalized as a linguistic tool in English. *Kairos* can be translated "time," but that is precisely why we need the Greek word. Time for us tends to mean chronological time . . . for which the Greeks had a special word, *chronos. Kairos,* on the contrary, means time as a moment filled with special and opportune content. Obsessed as we moderns are with chronology, having organized life around the clock, it is hard to envision that, for many of the ancients, time was not primarily a matter of succession, but of content. The names for months, for example, often described what happened in those months . . . the month of ripening ears, the month of flowers, the months of perennial streams, etc.

It is from a linguistic world like this that *kairos* comes. *Kairos* is the time when the circumstances are such that *opportunity* is presented to us. A sense of *kairos* is a sense of knowing when the time is ripe for the new. Involved too is a sense that when the circumstances are not ready, all creative effort is doomed to sterility. It is the sense of *kairos* that we see in Friedrich Engels when he with some overstatement approves the idea "that revolutions are not made intentionally and arbitrarily, but that they were always and everywhere the necessary result of circumstances entirely independent of the will and guidance of particular parties and whole classes."[52] Reflecting back on the preparatory role of work for creativity, it might be well to remind Engels that, not always, but at times, the *kairos* can be helped along especially at the corporate and political level of life where decisions have a massive effect for good or ill. Still, the main message of *kairos* is watchful patience and a special alertness when the harbingers of opportunity begin to appear.

Of course, ripeness is not all, as Koestler points out in his *The Act of Creation.* The opportunity may ripen and languish unpicked upon the vine. Or it may wait a long time before the genius watches the apple and the moon and makes the connection or sees that the slave too is a man, or perceives that the state is not divine and that conscience is not a serf in the fiefdom of government.

It is also possible that the genius will arrive, draw the creative conclusion, and be ignored. This can happen in science. It can happen more easily in morality. Gilbert Keith Chesterton, commenting on the drab moral quality of most Christians, could comment that Christianity had not failed; it simply had never been tried. There is more than the telling *bon mot* here. A creative moment in morality can have a long infancy. Lip service can be paid to it. Pomp and circumstance can attend it, and yet its demanding vitality is such that it is successfully repressed and not admitted into full communion with the lesser ideas that rule with jealous hegemony.

Withal, there is *kairos*, and the creative rise to its scent. In *The Structure of Scientific Revolutions*, Thomas Kuhn argues that creative moments occur on the occasion of an impasse. In science, for example, new problems can arise that cannot be solved by the established logic. No matter what the scientist tries, the solutions elude him. When this happens, it means that the prevailing scientific paradigm is proved inadequate and must be abandoned. It is the time for rejecting the old models of thought and inventing new ones. This is so, says Kuhn, even beyond science: "Just as scientific revolutions are inaugurated by a growing sense that the existing paradigm has ceased to function adequately, political revolutions are inaugurated by a growing sense that the existing institutions have ceased adequately to meet the problems posed by an environment that they have in part created."[53]

An example of impasse-opportunity can be found today regarding corporations. Professor Christopher Stone, author of *Where the Law Ends: The Social Control of Corporate Behavior*, remarks that "every area of American Law has been outmoded by this new phenomenon, the corporation."[54] Tort law could do fine, for example, for cases where one man struck another. It is not at all suited for handling cases where several corporations so pollute the environment that a number of persons die but only after some fifteen or twenty years. Corporations can pollute, allocate funds for the routine payment of fines, and go right on polluting. Stone has a number of suggestions for a creative reaction to this impasse. For example, the court could appoint in the corporation a temporary vice-president for environmental affairs, who would be an acknowledged expert in this field, give him special powers, and keep him in office until socially responsible procedures have been established. In other words, instead of just slapping futilely at corporations who are large enough to react less than does an elephant to a fly, society could enter into the managerial structure of the offending corporation and redirect policy.

The idea would seem to be one whose time has come. Society after all may enter into the structure of a family appointing guardians other than the parents when social and individual good require it. And a family is really a private enterprise. Corporations are not really private enterprises. What they do may enter into our lungs and blood streams and affect the genetic structure of our children. That makes a corporation a very public enterprise. As a rule of thumb, one would expect corporations to react to Professor Stone's suggestion with the enthusiasm that Caesar would have shown to the idea of a parliament. There is, of course, no simplicity to this problem or to any solution, but the time seems ripe because of the current impasse to create new ways of dealing with this new situation so that social good and vigorous business could blend. It may be time for corporate business to learn, in Stone's words, "that if the public interest is paramount, everyone, including the corporations, will prosper."[55]

The sense of *kairos* should also, by reason of impasse, at this time be eliciting creative response from the international community. For example, though there is still some nostalgic passion for it, the United States is forbidden by the facts from indulging in isolationist fantasies. Until recent years, we celebrated the advantage of the two great oceans that cut us off from the travail of the rest of the world. Aside from the hostile tribalism betrayed by such sentiments, we are now factually implicated with all that goes on beyond those oceans and even at the floor of those oceans.

> Twenty years ago the United States was virtually self-sufficient in the essential raw materials needed for industrial production. According to the National Materials Policy Commission, the United States will, by the year 2000 depend on imports for more than 80 percent of these materials.[56]

Realistic and creative policies that acknowledge that national independence is passé would grow out of this situation. As the *Second Report of the Club of Rome* says, "Cooperation is no longer a

schoolroom word suggesting an ethical but elusive mode of behavior;
cooperation is a scientifically supportable, politically viable, and absolutely essential mode of behavior for the organic growth of the
world system."[57] Here survival needs are forcing us to new frontiers.
Creativity will enter in, if it does, by fashioning the preternational
forms and structures that will with a terrible struggle begin to transcend the tribal instincts of nation-states and the profit-monism of
international corporations.

Aside from the exigencies of practical impasse, creativity may be
stimulated by the perceived preciousness of one alternative that may
be lost if creativity does not come to the rescue. Here creativity is
the child of love, and of love's need to hold fast. An example: Some
years ago, at the Catholic University of America I presented a case to
a class and asked them to illustrate their approach to ethics by exploring all of its implications. The case was that of a hypothetical
lady, one Mary Malfortuna. I presented it in this fashion:

> Mary was a strikingly beautiful woman who was also very
> sensitive and gentle of spirit. She had been married for
> some six years to Tim. Tim was not very beautiful. He was
> three inches shorter than Mary, bald, and a bit rotund. Per-
> sonally, he was lovable and Mary loved him. In the early
> years of their relationship, Tim had been neurotically inse-
> cure, simply unable to believe that this beautiful woman
> loved him as he loved her. His jealousy was a torture, ut-
> terly unwarranted, and strained the stability of the mar-
> riage. Mary, however, was exquisitely patient, and after two
> children and six years, Tim had come to believe, in peace,
> that Mary Malfortuna loved him. Tim, in fact, was so
> happy that he neglected his health and became quite ill
> with tuberculosis, requiring hospitalization for up to six
> months. Mary rose to the occasion, got a part-time job,
> cared for the children, and rushed back and forth to visit
> Tim. After some months of this some of her old friends
> sent over a baby-sitter and prevailed on Mary to join them
> for a fun evening. Unfortunately, the bartender had a
> heavy hand, and Mary, tired and elated as she was, overin-
> dulged. An old friend, with whom she had had a brief but
> intense intimacy, long before her marriage to Tim, drove
> Mary home. There was talk of old times, laughter, and with
> one thing leading to another, Mary and her friend impul-
> sively made love. As luck would have it, Mary Malfortuna

got pregnant. The question was, should Mary have an abortion or risk the destruction of her happy marriage? Mary was uneasy about the prospect of abortion but not entirely opposed to the idea. She felt that some abortions are morally justifiable.

One of the students who reacted to this case was a Catholic nun. Though theoretically convinced that abortion might at times be moral, her affective response to any abortion was decidedly negative. Her reply is not presented as "the right answer," for in an exclusive sense there is often no such thing in ethics. Rather her reaction illustrates the arousal of the imagination in defense of what is felt as precious. Again in summary, her answer was this:

> When active persons go through an illness with a prolonged period of convalescence and forced inactivity, it is often thought helpful to suggest counseling and therapy to help with adjustment and prepare for the gradual transition to active life. Rather than aborting, Mary could first of all go to the counselor or therapist and reveal the problem. After Tim had a comfortable relationship with the counselor, Mary could reveal her pained situation to him, anticipating the supportive backup of the counselor. She could explain that she did not opt for abortion though this was easily feasible, because she did not want to face any crisis alone without Tim . . . even this one that she had brought on herself. She could say that she decided that their marriage was strong enough to take this, and ask that Tim's love take the form of mercy . . . something that she needed now from Tim more than anything she ever needed or asked in their years of love together. Knowing that she could have hidden the event from him, Tim would actually have greater reason to trust her and believe in her love. Stronger than the suspicion—"If she did this once, then she etc. . . ."— would be the realization that "if she could tell me this, she could tell me anything." Also, since he did love her, his desire to ease her pain by complete forgiveness would be the dominant emotion. Finally, in a unique way in their marital history, Tim would be in the position of strength, giving support where support was desperately needed.

The reply is not given as infallible, but as illustrative of imagination at work in defense of a perceived value. The solution may indeed have been wrong and the revelation of the indiscretion plus the child that came from it may have been enough to end the possibilities of that marriage. And maybe a quick, private abortion would have been better. On the other hand, the proposed solution did develop a possible alternative and thus enlarge, as imagination should do, the ethical consideration of the case. Imagination will do this when someone cares enough about one of the value alternatives. Love is the mother and father of invention.

Beyond this particular case, it is clear that a lack of imagination is often traceable to a lack of love. It betokens a lack of caring about one or more of the elements of the ethical equation. This shows further the grounding of moral imagination in the affective foundational moral experience. A weakness at that level makes for a dearth of imagination in the facing of specific issues.

The final condition for moral creativity could be called *at-home-ness*, or the absence of alienation. The process of alienation is completely antithetical to the process of moral creation. Creation expands and reaches out; alienation cringes and turns in. Moral creation is a force of integration which connects the previously unconnected in the direction of greater and deeper unity. Alienation is disintegration and a lived repudiation of the foundational moral experience. Creative power grows out of and enhances kinship with all that is. To be converted from our alienation from the persons and things of earth, to break down the artificial barriers that we build and revere on the basis of nation, race, sex, status, or age, is to be readied for creativity. It prepares you to know what only those who are and feel at home can know. A stranger could not know *what is*, much less *what could be* in a home.

H. Richard Niebuhr expresses the experience of at-home-ness:

> . . . we were blind in our distrust of being, now we begin to see; we were aliens and alienated in a strange, empty world, now we begin sometimes to feel at home; we were in love with ourselves and all our little cities, now we are falling in love, we think with being itself. . . .[58]

Niebuhr sees that this leads to "an ethics of universal responsibility." As such, "it is the ethos of citizenship in a universal society, in which no being that exists and no action that takes place is interpretable outside the universal context."[59] Alienation is the natural enemy of such an ethics. Creativity, on the contrary, would be its natural child.

Imagination Astray . . .

Nothing is so sacred that it cannot be profaned. Creative imagination, seen by the ancients as a divine power housed in us, can be diverted. We can be monstrously as well as morally imaginative. The present world arsenal with its capacity to blot out all life on the planet many times over is a macabre tribute to the misuse of imagination. And with all of this achieved, evil imagination is not still. Farfetched schemes are theoretically probed about more diversified modes of killing, including such things as guided tidal waves, changes effected in the electrical environment to affect brain performance, laser death rays, and almost unstoppable, computerized, robot "tanks" containing a rich repertoire of nuclear and other kill-power.[60]

J. Bronowski says that his study of the creative mind began in 1945 when he was driven in a United States jeep through the ashy ruins of Nagasaki. It was night and he had not sensed right away that he had moved from the open country to the "city." The city was a dark and desolate ruin. The only sound he heard was that of an American military radio playing the popular tune "Is You Is or Is You Ain't Ma Baby?" It was a peak moment of truth for Bronowski. What he saw in it was "civilization face to face with its own implications. The implications are both the industrial slum which Nagasaki was before it was bombed, and the ashy desolation which the bomb made of the slum. And civilization asks of both ruins, 'Is You Is or Is You Ain't Ma Baby?'"[61] The question required distinct answers. The slum mainly represented a failure of imagination. The "ashy desolation" was the fruit of perverse imagination.

The extinction of life on our planet is no longer an apocalyptic dream. It is now a scientific possibility. Imagination can enhance life, or end it. Bronowski asks: "Has science fastened upon our society a monstrous gift of destruction which we can neither undo nor master, and which, like a clockwork automaton in a nightmare, is set to break our necks? Is science an automaton, and has it lamed our sense of values?"[62]

Science of course cannot be blamed for the perversions of our possibilities. Science is the errand boy of the culture, and does the culture's bidding. In that same culture there is the tender but hope-filled power of moral imagination, our primatial talent as moral beings. That exquisite power is the source of whatever humanizing good the future of persons might hold. Human redemption is only achieved through the grace of creative moral imagination.

NOTES—CHAPTER SIX

1. Rubem A. Alves, *Tomorrow's Child* (New York: Harper & Row, 1972), pp. 67–68.
2. J. Bronowski, *Science and Human Values* (Harper & Row, Harper Torchbook, 1965), p. 15.
3. Ibid.
4. Ibid.
5. Ibid., p. 13.
6. Ibid.
7. Ibid., p. 18. Bronowski says: "The discoveries of science, the works of art are explorations—more, are explosions, of a hidden likeness" (p. 19).
8. Arthur Koestler, *The Act of Creation* (New York: Dell Publishing Co., Laurel Edition, 1967), p. 96.
9. Ibid., p. 27.
10. Ibid., p. 123.
11. Ibid., p. 109.
12. Ibid., p. 144.
13. Ibid., p. 156.
14. Ibid., p. 157.
15. Henri Bergson, *The Two Sources of Morality and Religion* (Garden City, N.Y.: Doubleday & Co., Inc., Anchor Books, 1956), pp. 76, 78.
16. Ibid., p. 78.
17. Hannah Arendt, *The Human Condition* (Garden City, N.Y.: Doubleday & Co., Inc., Anchor Books, 1959), p. 289.
18. Ibid., p. 291.
19. Cyril Burt, foreword to Koestler, *Act of Creation*, p. 13.
20. John R. Platt, *The Excitement of Science* (Boston: Houghton Mifflin Co., 1962), pp. 64–65.
21. See Koestler, *Act of Creation*, p. 158. See Platt, *Excitement of Science*, p. 76.
22. Nicolas Berdyaev, *The Destiny of Man* (New York and Evanston: Harper & Row, Harper Torchbook, 1960), p. 136.

23. Loren Eiseley, *The Firmament of Time* (New York: Atheneum, 1960), pp. 4–5.
24. Platt, *Excitement of Science*, p. 8.
25. Ibid., pp. 75–76.
26. Bergson, *Two Sources of Morality and Religion*, p. 43.
27. Ibid., p. 46.
28. Ibid., p. 47.
29. Ibid., p. 46.
30. Quoted in Koestler, *Act of Creation*, p. 17.
31. Ibid., p. 88.
32. Ronald A. Knox, *Enthusiasm: A Chapter in the History of Religion* (New York: Oxford University Press, 1961), p. 591.

>   FRÈRE TROPHIME: *L'inertie est le seul vice, Maître Erasme;*
>   *Et la seule vertu est . . .*
>   ERASME: *Quoi?*
>   FRÈRE TROPHIME: *L'enthousiasme!*

33. Rollo May, *Love and Will* (New York: W. W. Norton & Co., 1969), pp. 123–24.
34. Bergson, *Two Sources of Morality and Religion*, pp. 74–75.
35. Ibid., p. 75.
36. Jacques Maritain, *Creative Intuition in Art and Poetry* (New York: Meridian Books, 1955), p. 188.
37. Quoted ibid., pp. 187–88.
38. Immanuel Kant, *Kritik der Reinen Vernunft*, edited by R. Schmidt (Leipzig, 1944), p. 95; quoted in Josef Pieper, *Leisure the Basis of Culture* (New York: New American Library, Mentor-Omega Book, 1963), p. 25.
39. Bernhard Jansen, *Die Geschichte der Erkenntnislehre in der Neueren Philosophie* (1940), p. 235; quoted ibid.
40. Pieper, *Leisure*, p. 26. The reference to Heraclitus is Fragment 112 (Diels).
41. Ibid.
42. Aristotle, *Metaphysics*, Bk. I, Chap. 1, 981b, 22.
43. Aristotle, *Nichomachean Ethics*, Bk. 10, Chap. 7, 1177b, 5.
44. Pieper, *Leisure*, p. 41.
45. Quoted in Koestler, *Act of Creation*, p. 142.
46. Quoted in A. D. Lindsay, "Introduction to Volume I," in David Hume, *A Treatise of Human Nature* (New York: Dutton, Everyman's Library, 1964), p. vii.
47. Arnold J. Toynbee, *A Study of History*, Vol. 8 (New York: Oxford University Press, A Galaxy Book, 1963), p. 90. He is speaking of Syria "in the broad sense in which this term had been used, in the vocabulary of physical geography, to cover an area bounded by the North Arabian Steppe, the Mediterranean Sea, and the southern es-

carpments of the Anatolian and Armenian plateaux." The Oxus-Jax-artes Basin is in Central Asia.

48. Ibid., p. 91.

49. Ibid., p. 97.

50. Ibid., p. 92. For example, since the sixth century B.C., "The Oxus-Jax-artes Basin had been included successively in four full-blown universal states—the Achaemedian Empire, the Arab Caliphate, the Mongol Empire, and the Russian Empire—and in three other empires—the Seleucid, the Bactrian Greek, and the Kushan . . ." (ibid., p. 96).

51. I John 3:2. In Christian experience the idea of the reign or kingdom of God was heavy with a sense of the "not yet." There were two beliefs basic to the theology of the reign of God, one in the present tense and one in the future. First, it is believed that God is actively at work in the present, building a new earth and inviting us to join in the adventure. Second, in the spirit of "it has not yet appeared what we will be," the present is relativized by what is yet to be achieved. This was the subversive core of Christianity. It de-divinized the status quo.

52. Friedrich Engels, quoted from a manuscript of 1847 in Hannah Arendt, *On Violence* (New York: Harcourt, Brace & World, Inc., 1969, 1970), p. 12.

53. Thomas Kuhn, *The Structure of Scientific Revolution* (Chicago: University of Chicago Press, 1966), pp. 91–92. See also F. S. C. Northrop, *The Logic of the Sciences and the Humanities* (New York: Meridian Books, 1959), p. 17, where he notes that "inquiry starts only when something is unsatisfactory. . . ." Similarly, see Morris R. Cohen and Ernest Nagel, *An Introduction to Logic and Scientific Method* (New York: Harcourt, Brace & World, 1934), p. 392.

54. Christopher D. Stone, "The Corporate Fix," *Center Magazine*, 9, No. 4 (July–Aug. 1976), p. 20. The article is drawn from a discussion conducted by Mr. Stone at the Center for the Study of Democratic Institutions.

55. Ibid., p. 22.

56. Mihajlo Mesarovic and Eduard Pestel, *Mankind at the Turning Point: The Second Report to the Club of Rome* (New York: New American Library, A Signet Book, 1976), p. 84.

57. Ibid., p. 111.

58. H. Richard Niebuhr, *The Responsible Self* (New York: Harper & Row, 1963), pp. 177–78.

59. Ibid., p. 167.

60. See the chilling book edited by Nigel Calder, *Unless Peace Comes* (New York: Viking Press, 1968). A number of experts in this vol-

ume discuss the sick possibilities that are not beyond the reach of science.

61. Bronowski, *Science and Human Values*, pp. 3–4.
62. Ibid., pp. 69–70.

CHAPTER SEVEN

CONSISTENCY AND SURPRISE

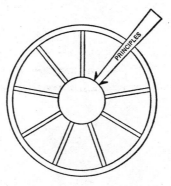

In today's ethical climate, moral principles are under regular attack
. . . almost, it would appear, on principle. Anyone who prizes the
moral constancies housed in principles is liable to charges of having a
classicist mentality, contextual insensitivity, a natural law bias, or
some related blight. Sometimes the charges have grounds. But sometimes they flow from the mood of a time in which flux has been
normalized and change is felt to be so promising that constancy is
suspect . . . whether it be in the form of principle, personal commitment (marriage or any form of loyalty), tradition, or whatever wears
the badge of established respectability.

The pendulum is an apt symbol of intellectual life and of our
tendency to go from one extreme to another. There is excess in the
reaction against principled moral wisdom, but that excess is a reaction against an excess that was. In the past, we had too much

confidence in our ability to imprison reality in our generalizations. Ultimately moral values are rooted in touchable persons and things. Moral principles are intellectual generalizations. They instruct and they prevent superficial reactions based on *prima facie* evidence. But again, "human actions are good or bad according to the circumstances." Because of this, there is an element of the unique and the unrepeatable in every moral case. Not all moral meaning is generalizable. And yet there is valid generalization.

The human mind is engaged full-time in making sense and keeping confusion at bay. Even while we sleep, the brain is active. It is badgered by literally billions of data. If all these data were unrelated and unalike, the mind, in self-defense, would go mad. Fortunately, it is equipped with a special talent for organizing the mass of images. The mind has both the power and the urge "to crack the kernel of the particular in order to liberate the universal."[1] It is able to discover those similarities that are the grounding of generalization. Generalization brings relief from the enormity of mental chaos that would obtain if there existed only atomistically individuated things, persons, and events . . . unrelated and unalike. We make sense of reality by finding illuminating patterns and common denominators. "From one learn all" (*ex uno disce omnes*), said the ancients, and in valid generalization, this is to an extent done.

Beyond this you can also say (which the ancients did not say in so many words), "From all learn one." You learn about the forest from the tree and about the tree from the forest. The universal that we liberate by cracking the kernel of the particular comes back to illumine the particular. In universalizing, we manage "to leap beyond, yet nearer bring" in Walt Whitman's phrase.[2] By seeing the individual reality in the light of comparison to that which is common, it becomes more understandable. Comparison reveals aspects that could be lost to the isolated gaze. The experienced attorney will see more in an individual case than his inexperienced colleagues because his broader base of comparison brings hidden likenesses to light. No amount of study of the individual case can yield the breadth of perspective that "general" knowledge makes possible. In fact, without valid generalizations there can be no perspective.

An age that denigrates principles is open to ethical shallowness. "Marry the spirit of the times, and you shall soon be a widow" is an old saying. Principles, by proffering the insights of our forebears and giving perspective, are a hedge against such bereavement. They protect us from ephemeral views that would otherwise be overwhelming in their influence. They relate to Santayana's truism that those who do not know history are destined to repeat it. Principles are the voice of history and the moral memory of the species. Without them we would be like an amnesiac, without history or perspective. Principles do not give us a blueprint of the present or of the future but they do broaden us with a sense of history, thus giving us some depth and making us less vulnerable in our admittedly fallible projections.

On the Distinctive Nature of Moral Principles . . .

What, then, are moral principles and what do they do for us in ethics? Moral principles are the repositories of the collective moral experience of our forebears. In philosopher John Dewey's words, they represent the "gathering together of experiences of value into generalized points of view."[3] He goes on: "Through intercommunication the experience of the entire human race is to some extent pooled and crystallized in general ideas. These ideas constitute *principles*."[4]

Moral principles, then, are culturally based propositions or generalizations about what befits or does not befit the behavior of human beings. In form, principles can be positive (Keep promises) or negative (Do not kill); very generic (Do good and avoid evil) or quite specific (Thou shalt not commit adultery).

Moral principles are not, of course, just empirical generalizations of the sort one finds outside of ethics. In mechanics, for example, one might come up with the principle that a particular engine will operate most efficiently at an incline of three degrees. This would be learned by observation of the performance of the engine at this and other angles of decline. Likewise, generalizations about the boiling point of various liquids can be based on simple uninvolved observation. This is not the way moral generalizations are derived.

Moral principles are as unique as moral experience itself. The experiencing and observing that produce them are not of the scientific sort. Moral principles are derivatives of the foundational moral experience and thus have their roots in affectivity and in faith as well as in observation, memory, and imagination. A moral principle expresses an influence drawn from the perceived value of persons and their environment. It is a conclusion about how persons should behave and be treated in view of their perceived value. Because of their value, they should not be killed, exploited, or deceived; and, positively, because of their value they deserve truth, fidelity, and caring, etc. Principles are the voiced specifications of the foundational moral experience.

Moral principles relate to creative imagination, since they preserve in propositional form the creative insights of the species on what does or does not enhance our evolution from barbarity toward genuine humanity. They are the creative insights that achieved tenured status in the culture. And so, again, moral principles are distinctive, as is moral imagination when compared, for example, to technological imagination. The difference is qualitative and points us beyond the quantifiable to the deeply personal roots of ethics.

The Empirical Roots of Ethics . . .

Though it is true that ethical principles are not derived in the manner of the principles of the physical or social sciences and cannot be thought of in that sense as merely "empirical generalization," it still remains true that moral experience is grounded and consummated in the empirical order. Principles do not come to us straight from the gods of Olympus or of Sinai, although principles often appear under religious auspices, and religions properly explore the linkage between moral standards and the mystery of the sacred. The Ten Commandments, drawn from the Jewish Scriptures, for example, are presented in that religious literature as of miraculous origin. Scholarship, however, can show their dependence on previous codes such as the Code of Lipit-Ishtar, the Code of Eshnunna, the Code of Hammurabi, and the Hittite Codes. The Commandments are primitive by contemporary standards and marked by the limits of tribal consciousness, but they do show where moral evolution was among the ancient Jews and surrounding peoples. They also illustrate the halting fashion in which we become aware of the moral implications of our reality, and they make us wonder how primitive our present conceptions will appear to future and hopefully more sensitive generations. At any rate, they do illustrate the relationship of principles to the empirical order.

The contextual, empirical basis of moral principles can also be illustrated by an example which presents a very specialized situation and the moral principle that developed to meet its human needs. At one time it was a principle among the Eskimos to practice a kind of socially motivated geriatric suicide. To relieve critical population pressures in the face of severely limited food supply, some of the older folks would resignedly go off to die on an ice floe. In the absence of alternatives, this could be judged a tragic but moral practice. It was the best they could do to survive, since all might have died without this release. One could not, however, rip this moral principle out of that specific empirical context in which it was temporarily defensible and say that this would be a good practice for others to whom more benign alternatives are available. Principles derive from circumstances, and circumstances make moral reality distinguishable and specific.

Not all principles have such a narrow empirical base as this particular principle of the Eskimos. Some principles can be articulated as relevant to any context imaginable. The prohibition of rape, lying, and violence are among these, as is the positive principle that urges us to revere and nourish life. But these principles too were learned in the concrete circumstances of life, and they cannot be applied except in dialogue with the realities of the concrete order. In circumstances of self-defense, the very desire to revere and nourish life may press us to kill when no other alternatives for the protection of the innocent are available. The ethical principle of licit killing in self-defense is born of this. *Ethics, in fact, can be seen as a dialogue conducted by the moral agent between the moral meaning found in principles and that found in the unique circumstances of the case.* Principles are thus tied to the empirical order by reason of their origin and their application.

Deep down in good principles there is contact with the sanctity of life. Principles may be skewed or reflective of outmoded data or myths, but we should not part with them without due process. Therefore if we find in our cultural reservoirs principles urging the counterproductivity of violence, the fitting conjoinment of sexual exchange and committed friendship, the duty to company with a dying person and not hasten his death, or principles that affirm the value of compassion, truth-telling, sincerity, etc., we should pause at length before the counsel of these principles before leaving them for a more morally valuable alternative. Only one who is steeped in principles has the moral maturity to depart from principles safely.

The Quest for Universals . . .

Immanuel Kant said: "I should never act in such a way that I could not also will that my maxim should be a universal law."[5]

Other ethicists too have placed great stress on the universalizability of moral principles, and the reasons for doing so merit attention. There is some basic wisdom in the attempt to universalize. For one thing, it makes us less liable to caprice and self-serving rationalization. Universalizability means that moral decisions are not simply intuitive and ad hoc. If one were to conclude that he ought to do *x* in circumstances A-B-C, he should be willing to universalize his insight by saying that anyone in circumstances A-B-C should do the same thing.

Kant's influence on ethics in this regard has been enormous, and so, even though his thesis is replete with problems, it is well to see what he was up to. Kant says that if someone were to refrain from making a false and insincere promise simply because the long-term consequences would outweigh the short-term gains, there is little or no morality at work. It was clear, Kant said, that such a decision would be "based only on an apprehensive concern with consequences" in a self-serving sense.[6] The universalizing test is what brings you into real functioning morality.

> Would I be content that my maxim (of extricating myself from difficulty by a false promise) should hold as a universal law for myself as well as for others? And could I say to myself that everyone may make a false promise when he is in a difficulty from which he otherwise cannot escape? I immediately see that I could will the lie but not a universal law to lie. For with such a law there would be no promises at all, inasmuch as it would be futile to make a pretense of my intention in regard to future actions to those who would not believe this pretense or—if they overhastily did so—who would pay me back in my own coin. Thus my maxim would necessarily destroy itself as soon as it was made a universal law.[7]

Kant had a sufficiently dismal view of human nature to know that our persistent ploy is to have double standards, one for self and one for others. Kantian universalizing certainly fights that.

Kant, however, was also concerned to give the common man solid grounds for moral living. He believed he had achieved this too.

> I do not, therefore, need any penetrating acuteness in order to discern what I have to do in order that my volition may be morally good. Inexperienced in the course of the world, incapable of being prepared for all its contingencies, I ask

myself only: Can I will that my maxim become a universal
law? If not, it must be rejected. . . .[8]

Kant was a typical eighteenth-century man, unrealistically in love
with the powers of abstract reason. His position is open to both practical and theoretical criticism. One might suspect that his views were
well suited to the simplicities of his Königsberg and that his theory
might do well if the world were Königsberg writ large, but even in
his day his moral theory put him on the defensive.

A French writer, H. B. Constand de Rebecque, took Kant to task.

> The moral principle, "It is a duty to tell the truth," would
> make any society impossible if it were taken singly and un-
> conditionally. We have proof of this in the very direct con-
> sequences which a German philosopher has drawn from
> this principle. This philosopher goes so far as to assert that
> it would be a crime to lie to a murderer who asked whether
> our friend who is pursued by him had taken refuge in our
> house.[9]

Kant acknowledged that he was the German philosopher in question and then stuck manfully to his conclusion. "Truthfulness in
statements which cannot be avoided is the formal duty of an individual to everyone, however great may be the disadvantage accruing to
himself or to another."[10] Quite simply, then, Kant would not be the
man you would want to stand between you and someone intent on
murdering you—at least if Kant knew where you were. (Aristotle or
Thomas Aquinas would take better care of you, as we shall see mo-
mentarily.)[11]

Given Kant's theoretical position, it is not surprising that the consequences would talk back and put Kant into this absurd position.
Kant's imperative comes from his view of the law of reason. "Reason
must regard itself as the author of its principles. . . ."[12] The ground
of obligation "must not be sought in the nature of man or in the circumstances in which he is placed, but sought *a priori* solely in the
concepts of pure reason. . . ." Any precept "so far as it leans in the
least on empirical grounds . . . may be called a practical rule but
never a moral law."[13] Affectivity and feeling are minimized in Kant's
view, since "feelings naturally differ so infinitely in degree that they
are incapable of furnishing a uniform standard of the good and
bad. . . ."[14] Kant is a major force behind the downgrading of

affectivity in modern ethics. Obviously, affectivity would "contaminate" the abstract world of reason that he was constructing.[15]

At any rate, cut off from empirical considerations and the affectivity that would help us plumb the moral meaning there, Kant builds a grid into which he would fit reality willy-nilly, and reality is just too diverse and surprising to be so circumscribed. On Kant's example of truth-telling, common sense and good ethics must say with Dietrich Bonhoeffer that Kant has "unintentionally carried this principle *ad absurdum*"[16] and common sense and good ethics also must stand with Monsieur Constand de Rebecque in his reaction against the "German philosopher."

Unwittingly, Kant illustrates why it would be better to use the term "generalization" rather than "universalization" in ethics. Universalization can be achieved only if we, with Kant, pretend to the impossible, making reason the *a priori* author of its own principles and by refusing to lean "in the least on empirical grounds." Though ethical knowing is a distinctive approach to the data of the empirical order, it still is knowledge of what is real and possible in that order. If our abstractions from the empirical order cut all links to that order, they float free and meaninglessly away from human relevance. The purveyor of such detached abstractions will find himself standing with Kant confessing the whereabouts of the victim to the prospective murderer—or in some equally absurd posture. It is in the empirical order that the mind develops principles. It is there also that principles can be tested and corrected.

The fallacy of saying that *x* is right if everyone should do it in circumstances A-B-C is that, in the concrete, there will never be anyone like the agent who is doing *x* in A-B-C; neither will there be an A-B-C exactly like this A-B-C. Ethics is not a judgment of physical qualities like heat or color, but of relationships in process. The web of relationships can never be entirely identical in different cases.

In sinning by abstraction, universalization passes over the fact that valid moral principles vary in their elasticity or openness to exceptions. One would be strained to find an exception to the prohibition of rape (precisely because of the circumstances implied by that term), but this is not the case with truth-telling.[17] To protect other values, like the life of an intended victim, or a legitimate secret, exceptions to truth-telling must be made. Excessive confidence in universalizability misses the complexity of principles and thus the complexity of moral life.

It is not a stretched lyricism to say that ethics is the mind of love. Love is a positive response to value. Ethics seeks to understand the appropriate response to value amid the complexity of life. The presupposition of ethics is that being moral means loving well, just as being immoral means a deviant response to value. This essential relationship of ethics to love is a good check to our tendency to sacrifice intellectual packaging and all-enveloping universals. Teilhard de Chardin states the indictment well:

> Love is the most universal, the most tremendous and the most mysterious of the cosmic forces. After centuries of tentative effort, social institutions have externally dyked and canalized it. Taking advantage of this situation, the moralists have tried to submit it to rules.[18]

Teilhard would not deny the validity of principles, and moral principles abound in his writing. His objection is to the narrow-mindedness and littleness of many moralists who, with undue confidence, reduce ethics to map making. In so doing, they underestimate and trivialize love, that "primal and universal psychic energy" which, however much we reflect on it, remains "huge, ubiquitous and always unsubdued."[19] Whoever would study ethics must be modest before they can be wise. Only the moral teacher who knows his limits can be trusted.

Moral principles must be somewhat solid and somewhat elastic. They must be solid enough to preserve and make available the creative moral wisdom they encapsulate, and they must be malleable enough to yield to or be reshaped by more humanizing understandings. To know about principles is important not just for this particular chapter which is considering principles formally, but for an understanding of ethical epistemology generally. Principles are not all, but they are close to the center of ethics. In knowing how they operate in ethical inquiry, we will know much about how the knower knows in moral matters. For this reason, we will now look at principles from the viewpoint of moral evolution.

Principles are not the center of ethics; the discerning subject is. If the discerning subject surrenders his unique role and reduces moral knowledge to conformism to rules, moral evolution halts. The person, the source of creativity, has defected.

Principles, along with authority, group experience, and other external aids, do not do our understanding for us. First of all, the discerning moral agent has access to what is unique in the case before him. In this sense, he is the irreplaceable, immediate arbiter of what the situation means. Though it has been said that "no one is a judge in his own case" since his vision may be biased by his interests, it can nevertheless be said that no one else can ultimately judge the case as he himself can. He alone has direct access to the concrete reality of the value situation. Judging alone, entirely apart from the social and cultural resources is actually psychologically impossible, since we are conditioned by the environment in which we know. It is also folly not to rely consciously on those resources. However, with all that relying done, moral judgment is not shifted to the environment. John Dewey rightly condemns the belief that "moral rules exist just as independent deliverances on their own account, and the right thing is merely to follow them. This puts the center of moral gravity outside the concrete processes of living."[20] It shifts the decision process from the agent to the tool. Again Dewey: "It fixes attention not upon the positive good in an act, not upon the underlying agent's disposition which forms its spirit, nor upon the unique occasion and context which form its atmosphere, but upon its literal conformity with Rule A, Class I, Species 1, subhead (1), etc."[21] What Dewey is against is the effort to use principles as though you could inventory and catalogue the entire moral life and put its contents into definitely labeled pigeonholes. This would amount to a despair of being able to do ethics, a despair about our ability to think.

What principles properly do is supply a deeper view of the context of a case, so that the discerning subject may the better discern. They cannot supply for the powers of the subject to understand the moral dimension of life. Only the subject can bring the affectivity, imagination, and dimensional sense which yield insight and understanding. If ethics were just a matter of conforming to external norms, there could be no moral evolution or creativity or spontaneity. Obedience, not creativity or sensitivity, would be the quintessential mark of moral man. Ethics would be reduced to a static science of rules.

A Practical Objection . . .

Something that sounds theoretically sound might only be an abstractionistic flight of mind. We serve the mind well by pausing betimes to see whether our theory can be translated into the experience of life. Thus, would a father who is quite convinced of the theoretical limits of ethical generalizations be prepared to pass this on to his young and newly dating daughter?

Would he say: "Remember, dear, there are external norms regarding how you should behave with your friends, but do not believe that the right thing is merely to follow them. This would put 'the center of moral gravity outside the concrete processes of living.' (Dewey's words, dear, not mine.) Remember only you 'can bring affectivity, imagination, and dimensional sense which yield insight and understanding.' If we were slaves to moral norms, 'there could be no moral evolution or creativity or spontaneity.' Now, go out, dear, and have an evolutionary, creative, and spontaneous evening."

The answer to this question-objection can be found to a large extent in the psychologists who have studied the stages of moral development. Ethics must work on the assumption that moral maturity is attainable. Persons who have not yet grown to moral maturity will show the signs typical of their stage of development. They will need a greater protective reliance on authority figures and external norms. There is no saying what they will do, but a mode of ethics that is geared to maturity would not seem real to them in all of its elements. There are a lot of problems in value counseling among the immature. Ethics is not directly responsible for them. At times it has *attempted* to be by lowering its sights and aiming at the immature— offering, in effect, fixed guidelines for those whose moral development is at a lower phase. Ethics should be geared to the subject who has achieved some of the autonomy that goes with psychological maturity.

Thus, the address to the daughter was misplaced. The speaker did not know to *whom* he spoke. Neither did he appear to know the *where* and *when* of her existence, and he was appallingly insensitive to *alternatives* and *foreseeable effects*. The young lady deserved better parenting, with moral counseling suited to her stage of development. And she deserved a rich experience of the ineffable value-communication that transpires in a loving relationship between parent and child wherein a consciousness of moral values is engendered that can only later be reflectively understood.

The point, then, is that principles must serve and illumine the discerning moral agent without being put in the place of his freedom. In a legalistic structure of morality, this displacement of freedom is what happens. The result is a hardening of the moral arteries and a blocking of moral creativity and evolution. Properly used, principles can support mature evolution and can provide a milieu in which creativity can be distinguished from caprice.

The History and Sociology of Principles . . .

Principles are the language of social beings living in history, and principles show the marks of their native condition. A highly rationalistic ethics which takes little cognizance of social and historical processes would tend to bypass this and imply that one could come upon his moral principles simply by looking inward at the laws of his mind. One might indeed discover in this fashion that the whole is greater than any of its parts, but mere introspection is not the adequate source of the principles that fill our moralscape. It is important to note this so that there can be some critical reflection regarding the principles to which we are heirs. Principles will bear the assets and the debits of social, historical existence. They must not be uncritically received. Principles capture the low as well as the high points of moral consciousness. It is intellectually chastening and healthy for a critical ethics to see that some principles that were long ensconced and apparently of the highest pedigree have come to be seen as wrong and immoral. Some examples of this will temper undue confidence in principled and established moral viewpoints.

For the first example, we can turn to slavery, an all too recent phenomenon in our history. Slavery was surrounded and sustained by a number of well-established ethical principles which were both religiously and legally blessed. There is grim witness here to the fact that accepted principles can be the repositories of iniquity. Since this is a failing that is not limited to the past, the following historical examples can serve to place us on guard in the present. What is needed is a habit of mind that attends to the social and historical influences of the accepted, principled wisdom. This then could lead us to refinement of our principles or, in some cases, as in slavery, to radical rejection.

As slavery grew in the majority of Christendom's overseas dominions, church thinkers "readily found sanctions in tradition whereby slavery might exist under the church's official favor."[22] The Council of the Indies, after conferring with theologians, jurists, and prelates of the Church, was able to assure the King of Spain that

> there cannot be any doubt as to the necessity of those
> slaves for the support of the kingdom of the Indies . . . ;

and [that] with regard to the point of conscience, [the trade may continue] because of the reasons expressed, the authorities cited, and its longlived and general custom in the kingdoms of Castile, America, and Portugal, without any objection on the part of his Holiness or ecclesiastical state, but rather with the tolerance of all of them.[23]

Prestigious groundwork had long been laid for such favor. Saints Ambrose, Isidore of Seville, and Augustine had rationalized slavery as being, like all secular instruments of coercion and government, part of divine retribution for the fall from grace. Martin Luther thought it clear from Scripture that both masters and slaves had to accept their status, since the earthly kingdom could only survive if some men were free and some slaves.[24] A number of functioning moral principles flowed from this and found expression and support in the common law of the land. Children could be separated from parents and husbands and wives be separated when sold. A North Carolina judge wrote in 1858: "The relation between slaves is essentially different from that of man and wife joined in lawful wedlock . . . for with slaves it may be dissolved at the pleasure of either party, or by the sale of one or both, depending on the caprice or necessity of the owners."[25]

As a hedge against our tendency to overestimate our civility, it is well to note the recent date of that North Carolina judge's pronouncement. Given the slow pace of moral evolution, it would be rash to suppose that we have since turned our souls inside out and banished all traces of the atrocities that made American slavery possibly the cruelest in history.

The principles that came to be accepted regarding women should also stir a critical view of principles, since it shows how ossified conscience can seek refuge in principle. An editorial which is, again, of comparatively recent date gives a sample of what is now being widely documented in women's studies. In the New York *Herald* editorial of September 12, 1852, it said:

How did women first become subject to man, as she now is all over the world? By her nature, her sex, just as the negro is and always will be to the end of time, inferior to the white race and, therefore doomed to subjection; but she is happier than she would be in any other condition, just because it is the law of her nature. . . .[26]

The law of nature is usually synonymous with accepted moral principles. Full many a time, as George Bernard Shaw observed, the customs of the tribe are thought to be the law of nature. Indeed, since the sacred is the ever-attendant penumbra of the moral, the laws of nature are easily thought also to be the laws of God. The moral principles operating here very often represent, in the Marxist phrase, "a tissue of lies" covering over some basic pattern or exploitative power and aggrandizement.

Sometimes what is actually going on in culturally dominant moral principles is less malignant than that and is simply a pretentious front for what is perceived as sheer necessity. The development of the divine right of kings in the sixteenth century is an example of that. This theory, which climaxed in the absolute monarchy of Louis XIV, would appear at first look to have been a theoretical defense of absolutism against constitutionalism, or of autocracy against democracy. In point of fact, the heart of the matter was that a strong feeling developed during the inconclusive and debilitating religious wars that there was just no other way to get effective government in France. All the theological elaborations which quoted Scripture to funnel the authority of God through the King, and the philosophical efforts to translate the feudal law of primogeniture into a general law of regal succession, were subsequent and subordinate to the need to get the French house in order and to survive.[27]

This is instructive on the meaning and nature of principles. The external form and defense of the principle may be purely accidental to the reality being pursued. The reality pursued might not be unworthy, but there is self-deception afoot in the rationalization offered. It is the job of ethics to be on the alert for such deceptions. In the principles that surrounded the institution of slavery and in those supporting the subjugation of women, the principles amounted to malignant fallacies used to justify exploitation. Less strikingly malignant, since it may have served as a temporary expedient for curtailing violence, was the divine right of kings. The underlying danger, of course, was not subtle and the presence of less drastic alternatives for peace seems to undercut any retrospective defense of this idolatrous theory. Yet this idolatrous theory took hold. As George H. Sabine writes: ". . . if the importance of a political doctrine depends partly on the number who hold it, the theory compares favorably with any political idea that ever existed, for it was believed with religious intensity by men of all social ranks and all forms of theological belief."[28]

Principles, then, have the potential to be directed to ignoble or shortsighted ends, however elegantly bedecked they are with rationalization. Principles can also, however, enshrine what is in itself a good moral value but become a block to moral evolution by absolutizing that value. Principles containing absolutized values are actually more dangerous than principles harboring exploitative options such as slavery and the downgrading of women, since they wear a more credible mask of respectability.

An example of this, and one of considerable and enduring influence on the American scene, is the theory of private property in John Locke, who was a major influence on early American thought. Though he spoke of the natural rights to "life, liberty and estate" (property), Locke placed outstanding emphasis on the last of the three. The right to property seems to be in his thinking the paradigmatic natural right and it got a lion's share of his attention. There were other traditions on this point from which Locke was departing. Some had held, for example, in the Middle Ages that common ownership is more perfect than private ownership and that the latter only developed as a result of "the fall of man." Locke, however, made it *the* fundamental right. Indeed, a major purpose for society and government is to protect that basic right.

Locke's philosophy here, it is clear, did not proceed from disinterested speculations conducted in a detached tower of learning. As R. R. Palmer comments, "His philosophy of private property can be regarded as an expression of the landed classes of England in their claims against the king. . . ."[29] He was articulating a vested interest.

The founding fathers of the United States were thoroughly imbued with the writings of Locke, and although Locke's "life, liberty and estate" became "life, liberty and the pursuit of happiness" in our foundational documents, the self-evident claims of private property made their way into our national credo. Locke really could not prove his assertion that "life, liberty and estate" were incontestably natural rights. In the ultimate analysis, he was an intuitionist who would have to stand with Thomas Jefferson and proclaim these truths to be self-evident.[30] Claims of self-evidence, of course, are bewitching. They demand admission without a check of credentials. They aggressively imply a certain obtuseness in anyone who would not see what is presented as obvious. Such claims have the advantage that accrue to gall. Realistic ethics must challenge them, since they are likely to slip into communal consciousness with immunity to chastening criticism. Unchallenged, they can reign as untested moral principles and blind all the ethics that is done under their unsuspected sway.

Any right that is absolutized and given an ontological, *in se* validity is in a disordered state. Principles (and rights) exist in relational tension with one another. Moral discernment must determine which principle applies (if any principle does) in a situation. No principle(s) should be thought to have permanent relevance. Property rights are, of course, limited in the United States, as in any functioning nation. Taxes are an obvious limit to the right to estate. Yet there is a discernibly Lockean absolutism subliminally and often more obviously present in the American defense of property rights and private enterprise. When conjoined to liberty, another sacred member of the Lockean triad, this absolutism takes on an added strength. We saw it operating in its purest form in the call to shoot looters during the riots of the 1960s. In what was a sure sign of *absolutizing*, death was seen as a fitting penalty for the violation of property rights. We also saw it working in the violent reactions to civil rights boycotts and in the foundation of private academies to exclude blacks which amounted to using private property "rights" as a weapon against black persons. The judicial system has reacted against this, but it has its work cut out for it, since the mentality here is nourished in deep springs. Absolutized rights of freedom and ownership can render nugatory the more basic claims of persons to justice and respect. And the mischief is all the more difficult because it is done by men of principle.

To see this mischief at work in the bold relief of caricature, we can turn to Ayn Rand, who wrote in 1963 that the civil rights bill was a gross violation of individual rights. As she saw it, the government would be violating the right to private property if it forbade discrimination in privately owned businesses. The passage of such a bill would constitute in Rand's view the most serious violation of property rights in the history of our nation.[81]

We cannot blame poor Locke for all of our biases, but his is one of the shadows that fall darkly upon those sentiments of Ayn Rand. The civil rights movement was arguably one in which the morally creative spirit was moving forward in truth. This instance of moral evolution ran headlong into entrenched principles regarding liberty and estate in an example of typically American absolutism. This is a

classical conflict in which moral evolution is resisted *on principle.*
The conflict, of course, is not over.

The problem of principles containing absolutized values may show
up in subtler form in the theory of justice put forth by philosopher
John Rawls. Rawls has come under criticism for his position that
"liberty can be restricted only for the sake of liberty."[32] Taking him
to task on this, L. Harold DeWolf writes:

> Rawls believes that rational persons in the conditions he
> has specified would place so high a value on liberties that
> no restriction could be placed upon them for the sake of
> economic benefits or social status. . . . Some readers, in-
> cluding me, would quarrel with his placing an absolute pri-
> ority on liberties above economic goods. It is often argued
> by champions of Marxian socialism that economic goods
> are more basic than political liberties and it must seem so
> to many persons who are on the verge of starvation.[33]

DeWolf goes on to argue that Rawls's doctrine that "liberty can
be restricted only for the sake of liberty" would seem to imply that
incarceration should never be used for property crimes. Unless it
could be shown that the property loss caused a liberty loss, the liberty of the offender could not be restricted for the sake of material
loss. DeWolf admits that Rawls did not discuss this matter explicitly, but he does ask: "In fact, does not the pressing of this question
cast further doubt on the sharp distinction between liberty and all
other values and even more on the absolute priority he had given to
liberty?"[34]

The upset caused by the unbalanced emphasis of certain values
and certain principles is far-reaching. The American unbalanced fas-
cination with liberty and the right to private property exemplifies
this. Its influence can be found in pivotal political and economic
concepts such as "the national interest," "private enterprise," and
"free trade." Here is where we can see the link between ethics and a
science such as economics where moral principles are also at work. A
value-conscious economics would probe deeply into its presuppositions to see what assumptions and principles it has been carrying
regarding the primacy of liberty and individual ownership and how
these affected the conclusions and form of economic theory. Economics does not function without specific attitudes on what man is
and what befits him. These are foundational ethical considerations,
and they should be checked. As the economist E. F. Schumacher
writes: "Economists themselves, like most specialists, normally suffer

from a kind of metaphysical blindness, assuming that theirs is a science of absolute and invariable truths, without any presuppositions. Some go so far as to claim that economic laws are as free from 'metaphysics' or 'values' as the law of gravitation."[35]

The economist, of course, is up to his neck in moral values, treating some value options as absurd and others as "the law of nature." Again Schumacher:

> The modern economist is used to measuring the "standard of living" by the amount of annual consumption, assuming all the time that a man who consumes more is "better off" than a man who consumes less.[36]

Schumacher compares this moral and economic stance to Buddhist economics where quite different moral value selections have been made. A Buddhist economist would consider this consumption approach "excessively irrational: since consumption is merely a means to human well-being, the aim should be to obtain the maximum of well-being with the minimum of consumption."[37] In self-defense, the Buddhist economist can point out that in their system "amazingly small means lead to extraordinarily satisfactory results."[38] The Buddhists also look on the use of nonrenewable goods as violent unless the use is indispensable. Westerners, on the contrary, seem to feel that human work is the only expenditure that counts, displaying little sense of being part of an ecosystem. And work is something of a necesary evil for the Westerner to be dispensed with entirely by automation if possible. For the Buddhist, work is a creative, socializing enterprise that has a value in itself. The Buddhist, in other words, has different principles.

The stress in Buddhist economics is to maximize human satisfactions by the most humanly suitable patterns of consumption. The Western economist is out to maximize consumption by the best patterns of productive effort. As Schumacher comments:

> It is easy to see that the effort needed to sustain a way of life which seeks to attain the optimal pattern of consumption is likely to be much smaller than the effort needed to sustain a drive for maximum consumption. We need not be surprised, therefore, that the pressure and strain of living is very much less in, say, Burma than it is in the United States, in spite of the fact that the amount of labour-saving machinery used in the former country is only a minute fraction of the amount used in the latter.[39]

The point here is not that we must convert to the Buddhist moral
value system, but that both Buddhist and other theories of economics are replete with moral principles. Though economics may be
defended as a legitimate and distinct discipline, it may not be
presented as an ethics-free system. It is replete with estimates of
what befits persons as persons and that is the stuff of ethics.
Schumacher's comparison to another kind of economics provides the
contrast to make the point clear. Many moral principles arising out
of the culture are assumed by the social sciences, given new shape
and emphasis, and returned to the culture with new force and
significance. The term "value-free social science" is a crude example
of false labeling. Principles, then, do not drop down on us from the
untainted realms of rarefied intellectuality. Like ourselves, they have
a history. Critical ethics requires that we look to the historical and
sociological roots of our principles. We cannot naïvely think of principles as immaculately conceived.

The Rapport Between Principles and Ideals . . .

Some principles house practical norms. Some contain ideals, and it
is to these latter that we may now attend. Ideals and idealists are a
practical problem. They are discontent by nature, pointing toward
something which is not yet. They also represent a call to self-criticism and are therefore potentially unpleasant. For this reason, idealists with their invitation to self-criticism are not well received in society. As Reinhold Niebuhr writes:

> Even those tendencies toward self-criticism in a nation
> which do express themselves are usually thwarted by the
> governing classes and by a certain instinct for unity in soci-
> ety itself. For self-criticism is a kind of inner disunity,
> which the feeble mind of a nation finds difficulty in distin-
> guishing from dangerous forms of inner conflict. So nations
> crucify their moral rebels with their criminals upon the
> same Golgotha, not being able to distinguish between the
> moral idealism which surpasses, and the anti-social conduct
> which falls below that moral mediocrity, on the level of
> which every society unifies its life.[40]

By a fortunate compensation, however, ideals are powerful. There
has never been a major turning point in history which was not pregnant with idealism. In spite of all the pragmatic and petty concerns

that characterize all of human life, and to which the American Revolution was not immune, that revolution could not be understood outside of the idealism that surfaces persistently in the documents and history of that period. And many students of communism would agree with Harold Laski when he says that "communism has made its way by its idealism and not by its realism, by its spiritual promise, not its materialistic prospects."[41]

There is no perfect distinction between ideals and principles because ideals also appear in the form of principle. There are three concentric aspects to ideals that make them special: They have a future referent; they are subversive; and they are gradually and never fully realized. They point to what is not yet and they beckon. Some principles such as those directing you not to kill, steal, or vandalize are not offering ideals but rather are spelling out the requirements for survival right now. Idealistic principles (or, simply ideals) point to what would be a better way of living. They are futuristic.

Second, and related, they are subversive. They undercut the moral heresy that all is as all should be. They contradict the comfortably accepted wisdom which has settled for less and the rationalistic reductionism that has made all things neat. For example, the ideal of internationalism and interdependency has been nagging us in recent decades. It is, of course, an utterly subversive notion, implying that states should no longer putter around like unacquainted shoppers at a fair. Doing one's own thing internationally is losing its respectability. In a departure from what was always held sacred, the Report of the Commission on International Development dares to give voice to the new ideal by observing matter-of-factly that historical developments have

> . . . changed the whole concept of national interest. Who can now ask where his country will be in a few decades without asking where the world will be? If we wish that world to be secure and prosperous, we must show a common concern for the common problems of all peoples.[42]

This kind of thinking goes to the roots of established approaches to tariffs and trade. It raises the strange idea of world income tax to bring needed aid to less developed nations in a systematic and not in a sporadic, *ad hoc* fashion. Those nations which are the sources of various raw materials can no longer be treated like a fish market where one can go at will to buy with little notice of the sellers.

Those sellers are now, in the words of the above-mentioned report, our "partners in development." This radically subverts the rugged individualism of the old nation-state, and rattles the foundations of the value system that has supported traditional statecraft. What this well-grounded idealism does is to question the whole frame of reference in which we moved along with the moral principles that made sense in that frame of reference. This is subversion of the greatest imaginable sort.

Ideals are not only futuristic, and subversive, but are also only gradually and never completely realized. Equality, for example, is an ideal of long standing, especially since the rise of democratic theory. Nevertheless, anthropology can tell us that "the need for leadership and the universality of the power drive, no matter how it may be culturally camouflaged, are responsible for the fact that there are no genuinely equalitarian societies."[43] In like wise it may be said that there are also no just societies or free societies. This does not mean that justice and freedom are chimeric or illusory. They are horizons toward which we move, and the more we set our vision on them, the more does our moral existence reflect their light.

Idealistic movements, therefore, must be patient. Ideals do not have the instant success that the forward pass had in football when it was first conceived. Ideals get smothered in lip service and the hegemony of lesser visions is not easily unsettled. In the United States, July 4 is celebrated, for the most part, by political Tories who would never have joined the original Revolution. Yet they would vote for no one who did not proclaim the ideals of that Revolution. Moral evolution may lurch forward at rare times, but in general the pace is glacierlike. It is those who are patient who shall possess the earth.

The final word on ideals should be hope. Without attempting to romanticize Buddhism, which has its own intrinsic deficiencies, we can turn to it again for a hopeful example. The fundamental principle of Buddhist ethics is that all men should develop an attitude of compassion and of "true friendliness." This ideal admittedly sounds ethereal and too delicate for the harshness of human life as it really is. The success of the ideal, however, is encouraging. Hajime Nakamura, a Buddhist scholar, writes:

> The practical results of the development of compassion
> have been seen in the way that Buddhism has softened the

rough warrior races of Tibet and Mongolia, nearly effacing all traces of their original brutality. In Japan, also, according to statistical reports, cases of murder or assault are relatively rare in districts where Buddhist influence is strong.[44]

The record of idealism does not leave us devoid of hope.

The Problem of Exceptional Cases . . .

Our principles are open to surprise. Proudhon's passing remark, "The fecundity of the unexpected far exceeds the statesman's prudence," is one that has application to moral principles. Principles increase our consciousness within the realm of the expectable. But the fecundity of reality has a broader reach than that. Put in another way, morality dictates not only rules but exceptions to those rules.[45] As Aristotle put it, "The *data* of human behaviour simply will not be reduced to uniformity."[46] There are moments of ultraobligation and heroism for which there are no rules. There are unchartable situations and decisional problems that do not so much go against principles as beyond them.

In ethics, neither principles nor exceptions can claim a higher status or a greater legitimacy. Both are an expression of and a reaction to the perceived value of persons. Both enjoy equally sound credentials. Why then are exceptions so often on trial. Joseph Fletcher, for example, in his *Situation Ethics*, excited an unbelievable furore by putting forth some likely exceptions to worthy principles. One of them in particular received the widest attention in discussions of morality. This was the "sacrificial adultery" of one Mrs. Bergmeier. As Fletcher tells the story, Mrs. Bergmeier was picked up by a Russian patrol while she was foraging for food for her children. She was taken to a Russian prison camp. There she learned that she could be released from prison for only two reasons: illness requiring hospital facilities, in which case she would be sent to a Soviet hospital; or pregnancy. In the event of pregnancy, she would be sent back to Germany as a liability. After some consideration, Mrs. Bergmeier prevailed on a friendly camp guard to impregnate her. He obliged. When her pregnancy was verified, she was released and sent back to Berlin where she was reunited with her husband and family. As Fletcher reports it: "When the child was born, they loved him more than all the rest, on the view that little Dietrich had done more for them than anybody."[47] Fletcher queried whether Mrs. Bergmeier had not indeed done "a good and right thing." The furore ensued.[48]

What Fletcher did was to bring attention to cases where exceptions to supposedly absolute principles seemed to make sense. In Mrs. Bergmeier's case, it did indeed seem that a higher principle of maternal love and caring for her family seemed to take precedence over the principle prohibiting extramarital sexual exchange. Yet the exception was subjected to a heated trial. Why?

Exceptions to moral principles are put on the defensive for a number of reasons, one of which would seem to be worthy. This worthy reason is that exceptions can run away from the value housed in the principle. A good exception moves beyond the principle to a truer realization of value; a bad exception contradicts the principle. In Mrs. Bergmeier's case, one might sense the problems that little Dietrich might someday have, or the possible problems for the guard who fathered a child he would never know, etc. After considering all of the circumstances, however, one might conclude that, notwithstanding the risks, the Russian prison code contained a remarkably benign loophole and Mrs. Bergmeier was well advised to avail herself of it. The iniquity was upon the heads of those who caused society to be so disordered that persons could be put in such straits. Mrs. Bergmeier's activities come within the realm of the morally defensible. It can be seen as a good exception to a good principle which in no way threatens the value the principle contains.

Well before Fletcher and Bergmeier, Augustine speaks of the instance of a wife who submitted herself sexually to her husband's captors at her husband's request in order to purchase his freedom from captivity and death. In commenting on this case, a conservative Catholic moralist of some years ago observed that Augustine "does not dare to define that these spouses sinned, and he permits everyone to think what he will since these spouses 'in no way judged that in these circumstances that act was adultery.' "[49]

To reach such conclusions is not to say that any departure from pledged sexual exclusiveness is moral. Such a conclusion would sin by abstractness. It would ignore the perceptible value of promissory fidelity and it would overlook the unitive and symbolic power of the sexual encounter. This can serve as an example of the problems posed by overly facile exceptions to principles. The principle in question could be stated this way: When persons have pledged themselves to a union characterized by sexual exclusivity, they should be faithful to their common pledge. This does not prejudge relationships where no such pledge is implicit or expressed or where it has lapsed and another kind of relationship has ensued. This would be a qualitatively different matter, not to be lumped together with the principle as stated. Permit me to elaborate this principle at some considerable length, since it has broad application and can serve to show the legitimacy and illegitimacy of exceptions, as well as the nature and development of principles.

Persons may bind themselves in a union (whether in marriage or in a less formal way) in which the promise of sexual exclusivity is an important and meaningful component of the relationship. A promise like this can exist in such an existentially binding way that breaching it would induce a disturbing experience of guilt—and not neurotic guilt which is traceable to no reasonable cause. This guilt, rather, would arise from a realization that infidelity in this kind of relationship changes the relationship in some substantive way. The guilt would be validated by the recognition that the other party would be seriously hurt and disappointed if he or she knew of it. It would, in a word, violate expectations that have been created by the kind of commitment that the two have made in developing a relationship of tenderness and trust. If unrevealed, it introduces an element of untruth where perfect sharing in truth had been the worked-at ideal. If revealed, it would require either reconciliation and a restoration of the previous kind of relationship (one marked by this form of trust) or a serious alteration in their mode of relating.

A promise should not be thought of in merely legal terms, which are geared to the more manageable needs of an external forum. A promise creates expectations in a person and takes on special form and force because of the specific attitudes the promiser has to the recipient of his promise. Following this, fidelity becomes a specifying mode of this communing of persons. A departure from the promise works changes at the level of intensely personal attitudes. A broken promise can thus change the promiser *and* his relationship to the beneficiary of his promise. Communion between the two persons is altered, possibly in a way that will seriously hamper or even reverse the process of intimacy that has been going on.

In so saying, I am not excluding the possibility that some breach of promise might occur impetuously, without deep investment of the person. In such a case, the breach might have minimal impact on the fidelity-relationship. Repeated occurrences of such impetuosity would indicate, however, that the person either lacked the psychological maturity for fidelity, or was allowing the commitment to erode, or that the commitment and the relationship had been altered substantially through a gradual succession of circumstances that weakened the bond.

The promise is not the only morally relevant factor here. There is also the powerful symbol of sexual exchange. A union marked by sexual fidelity is a special kind of promissory relationship. The sex makes it special. Sexual questions in ethics are often spoken of without first clarifying *what* sex is. The very question would seem calculated to evoke snickers. Such a reaction is out of order, since sex in humans, like everything in humans, is more than it appears to be. At one level, sex reflects the nonrational and purely physical in us. It releases unconscious springs of playfulness and relaxes tensions and frictions born of the struggling, deliberative part of our life.

Beyond this, sex is also a natural liturgy—a term that calls for immediate explanation. A liturgy consists of symbolic activity which communicates through physical gestures and material things. The physical activity is not primary and it will vary in *contrived liturgies*. In the liturgy of greeting, for example, the physical part will vary from bow to handshake to the rubbing of noses. What is intended is substantially the same in all. *Natural liturgies*, on the contrary, are the ones that we do not make up. They unfold without contrivance, although variety will occur in the manner of their unfolding. Before showing that sex is one of these, a look at another natural liturgy will clarify whereof I speak.

A meal is a natural liturgy. In humane conditions, the table is not a trough. In normal circumstances, persons who dine together are not just united by hunger. They are not just intent on consuming proteins and carbohydrates. Normally we do not invite people there because they are notoriously hungry. Food there must be, but the food will be the material substrate of so much more that is *symbolized* when persons eat. The meal is more than an ingestion event. When persons eat together, it is a social and socializing event. Though it may seem detachedly lyrical to say it, love and respect are essential components of human eating. As a practical proof of this, consider what happens when you eat with someone you seriously dislike. The resultant indigestion bears witness to the fact that foodstuffs and a common table do not a meal make. By its nature, a meal is a community-building phenomenon. You can of course eat with strangers, but given the communicational dynamism of the meal, they will probably not remain strangers.

Similarly, sex is a natural liturgy. It does, of course, as was said, meet physical needs such as relaxation. At times, it will do little more than this. But sex is also communication and symbol. In-depth sexual exchange, especially when repeated, has a power to be personally as well as physically interpenetrating and copulatory. Sex is a force for intimacy as well as for physical release and fun. It has a power to engender and express endearing emotions and exquisitely personal expectations. This, of course, varies in accordance with culture and circumstance, but in no culture does sex remain throughout frivolous and merely physical.

Recreational sex is possible. You can have sex and keep the "spiritual" elements in abeyance, just as it is possible to eat with strangers. There may even be in a culture (or in a person) a protracted period of recreational sex as anthropologist Malinowski saw among the Trobrianders. Yet even with the Trobrianders, the intimitizing power of sexuality is eventually felt.[50] The unitive efficacy of sex, which stretches from the physical sexual organs through the emotions, reaching to the center of personality, is missed by much contemporary sexual naïveté. But this is what sex is.

Applying all of this to the principle of promised sexual fidelity, the conclusion which presents itself is that exceptions to this principle are not to be facilely entertained. It would, of course, be true that not everyone is psychologically able to refrain from extraneous sexual gratifications as a living out of a fidelity-relationship, or that some would come to be capable of such only after what could be called a very halting start. The fidelity-relationship may not bloom all at once; it may be that the inner persistence of stubborn love may bring it through storms to maturity. If, however, we are speaking, as ethics must, of what befits persons who have achieved some maturity, justifiable exceptions to the sexual fidelity principle would require extraordinary circumstances. Both the sex and the promise in the fidelity-relationship are creators of expectations. The betrayal of expectations is no slight matter between sensitive persons. Love is a unitive force. The betrayal of expectations, to the degree it is disunitive, is unloving. Herein lies its moral significance.

The conclusion reached here is not based on an assumption that principles are not open to exceptions. Generalities cannot deal adequately with all that is unique and particular in life. The position here is based on the personal reality which the fidelity principle addresses. A relationship of pledged sexual fidelity opens persons to new possibilities and to new vulnerabilities. This, in the name of realism, cannot be ignored. This real experience of real persons is what the famous sexologists William Masters and Virginia Johnson refer to in describing a union characterized by a "commitment of concern." They mean by this

> . . . a bond in which a man and a woman mutually meet their obligations not because they feel *compelled* to but because they feel *impelled* to do so. . . . They expect to be faithful because they want to be. Furthermore they realize that if either or both of them must seek sexual satisfaction with other partners, the circle of commitment will have been broken. The more satisfaction they find with other people, the fewer satisfactions do they need from each other; and the less they need from each other, the easier it is for them to go their separate ways.[51]

Masters and Johnson reach what would have to be called conservative conclusions regarding "open marriage" or a "swinging" life style, arguing that these approaches will ultimately not even prove sexually satisfying. They point to the human need to be fully accepted. "The need to be recognized and accepted as a unique individual, to have an emotional identity as specific and singular as one's fingerprints, is crucial to an intimate relationship."[52] It is their contention that this experience is best achieved in an intimacy marked by commitment and sexual exclusiveness. Their complaint is that

> the idea that sex functions naturally when it is "lived" instead of "performed" seems to escape many people. That sex can be "lived" in marriage or in a deep and continuing commitment seems to have escaped almost everyone.[53]

What they are arguing for here, largely based on the sexual and over-all personal experiences of persons they have surveyed, is that the principle of sexual fidelity in a relationship is valid. They are, of course, concerned to stress the sexual perquisites that attach to such a union. What they conclude is that making exceptions to this principle should be a matter "of last resort" because "it carries with it the potential of a cure that is as unsatisfactory as the problem to be cured. . . ."[54]

Word shifts often indicate what is going on in a culture. The word "adultery" is sometimes described as being at least obsolescent. It was succeeded by "extramarital sex," a term that is somewhat less judgmental, and then, more recently, by "comarital sex," which may even be tinged with connotations of approval. What these words signal is an ongoing reappraisal of what befits or does not befit the marital union. Even more basically they imply an informal, and sometimes formal, reassessment of what marriage is. This is what makes it relevant to the discussion of principles and exceptions. When you entertain more and more exceptions to a basic principle, it may mean either that the proper elasticity is being discovered in the face of mounting complexification, or it might mean that the value in the principle is receding from view. It is this latter possibility that makes some critical pause in the face of new exceptions commendable. This is the good reason for putting exceptions on trial.

There are some bad reasons. One of them is the phenomenon that has merited many names. I have referred to it as the domino theory. Other images are used such as the wedge, or the camel's nose under the tent, or the finger out of the dike, or the slippery slope, or even the parade of horrors. The problem envisioned by all of these terms is that of uncontrollably cascading effects once you allow an exception to what had been thought to have been a solid principle. It is this fear that is behind the hesitancy to admit even a reasonable exception to an iron-clad principle. If you grant A, which seems reasonable, then you will logically have to grant B and C and D, which do not seem reasonable. If you puncture the principle with exception A, then exceptions B, C, and D will collapse upon you. Therefore, for safety's sake, do not grant A.

What is to be said of this fear of the domino effect? On the one hand it represents a salutary fear. Sociopsychologically, it is possible for a pendulum effect to take place in society when that society leaves the contrived security of an absolutized principle and begins to make distinctions and to exercise freedom in a new area. The movement is from not doing ethics to doing ethics, and many persons can be expected not to make the switch. This exposes a society to the same peril that a maturing child faces when it moves from reliance on paternal and peer authority toward some moral autonomy. There is a danger here that should not be minimized. It is a danger, however, that has to be faced unless we opt for an arrested adolescence in the child or in the society.

The basic question is: "Shall we ban the use for fear of the abuse?" An old Latin axiom replies to that question wisely: *Abusus non tollit usum,* meaning that because something can be abused does not mean that it cannot be intelligently used. The possibilities of foreseeable abuse would have to be taken into sensitive account, since the responsibility for the containment of possible abuse is intrinsic to freedom. The tempting and seemingly safer path is to foreclose on freedom for fear of the abuse. In truth it is likely to be less safe, since life will probably flow around our prohibition and do so without the discerning presence of a realistic ethics. Greater abuse is likely, since action will move forward without reflection. Such a situation rather seems to remand us to the neglected powers of our creative imagination where the price of freedom is to be paid. A critical pause before new exceptions, therefore, is very much in order, provided it does not lead to a catatonic state of rigidity.

At the level of ethical theory, the domino fear of runaway exceptions is weak for two principal reasons: It shows a lack of an empirically grounded ethics, and second, it represents a kind of crypto-utilitarianism. One who allows for the morality of exception A need not choose to allow for B, C, and D for the excellent reason that B, C, and D are not A. Ethics is not done by deductive logic alone. The exception is not related to the principle as the puncture to the balloon. Principles are applied in experiential dialogue with the circumstances. The unique aspects of one situation do not transfer over into the analysis of all similar cases. Still, this imputation is very much with us.

In my study of the morality of mercy death, I have found that the most frequent objection to mercy death in the literature on the subject is some form of the domino theory.[55] Though there are many twistings and turnings in the presentation of this objection, the thrust is toward saying that possible abuse cancels out use. For example, a report by a working party of the Anglican Church entitled *On Dying Well* addressed the subject of mercy death. At one point the study grants that there is not an absolute principle against taking innocent human life. There are cases in war, for example, where a man trapped in a blazing gun turret or wounded men who faced death by torture if left on the battlefield were shot by their comrades. The Anglican study says that it is not possible to say that those who killed in such desperate situations acted wrongly.[56] Noting that these cases are outside the medical field, the study is initially reluctant to qualify the principle prohibiting the termination of innocent life in the medical field. "Our fear is that, if the principle is once so qualified as to allow for the altogether exceptional cases, it will be regarded as no longer binding in the ordinary conduct of life."[57] I mentioned that persons using the domino theory tend to twist and turn. This is certainly true in the Anglican study, which is further complicated by being the work of many hands, not all of them co-ordinated. Elsewhere, within a few pages, the study says that it is difficult to maintain the position that "euthanasia" is always and everywhere wrong, and it even allows that in certain cases the teaching of Jesus would seem to "legitimize at least some instances of euthanasia."[58] Still their statement of the domino objection quoted above is perfectly typical. If the principle is modified to allow exceptions, it may no longer be regarded as binding in ordinary cases. Their suggestion is that if we allowed one case, we could never draw a line. It has, of course, been aptly said that ethics, like art, has the task of knowing where to draw lines. And neither ethics nor art can avoid drawing lines. Domino thinking would commit us to universalization wherever difficult cases are involved. Of course those who use domino thinking to support a universal moral veto of mercy death do not use it elsewhere where they are doing ethics beyond the shadow of a controlling taboo.

An example can help to keep us closer to the empirical order. Huntington's disease is an inherited, incurable disease of the nervous system which has its onset somewhere between the ages of thirty-five and forty-five. It is known crudely as Huntington's *chorea*—from the same Latin root from which we have the word "choreography." The reference is to the fact that as this disease develops—and it takes ten to fifteen years to kill—the patient evinces continuous, involuntary, and unco-ordinated movements and flailings of the limbs and face, loss of articulate speech, slow mental deterioration, and loss of bladder and bowel control. Death often has its immediate cause in infection and in the total muscle exhaustion caused by the flinging of the arms and legs. Understandably, death is often caused by suicide.[59]

There are obviously macabre aspects in the development of this disease. If someone was afflicted with it and decided to bear it as long as possible, but at a certain point decided to end his life so as to spare himself and those who would have to care for him during the terrible spectacle of this final suffering, I would see the decision as quite defensible. I do not believe it would indicate that the patient would be displaying immaturity or shallowness in the face of the tragic. Neither do I think this patient would be throwing open the floodgates to every manner of exception to the lifesaving principle. I believe he would be taking one of the moral though tragic options available to him and quite reasonably defensible in these special circumstances.

Those who would shy from this conclusion on the grounds that it would be impossible to hold back a continuous and abusive expansion of exceptions are identifiable as utilitarians though they would hasten to deny it. Reductively, the abuse argument implies that even if this exception seems to be a good exception, nevertheless, because of the greatest good of the greatest number, it must be deemed immoral. The contention seems to be not that this exception is abusive and thus wrong, but that it would open the door to abuses. The good in this particular exception is simply written off in view of the alleged requisites of the common good. The *one* is sacrificed for the *many* in a classically utilitarian manner.

There is, furthermore, a missing link in the argument. It is not *shown* that this would open the door to abuses. If this were shown, this exception would be intrinsically part of a train of abuses, a kind of trigger mechanism, and thus would be morally linked to the subsequent abuses. Instead, the coming of the subsequent abuses is taken as certain *and* certainly related to this exception as effect to cause. The burden of proof is upon those who would make such extraordinary and gratuitous assumptions. To be concrete, I submit that a person with Huntington's disease has an arguable moral right to end his life when the course of his disease becomes for him unbearable and bizarre. (He also, of course, has a right to live his life to the end. What persons can bear varies.) To say that this is not a defensible exception to the life-preserving principle on the grounds that a series of evils will flow from it will not stand as an argument unless the grounds for these dire predictions are established and the causal link between this exception and those foretold evils is demonstrated.

Clearly, one would not use this argument from predicted abuse in an area where the vested interest of taboo is not present. In fact, a far stronger case could be made to prove that all acts of violence in self-defense and in war are immoral. There the abuses could be historically documented *ad nauseam*. But because these are culturally blessed exceptions, the argument from potential abuse is not used in the way that it is used against mercy death.

The Lure of Essences . . .

It is not only in ethics that the special and the unique is suspect. In the field of science, for example, it has been necessary to counterattack the influential Aristotelian view that science is a pursuit of the knowledge of universals. As Aristotle put it, "Scientific knowledge is judgment about things that are universal and necessary, and the conclusions of demonstration, and all scientific knowledge, follow from first principles. . . ."[60] Against this it is contended that sciences such as the biological and the biomedical are primarily focused on achieving knowledge of particulars. This discussion is not of a "purely theoretical" sort. The differences here affect the foundations of one's approach and the results are practical. With regard to medicine, for example, a particularist stress would mean that the behavior of particulars is not predictable through deduction. This affects, for example, the concept of malpractice, since, if the behavior of particulars cannot be deduced always or completely from general principles, the physician is not liable for those failures that follow from the special nature of particulars.[61]

The generalist attitude in science is not unrelated to the universalizing thrust in ethics, since paradigms and attitudes pass from one discipline to another in the cultural mix. A more direct relationship of the Greeks and their stress on the common over the particular has been cited by philosopher Edmund J. Egan. He mentions how the Pythagorean dualism listed under the Good such qualities as light and unity, and under Evil such things as plurality and chaos. This, of course, puts what cannot be draped in commonality at a decided disadvantage. In the thought of Plato, this tendency continues. Egan comments that "this emphasis was to have in Plato's thought a deeper and . . . a damaging issue. For Plato, mathematician-moralist, the Pythagorean rejection of disharmony and disorder was developed and broadened into a rejection of the subjective, the unpredictable and the variable."[62] In Aristotle the problem is complicated by the difficult question of individuation in his philosophy and of the perception of matter as a principle of unintelligibility. As Egan comments:

As a principle of unintelligibility, furthermore, matter would in this function make the individual less knowable, hence less valuable, than the species of which it was a member. . . . This might be interpreted as an exaltation of essence which in human terms would translate into the primacy of the common."[63]

A belief in the "primacy of the common" and the greater knowability of the general is the motive force underlying undue confidence in universals. For a corrective, I turn to something else in Aristotle, to Thomas Aquinas, and to the common sense that is born of experience. Aristotle uses the category of "practical wisdom." The happy yield of practical wisdom is that those who have it "can see what is good for themselves and what is good for men in general." They can tell what sort of things "conduce to the good life."[64] Practical wisdom is not "concerned with universals only—it must also recognize the particulars; for it is practical, and practice is concerned with particulars."[65] In a remark that cannot be encouraging for young ethicists, Aristotle says that "it is thought that a young man of practical wisdom cannot be found."[66] (Young men, however, need not despair. They are quite capable of becoming mathematicians. While "young men have no convictions" about things related to experience, "the essence of mathematical objects is plain enough to them.")[67]

So the particular is not an orphan in Aristotle. His student of many centuries later, Thomas Aquinas, also provided a sensible treatment of ethical particularity. In fact, Thomas saw the possibility of exceptions to very basic principles so that in certain circumstances one could morally and licitly take the property of other persons, have sexual relations with someone other than one's wife, and even directly kill one's self or another innocent person. Thomas distinguishes between speculative and practical reason. It is the latter that has to do with human behavior. Regarding the principles of practical reason that have to do with ethics, Thomas says: ". . . although there is some necessity in the common principles, the more we descend into particularities, the more frequently do we encounter defects."[68] The "some necessity" means that generally a moral principle will be applicable and relevant in the type of case to which it refers. The principle is good and useful. It is not, however, without what Thomas calls "defectus," deficiency, limit. There are times and circumstances when it does not apply. At times it would be positively harmful and irrational to insist on the principle. This would occur in cases where greater values than those contained in the principle supervene and prevail.

As an example of a good principle that is open to exceptions, Thomas gives: *Things held in trust should be returned upon request.* Normally this is true and applicable. However, if someone came back to claim something which you had held for him in trust for the avowed intention of doing some manifest evil with it, it would be both harmful (*damnosum*) and irrational (*irrationabile*) to conform to the principle. In that case you would be morally justified in keeping what belonged to this person, at least till circumstances changed.[69]

There is one more striking point in Thomas in this regard that should be noted. Thomas says that in a sense truth is not the same for all men in matters of behavior. ". . . in speculative things, truth is the same for all men. . . . In matters of behavior, however, truth of practical moral rightness is not the same for all with regards to that which is particular but only with regard to that which is in common. . . ."[70] This is a most notable allowance to the meaningfulness of that which is unique and special and ungeneralizable. If all moral meaning were generalizable, then the truth would be the same for all men and Thomas' dramatic statement would not be necessary.

Earlier I mentioned that Thomas Aquinas allowed some remarkable exceptions in areas of sexuality and life-taking. For a Dominican monk writing in the thirteenth century, this might seem surprising. However, Thomas did manage to eat his cake and have it too regarding these cases. The exceptions came into Thomas' discussion of principles and exceptions because they occurred in the Bible or were done by saints of the Church and therefore had to be defended in Thomas' view. Samson had committed suicide by pulling the building down on himself; Abraham consented to directly kill his son, Isaac; Hosea appeared to have been implicated in sexual sin. Thomas had several ways of justifying these events, such as by saying that they were done by divine command. Thus he could say regarding Hosea that "intercourse with any woman ordered by a mandate of God is neither adultery nor fornication."[71] This certainly seemed to get Thomas off the hook, since a mandate from God would seem hard to come by. However, Thomas did not lapse into a crude nominalism or voluntarism here of the sort that would say that something is good because commanded by God. As an ethical realist, Thomas held that nothing could be commanded unless it was good. God is also bound by the order of justice and "beyond this order, God can do nothing."[72] God's role here was to *reveal* that this was a good exception in the circumstances. He was not making it good by mandating it; he was revealing that it was good. Thomas was not prepared to admit that persons could come up with this insight by themselves. Here Thomas was inexorably a child of his times. Nevertheless, despite his *deus ex machina* approach, Thomas had room in his theory for these exceptions.

Thomas did not find himself in the bind that Immanuel Kant did. He would not have to tell the prospective murderer where his victim was hiding. In fact he could give incorrect information to the desperado and find no problem justifying it morally within his system. The truth-telling principle would have run into particularities where it did not apply.

Leaving both Aquinas and Kant behind us, it is possible to illustrate these situations where a principle ceases to apply in the following manner:

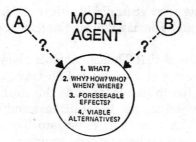

The moral agent is central to the diagram, conducting a dialogue between the moral situation, revealed in its fullness through the reality-revealing questions from the hub of the wheel model, and the potentially relevant moral principles. In the case of telling the murderer about his victim, principle A represents the truth-telling principle. However, in this case, as in most cases in life, there is more than one principle making its claim to valuable relevance. Principle B is the principle that says that you should save innocent life from destruction when it is within your power to do so. The ethical question is: Which principle connects most valuably with the concrete circumstances of the case? Which principle best serves the personal values at stake? It is not, therefore, a question of sticking with your principle, but rather a question of which principle you should stay with. You cannot have it both ways. One principle must be discarded—that is, denied application. If you tell the truth, you do not save life.

Some situations may call for rigorous administration of criminal justice. Others may call for leniency and mercy. You cannot have both. It is the role of the moral agent (in criminal justice, the judge or jury) to decide which principle best complements the value needs of the situation.

Some cases will not be of the either-or sort. At times the values of several principles may have to be blended by the moral agent in his act of moral judgment. Suppose a patient comes into the hospital with a massive coronary. In the opinion of the attending physician, which he voices to the nurses after the examination, the patient's heart is so critically damaged that death will probably occur any minute. When the doctor returns to the bedside of the patient, to his surprise, the patient opens his eyes and says weakly: "How bad is it?"

One winces to think what Immanuel Kant would say were he the physician. More realistically, the doctor would have to consult the principled values that hover over his decision. One is truth-telling. The patient, especially a moribund patient, has a right to know the truth. He may want to use his last moments of consciousness to be reconciled with a loved one, to change his will, etc. A lie occurs when you deny the truth to which someone has a right. To say "You're doing beautifully and you're going to be just fine" would be a lie. On the other hand, the doctor knows that his is a fallible skill. He has been surprised before, though never in a case like this. Still, he is fallible. He somehow has to give the patient the minimum of peace that might allow the stubborn and surprising healing powers of the body to have a chance. He cannot say, even though he thinks it: "You could die any minute now." This information would be self-fulfilling and it would give no chance to the remote, but not negligible possibility of recovery. Thus the doctor might well decide to accept something of the truth-telling principle and something of the lifesaving principle. He would tell the patient that he had had a serious heart attack but would cushion this with the assertion that he was in good hands and that it was very important to rest and give the heart a chance to heal. The delicate task of the doctor (and here *how* becomes massively important in the ethical equation) would be not to make the cushion so prominent as to blot out the news of the danger and not to so stress the bad news as to create an immediate panic that could stop the beating of an even healthier heart.

The doctor's dilemma illustrates the kind of sensitive orchestration that has to be done in moral living. No problem would exist if ethics could be reduced to the simple application of one relevant principle to the case. Neither life nor the ethics that seeks to meet its challenges reflectively is so simple.

The example of the dialogue conducted by the moral agent between principle A or B and the concrete situation, like every example, limps. It could imply that there is always some relevant principle out there waiting to be connected to the case at hand. In effect, it could imply that life can be captured in principles if only you find the right one. And that would be an error. There is the inimitable and the unrepeated. There is the unchartable, ungeneralizable moment when the confluence of events and relationships is such that all the maps that our principles contain are unprofitable servants. A principle, after all, is not a decision, but only the background of a decision. It is the voice of experience past and, however helpful, it is inevitably limited in the face of the truly new. Moral wisdom requires that our sense of uniqueness not be dulled by the more manageable sense of what is generally true.

Perhaps this is a message that is come of age. Perhaps this is the age of particularism and heightened awareness of differentials. Special preaching of this might not be needed now. Maybe the prophet of today is someone like Clyde Holbrook who laments: "It seems that there is nothing that all human beings as human beings should know or be concerned about."[73] He calls for a renewed sense of *humanitas*, a sense of what is humanly universal upon which we can build our collective future. We have become intensely aware of cultural conditioning, and culture is realized in particular form. This suggests that all is particular and that intimations of universality are mistaken. Against this possibility, Holbrook enters his plea: "Although our conception of *humanitas* may be conditioned and even narrowed by the limitations of our own cultural experience, we should not deny the measure of universality in that conception, nor elevate cultural conditionedness to the status of an educational philosophy."[74]

There are concrete witnesses to what Holbrook says. There is that outstanding moment in human history, December 10, 1948, when the General Assembly of the United Nations adopted the Universal Declaration of Human Rights. This historic document, through its preamble and thirty articles, lists a number of ideals and principles that are of potentially universal appeal. Freedom of conscience and assembly, protection from discrimination on grounds of "race, color, sex, language, religion, political or other opinion, national or social origin, property, birth or other status," the right to fairness in work and pay, the right to marriage, and the right to rest and leisure—just to cite a few of the many things on which there is so broad a consensus. Surely this sampling of universal rights must in some way touch on bonds that transcend all the variables.

Aristotle was cited earlier in defense of particularity: "The *data* of human behaviour simply will not be reduced to uniformity."[75] But it was that same Aristotle who admired Pericles and men like him because they could see not only "what is good for themselves" but also "what is good for men in general."[76] Humanity is served when we crack the particular and liberate the universal while losing sight of neither.

NOTES—CHAPTER SEVEN

1. The phrase is that of the poet Stanley Kunitz, used by him during a reading of his poetry at Northwestern University May 1, 1959, and quoted in Glenn D. Paige, *The Korean Decision* (New York: The Free Press; London: Collier-Macmillan Ltd., 1968), p. 10.
2. Walt Whitman, "Songs of Myself," XLII, in *Leaves of Grass.*
3. John Dewey and James H. Tufts, *Ethics*, rev. ed. (New York: Henry Holt & Co., 1932), p. 304.
4. Ibid.
5. Immanuel Kant, *Foundations of the Metaphysics of Morals*, translated by Lewis White Beck (New York: Liberal Arts Press, 1959), p. 18.
6. Ibid., p. 19. Kant's horror of consequentialist thinking is based on the supposedly selfish motivation involved in such calculation. See ibid., pp. 10, 16, 17–19. He opted for founding moral obligation in a law of reason which breeds a duty that is quite independent of extraneous considerations.
7. Ibid., p. 19.

8. Ibid.

9. Quoted by Immanuel Kant in "On a Supposed Right to Lie from Altruistic Motives," in *Critique of Practical Reason and Other Writings in Moral Philosophy* (Chicago: University of Chicago Press, 1949), p. 346.

10. Ibid., p. 347.

11. Interestingly, Kant, in defending himself, takes a consequentialist turn in spite of his deontological stance. The lie is wrong because "so far as in me lies I cause that declarations should in general find no credence, and hence that all rights based on contracts should be void and lose their force, and this is a wrong done to mankind generally" (ibid.). There was also a consequentialist thrust to the argument on the false promise quoted above. No deontology can remain aloof from the moral import of consequences without becoming absurd.

12. Kant, *Foundations of the Metaphysics of Morals*, p. 67.

13. Ibid., p. 5.

14. Ibid., p. 61.

15. Lewis White Beck attempts to defend Kant on this point. He writes: "Almost everyone else at that time was accentuating feeling at the expense of reason as the exclusively legislative moral faculty. . . . Though he never admitted that feelings could generate a genuine moral disposition, or desire for happiness could function as a moral motive. Kant was quite aware of the 'synergistic' relationships between reason and empirical character." Synergism, however, is not enough to give its due to the affective component of moral knowledge. For Beck's comments, see "Introduction: Kant and His Predecessors," in *Critique of Practical Reason and Other Writings in Moral Philosophy*, p. 42.

16. Dietrich Bonhoeffer, *Ethics*, paperback ed. (New York: Macmillian Co., 1965), p. 369, note 1.

17. Some words have a negative moral judgment built in. For example, murder implies unjust killing. One could not look for an exceptional case where murder would be acceptable. Similarly, lying implies unjustified failure to communicate truth. There can be no "good lie," since that is a contradiction in terms. Other terms like "homicide" are morally neutral.

18. Pierre Teilhard de Chardin, *Human Energy* (London: Collins, 1969), p. 32.

19. Ibid., p. 33 and p. 32.

20. Dewey and Tufts, *Ethics*, p. 307.

21. Ibid., p. 306. Dewey is here attacking what he calls "casuistry" in which the entire moral life is inventoried and catalogued. This amounts to a deviant form of reliance upon principles.

22. Stanley M. Elkins, *Slavery* (New York: Grosset & Dunlap, Universal Library Edition, 1963), p. 69.

23. "Minutes of the Council of the Indies" (1685), quoted ibid.

24. See David Brion Davis, *The Problem of Slavery in Western Culture* (Ithaca, N.Y.: Cornell University Press, 1966), Chapters 3, 4, 7, and passim.

25. Quoted in Elkins, *Slavery*, p. 54.

26. Quoted in Ashley Montague, *The Natural Superiority of Women*, new rev. ed. (New York: Collier Books, 1974), pp. 28–29.

27. For a discussion of the divine right of kings, see George H. Sabine, *A History of Political Theory*, 3rd ed. (New York: Holt, Rinehart & Winston, Inc., 1961), pp. 391–97.

28. Ibid., p. 393.

29. R. R. Palmer, *A History of the Modern World*, 2nd ed., revised with collaboration of Joel Colton (New York: Alfred A. Knopf, 1960), p. 286.

30. Locke said that moral knowledge can be as certain as mathematics. As Vernon J. Bourke writes, "There is a certain quality of idealistic intuitionism involved in this claim. Our moral ideas are 'archtypes' like our mathematical ones; . . . So, in the end, Locke's empirical ethics is transmuted into an ethical intuitionism." Vernon J. Bourke, *History of Ethics* (Garden City, N.Y.: Doubleday & Co., Inc., Image Books, 1968), Vol. 1, pp. 204–5. And George H. Sabine: "That all individuals are endowed by their creator with a right to life, liberty, and estate, aside from all reference to their social and political associations, is certainly not a proposition for which any empirical proof can be given." Sabine, *History of Political Theory*, p. 529.

31. Ayn Rand, *The Virtue of Selfishness: A New Concept of Egoism* (New York: New American Library, Signet Books; copyright © 1961, 1964 by Ayn Rand; 1962, 1963, 1964 by the Objectivist Newsletter, Inc.), p. 134. Rand adds in a note that the bill was passed in 1964 "including the sections that violate property rights."

32. John Rawls, *A Theory of Justice* (Cambridge, Mass.: Belknap Press of Harvard University Press, 1971), p. 302.

33. L. Harold DeWolf, *Crime and Justice in America* (New York: Harper & Row, 1975), p. 158. In fairness to Rawls it should be noted that he does allow that freedom may have to be curtailed due to "social conditions." He is not an absolute libertarian. "The denial of equal liberty can be accepted only if it is necessary to enhance the quality of civilization so that in due course the equal freedoms can be enjoyed by all." Rawls, *Theory of Justice*, p. 542.

34. Ibid., p. 159.

35. E. F. Schumacher, *Small is Beautiful* (New York: Harper & Row, Perennial Library, 1975), pp. 53–54.

36. Ibid., p. 57.
37. Ibid.
38. Ibid.
39. Ibid., p. 58.
40. Reinhold Niebuhr, *Moral Man and Immoral Society* (New York: Charles Scribner's Sons, 1932, 1960), pp. 88–89.
41. Quoted ibid., p. 163.
42. Lester B. Pearson, *Partners in Development: Report of the Commission on International Development* (New York: Praeger Publishers, 1969), p. 9.
43. Ralph Linton, "The Problem of Universal Values," in Robert F. Spencer, ed., *Method and Perspective in Anthropology: Papers in Honor of Wilson D. Wallis* (Minneapolis: University of Minnesota Press, 1954), p. 160.
44. Hajime Nakamura, "Unity and Diversity in Buddhism," in Kenneth W. Morgan, ed., *The Path of the Buddha* (New York: Ronald Press Co., 1956), p. 387.
45. Some ethicists make an effort to distinguish rules and principles. John Dewey, for example, tries to do this but then has to admit that "the word 'rule' is often used to designate a principle—as in the case of the phrase 'Golden Rule.'" Dewey and Tufts, *Ethics*, p. 309. This is also true of "the principle of double effect." The effort to render ethics unnecessarily tedious by distinctions that do not hold up in usage is both pedantic and unkind.
46. Aristotle, *Nichomachean Ethics*, Bk. 5, Chap. 10, 1137b, 14. The translation is that of J. A. K. Thomson. The translation of W. D. Ross is: "about some things it is not possible to make a universal statement which shall be correct." See Richard McKeon, ed., *The Basic Works of Aristotle* (New York: Random House, 1941), p. 1020.
47. Joseph Fletcher, *Situation Ethics* (Philadelphia: Westminster Press, 1966), pp. 164–65.
48. See Harvey Cox, ed., *The Situation Ethics Debate* (Philadelphia: Westminster Press, 1968).
49. Augustine, *De Sermone Dom. in Monte*, Lib. 1, c. 16. The moralist who commented on this was D. Prummer in his *Manuale Theologiae Moralis*, ed. 8a (Friburgi Brisgoviae: Herder and Co, 1935), I, 111, 1. The example of Augustine was recalled to my attention by my colleague Dennis Doherty upon reading this portion of my manuscript. He alludes to the incident and Prummer's comments in his book *Divorce and Remarriage* (St. Meinrad, Ind.: Abbey Press, 1974), pp. 185–86, note 8.
50. See Bronislaw Malinowski, *The Sexual Life of Savages* (London: George Routledge & Sons, 1932), Chap. 3.

51. William H. Masters and Virginia E. Johnson, *The Pleasure Bond: A New Look at Sexuality and Commitment* (New York: Bantam Books, 1976), pp. 269–70.

52. Ibid., p. 271.

53. Ibid., p. 195.

54. Ibid., p. 196. Though Masters and Johnson in this book are, as would be expected, arguing with a good deal of reliance on interviews and surveys—i.e., on a rather empirical approach—it is also clear that they are doing ethics and taking definite positions on the derivation of principles, the generalizability of moral meaning, etc. Another example of the ubiquity of ethics.

55. See Daniel C. Maguire, *Death by Choice* (Garden City, N.Y.: Doubleday & Co., Inc., 1974); (New York: Schocken Books, 1975), pp. 131–41.

56. *On Dying Well* (Church Information Office, Church House, Dean's Yard, SW1P 3NZ, 1975), pp. 10–11.

57. Ibid., p. 11.

58. Ibid., p. 23. On p. 18 it also says that euthanasia would seem wrong "where there are other means available of exercising care and compassion towards a person in his dying and of relieving his ultimate distress. . . ." The notable weakness of this study is that it confuses ethics and law, moving from ethical to legal considerations without making the necessary distinctions. It is interesting, however, that, while leaning heavily on the domino objection, this study does allow the morality of euthanasia in certain cases.

59. For a discussion of some of the moral problems surrounding Huntington's Disease, see Michael Hemphill, "Pretesting for Huntington's Disease," *Hastings Center Report* 3, No. 3 (June 1973) pp. 12–13. And Frank R. Freeman, "Pretesting for Huntington's Disease: Another View," *Hastings Center Report* 3, No. 4 (Sept. 1973), p. 13.

60. Aristotle, *Nichomachean Ethics*, Bk. 6, Chap. 6, 1140b, 31.

61. On this, see H. Tristram Engelhardt, Jr., "The Roots of Science and Ethics," *Hastings Center Report* 6, No. 3 (June 1976), p. 36. Engelhardt summarizes the view in this regard of Samuel Gorovitz and Alasdair MacIntyre. See Samuel Gorovitz and Alasdair MacIntyre, "Toward a Theory of Medical Fallibility," in H. Tristram Engelhardt, Jr., and Daniel Callahan, eds., *Science, Ethics, and Medicine* (Hastings-on-Hudson, New York: Institute of Society, Ethics and the Life Sciences, 1976).

62. Edmund J. Egan, "The Transformation of Ethics and Heterosexual Consciousness," *Cross Currents* 23, No. 2 (Summer 1973), p. 171.

63. Ibid., p. 173.

64. Aristotle, *Nichomachean Ethics*, Bk. 6, Chap. 5, 1140b, 9, and 1140a 27.

65. Ibid., Chap. 7, 1141b, 15.
66. Ibid., Chap. 8, 1141a, 14.
67. Ibid., 15–19.
68. Thomas Aquinas, *Summa Theologica* I II q. 94, a. 4, in corp. ". . . *etsi in communibus sit aliqua necessitas, quanto magis ad propria descenditur, tanto magis invenitur defectus.*" Thomas does allow for immutable principles regarding morality, but these are highly generic and can thus afford to be immutable. They are such things as: Evil should be avoided and Justice should be observed. John Giles Milhaven, in an excellent study on Aquinas and moral absolutes, lists ten such overlapping immutable principles in Aquinas. See John G. Milhaven, "Moral Absolutes and Thomas Aquinas," in Charles E. Curran, ed., *Absolutes in Moral Theology?* (Washington, D.C.: Corpus Books, 1968), p. 169. On the inconsistent terminology in Thomas and the difficulties this presents, see Eric D'Arcy, *Conscience and Its Right to Freedom* (New York: Sheed & Ward, 1961), pp. 69–71.
69. ". . . *deposita sunt reddenda. Et hoc quidem ut in pluribus verum est: sed potest in aliquo casu contingere quod sit damnosum, et per consequens, irrationabile, si deposita reddantur; puta si aliquis petat ad impugnandam patriam. Et hoc tanto magis invenitur deficere, quanto magis ad particularia descenditur. . . .*" Ibid. Notice these final words: The principle will be more and more open to exceptions the more you descend into the particulars of life.
70. "*Sic igitur in speculativis eadem est veritas apud omnes. . . . In operativis autem non est eadem veritas vel rectitudo practica apud omnes quantum ad propria, sed solum quantum ad communia. . . .*" Ibid. I have translated "*propria*" as particular. It refers to that which is proper and unique as opposed to "*communia.*"
71. Ibid., a. 5, ad 2.
72. *Summa Theologica* I q. 105, a. 6, ad 2. ". . . *ordo iustitiae est secundum relationem ad causam primam, quae est regula omnis iustitiae. Et ideo praeter hunc ordinem, Deus nihil facere potest.*" For further references on these exceptions in Aquinas, see II II q. 64, a. 5, ad 4; II II q. 154, a. 2, ad 2; *De Malo,* q. 3, a. 1, ad 17; *De Potentia Dei,* q. 1, a. 6, ad 4; *In III Sent.,* d. 37, a. 4.
73. Clyde A. Holbrook, "The Erosion of Humanitas," *Worldview* 17, No. 7 (July 1974), p. 35.
74. Ibid., p. 39.
75. Aristotle, *Nichomachean Ethics,* Bk. 5, Chap. 10, 1137b, 14.
76. Ibid., Bk. 6, Chap. 4, 1140b, 9–10.

CHAPTER EIGHT

ON REASON AND RELIANCE

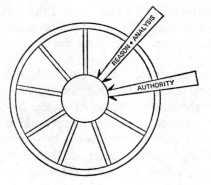

In this chapter I am speaking of two further and significant modes of moral evaluation: *reason* and *authority*. Both are broad avenues whose roles in ethics will be fleshed out by a number of other things treated throughout this book. Reason and authority function throughout all of the human processes of thought. My concern here is to show how they contribute to ethics. First to reason.

Reason, in the words of the Oxford English Dictionary, is "the guiding principle of the human mind in the process of thinking." That, obviously, is quite generic, and in this broad sense would overlap with much that is covered by the other evaluational processes (spokes) in my wheel model of ethics. Reason, in fact, is as broad as human life. We can see it at work everywhere from science to poetry, though with varying degrees of ascendance and in varying forms. The way we reason is qualified by the challenge we address.

In mathematics, reason can reach high levels of abstractness, and in the sciences it will work between and combine the theoretical and the practical.

In ethics, one would expect reason to take on and reflect the nature of moral experience. If it simply functioned here as it does in other areas of experience, it would mean that moral experience is not distinctive or that reason is not fully drawn into the service of moral meaning. If, for example, reason equates ethics with some elements of mathematics (and this has happened), reason will to some degree pervert where it seeks to serve. The Pythagoreans, for example, felt that numbers and proportions constituted the basis of reality. This was their dominant metaphor. Since our thought bears the marks of our metaphors, we find that the Pythagoreans took the idea of the mathematical mean and, in ethics, made good behavior the mean between two extremes. The metaphor and the mathematical bias were not useless, but they did introduce a certain abstractness and artificiality that did not always meet the demands of the mysteries of moral meaning.[1]

To show the proper role of reason in ethics, I will list some of its tasks, show how it relates to other evaluational processes, and in this way indicate the distinctiveness of reason in the workings of the mind of the moralist. I see reason as working intelligence. It has more to do with perspiration than with inspiration. Reason is not the mind waiting in passive intensity the gifting touch of the creative muse. It is, rather, the mind throwing itself into the tasks of truth-finding.

Reason is combined with analysis in this spoke of the wheel model to emphasize its laboring function. Analysis comes from the Greek meaning to loosen up or to break up. Early impressions, in ethics or elsewhere, come to us in largely undifferentiated globs. Reason and analysis break them up and sort them out so that we can know what it really is that we are talking about. This is sometimes a mammoth operation. Everyone has some idea of what a multinational corporation is. Without a lot of perspiring reason and analysis, however, that idea will remain at the level of an impressionistic mass and no realistic ethics of the MNC will be done. The MNC has to be judged morally, since it is a principal agent in the community of persons and has deep effects on the quality of life. Judging MNCs ethically, however, is no simple matter given the new economic and political complexities that they have foisted upon us. We are only at the first stages of the analysis of these entities. The reasons and analysis process will broaden but it must go on or the MNC will slip beyond the pale of moral consciousness. As Aquinas said, "To order is the function of reason."[2] If reason is not functioning, then disorder is the result. The moral import of the MNC is too profound to go unordered by moral reason.

Reason has its work cut out for it in every area of moral experience. Among its critical tasks: to find and compare ethically meaningful empirical data; to search for the unasked questions; to test the regnant authorities before which minds may be playing dead; to cope with the inevitable partiality of our knowledge; to jog the lazy memory; to fight the allure of too facile consensus; to break the strangle hold of habituation; to check our myths and other filters; to solve the conflicts between and among principles; and to tend to the reformulation and correction of principles in view of new experience. In a word, reason works to be critical and to fight the superficiality that is the fruit of homework undone.

Reason must also make sure that the mind stays in process. The mind, to take its ease, might well pretend that reality is not mobile or that it will stop to be photographed. In fact, the mind is not best compared to a camera, which reflects without animation what is there. Human knowledge is interaction between the knower and the known. The knower filters and projects, and introduces incoming data into his subjectivity. We are changed by our contact with the world, and as a result of that, we come to know it in different ways. Old eyes and young eyes look at the same things, but the resultant knowledge is different. A major function of reason is to remind us that life is in process. If we forget, we can be put into the predicament of the compulsive better who, while watching a football game on television, lost ten dollars on a play, and then lost another ten on the instant replay. He mistook the past for the present, as will anyone who loses the sense of process.

Thus far, obviously, we have not shown that reason in ethics is distinctive. All of the above chores could in some proper way be commended to the reasoning political scientist as well as to a reasoning moralist. So for distinctiveness, we must push on.

Reason and Affection . .

Ethical reason is in pursuit of moral values. Values, however, are appreciated affectively as well as intellectually. Thus ethical reasoning is especially bound up with affectivity. This does not mean that ethics is reducible to affectivity in the sense that I shall describe the appreciative, prizing function of affection in the following chapter. It is, however, infused with the affective response that makes moral inquiry meaningful. A value is a perceived good, and the primary response to value is in the affections. By the definition of R. B. Perry, "Value is any object of any interest."[3] If we are interested, it means that we are not just cold, detached, and purely intellectual in our approach as we might be when thinking about the sum of the angles of a triangle. When we think and talk values, the will is involved.

Of course, the will is also involved when you are reasoning and thinking about how to get your car started when it has stalled. Getting it started is a good and a matter of interest, and affectivity rises to it. Figuring out what is wrong under the hood, however, is not an intrinsically affective achievement. Affectivity prods you to think in this case, but it is not integral to the thought process as it is when one reasons about moral values. Thinking about that engine touches on what you need. Thinking about moral values touches on what you are. Your feelings and affectivity will be implicated in moral reasoning in a way that can be called intrinsic.

Ethical reason relates to the foundational moral experience. It is an agent of that experience. Were a person in no way immersed in that experience, the material that is the concern of ethical reason would be blurred and only partially known. The situation would be like that of a person born blind who hears about colors. He could understand what science would explain about the physical perception of various colors, and he could even make true statements about colors, but he would have no experiential base from which to know them. He could know about them, but he could not know them. Similarly the affective faith experience that founds ethics is the ground of ethical meaningfulness. Reasoning about nonmoral matters does not have this same rootage in affectivity and faith.

When Garrett Hardin in his "lifeboat ethics" argues that the dispossessed of the world will have to be allowed to perish in their hunger, there is the ring of reason about it, and not a few have pronounced it reasonable. However, what he is doing here is reasoning about persons as though they were not persons. Tribal-fashion, he has cut off a large segment of humanity from full status in humanity. With that done, he can reason, in a way that many find convincing, that these depersonalized beings cannot be helped by being fed any more than cancer cells are helped by being fed. The malignancy just grows. The defect in this reasoning is affective.

There are defects at other levels also, starting with his dominant metaphor of the lifeboat. He has missed the reality of human inter-dependency and thus the fact that the human family is on one single lifeboat. He also underestimates the impatience and ingenuity of the dispossessed. But in a way that illustrates the affective component of moral reason, he defects at the level of caring. His reasoning process does not show signs of being shaped by the perceived worth of these masses of persons. His reason falters, therefore, not just because of the broader defects in rationality, such as false analogies, mistaken metaphors, unawareness of alternative and consequences, but also because his moral reasoning (which is classically tribal) is lamed at the level of foundational affectivity.

Analytical philosophers who are concerned with what it is that makes statements specifically moral will note that I see Hardin as doing ethics because he is talking about what does or does not befit the *humanum*. However, he is doing it poorly, for the reasons offered. No one functioning in society with passable success is quite like the man born blind. A complete psychopathic blackout of the value of persons and their environment is not imaginable in anyone who is coping socially. The *bête noire* of our example, Garrett Hardin, makes many meaningful and sound ethical statements throughout his various writings. The defect found here was in one specific area where apparent distortions at the level of caring had visible and practical effects on his ethical position.

I am not allowing that Hardin's affective deficiencies put him into the realm of the amoral or nonmoral. While discoursing about what befits persons as persons, he depersonalizes some persons to bring advantages to other persons. His moral experience is segmented; his conclusion thus is not nonmoral, but immoral. Something similar happens in the calculations of military planners who coldly and tearlessly discuss the civilian losses in projected nuclear or counterinsurgency actions. The economist also may be repressed in his moral affect as he unfeelingly assesses levels of "acceptable unemployment." In all of these instances, reason becomes technologized and demoralized. It tends to treat some persons as nonpersons while remaining sensitive to some of the other needs of other persons. It is the awareness of persons as persons that implicates reason in affectivity.

This does not mean that persons whose reason is sensitized to the value of persons will all reach the same conclusions. Their sensitivity will not yield a detailed code of do's and don'ts. They may even in some circumstances reach conclusions that indicate that killing people might be tragically but morally called for. Reason that is not desensitized, however, would do this in Augustine's "mournful mood." Even moral reason which has not been stripped down to the level of bare technological considerations may be drawn to painful conclusions amid the complexities and radical imperfections of human life at this early point in moral evolution.

Finally, on the symbiosis of reason and affectivity in ethics, it should be noted that reason always stands on the brink of rationalization. The thrust of the affections can easily be self-serving. This is why ethical method has to be a system of checks and balances, as the various evaluational processes illustrated by the spokes of the wheel model will illustrate. Our immediate, and not always worthy purposes, can present themselves as the inexorable dictates of pure moral reason. This kind of rascality is an indigenous problem of ethics. Aristotle speaks to it. He notes that "someone may say, 'We all aim at what appears to us to be good, but over this appearance we have no control.' How the end appears is determined by the character of the individual."[4] A misguided wish is often father to the ethical thought. In value matters we can come to see what we want to see. The difficulty is in distinguishing real good from apparent good. Aristotle does well to spotlight the role of character in this.

Character, as I will discuss further in the next chapter, has a cognitive role, since merely apparent good will not ring true when brought within the dynamism of a character geared to the really good. Our impressions about morality resonate within our characterological orientation. This is just fine, and gives us a kind of instinctive divining power for discovering the truly moral—if ours is a good character. If not, the good that seems most congenial to us may be only apparent. What makes this so difficult is that no one thinks he or she has a bad character—outside of rare moments of major moral conversion. We admit to misdeeds, but always with the firmly implied suggestion that these are atypical of our over-all orientation or character. Of our general dispositions and characters Aristotle said: "Their beginning is something we can control, but as they develop step by step the stages of their development elude our observation—it is like the progress of a disease."[5] Again, a system of checks and balances built into one's ethical method is the only guard against this natural hazard.

Reason as the Forebear of Creativity . . .

With reference back to Chapter Six, this point can be briefly made. The creative muse, however much a gift her interventions are, is most likely to be received by "the prepared mind." It is not pure luck or sheer grace that explains a creative contribution. Hard-working reason and analysis are the preparing forces that make straight the way for the creative insight. Referring back to the image of the detective, the more clues we have gone out and gathered, the more likely are we to have the creative insight which discovers the answer and solves the case. Also, the tasks of reason listed above (p. 263) are a spelling out of the kind of preparation that has to be done if creative fortune is to visit. If reason is stagnant and unalert, the mind will be dulled by unasked questions. And a closed mind is a poor target for the creative muse. If reason is not checking our filtering myths we shall be seduced by our own imaginings and abstractions. Another block for creativity. If reason does not check the godly authorities to whom our minds may be bound in unknowing servitude, the mind will be unaware of even the need for creative break-throughs. Similarly, reason can serve to prepare the mind by bringing critical thought to the discovery of superficial consensus and ideological blinders. Reason can provide the research and the solid information base that are the prerequisites for creative fecundity.

Reasonable or Rationalistic . . .

Reason has two verbal relatives in *reasonable* and *rationalistic* that are scarcely on speaking terms. The one has felicitous connotations, the other does not. Reasonable, the good relative, is not just the adjective that relates to reason. It has a broader meaning and is instructive about the role and nature of reason. To be called reasonable is a compliment. No one would want to be considered anything else. Wrong, maybe, but never unreasonable! Reasonable connotes an openness to reality and to being, along with a kind of balance and thoroughness. In a notable way, this sense of reasonableness emerges in the "reasonable man" criterion employed in court decisions. Such usage exemplifies jurisprudential confidence in the reasoning mind

and in the category of reasonableness. It amounts to saying that the
reasonable is equivalent to the good, the legal, and the proper. The
word "reason" does not bear all of these connotations in general
parlance. It should, however, bear them in a thoughtful ethics. As
Josef Pieper says of reason in ethics:

> *Reason* includes a reference to reality; indeed it is itself this
> reference. "In accord with reason" is in this sense that
> which is right "in itself," that which corresponds to reality
> itself. The order of reason accordingly signifies that some-
> thing is disposed in accordance with the truth of real
> things.[6]

With this in mind, it could be said that that which is reasonable is
moral. Without all of these distinctions in mind, however, this could
not be said, since the term, in common speech, can also entertain
connotations of casualness in deciding what is right. "As long as you
are being reasonable . . ." Reasonable does not always imply the serious work that reason does. With these qualifications, however, and
with the full meaning of *ethical* reason in view, it is possible to say
that the good and the reasonable are as one.[7]

If there is danger in so saying—and history suggests that there is—
it ties into the words "rationalistic" and "rationalism." Rationalism
cannot be caught in a neat definition. It can, however, be described
and shown forth in examples. Rationalistic thinking is, in an Irish
colloquial expression, "entirely too smart." It is reason shorn of its
necessary modesty. It is also often moral reason cut off from collaborative affectivity. It is heartless head of the sort that recalls Shakespeare's phrase: "Sicklied o'er with the pale cast of reason." Rationalism is also fastidious and simplistic, prone to tidiness even
when the truth is sloppy. Much devotion to reason has turned rationalistic.

The roots of "right reason" theories of ethics explain this. As mentioned above, the Pythagoreans were an early influence on the understanding of reason. Historian of ethics Vernon Bourke credits the
Pythagoreans with the beginning of the approach which sees the
good as that which is rational and intelligible. He goes on to say:

> It is quite possible that Aristotelian and medieval theories
> of right reason (*recta ratio*) as the norm of ethical judg-
> ment are directly indebted to Pythagorean intellectualism.
> The classic Greek respect for the life of reason (*logos*) is al-
> ready evident in the early Pythagorean teachings.[8]

The mathematical bias of the Pythagoreans had to give a highly intellectualistic cast to the idea of reason. The mathematical paradigm simply is not conducive to a conception of ethical reason that integrates intellect and affectivity.

The Stoic philosophers were also a major influence in the historical understanding of reason in ethics. As Bourke says to them:

> As much as Hegel, the Stoics thought that the world is completely rational in character. There is a reason (logos) for everything that occurs. . . . the Stoics saw all things as interrelated in a comprehensible manner. . . .[9]

Such a view is not sufficiently hedged by a sense of mystery. And it is precisely this sense of mystery and the modesty it engenders that are sorely lacking in rationalistic thinking. The hubris of rationalism is to think that the mind can take the measure of the real. Stoic pan-rationalism encouraged this. There are overdrawn expectations of cosmos and too great a hunger for patterns in Stoic rationalism that found their way into much of the ethics of right reason.

Catholic ethics in the past invested heavily in this kind of rationalism. It led to a kind of overconfidence in the ability of the mind to discover universal patterns. Thus in sexual ethics, contraception, nonmarital sex acts, and remarriage after divorce were always and everywhere wrong. For example, Arthur Vermeersch, arguing the absolute immorality of contraception, said that what was discovered here was "the essential order which man should observe in his use of the conjugal act." No Stoic would demur at the idea that the mind can discover such an essential "order" in nature. Vermeersch goes on to show how abstract rationalistic thinking can get. It can even prescind from the good or harm done to the persons about whom and for whom ethics is presumably done. All weight shifts to the perception of order. "This argument is free from any consideration" of what this means "for the private or the common good." He goes on:

> True, the provident God himself, while He lays down the order to be kept, is the guardian and protector of the common good. But we should not weigh what advantage or harm each act may bring in order to determine from this that there is a serious or light fault. Mortal sin . . . is formally an act substantially against order laid down by divine law, but not formally an act against the common good.[10]

This is a chilling thought, and shows the wisdom of Sartre's observation cited above that the greatest evil of which man is capable is to treat as abstract that which is concrete. Rationalism is not harmless. When it comes home to roost, it can be cruel. In Vermeersch's rationalism, once reason has captured the essential order, contradictory indications in the form of harm to persons may be ignored. And to add sacrilege to injury, it was all blamed on God! Thus a couple who had compelling reasons not to have another child could not achieve this effect by contraception or by sterilization which was proscribed by similarly rationalistic thinking. What the result would be and what it would do to their lives was not a matter for consideration, since the moralists had found for them the "order laid down by divine law." Fortunately, this approach has been abandoned by all but a rugged minority of Catholic moralists. The historical development of such a system, however, stands as a witness to the mind's lugubrious ability to be bewitched by its own schemes. Reason's task is not to come up with "definitive" charts of reality.[11]

Reason in Recess . . .

Not every age believes with Dante that reason in man "is especially his life and the actuality of his noblest part."[12] Because of the abuses of reason and because reason is work, it is at times less revered. Our age is inclined to bypass the laborious horizontal explorations of ethical reason and to move by a vertical stroke to simplistic moral conclusions. The philosopher E. W. Kluge is of the opinion that "if there is one thing that characterizes the current moral scene, it is the abandonment of deliberate reason in favor of unreasoned personal preference."[13] Such an approach leaves us at the mercy of whimsy even though whimsy may defend itself in terms of conscience. What Kluge sees are the shadows of Dada. Ethics in any age must be an apologist of reason, but especially in an age when reason recedes before the seductive simplicities of caprice.

Authority and the Art of Reliance . . .

When all the praises of reason have been sounded, it remains quite probable that most of our moral opinions are not the result of a reasoning process, but are directly due to the influence of someone we admire or love or to the influence of traditional and accepted wisdom which we have never questioned. Reliance on authority of one kind or another is probably the most common form of moral evaluation, even among those who feel themselves highly independent and "liberated." Everyman has his authorities; we are all more docile than we suppose. What we accept on authority we may come to understand and appropriate through our own cognitional experience, but acceptance without critical examination is commonplace. As psychologist E. R. Goodenough writes:

> The great majority of men . . . take their patterns of conduct from their society or traditions, get them ready-made as blueprints. . . . This is by no means the attitude of simple and weak minds alone. Often the human mind fears itself, and we shrink from our own thinking.[14]

Reliance on authority in doing ethics, then, might seem at first blush to be a problem, a defection from the work of intelligence. However, in presenting authority as one of the evaluational processes of ethical method, I am viewing it positively, as a resource for understanding. Like all the other evaluational resources and processes (illustrated by the spokes on the wheel model), authority can be used or abused. The study of authority, however, is fraught with some special difficulties. In a time that is marked by the steady slaughter of sacred cows in Church and State, and by the successful debunking of sacred and secular oracles, we might easily indulge in the illusion of thinking ourselves free at last and independent of all authority. First, then, let us see reliance on authority as an eternal fact of life, and then move on to see its potential for use and misuse in ethics.

Two centuries ago, Adam Smith addressed the subject of our natural credulousness.

> . . . the man scarce lives who is not more credulous than he ought to be, and who does not, upon many occasions, give credit to tales which not only turn out to be perfectly false, but which a very moderate degree of reflection and attention might have taught him could not well be true. The natural disposition is always to believe. It is acquired wisdom and experience only that teach incredulity, and they very seldom teach it enough.[15]

It is no less true today that persons, even the sophisticated, are conspicuously prone to "buy a bill of goods" with uncritical acceptance. There are a number of perennial authority sources to whose sway none of us should facilely claim immunity. Let us look at some of the more potent forms of authority that operate in our social world such as peer authority, expertise, religious, crypto-religious, and tribal authority, tradition, and charisma.

First, there is the imperious authority of the peer group that imposes a view of life and its values upon all regardless of age or education. It is no easy task to stand apart from the dictates of the peer group. (Neither, as we shall see, is it a virtue always to attempt to do so.) What the peer group does among young and old is to establish an evaluational orthodoxy. It takes courage and strength of mind to depart from that orthodoxy. And staying within it is not without its alluring satisfactions. As psychologist Paul W. Pruyser says: "To be orthodox is to be loved by our important orthodox love objects, to be considered lovable by them, and thus to have self-respect."[16] Moral value positions are closely linked to our emotions and to our sense of identity. Dissenters against established positions are perceived as a threat. Hence the peer group consensus will be re-enforced by a number of sanctions ranging from excommunication to ridicule. This phenomenon is as visible in countercultural groups as it is in monasteries or board rooms. The devotees of a hippie commune, with all of their avowed commitment to doing one's own thing, are permitted few deviations regarding dress, language, recreational forms, or moral attitudes. Though they have substituted one orthodoxy for another, they have not stepped outside the dynamics of authority. Fads and special options are enforced there as everywhere.

Another perennial authority that has taken on new force is the expert. He is the only relief from swelling complexity and an essential authority in a time when the idea of universal knowledge is seen as chimeric. The problem with the expert is that he can become an oracle and can command even our common sense to recede before the prestige of his special qualifications. This problem is illustrated by the subcommittee that is sent away to study a complicated matter and returns with faulty findings. It takes a special kind of courage to rise up before the authority of those who have done the research on this and who come to us wearing the mantle of expert authority.

Expertise has gone mechanical in our day with the advent of the computer. The computer adds to expertise the attractiveness of apparently unalloyed objectivity. By attributing intelligence to the computer, an attribution that is ambiguous at its very best, we have made the computer the modern oracle. We repair to it with expectations it cannot meet, looking for answers it cannot give. It should not have been necessary for Claire Sterling, writing of the plight of the countries of the Sahel, to remonstrate that "there is no need for a million-dollar MIT computer study, one of the U. S. AID's more exotic contributions, to figure out how the Sahel can be turned into a paying proposition."[17] Here and elsewhere, the temptation is to try to transfer the burden of ingenuity from the creative spirit of persons to the machine that symbolizes to us redemption by expertise. The aura of the computer hangs heavily over the academic world, where more critical intelligence should be anticipated. Studies and articles buttressed by masses of computerized data have an immediate prestige even if the yield in truth is negligible. The very fact of computerization lends its own special kind of authority and prestige. As Fred Hapgood comments: "Every culture has its juvenile embarrassments; misdirected enthusiasms which fail dramatically and in retrospect seem to say something humiliating about the civilization that pursued them. The great computer craze of the late fifties and the sixties is such a case."[18]

Some fear that the stunning miracles of the electronic age may lead to more than "juvenile embarrassment." Zbigniew Brzezinski writes: "In the technetronic society the trend would seem to be towards the aggregation of the individual support of millions of uncoordinated citizens, easily within the reach of magnetic and attractive personalities effectively exploiting the latest communication techniques to manipulate emotions and control reason."[19]

Authority always operates powerfully in religious and cryptoreligious contexts. Wherever the aura of the sacred accrues, there is a tendency for critical judgment to give way to awe. Since moral experience brings us into contact with the phenomenon of sacredness, one could expect religiously tinged authorities to operate here. And, of course, the major religions have been active in assuming an authoritative role in matters moral. We find an authoritative moral teaching or scripture in most religions; the Vedas of the Hindus, the Koran of the Muslims, the Dhamma of the Buddhists, the Bible of the Christians, and the biblical and talmudic writings of the Jews. Religions have met a socially felt need in spelling out the meaning and shape of the good life. As Karl Mannheim writes:

> In every society there are social groups whose special task it is to provide an interpretation of the world for that society. . . . Thus the magicians, the Brahmins, the medieval clergy are to be regarded as intellectual strata, each of

which in its society enjoyed a monopolistic control over the moulding of that society's world-view. . . .[20]

Those who fulfill this priestly role may not always be within a formally religious agency. As Mannheim says, those who fulfill it in our society may be those we refer to as the "intelligentsia." What is important to note is that much that is numinous in character is located within the apparently secular. Nationalism and patriotism have been recognized as "full of gods." A nation is no merely pragmatic association of persons, but is rather a social entity endowed with a sacred mystique that can evoke complete devotion from its citizens even to the point of the "supreme sacrifice" of their lives. National heroes assume a kind of sainted role, and the foundational documents and constitutions of nations acquire a biblical quality. National sacredness also overshadows those who hold high office so that they achieve an authority that is not without sacral tones. In ancient times (and the term "ancient" is very relative and should not connote that which is utterly and uninfluentially distant from us) the national leader was thought to be a god. There has been movement away from this, as when, for example, the Emperor Aurelian renounced his claim to be a human god and declared himself with only slightly less pride to be no more than God's vicegerent on earth. In the modern state the sacrality of the leader is more muted, though it shows through in inaugural ceremonies and in the priestly trappings and protocol that attend officials of state. We have not yet outgrown the sacralized tribe. Sacralized civil authority, then, is extant. It is visible in caricature form in the "super-patriot" whose zeal could only be described within the categories of religious devotion. It also can appear in more subtle form in the conceptualization of citizenship. Religious authority, whether implicit or explicit, remains a major force in the valuations of both private and political ethics today.

Tradition is another common authority. Tradition breeds familiarity, and the familiar is likely to seem reliable and true. Psychological studies have shown what advertisers have always banked on, that mere familiarity makes something seem attractive, regardless of its merits.[21] The "traditional" has some likely claims to reliability, since that which has stood the test of time is probably not without some merit. However, since error can become as traditional as truth, this authority too must be tested.

Charisma is another widely influential form of authority. The term need not be limited to the magnetic qualities of political figures, but refers to the personality strengths that are present more or less in almost everyone by virtue of which we can sway and influence others. In any group, charisma will function and will exert a kind of blind influence on the group members. Charisma has many ingredients. The attractiveness of persons,[22] the attitudes and confidence they project, the emotions they engender, etc., all give persons more or less influence or charisma. Achievement also lends charisma, as does the mere fact of being famous. Nations can gain charisma because of inspirational achievements (as the United States did in the idealistic Revolution of 1776) or simply because of their technological prowess. The forces that generate charisma might be worthy or quite irrelevant. For this reason, a sensitive ethics must alert persons to the presence of charismatic influences in their thought processes. Again, charisma can function negatively or positively, but the point here is that it is a pervasive force where persons interact and evaluate.

Authority functions in myriad forms, and the human mind accepts on authority ethical positions that it has not thought through. But what of the widely heard contention that authority is withering in our day as all forms of traditional authority come under attack? That there has been a change is undeniable. As Pierre Delooz observes: "The exercise of authority has changed within the space of a single generation, and so abruptly and fundamentally that the relationships between men and women, parents and children, employers and employees, officers and their subordinates, parish priests and their flock, etc., are all being challenged and reassessed."[23] Delooz suggests two important reasons for this. First, the flow of information has relativized the power of traditional authority figures. But more basically, authority "is no longer regarded as a value, but only as the precondition of a value: efficacy. . . . Caught in the growing flow of information and forced to yield to the imperatives of efficacy, authority in the traditional sense cannot recover from the blow."[24]

What this represents is not so much a failure of authority as a maturation of it. The idea of efficacy implies that authority must show that it is trustworthy and that it promotes the good. Authority must be earned; it does not come *ex officio*. This is certainly progress and a move away from magical forms of oracular authority. As a trend it is to be welcomed.

The Good Side of Authority . . .

Excessive reliance on authority is a one-rubric approach to ethics which ultimately represents a despair of our capacity to know. There is, however, a healthy reliance on authority which is part of an integral approach to ethics. Proper reliance on authority is both a practical necessity and a community-building form of trust. Dependence on authoritative sources is required by our finitude. Complexity is expanding exponentially, and as a result knowledge is more specialized. The dream of comprehensive knowledge has passed, and any attempt to retrieve it would condemn us to superficiality and frustration. Reliance on authority, of course, must be critical and not naïve. We must first of all be aware of the authorities who are influencing us, and to that end I listed examples of pan-human types of authority. Furthermore, the authority source must be tested and seen to be credible and trustworthy. When possible the mind should not rest with the extrinsic contact with truth afforded by accepting something as true on the authority of another. It should attempt to know what it accepts when that is feasible. And finally, authority must be seen as but one of the many processes by which we grope toward the truth. It is not the only one. We cannot rationally succumb to the oracular instinct and let authority do our thinking.

The first positive role of authority, then, is pragmatic. We need help, and in accepting authority we get that help from those sources that we judge reliable. There is a deeper meaning to authority, however. Authority is a personalizing and community-building form of trust. The inclination we have to rely on the opinions of others is not just pragmatic; it is also a manifestation of our social nature. As David Hume wrote: "No quality of human nature is more remarkable, both in itself and in its consequences, than that propensity we have to sympathise with others, and to receive by communication their inclinations and sentiments, however different from, or even contrary to, our own."[25] Authority can only function in an atmosphere of trust. In a matter of merely technical expertise, the trust element will be less important than the indicators of genuine knowledgeability. When authority functions at a more personal level, however, a process of trust is in effect.

Authority in moral matters operates powerfully within a matrix of personal exchange. We will trust the value inclinations of persons whom we find worthy. Those factors that hinder personal relationships also block the functioning of authority. In fact the deeper and fuller a relationship is, the better will the parties of that relationship become authorities to one another in moral discernment. A true friend is a moral authority to us even if we rarely think of it that way. True friendship breeds trust in the value orientation of the friend.

Acceptance of authority is not just an impersonal acceptance of a known source of information. It is also a personal response to the personal source of that authority and thus is a socializing act. Acceptance of authority involves a favorable assessment of the moral qualities of the personal source. As Aristotle wrote in his *Rhetoric*:

> Persuasion is achieved by the speaker's personal character when the speech is so spoken as to make us think him credible. . . . It is not true, as some writers assume in their treatises on rhetoric, that the personal goodness revealed by the speaker contributes nothing to his power of persuasion; on the contrary, his character may almost be called the most effective means of persuasion he possesses.[26]

Thus, authority is not an alien intrusion on the autonomy of rational man, but is rather part of a system of reliance and trust that not only increases our contact with truth but also intensifies relationships among persons. Again, this is a normal part of developing moral consciousness. Inability to accept authority influences is a social and psychological problem and a problem in ethics.

Some years ago, when speaking at the University of Pennsylvania, the existentialist philosopher Gabriel Marcel was asked how he came to change his attitude toward a personal value question he had discussed. His reply, which was perfectly existentialistic, was simple: personal encounters. Nothing else, he insisted, ever makes us change important value assessments. We need not be as absolute as Marcel to accept the authoritative power that operates through the medium of friendship and trust and to see authority as indigenous both to the socialization process and to moral discernment.

Conclusion . . .

Reason and reliance on moral authority, though apparently as antithetical as independence and dependence, are conjoined in the service of moral truth. Each are ways in which our pluriform consciousness seeks attunement with the really good as it emerges in the swirl of social and historical existence. Reason and authority are both broad concepts, and the fuller meaning of each for ethics will be seen in the elaboration of other parts of this ethical method. Reason is involved in the whole expository phase of ethics and is a motor or collaborative force in most of the evaluative processes. Authority operates in a number of ways aside from those mentioned in this chapter. Principles, for example, come to us with the authority of cultural acceptance often religiously and legally fortified. Also the discussion of *group experience* will illustrate the ways in which the individual is drawn into the moral patterns of the group. Here the attempt has been to show, as any exposition of ethical method must, how the mind should pursue moral truth through the work of reason and the virtue of reliance.

NOTES—CHAPTER EIGHT

1. Aristotle's use of the golden mean was credited by him to Pythagorean thought. See Aristotle, *Nichomachean Ethics*, Bk. 2, Chap. 6, 1106a 14–1107a 25. Thomas Aquinas followed Aristotle on this. However, both Thomas and Aristotle moved beyond the symbols of mathematics in their ethical epistemology and developed a broader and more elaborate system of ethics. Their devotion to "the mean," however, is strained at times and shows the hazards that beset those who are touched by the long shadow of Pythagoras.

2. Thomas Aquinas, *Commentary on the Nichomachean Ethics*, Bk. II, Lectio 3; translated by C. I. Litzinger (Chicago: Regnery, 1964), Vol. 1, p. 126.

3. R. B. Perry, *General Theory of Value* (New York: Longmans, Green, 1926), pp. 115–20.

4. Aristotle, *Nichomachean Ethics*, Bk. 3, Chap. 5, 1114a 32. Translation is that of J. A. K. Thomson.

5. Ibid., 115a, 1, p. 92. "Character" in this translation is obviously interpretative on Thomson's part and is not an anachronistic attempt to insert Aristotle into the modern ethics of character.

6. Josef Pieper, *The Four Cardinal Virtues* (New York: Harcourt, Brace & World, 1965), pp. 115–56. Pieper is discussing the meaning of reason in Thomas Aquinas, noting that in Thomas it is used realistically, not idealistically or rationalistically, that it has none of the

connotations of the *ratio* of the Enlightenment, and that it is not spiritualistic. For a fuller idea of Thomas, it is well to look at his idea of *ratio practica*, the role of prudence in ethics and the relationship of prudence to the moral virtues, and to knowledge by way of connaturality.

7. Natural law theories of ethics would find this a very compatible idea in view of the prominence of the notion of "right reason" in that tradition. There is much variety in natural law theory, however. Sometimes it has a physicalist cast, sometimes it is highly rationalistic and idealistic. Its roots in Greek rationalism and its use of the metaphor "law" to describe ethics did not lead to uniformly happy results. The criticism of rationalistic thinking in this chapter is relevant to much, though not all, that is done in the ethics of natural law.

8. Vernon J. Bourke, *History of Ethics* (Garden City, N.Y.: Doubleday & Co., Inc., Image Books, 1968), Vol. 1, p. 16.

9. Ibid., pp. 131–32.

10. Arthur Vermeersch, S.J., *De Castitate et de Vitiis Contrariis* (Rome, 1921), p. 256, note 258; quoted in John G. Milhaven, "Towards an Epistemology of Ethics," *Theological Studies* 27 (1966), p. 230. Milhaven's translation.

11. Heinrich A. Rommen, writing on the natural law, shows the divine exemplarism that came into this approach. "The order of all being has its principle in God: as order of essences in God's essence, as created existing order in God's will. The essences of things, as first creatively conceived by God's intellect, are, once established, unalterable. This order of the world is the eternal law. . . . The natural moral law is therefore the eternal law for rational, free beings." Heinrich A. Rommen, *The Natural Law* (St. Louis, Mo.: B. Herder Book Co., 1947), pp. 178, 181.

12. Dante, *Convivio*, II, 1, and III, 15.

13. Eike-Henner W. Kluge, *The Practice of Death* (New Haven: Yale University Press, 1975), p. viii.

14. E. R. Goodenough, *The Psychology of Religious Experiences* (New York: Basic Books, 1965), p. 120.

15. Adam Smith, *The Theory of Moral Sentiments* (New York: Augustus M. Kelley, 1966), pp. 494–95.

16. Paul W. Pruyser, A *Dynamic Psychology of Religion* (New York: Harper & Row, 1968), p. 272.

17. Claire Sterling, "The Making of the Sub-Saharan Wasteland," *Atlantic* 233 (May 1974), p. 104.

18. Fred Hapgood, "Computers Aren't So Smart, After All," *Atlantic* 234 (Aug. 1974), p. 38.

19. Zbigniew Brzezinski, "The Technetronic Society," *Encounter* 30, No. 1 (Jan. 1968), p. 19.
20. Karl Mannheim, *Ideology and Utopia* (New York: Harcourt, Brace & World, Inc., A Harvest Book, 1961), p. 10.
21. See Robert Zajone, "The Attitudinal Effects of Mere Exposure," *Journal of Personality and Social Psychology Monograph Supplement*, 9 (1968), pp. 1–27.
22. On the influence of even merely physical attractiveness on our judgments, see Elliot Aronson, *The Social Animal* (New York: Viking Press, 1972), Chap. 7.
23. Pierre Delooz, "The Western Family," *Cross Currents*, 23 (Winter 1974), p. 432.
24. Ibid.
25. David Hume, *A Treatise of Human Nature*, Vol. 2, Pt. I, Sec. XI (London: J. M. Dent & Sons; New York: E. P. Dutton & Co., 1962), p. 40.
26. Aristotle, *Rhetoric*, Bk. I, Chap. 2, 1356a 4–5, 10–13.

CHAPTER NINE

THE FEEL OF TRUTH

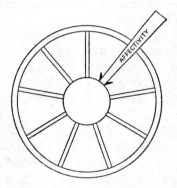

Great truths are felt before they are expressed.
Teilhard de Chardin (The Vision of the Past)

Like great works, deep feelings always mean
more than they are conscious of saying.
Albert Camus (The Myth of Sisyphus)

All moral experience is grounded in affectivity, in the foundational moral experience of personal value. As John Dewey said: "Affection, from intense love to mild favor, is an ingredient in all operative knowledge, all full apprehension of the good."[1] In this chapter, however, I am not just speaking of the grounding of ethics in affectivity. I am speaking more specifically of how a recognition of the cognitive nature of the affections can afford a higher level of moral awareness. It is my contention that a systematic account must be taken of the value awareness—admittedly sometimes somewhat ineffable—that comes to us through that expression of our subjectivity that we call feeling or affection. Ethics should take account of this as it goes about addressing particular cases.

Much influential thinking has been impaled on the fallacious dichotomy which divorces feeling from intelligence and affectivity from knowledge. It is my contention here that feeling is a knowing experience and that extreme mischief has been wrought, especially in ethics, by the failure to recognize this. Whether we take account of them or not, our feelings rise in the face of a morally adjudicable situation. And they do not arise as neutral outbursts, but as informed, evaluative reactions. Feelings may be mixed and contradictory just as abstract and intellectualized reasonings may be. Nevertheless, those feelings are a cognitive reaction, not a sideline eruption that takes place off the field, of knowing.

We do not have to plan for this to happen or pause to summon the *votum* of the heart, though we may have to plan to listen to it. The awareness that comes through feeling is spontaneous and quite integral to the knowledge of morality. Feelings, of course, may be repressed or encouraged in certain intrapsychic or cultural milieus, but they cannot be expunged.

An example might illustrate the natural appearance of evaluative affectivity. The purpose of the example is to show that feelings enter into an evaluative role with or without invitation, and, second, to suggest the positive value of those feelings. As was said above, all of the evaluative processes and resources illustrated by the spokes of the wheel model can be abused. It is their potential positive use that I am stressing by incorporating them within the framework of ethical method.

A Radical Plan for Good Breeding . . .

The science of genetics has pointed out the progressive deterioration of the human gene pool. It is no longer only the genetically fit who survive. The unfit now not only survive but enjoy prolonged fertility and thus can unleash their unfitness into what becomes the genetic destiny of posterity. Natural selection is not functioning as a screen, and the result is an increasing phenomenon of negative feedback whereby gene-based imperfections are spreading throughout the species. Modern technology causes more and more genetic damage, and that same technology helps genetically damaged people to live longer and to spread their genes by reproducing. Some envision a human race eventually so stocked with damaging genes that the whole race will be sick and consumed in medicinal care of itself.[2]

One temporary solution suggested by Herman J. Muller gives us an opportunity to see how feeling functions in ethics. It is very difficult to hear of this proposal without having an emotive response which is also evaluative. Muller suggested that we obtain and freeze the sperm of superior men, men such as Einstein, Pasteur, Descartes, and Lincoln. No "reasonable" woman could object to being fertilized by such men. The sperm would be preserved for as much as twenty years to ensure that the judgment of their superiority was not amiss. A panel would then judge after this period which of the men still seemed sterling genetic sources. Then their sperm could be used in a voluntary program of artificial insemination by couples who were conscious of their own genetic limitations and were anxious to strike a blow for genetic improvement within the human species.

This offers to us the picture of a noble and enlightened wife importuning her less enlightened but docile new husband in words something like this: "You know, darling, that you are the joy of my life and the fulfillment of all my dreams of love. Genetically, however, as we both know, you are, relatively speaking, something of a disaster. Therefore, let us repair to the frozen sperm bank, and select there the choice sperm that will help turn the tide of the deteriorating human gene pool."

Muller's suggestion is a scientific option that is also a matter for moral judgment. Aside from its scientific feasibility or nonfeasibility, it is a course of action that befits or does not befit the reality of what persons are; that is, it is either moral or immoral. Before one begins a complete ethical analysis of the suggestion by asking *what* the plan is in its *prima facie* physical appearance, what effects are imaginable, what alternatives could be found, etc., someone hearing the suggestion for the first time would not begin the questioning process without a preliminary stance. The very suggestion would evoke some affective response. With most persons, this response would be negative, or at least very hesitant and uneasy. One might even be aghast at the idea. On the other hand, one might also respond with fervid enthusiasm for the project.

These responses are affectivity, feelings, *Gemüt* at work. They give us an initial position on the subject even before we begin the kind of systematic analysis that this suggestion of a Nobel prize winner merits. In this reaction we are already doing ethics, though not in all the ways that a full ethical treatment would dictate. We are, nevertheless, reacting evaluatively to a proposal. We have a preliminary, tentative position on whether this proposal is or is not compatible with the implications and genuine meaning of personhood, whether it really seems to view persons as persons with all of their unique needs and possibilities. This affective response is a response of ethics. It also qualifies as a kind of knowledge. If knowledge is awareness, then, in reacting affectively in this matter, I am affectively aware, and probably in a pronounced and heightened way, of the rapport between this proposal and personhood as I understand it. Whether the affective response is positive or negative, it means that I am not entirely unknowing about the moral import of this matter.

It is possible that an unlettered person might not be able to say anything to explain or defend his reaction, yet he would have a definite reaction and would not be neutral on the matter. It is possible, also, that a person might go on to think about his first feelings on the matter and reverse his position. A negative emotional reaction might, upon further reflection, yield to a determined judgment that this is truly a bold new idea whose time has come—one which only nonreflective recalcitrance could resist. But this would only be because of change within a process that was *at every level*, in varying ways, cognitive. It would not be a movement from not knowing to knowing, but from knowing to knowing better, if the latter position became established.

To shrink from something in a reaction of abhorrence, even if the "shrinking" cannot be articulated by the person except in expletive, is an act of knowing awareness. If one heard an eloquent defense of that reaction later, one would say: Yes, that was exactly what I *felt*, although I could not explain it in words.

Let us suppose that one reacted with a sense of abhorrence and shock to Muller's idea. He might then undertake to study the matter. His study might conclude that the plan is skewed for many reasons including the following: The sperm could undergo significant mutations in this frozen state; unsuspected recessive traits might exist in the sperm of these great men only to surface in their progeny; psychosocial collisions could result if the intended goals are achieved and a very superior child is born into a very mediocre family environment; the decision of who is the ideal type and why he is ideal is rather arbitrary; etc.

When these and other reasons were marshaled, one could then

accost Muller's idea with a highly informed critique. The final articulated conclusions, however, would not differ from the initial affective response. The work of ethical inquiry would be confirmatory. Confirmation, however, is a re-enforcement of the known. Something happened in the affective reaction that must be called knowledge, and that knowledge is justified in the subsequent rational analysis.

There is an obvious difficulty to be confronted here. I am speaking as though we could have affective response cut off from or preliminary to all intellectualization and conceptualization, as though the wet of emotion and the dry of intellection could have separable existences in a person. This is not the case. Feeling, "emoting," abstracting, and reasoning are all operations of the person, not detachable faculties that can be conveniently taken aside and studied in isolation from the others as one could study the foot while paying no heed to the ear. Knowledge of certain facts or abstract knowledge may be virtually free of affectivity. But affection pervades all moral knowledge, since a complete absence of caring would render all moral categories meaningless. Furthermore, even a decidedly emotional response to a case such as that of Muller is not severed from previous intellectual and conceptualized experiences. As John Dewey writes:

> The results of prior experience, including previous conscious thinking, get taken up into direct habits, and express themselves in direct appraisal of value. Most of our moral judgments are intuitive, but this fact . . . is the result of past experience funded into direct outlook upon the scene of life.[3]

In moral knowledge, there is no purely emotional reaction and no purely conceptualized judgment. Conception and affection are essentially intertwined. Still, the distinction between the two is not a distinction without a difference. Affective knowledge is not the same as conceptualized knowledge. Abstract, conceptual knowledge can be distinguished from an affective and emotional response. The problem is that the distinction has been too drastically made and emotion has been considered something precognitive or pretercognitive. Affective knowing should be seen as a genuine though different kind of knowing. It calls for completion, and the mind should move on to other kinds of knowing to find that completion. Otherwise it will not be able adequately to give reasons for its position. Neither will it know, without the intellectual work of comparison, whether its position is the result of bias or of genuine insight.

To quote Dewey again: "As Aristotle remarked in effect a long time ago, the immediate judgments of good and evil of a good man are more to be trusted than many of the elaborately reasoned out estimates of the inexperienced."[4] But Dewey goes on to note pointedly that "there is no such thing as a good man—in an absolute sense. Immediate appreciation is liable to be warped by many considerations which can be detected and uprooted only through inquiry and criticism."[5]

The moral and psychological story of each of us is scarred and twisted. There is no ideal observer of things moral and there is no infallible feel for moral truth in any of us. Affectivity cannot be the only spoke in the wheel of moral inquiry. D. H. Lawrence's "what our blood feels is always right" must be balanced against Adolf Hitler's "I think with my blood."

Feeling and Character as Conduits of Truth . . .

I have already spoken of the relationship of character to reason. I now propose to show more of its nature and its relationship to our affections. Character is another bruised term in ethics. It has picked up a number of unfortunate connotations such as excessive rigidity and stodginess. It also has a ring of quaintness about it. This is a pity, since the reality of character is basic to an understanding of the moral life. Character is the embodiment of a person's moral orientation. It is the timbre of a person's ingrained moral quality. It takes its form from the values one has invested in. It is the moral thrust of the personality that is given its direction from the decisions of our moral history. Character is not innate but rather results from what we have done and how we have chosen within our moral environment. Aristotle puts it this way:

> . . . by doing the acts that we do in our transactions with other men we become just or unjust, and by doing the acts that we do in the presence of danger, and being habituated to feel fear or confidence, we become brave or cowardly. . . . Thus, in one word, states of character arise out of like activities.[6]

Character refers to the awesome fact that morally we come to be what we do.[7] Character is the form or kind of person we have chosen to be. It is not a superficial disposition or directioning, but is rather that moral substance which developed out of the values with which we identified in our choices. Of course, what has been said about freedom applies here. No one is entirely free. In the development of character, the cultural and physical environment have their enormous enabling or limiting influence. Still, the person is not a mindless piece of cork helplessly adrift. We exercise some directioning power so that we can be termed in some decisive sense free and in some decisive sense the architects of our character.

Character reflects the roots and the moral center of the personality. It has, therefore, a kind of stability. Atypical behavior contrary to the direction of the character is suspect. It is seen as "uncharacteristic." Sudden and major shifts in character are not to be looked for. A ruthless political operative, for example, who suddenly becomes morally transformed and religiously fervid is duly and properly suspect for a time. Character involves the direction of the person that has been established over the long haul. As such it has considerable momentum and cannot go immediately into reverse. The arc of moral conversion is broad, not narrow.

Obviously, there is no one who has a purely good or bad character. We are all amalgams of values and disvalues. Certain over-all moral traits are discernible in persons, however, and we are instinctively alert to these in "sizing people up." We do not perceive persons as a page filled with unconnected dots. We find connections and patterns, enough to make some judgment on "the kind of person" they are and the kind of thing they are likely to do. What we glimpse is called character.

Character, then, is a stabile directive moral orientation within the personality. But what does it have to do with feeling and affective knowledge? The tides of what we know move under the gravity of what we love and will. And what we love and will becomes part of us in the form of character. Character is thus a factor in moral knowing. It is, in Thomas Aquinas' related phrase, "the disposition or form by which the knower knows."[8] Character is the chamber in which new moral experience resonates, is interpreted, and known. It is a critical source of perspective in judging. The person who is equitable and just will judge matters of justice out of a sympathy for that value that will shape and condition his knowing experience. As Dewey says: "A person of narrow sympathy is of necessity a person of confined outlook upon the scene of human good. . . . Sympathy is the animating mold of moral judgment . . . because it furnishes the most efficacious *intellectual* standpoint" (Dewey's emphasis).[9] To speak of "a person of narrow sympathy" is to speak of ingrained orientation and tendencies—that is, of character.

Character comes from what we do and will—which is to say that it has its roots in the affections. We may know about moral values without their being a part of us. With moral values, as with persons, it is one thing to *know about* them and another to *know* them through the richness of multileveled personal encounter.

Affectivity, which engenders character, offers this fuller experience. What we merely know we can be detached from. Abstract intellectuality allows for distance. What we love we become. Love is a unitive and a lively force which gives things known a new vitality. It enfleshes them in us so that they become "second nature" to us. Knowledge that is shy of affectivity does not do this. The unjust man might be a whiz at ethical theories of justice. His intelligence of justice, however, is flawed by his lack of full experience of what it is about. His knowledge and awareness of what justice means is limited to one kind of potential knowing. He is weak at the foundational moral experience and thus does not have at his command what Bergson calls "the genius of the will."[10] The reasons of the heart, to which Pascal referred, will escape him. The foundational moral experience is the parent of character. Weakness there will lead to a flawed character and the possibility of distortions in moral knowledge.

Important qualifications must be added to this consideration. Just as there is no such thing as an absolutely good man, there is no such thing as an absolutely bad one. Both join the Ideal Observer in nonexistence. A total liquidation of sympathy cannot be imagined any more than one can imagine perfection in a human being. Also, the "good man" might have narrow experience and possibly he could profit from the "bad man," who may have garnered amid his iniquities a keen sense of relationship and predictability which would be valuable in assessing complicated moral matters. Thus it is not necessary simply to make a choice between the judgment of a good man or that of an expert who is not so virtuous. One would be well advised to hear from both.

Thomas Aquinas has an interesting viewpoint in this regard. He states that correctness of judgment can come about in two ways: through a perfect use of reason, or through what he calls a kind of affective "connaturality" with the matters being judged. So one person might learn about a moral value through the study of ethics. Another person, who has not studied ethics, might also judge correctly about it because he has embodied that value in his habitual disposition—or, we could say, his character. Thomas distinguishes between "learning" (*discens*) and "suffering" or "experiencing" (*patiens*). In the latter kind of knowing, love so blends the value into the reality of the person that it becomes "connatural" (second nature) to him. He can judge correctly about that value because he is so personally attuned to it. ". . . he has a correct judgment about these things according to a certain connaturality which he has to them." And connaturality comes "through love."[11]

Thomas is within the province of character here, since he is not speaking about a passing feeling but about the effect of a value established in a person through virtue. It is a stabile disposition or quality of the person brought about by his choice that connaturalizes him to the values being judged. The term "character" would accurately describe that.

Thomas' dichotomy between a "perfect use of reason" and knowledge by way of connaturality is a bit too neat. As I have argued, a good use of reason (and *a fortiori* a "perfect" use of reason) is not without the constitutive influence of affection. One could concede this and still find in Thomas a strong witness to the cognitive influence of character.

Some of Thomas' classical commentators are even clearer on the possibility of affective knowledge, in a way that stresses the idea that affectivity is insightful. Their contributions here are neglected in the history of thought. The seventeenth-century writer John of St. Thomas is certainly the strongest in the Thomistic line in this respect. He develops an explicit notion of "affective knowledge" which also ties in with the idea of character.[12] John follows Thomas in distinguishing (again a bit too neatly) the two modes of knowing and judging. One can know by study and disputation, or one can know from connaturality and affect (*ex quadam connaturalitate et affectu*).[13] John goes beyond Thomas in elaborating the difference between the two. The essential difference is that the second kind of knowledge is affective. This, of course, sounds like a confusion of the faculties of intellect and will. John faces up to this natural objection to the very idea of affective knowledge.

First of all, he does not slip off the hook by saying that affective knowledge is simply knowledge stimulated by love. Love, he admits, can make us attend more to learning and can make us apply ourselves more vigorously. It can act as an *efficient cause* to stimulate the knowing process. If you like mathematics, you will study it more and learn it better. Maybe that is all there is to say about the relationship of love and affectivity to knowledge. But John denies that this is all there is. While granting that love can do this, it can also do more. This intrinsic function of love does not change the species and form of knowledge that obtains. It is merely an external prodding force.

In affective knowledge, love acts as what he calls an "objective cause," transforming the relationship of the object known to the knower, and making for a different kind of knowledge as a result. When the object known is also loved, a formally distinct form of knowing takes place. The affections can "causally provide greater light" by rendering the object known more fully experienced. John admits that this is not easily understood or explained. "What is more occult or more hidden than the interior affections of the will?" he asks.[14] It is far easier, he says, to trace out the workings of purely intellectual knowledge. Still he presses on. In his exposition he reaches for different images than those customarily used to describe more intellectualized knowledge. Affective knowledge is less like *seeing* and more like "tasting" or "touching." The object that is loved as well as known is somehow "invascerated" within the knower. He experiences it as united to himself and hence related to himself with an entirely different sense of proportion and congeniality. Affective knowledge is just not the same as "naked" intellection.[15]

Furthermore, John says that the very concept of connaturality implies a permanent and not a transient disposition of the knower.[16] This makes his thought relevant to the discussion of character. He relates affective knowledge to a permanent disposition of the knower engendered by his affective orientation. There is solid insight in this that modern ethics can profit from.

On Delight and the Sense of Profanation . . .

Show me your delights and I will tell you what you are. In the phenomenon of delight (and its opposite, the sense of profanation) we have the most perceptible manifestation of the cognitive capacity of affectivity. The neglect of delight in modern thought and especially in modern ethics reflects our rationalistic unease with the awareness that comes through feeling. In the moral philosophy of persons such as Aristotle, Plato, and Thomas Aquinas, in contrast to most moderns, delight is given thoughtful consideration. Aristotle, for example, saw delight as a signal of where the heart or the character of a man is. He said that we must take as a "sign of states of character the pleasure or pain that ensues on acts." If we delight in doing the acts that pertain to a certain moral value, then this is a sign that this value has woven its way into our character. If we do these things but do them grudgingly and find them a burden, we have not incorporated the value into our moral fiber.[17] Delight arises from unimpeded and congruent activity.[18] In the same vein, Thomas Aquinas says that when our activity is connatural to us, it is delightful.[19] So it is that delights are the indices of character. Aristotle is willing to say in his *Ethics* that just as "truth is that which seems to the good man to be true," so too the delights of the good man can be taken as true and properly rooted.[20] The good man can therefore serve as a criterion of good and bad delights.

Notice that Aristotle's "good man" need not be learned or capable of impressive argument to be reliable. The reliance here is on his affective orientation in the face of a moral question. I have some reservations with regard to this position, but the significance of Aristotle's view for the idea of affective knowing is notable. That which is good vibrates and resonates delightfully—that is, it produces emotions of delight and pleasure—in him who is good. There is an affective response to a particular value option which is experienced as congenial, suitable, "connatural," quite in accord with one's moral orientation, and hence delightful. In the good man, this means that it is also good.[21] These emotional reactions of delight amount to an endorsement of that which is perceived. But endorsement proceeds from evaluative awareness and implies some kind of knowledge. Endorsement divorced from knowledge is just noise.

There is another aspect in the classical concept of delight that is helpfully suggestive. In discussing the effects of delight, Thomas Aquinas is guilty of taking some liberties with etymology. His transgression is pardonable, however, since the points he makes are valid —etymological foundations to the contrary notwithstanding.

Thomas suggests that delight (*delectatio*) comes from the word for broadening (*dilatatio*), and he then goes to work with this as a dominant metaphor. In delighting, we are stretched and enlarged as we somehow strain to make room for and contain that which comes to us as a new good. Delight is a reaction to that which is congenial and pleasant. The stretching and broadening effect of delight is part of the urgency of delight through which we attempt to take that which is delightful into ourselves to envelop it and enjoy it more fully.[22]

However he got to it, Thomas is on to something here. Delight is the bloom of pleasant experience and yet it does have in it elements of straining and stretching, even to the point of pain. Ecstasy is often described in terms of pain. The grimace that manifests extreme pain is not unlike the "grimace" of orgasm. Extreme delight, like extreme sorrow, can produce tears.

Many of the mystics who write of the supreme joy of their highest mystical moments turn to images of pain such as "piercing" and "burning" to describe their experience. Delight has an inner impatience and insatiability in it that seems to reach for more, even in the midst of fulfillment. A heightened need for union with the object of delight seems to characterize delight at its most lively pitch. Hence, the bittersweet or agony-ecstasy tension of intense delight. The dynamic here seems to be toward union and absorption. Delight seeks to take in that which delights and to be identified with it. Thus do we become our delights.

Here again, the significance of delight and affectivity for a complete knowing experience can be seen. Delight weaves its object into our being. If we delight in the value of persons and in those moral values which enhance and protect their preciousness, these values are absorbed into the tonality of our moral consciousness. Situations involving those values will be touching on the center of our delights and affections, and with all the help we need and may get from clever reasoning in assessing these situations, feeling also will instruct us and direct our reach for the truth.

The sense of profanation, of which I have spoken above,[23] is the nether side of delight. This is the sense of shock, aversion, and withdrawal that we experience in the face of that which offends the value of persons and their environment. If persons are the prime sacraments of delight, their violation in any way evokes the feeling of profanation. Sometimes that which is valuable is taken for granted. We are duly placid at best, inured at worst, to the delightful reality that is so familiar to us. Only after the sense of profanation that follows upon violation or destruction might we become sensitive to the delight that we in our apathy had missed. The emerging ecological awareness of this time might come to illustrate this. We used nature and subdued it abusively. As shock begins to register on our obtuse consciousness, there are signs of reawakening affections and enthusiasm for the earth that bore and sustains us. If this is more than lightly romantic and ephemeral, a new capacity to delight in the richness of the good earth might be born of the shock of ecocatastrophe.

When Affective Knowledge Is Disdained . . .

The psychology of ethics would be tidier if we could draw a sharp dividing line between the affective and the cognitive. As ever, tidiness is suspect, and in this case, it would seem clearly wrong. Cognitive awareness is not limited to what we describe as purely intellectual knowledge. The avoidance of the concept of affective knowledge is understandable. Many important figures and influences that hover over modern thought have borne witness against it. Kant spoke with little patience of "the alleged special sense, the moral feeling." The appeal to moral feeling, Kant said, "is superficial, since those who cannot think expect help from feeling. . . ."[24] Kant called ethics into "the court of pure reason" and many are they who harkened to him. Kant's reactions to the excesses of the "moral sense" ethicians was in turn excessive. Some point to Freud as a major culprit, who, as he got older, "became the more convinced of the essential insanity of our desires and of the need to repress the logic of the heart."[25] Scientific Marxism is also liable to criticism for classifying emotion as the breeding ground of ideological distortions. Christian spirituality, which was enormously influential in shaping Western consciousness, attached negative value to "concupiscence" in a way that stigmatized the emotional and affective side of personal life. Pragmatic currents in our achieving society banished the Maypole dancers and with them much of the valid claims of the Dionysian and sentimental forces of our nature.

On top of this, affective knowledge has suffered from ungainly defenders, as, for example, the ethicians of the "moral sense school." The moral sense people wanted to escape both an excessive intellectualism and skepticism. What they came up with was a kind of simplistic intuitionism that brought discredit to the idea of an affective element in human knowing. The "emotivists" also stress feeling but deprive it of truth value. Moral statements for them are evinced emotions, not true or false. Both these "noncognitive" classifications and most of their critics missed the cognitive aspect of affectivity.

Related too to the contemning of the affective is the pervasive cultural degradation of woman. While putting woman down, those things that were associated with woman—and this included affectivity—were concomitantly slighted. These are just some of the influences, enough perhaps to say that this debit in modern thought and especially in modern ethics is understandable and deep. The debit, however, is a damaging one.

It has, for example, led to a disparagement of the body, with consequences which are broad and unhealthy. It is in the affections that awe is begotten, awe before the *entire* miracle of life. The marvel of life is found in all of its phases from the biological to the spiritual. Unfortunately, there is in the best of modern intellectuals a bit of the Platonic tendency to make too sharp a distinction between the "philosopher" and the "philosoma"—between the "wisdom-lover" and the "body-lover," in Plato's terms.[26] That the body has its own wisdom is something that needs reasserting, and the affections do just that. It is body consciousness that saves us from our abstractness. It is too easy to forget that we are our bodies. He who wounds my hand wounds me. Ethics, then, which is a work sprung from reverence, needs emphatic reverence for our corporality too.

What is not needed, of course, is an overstress on the biological to the point where the biological becomes ethically normative. The Stoics were among those who sinned grievously in this way, blurring the lines between the biological and the ethical. This kind of thinking led, for example, to the conclusion that contraception, since biologically "frustrating," was therefore ethically wrong. Such a caricature should serve as a warning, but not as a block to a strong ethical respect for bodiliness. Those working in bioethics should take special heed here, since the controlling mind, drunk with its new powers which are seemingly boundless in their promise, could deafen us to the gentle claims which the body legitimately presses upon our consciences.

The lack of esteem for affectivity has also left us still primitives in moral education. Plato said that we should be brought up and educated from our youth in such a way that we would delight in and be pained by the things that we ought.[27] This outstanding challenge has not been impressively met.

Also, and more generally, ethics has gone forward with heartless head in command. There would, of course, be havoc if headless heart were in charge of human affairs. And yet there is a greater capacity for cruelty in heartless head. Ethics seeks the alliance of head and heart. Those ingenious military planners who coolly and ingeniously calculate in terms of megadeaths are an example of the perils of unfeeling mind. Those who would lyrically infer that politics could be done without reference to the category of power would be an example of headless heart. Heart and head together would be in pursuit of expressions of power that can be effective without resort to slaughter. In moral man, head and heart unite.

Affections keep us close to the flesh and find the reality of persons beneath abstractions and statistics. This is their contribution to the living mind in pursuit of values. Adam Smith criticized unfeeling teachers of morality:

> None of them tend to animate us to what is generous and noble. None of them tend to soften us to what is gentle and humane. Many of them, on the contrary, tend rather to teach us to chicane with our own consciences, and by their vain subtleties, serve to authorize innumerable evasive refinements with regard to the most essential articles of our duty.[28]

This, of course, has also contributed to the bad name that ethics has gained. The fault was not all that of the ethicists. Our culture is, as we have seen, cold and unreceptive to the beauty of the moral. We can afford to repeat the thought of Schopenhauer, who speaks a tongue quite foreign to us when he writes:

> The metaphysics of nature, the metaphysics of morals, and the metaphysics of the beautiful mutually presuppose each other, and only when taken as connected together do they complete the explanation of things as they really are, and of existence in general.[29]

The aesthetic connection escapes us. Dewey speaks of the natural recognition of beauty in conduct. Justice, he notes, is closely allied to the idea of symmetry and proportion, and so, he says, "the double meaning of the term 'fair' is no accident."[30] The Greeks seem more fully aware of the aesthetic dimension of the good. The Greek *sophrosyne*, which is unhappily translated "temperance," meant to the Greeks, as Dewey observes, "a harmonious blending of affections into a beautiful whole—essentially an artistic idea."[31] Even Aristotle's stress on the congruence of virtue and the proportionate mean implied "an acute estimate of grace, rhythm, and harmony as dominant traits of good conduct."[32] Such sensitivity is not at home in our culture. As Dewey concludes:

> The modern mind has been much less sensitive to esthetic values in general and to these values in conduct in particular. . . . The bleakness and harshness often associated with morals is a sign of this loss.[33]

The point here, of course, is not that the aesthetic and the moral coincide. We recall Tolstoy's comments on the ladies who wept in the theater at the touching beauty of the play but had no feeling for their coachmen who were freezing outside. Persons can delight in beautiful music and poetry and be indifferent to slaughter. The love of the beautiful can make successful excursions away from morality. Morals and aesthetics are not identical. The point here is that there is beauty in the values that make a person fully alive and flourishing as a person and a shallow, unfeeling culture can miss this beauty.

How Practical Affective Knowledge?

One of the very practical reasons why modern ethics has not sufficiently dwelt on affective evaluation is that it is no simple matter to say in a systematic ethical treatment just how one goes about plying his affectivity. To speak of moral principles, for example, is a more manageable task. There is a lot that one can get a grip on. One can discuss the relationship of the general to the exceptional, the meaning of universalizability, the history of principles, etc., with a reassuring feeling that this is indeed workable turf. In addressing particular cases, a number of principles of potential relevance have been formulated and may be summoned to test their applicability. In doing this, one can have a good sense of knowing what one is about. But, how, in attempting to analyze the moral import of a situation, does one summon affectivity? Should one repair to a meditation room and allow his feelings to play upon the cases at hand and then bring back a report on this to the table where the hard ethical analysis is going on?

These questions, of course, are misconceived. In setting up the wheel model of ethical method, I am not implying that all of the evaluational processes and resources signified by the spokes can be similarly employed in ethical inquiry. For example, one of the spokes yet to be discussed is humor and comedy. Obviously, one could not do ethics by reasoning and analyzing for a while, applying principles for a while, and then looking for the comic side of the matter.

What I am stressing in my method is that the unfolding of moral consciousness is pluriform. Sensitivity to the moral dimension of existence is not achieved only through reasoning or the application of principle or even through the exercise of creative imagination. An ethics that only stresses one or some of these is sinning by partiality. Such partiality has been a common failing in ethics. A complete ethics should seek to develop an awareness of all the ways in which consciousness awakens to the reality of the moral. Some of these are more easily describable processes. Some have no particular relevance to certain cases. Some will point us more toward the background and presuppositions of our thought and cannot be thought of as one in a series of similar tools. Some will involve something of all of these aspects.

So how does affectivity operate in ethical analysis? First of all, it is necessary to be aware of the fact that our evaluation *is* affectively as well as intellectually actuated. This point we have pressed up to now. If we were not aware of this, if we assumed that our ethical thinking was proceeding with limpid and undiluted intellectuality, we would not only be naïve but would also be the easy prey of untested affective forces. Our affective orientation is not infallible. And so, just as a lawyer wants to know the vested interest of his client in legal dealings, so do we have to be aware of where our feelings are pulling us and why. The vested interest that affects our thinking may make us more or less drawn to the truth.

Uncritical thought is the bane of good ethics, and whoever denies the cognitive side of his affectivity will not be proceeding critically. This is a negative consideration. Our feelings can lead us astray, and unless we are the perfect incarnation of Aristotle's "good man," the fact is that to some extent our feelings are fonts of fallacy. If I have not stressed this up to now, it was not because I wanted to belittle the potential debits of our volitional and emotional structure. This point has been made and indeed often overmade throughout history. I stress it now because misconceptions about the potential negative dimensions of affectivity could only have an unhappy yield along the way of ethical inquiry. No system of ethics can ignore this. Bigots, after all, speak from the heart. They are surely *Gemüt* people. Fanaticism also is an offspring of heightened affectivity. "The worst of madmen," said Alexander Pope, "is a saint gone mad." And a saint is clearly one in whom affectivity is ablaze. Affections, however, unaided by the discipline and analytical activities of working reason, can lead to chaos.[34]

Ethical inquiry, however, must also take advantage of the positive yield of affectivity. In studying particular issues in ethics, our antennae should be alerted to the wisdom of the heart. It could serve as a corrective for reason gone amuck. An example might illustrate this.

Not too many years ago, Catholic moralists were in almost perfect unanimity in teaching the indissolubility of marriage. Some historical exceptions had crept in, but these were tightly confined and the usual cases were met with a firm prohibition. Only death could dissolve the marriage bond. Persons who remarried while the former partner lived were "living in sin." This position was supported by a variety of intellectual arguments. To hold anything else would have been seen as a radical and unacceptable departure from orthodoxy.

Nevertheless, there were chinks in the armor of consensus. A number of people who accepted this view in the abstract sensed something wrong with it when faced with a concrete case of someone who entered a second marriage after the total collapse of their first. It was not that they could refute the arguments against their feeling and in favor of the official position. It was just that there was a "gut feeling," an instinct, a sense, that this second marriage, which they knew in its concrete reality, was something good and not something sinful. This indulgent view was seen by the learned as mere sentimentality at best.

Sentiment was of course at work in this phenomenon of dissent. Significantly, in fact, dissent in this and other matters of Catholic rigidity was more widespread in Latin countries where affectivity is less cowed. The intellectually learned would have done well to listen to it while heeding the words of Blaise Pascal: "We know truth, not only by the reason, but also by the heart. . . ."[35] Catholic intellectual opinion has shifted regarding divorce and remarriage.[36] The shift would have occurred sooner if this system of ethics had more respect for the witness of the heart in morality.[37]

Sometimes, in doing ethics, when we look for the witness of the heart, we will hear contradictory answers. The heart, like the intellect, does not specialize in unequivocal conclusions. Here, as in all situations of disagreement, sound ethics wants to hear both sides to find the part of truth that each may be presumed to contain.

Love and Our Social Future . . .

Sensitivity to affective evaluation is also essential in the ethical analysis of cultural trends. The heart has a sense of direction. There is in affectivity, as there is in creativity, a future referent. We cannot see the future, but we can do certain things in our effort to know it. We can analyze the past, justly expecting that it will overshadow the future in important ways. Second, we can analyze the causal factors operating in the present so as to make admittedly fallible, but not therefore useless, judgments about the kinds of effects that might continue into the future. This could all be a dominantly "intellectual" enterprise, and quite useful or even essential for ethics.

The heart, however, seems to have special prerogatives for conducting its own probes on the future. I have spoken before of the link between creativity and affectivity.[38] Love thrusts us toward the discovery of the possible that is latent in the actual. Love thirsts for the more that creative imagination discovers. Emotion has a maternal influence on the creative thought. Thomas De Quincey spoke of the heart as "the great *intuitive* (or nondiscursive) organ" and saw it as a symbol of "man in his highest state of capacity for the infinite."[39] Love, at its core, is impatient. It reaches for more. In assessing our moral future, we feel our way where we cannot see.

Notice the effective and futurist elements in Ruth Nanda Anshen's remarks about what seems to be taking shape in our culture. She writes:

> There is in mankind today a counterforce to the sterility and danger of a quantitive, anonymous mass culture; a new, if sometimes imperceptible, spiritual sense of convergence toward human and world unity on the basis of the sacredness of each human person and respect for the plurality of cultures.[40]

No matter how much supportive data it provides, quantitative analysis will never reveal the things Anshen speaks of here. No amount of such analysis will reveal the increasing perception of the "sacredness of each human person" or of emerging "respect" amid cultural diversity. Anshen is perceiving with heart and mind in mak-

ing this estimate of what is and what might be. Her concern is to see
the dynamics of social change both to assess what these augur for the
future and to make it possible for us to bring reflective consciousness
to bear upon that emerging future. Quite properly, though again
quite fallibly, she is looking to the affective shifts in the culture.
Good social changes are always rooted in affection, though they may
find their immediate stimulus in a variety of events. Ideals are the
power behind these changes, and ideals are helpless unless enfranchised by affection. Therefore, the discovery of affective shifts is a
major need for successful social ethics. The problem, of course, is
that this sounds so nebulous. And, from any viewpoint, the task is
not simple. It is, however, no more difficult, and indeed it overlaps
with what sociology does in studying the "unit-ideas" in a culture.[41]
Robert Nisbet, for example, in *The Sociological Tradition*, bases his
study upon what he sees as the five essential unit-ideas of sociology:
community, authority, status, the sacred, and *alienation.* These ideas
he sees as "timeless and universal" though their presence will ebb
and flow in history.[42] He sees them as underlying categories in Plato
and Aristotle, in the Roman philosophers of the first century B.C.,
and in the work of the early Christian philosophers. These categories
do seem useful for social analysis, so long as one does not become
dogmatic about their formulation. These are basic ideas and provide
vantage points from which to study a cultural shift in a society.
Major changes in all or even some of these ideas would mark a genuine revolution in culture. Clearly, all of these ideas are focal points
or constellations of a number of moral values in which we are, quite
inevitably, affectively implicated. As Nisbet says: "Major ideas in the
social sciences invariably have roots in moral aspiration." Applied to
the five unit-ideas on which he bases his study, Nisbet says: "The
moral texture of these ideas is never wholly lost."[43]

In studying a social setting with these in mind, one would be attempting to chart the direction and implications of new affective attitudes toward basic human values in a society. Immodest hopes for
precision here would be out of place, but the importance of the enterprise should be clear. Any effort to understand any moral question
would be impaired if we took no account of our influential cultural
matrix. These unit-ideas give us fixed points from which to know
something of that matrix. They are therefore useful tools for ethics.

It would be an improper conclusion to say that sociology and ethics
coincide when both are focused on social analysis through the prism

of these unit-ideas. Ethics is an explicitly normative art-science which focuses on very individual questions as well as social ones— without implying that individuality and sociality can be, in reality, utterly separated. The distinction of sociology from ethics can be said to be real but not complete. There is truth in Nisbet's statement that "the great sociologists never ceased to be moral philosophers."[44] Sociologists do wax normative at times, as do all social scientists. Given the nature of their subject material, it would be impossible for them to repress all normative judgments. This is also their human prerogative, and there is no harm in it if they know what they are doing and attempt to do it well. Ethics, after all, is not a private preserve with discreet boundaries of specialization into which only the initiated might proceed. Ethics is a pan-human concern. The formalized study of ethics seeks to give reflective treatment to the work and method of ethics so that the valuing animal which is everyman (including the social scientist) can do his valuing better. Stilted efforts to walk value-free through the field of values can only result in the surreptitious intrusion of unchecked normative judgments. Efforts to limit directive value judgments is something the social sciences can attempt in order to leave their beneficiaries as free as possible to do their own evaluating. In this sense, the value-free goal can be presented as an ideal that can serve good purposes without ever being reached.

Affective Relief from the Experts . . .

As mentioned in the previous chapter, one of the more oppressive though inevitable authorities in the modern world is the expert. He is a cure for vertigo in the midst of abounding complexity. The hazard is that the expert wears the mantle of privileged knowledge. It seems rash and immodest to question him because he has done work that you have not done and he bears credentials that you do not possess. Docility would seem to be his due. Docility, however, is something that can belong to the simple-minded or to a properly critical mind. Expertise is not infallible. It is borne by "vessels of clay" who have their own presuppositions, their own unasked questions, and their own vested interest in the conclusions they have already taken a stand on. They can be as wrong as they can be impressive.

The power of the expert can be relativized in two important ways:

First, by questioning. No expertise is beyond questions. Second—and it is not entirely distinct from questioning since it may inspire the question—there is the reality of what we call common sense or "horse sense" or intuition (when it occurs in women). This way of thinking is richly endowed with affectivity. It includes also the incipient intellectual insight that has caught a fleeting glimpse of the solution which is near but not yet grasped. This insight-affect which gives us a feel for the truth has its own valid credentials. The affections keep us close to earth and are less vulnerable to the seduction of abstraction. Affective knowledge has a way of getting to the point, and when we sense that it might be doing so, we should give it its say with all due reverence for contradicting authorities. Some examples at this point would help.

In their book *Open Marriage*, Nena and George O'Neill have a chapter titled "Love and Sex Without Jealousy." In it they say that

> the idea of sexually exclusive monogamy and possession of another breeds deep-rooted dependencies, infantile and childish emotions, and insecurities. The more insecure you are, the more you will be jealous.[45]

The O'Neills then accost the idea that this kind of jealousy is something that cannot be escaped.

> To begin with, we would like to lay to rest the idea that sexual jealousy is natural, instinctive and inevitable. It is none of these things. Jealousy is primarily a *learned* response, determined by cultural attitudes. In many societies around the world, including the Eskimo, the Marquesans, the Lobi of West Africa, the Siriono of Bolivia and others, jealousy is at a minimum; and in still others, such as the Toda of India, it is almost completely absent.[46]

Anyone who never heard of the Lobi or the Toda or the Siriono has to admit that the O'Neills know something he does not know. Part of the argument they advance is based on authority. If the Lobi, the Toda, et al. do not have it, "then it cannot be regarded as 'natural' to man's behavior."[47] Most people in our society presume that jealousy is a normal and natural response. The O'Neills allege knowledge that not all people have it and argue from this authority that it is learned and not natural.

One way of reacting to this position is to enter into a study of anthropology. Nearer at hand, however, is the experience that although jealousy can be neurotic and an indication of the need for therapy, jealousy in a love relationship can be an unneurotic fear of losing that which is precious. Rather healthy persons seem to have found a value in monogamy that is threatened by broader sexual exchange. Many people enjoy reading about open marriage (the O'Neills' book was on the best-seller list for almost a year), indicating that many find the idea a fascinating fantasy. But as Morton Hunt says in his extensive study of American sexual mores: "At the same time most people continue to disapprove of such behavior because they believe that when it becomes a reality rather than a fantasy, it undermines and endangers the most important human relationship in their lives."[48] Hunt's conclusion is that "no more than a tiny minority of Americans have yet attempted such open marriages, and fewer still have made them work."[49]

A number of people, then, who read the literature advocating extramarital (or comarital) sex reject it, not on the basis of a fully thought out refutation of the thesis, and not by establishing systematically that the Toda, Lobi, and Siriono have less developed personal appreciations of sex, but simply because they feel, in Hunt's words, that it "endangers the most important human relationship in their lives." Their feeling is not infallible. They may be wrong and a bit delayed in their cultural and moral evolution. But their intellectual papers are in order if they choose to honor this feeling and act on it. Feeling is not per se suspect. It is a way of knowing that has its own legitimacy, even in the face of contradicting expertise. This is an important resource to have, as long as it is not thought to be self-sufficient and the end of the thinking process. Modern life has even made it more needed. A sense of one's own ability to appreciate the good even prior to systematic intellectual defenses of that appreciation is an essential asset in an age where the tyranny of expertise is too little challenged.

Similarly in the political order, there is need for solid convictions about the value of common sense. The military budget is a case at point. Each year it allocates increasing billions of dollars for killpower. The justification offered for this allocation would boggle and has boggled the ablest of minds. It involves complex interpretations of foreign policy, the nature of disarmament negotiations which allegedly require more arms as bargaining chips in the effort to have fewer arms, and the national and international economy. The nonexpert easily retreats from the learned barrage that comes forth to account for this particular use of the national treasury. But the nonexpert is, again, not without resources. Without advanced degrees in economics and in military and political science, he might sense that the pressures for a swollen military budget derive from the fact that "some of the most powerful firms benefit from the defense economy to such an extent that they could not survive without it. . . . profits on military contracts are on the average substantially higher than those on nonsubsidized production in the free market economy. . . . the military contractor has an enormous competitive advantage."[50] One need not have grown up in the pushing and shoving world of the Washington lobbies to sense what these facts of life can mean.

Talk of converting militarily fixated industries or providing economic alternatives for communities supported by military works usually collapses into the language of infeasibility. Those who sense that vested interest and a lack of imagination are the problems here might know something that is escaping a lot of "experts." Regarding the national security argument for more weapons, the nonexpert could easily share Richard Barnet's observation that "a country that feels secure only if it has the power to kill its enemies 100 times over has problems that additional missiles will not cure."[51] The very idea of "overkill" should inspire an insightful uneasiness. Such insightful uneasiness does not require expertise.

A renewed appreciation of our affective capacities to perceive the good could help to restore confidence in the individual human spirit, bowed as that spirit is before the oracles of mass society. The danger inherent in this is simplism, and a too comforting feeling that we can divine the truth without exhaustive intellectual labor. That danger is met by awareness that what we sense affectively we do not possess. Affective knowing, like all knowing, is incomplete. But it is a knowing power that has been neglected in ethics. Compensatory overreliance would not be progress. But somewhere between neglect and overreliance lies richer understanding.

Where Principles Fade . . .

A final word on our affective approach to truth. Ethics is best seen as art-science. Like art, ethics cannot be done simply by following the rules. Guidelines and principles play an indispensable role, but they do not of themselves yield moral discernment. However well instructed we are by moral principles, there is a certain point when one's sympathy for the personal and contextual factors of a case attains crucial importance. The rules cannot tell you how to approach someone who needs help in such a way as to get their confidence. Rules may speak to this and be helpful. The experience of others can in this way be passed on—but only to a degree. The final judgment of the fitting way to proceed will be based on an immediate intuition and on a sympathetic sense of what this concrete situation requires. We move beyond rules to an extent and into the realm of affective perception and intuition when it comes to the basic ethical necessities such as contextual sensitivity, delicacy, tact, and a sense of timing and opportuneness.

Reality is process, and a moral decision involves a step into that process at the time deemed most fitting and potentially fruitful. To make this decision on very abstract grounds would be to operate at only one level of our cognitional capacity. To know the *kairos* when it obtains through a confluence of disparate events calls for both the genius of the intellect and the genius of the will. Sound ethics knows that the heart is wise in its fashion if we will but give it its due.

NOTES—CHAPTER NINE

1. John Dewey and James H. Tufts, *Ethics*, rev. ed. (New York: Henry Holt & Co., 1932), p. 296.
2. See, for example, Herman J. Muller, *Studies in Genetics: The Selected Papers of H. J. Muller* (Bloomington, Ind.: Indiana University Press, 1962); Theodosius Dobzhansky, *Mankind Evolving* (New Haven: Yale University Press, 1962); Gordon Wolstemhomme, ed., *Man and His Future* (Boston: Little, Brown & Co., 1963).
3. Dewey and Tufts, *Ethics*, p. 293.
4. Ibid.
5. Ibid., p. 299.
6. Aristotle, *Nichomachean Ethics*, Bk. II, Chap. 1, 1103b, 14–21.
7. The word "do" here is not taken narrowly as referring only to commission and not to omission. What we omit is often more morally significant.
8. Thomas Aquinas, *Summa Theologica* I q. 87, a. 2, ad 3. Thomas, of course, did not have the word "character" with its current significance in his vocabulary any more than Aristotle did. What he was talking about here was *habitus*. For the meaning of *habitus*, see

Summa Theologica I II q. 49, a. 1; II II q. 171, a. 2, in corp; I II, q. 49, a. 2, ad 3. What he says here about knowing through the habit is: "Things are not known through a habit as through a known object, but rather things are known through a habit as through a disposition or form by which the knower knows" (my translation).

9. Dewey and Tufts, *Ethics*, p. 297.
10. Henri Bergson, *The Two Sources of Morality and Religion* (Garden City, N.Y.: Doubleday & Co., Inc., Anchor Books, 1956), p. 58.
11. Aquinas, *Summa Theologica* II II q. 45, a. 2. "Correctness or judgment can take place in two ways: one way according to a perfect use of reason; in another way because of a certain connaturality to those things which are to be judged." Thomas is not as clear as some of his commentators on affective knowledge, but his writing points in this direction. As we have seen (Chapter Three) he saw faith as a kind of knowledge "existing within the genre of affection," and in the article quoted from here, his notion of connaturality has definite cognitive implications as does his statement that the cause of wisdom is in the will, "namely in love," even though its essence, Thomas insists, is in the intellect.
12. Joannes a Sancto Thoma, *Cursus Theologicus* (Quebeci: Collectio Lavallensis, 1948), a. 3, n. 78, p. 147; n. 81, p. 150; n. 82, p. 151; and passim.
13. Ibid., n. 45, p. 119.
14. Ibid., a. 5, n. 9.
15. Ibid., a. 4, n. 15, pp. 168–69; a. 4, n. 19, pp. 170–71. In developing the idea of affective knowledge, John of St. Thomas is working in the framework of a theology that has in many respects and for good reasons been abandoned. It would be a mistake, however, to miss the valuable insight developed in this theology and to reject them with the errors. No system of thought is either all innocent or all guilty with regard to error. Evaluation should operate like a strainer that preserves the contributions.
16. Ibid., a. 2, n. 10.
17. Aristotle, *Nichomachean Ethics*, Bk. II, Chap. 3, 1104b, 4–13. ". . . the man who abstains from bodily pleasures and delights in this very fact is temperate, while the man who is annoyed at it is self-indulgent. . . ."
18. Ibid., Bk. VII, Chap. 12, 1154a, 13–17.
19. Thomas Aquinas, *Summa Theologica* I II, q. 31, a. 1, ad 1: "*Quando constituitur res in propria operatione connaturali et non empedita, sequitur delectatio. . . .*"
20. Aristotle, *Nichomachean Ethics*, Bk. X, Chap. 5, 1176a, 15–19. Translation, Thomson, p. 300.
21. Obviously we can mistake a bad man for a good man so the good

man criterion like the modern judicial "reasonable man" criterion requires criteriology derived through a complete ethical method. This does not negate, however, our capacity to identify good persons with some reliability and use them as moral authorities.

22. Thomas Aquinas, *Summa Theologica* I II q. 33, a. 1, ad 1, ad 3. The terms Thomas uses here are such as *magnificari, dilatari, ad . . . interius capiendam, ampliatur, ut capacius reddatur.*

23. See Chapter Three.

24. Immanuel Kant, *Foundations of the Metaphysics of Morals,* translated by Lewis White Beck (New York: Liberal Arts Press, 1959), p. 61. Kant did allow that feeling had some closeness to morality, since it could be an unselfish admiration of moral beauty.

25. Rubem A. Alves, *Tomorrow's Child* (New York: Harper & Row, 1972), p. 46.

26. Plato, *Phaedo,* 67B. In this dialogue, Socrates is speaking to Simmias and says "that if you see a man fretting because he is to die, he was not really a philosopher but a philosoma—not a wisdom-lover but a body lover."

27. Plato, *Laws,* 653Aff.; *Republic,* 401E–402A.

28. Adam Smith, *The Basis of Morality,* 2nd ed. (London: George Allen & Unwin, Ltd., 1915), p. 500.

29. Arthur Schopenhauer, *The Theory of Moral Sentiments* (New York: Augustus M. Kelley, 1966), p. 8.

30. Dewey and Tufts, *Ethics,* p. 298.

31. Ibid.

32. Ibid., p. 299.

33. Ibid.

34. When I speak in Chapter Thirteen about the hazards of moral discourse, it will be clear that in many of these, there is affective mischief afoot.

35. Blaise Pascal, *Pensées* (New York: Washington Square Press, 1965), no. 282, p. 85.

36. See, for example, Dennis J. Doherty, *Divorce and Remarriage: Resolving a Catholic Dilemma* (St. Meinrad, Ind.: Abbey Press, 1974); L. Wrenn, ed., *Divorce and Remarriage in the Catholic Church* (Paramus, N.J.: Newman Press, 1973); S. Kelleher, *Divorce and Remarriage for Catholics?* (Garden City, N.Y.: Doubleday & Co., Inc., 1973). There is in Catholic doctrine the notion of the "sense of the faithful." This implies that the theologians should be sensitive to what the faithful felt to be true in matters of faith. This notion was never effectively applied to morals. If it had been, the churches would not have become locked into so many unrealistic and absolutist positions in moral issues.

37. In speaking about this particular form of dissent to an established

orthodoxy as "a witness of the heart," I repeat that there is no such thing as independent, subsistent affectivity or intellectuality. What this witness does seem to show is that in the face of a concrete personal situation, an uneasiness sometimes was obtained that had a strong affective component. Very often, too, affections were stimulated by the plight of divorced and remarried persons which did not point to new conclusions. The ease with which new views of this subject have been received in the Catholic population does indicate that weaknesses in the older absolutism were both felt and seen, and that this paved the way for a quiet transition.

38. See Chapter Six.
39. Quoted in Jacques Maritain, *Creative Intuition in Art and Poetry* (New York: Meridian Books, 1955), p. 109.
40. Ruth Nanda Anshen, "World Perspectives," an introductory comment for the books in the World Perspectives series, as in Ivan Illich, *Tools for Conviviality* (New York: Harper & Row, 1973).
41. The term is explained by Arthur O. Lovejoy, *The Great Chain of Being* (Cambridge, Mass.: Harvard University Press, 1942).
42. Robert Nisbet, *The Sociological Tradition* (New York: Basic Books, Inc., 1966), p. 7.
43. Ibid., p. 18.
44. Ibid.
45. Nena O'Neill and George O'Neill, *Open Marriage* (New York: Avon Books, 1973), p. 237.
46. Ibid., p. 236.
47. Ibid.
48. Morton Hunt, *Sexual Behavior in the 1970's* (Chicago: Playboy Press, 1974), p. 256.
49. Ibid., p. 361.
50. Richard J. Barnet, *Roots of War* (Baltimore: Penguin Books, 1973), p. 168.
51. Richard J. Barnet, *The Economy of Death* (New York: Atheneum, 1969), pp. 25–26.

CHAPTER TEN

KNOWLEDGE : COMMON AND UNIQUE

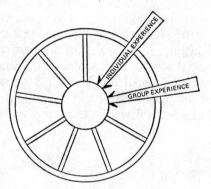

A medical treatise composed during the fourteenth century offers the following advice:

> The doctor should understand that in operations of this kind he may do more things than he finds written in the books. For not everything that can be done can be put into words; so a skillful doctor uses his own ingenuity, and in addition to what he reads, makes use of his own common sense. For, as Boethius says in his *De disciplina scholarium*, "He has but a poor head who goes on using things that others have found out and never finds out anything for himself."[1]

The advice applies also to ethics. Anyone engaged in moral evaluation truly has "but a poor head" if he "never finds out anything for himself." The individual knows some things that no one else knows

and has a capacity for discovery that is unique to him. This insight,
however, must be tempered by the opinion enunciated in the modern sociology of knowledge:

> . . . it is not men in general who think, or even isolated in-
> dividuals who do the thinking, but men in certain groups
> who have developed a particular style of thought in an end-
> less series of responses to certain typical situations charac-
> terizing their common position.
>
> Strictly speaking it is incorrect to say that the single indi-
> vidual thinks. Rather, it is more correct to insist that he
> participates in thinking further what other men have
> thought before him.[2]

In presenting *individual history* and *group history*, the point to be
made for ethics is this: Every individual is a unique font of ethical
wisdom. What is unique and original in our knowing potential, however, is not adequate. Not only is knowing rooted *de facto* in our social reality and history, but we should also systematically seek to
learn from the social sources of wisdom. Ethics must blend a reverence for personalized original insight with a sensitivity to what is
contained in the common fund of cultural and ethical traditions. It
must be critical of what is flawed in that fund and receptive of what
is sound.

The Fact of Group Knowing . . .

The idea of a completely original thought is an illusion. We are always debtors to our social matrix when we think. This does not
mean that we cannot transcend it and move creatively beyond some
of its strictures, but it does mean that when we transcend we do not
take off from nowhere. It is a common failing to bask in illusions of
independence and to ignore our radical and profound dependence on
the cultural womb that bore us. The danger in this is that we might
presume that we are discovering when we are only mimicking. We
might think ourselves a voice when we are only an echo. In so doing,
we would be likely to be uncritical about that which we are mirror-
ing. A person who is organically dependent on his environment, and
knows this to be so, is in a position to assess the legacy that has
come to him. The person who thinks, to repeat the words of George
Bernard Shaw, that the laws of his tribe are the laws of nature is not

likely to have critical questions about his tribal wisdom. If we are not aware of our cultural conditioning, we are locked into it.

Psychology and many of the social sciences have stressed the radical degree to which group influences affect us. Anthropologist Clifford Geertz, for example, sees all of our basic talents as dependent upon cultural conditioning.

> There is no such thing as a human nature independent of culture. Men without culture would not be the clever savages of Golding's *Lord of the Flies*, thrown back upon the cruel wisdom of their animal instincts; nor would they be the nature's noblemen of Enlightenment primitivism, or even, as classical anthropological theory would imply, intrinsically talented apes who had somehow failed to find themselves. They would be unworkable monstrosities with very few useful instincts, fewer recognizable sentiments, and no intellect; mental basket cases.[3]

Without stepping into the debate about what we could expect from the completely feral child, we can say that we are increasingly aware of the social sources of the individual person's mind-set. In what is called the process of primary socialization, every person is born into a social setting. In this setting, an interpretation of reality and its values already exists and this is mediated to the nascent mind of the merging person. We are born not only into the world but into a world view, a particular world view in which reality has been defined and assessed in a certain way.

Again, as Teilhard de Chardin says, nothing is intelligible outside of its history, and this is certainly true for the world view we inherit at birth. Cultures develop through a process of action and reaction. Within this field of action-reaction, societies produce their interpretations of the meaning of it all. Interpretations of reality will be as varied as the historical experience in which they evolve. No two histories are the same and no two historically interpretative reactions to those histories will be identical. Nevertheless, it is into one of these world views, with all of its specific value assumptions and positions, that we are planted at birth. We do not arrive with an independent world view of our own. But we do arrive with a thirst for meaning and a need to make sense out of this world into which we have been abruptly projected. But that thirst for meaning is absorbent before it can become judgmental and critical. Indeed, it may never arrive at any significant critical consciousness. At any rate, we absorb values and identify with them before we are in a position to step back and gain the necessary critical distance to assess them. That is why ethics must urge examination of the unconsciously assumed values of moral man. To think that we perceive moral values in anything like the way we see the starry sky above is seriously mistaken. To a significant extent, the "seeking" of moral values is a social experience, and even a creative moral insight is not without ties to the context in which our consciousness was formed. In a word, our sense of reality varies according to our social conditioning. As sociologists Berger and Luckmann put it: "What is 'real' to a Tibetan monk may not be 'real' to an American businessman. The 'knowledge' of the criminal differs from the 'knowledge' of the criminologist."[4] Knowing occurs in society, and the social setting in which it occurs gives it distinctive form, accent, and orientation.

Both how we know and what we know—that is, both the content and the method of our knowing—are strongly controlled by our cultural environment. Sociologists of knowledge point out two reasons for the strength of this influence. For one thing, the interpretations of reality that the significant persons in our life impose on us are posited as objective reality. At first, we do not distinguish the interpretation of reality from reality itself. The confidence this breeds is not easily shaken. Also, our sense of self-identity takes place in our early formation, and thus radical criticism of accepted values, values which are experienced as woven into one's self-image, is not facilely achieved. Second, the early socialization process involves much more than purely cognitive learning. As Berger and Luckmann say of it: "It takes place under circumstances that are highly charged emotionally. Indeed, there is good reason to believe that without such emotional attachment to the significant others the learning process would be difficult if not impossible."[5] Attitudes and value options which are linked to our early process of self-identification and ensconced in our emotional history have an inherent stubbornness. That would be good if the socialization process was good, but since no such process is perfect, the problem of conversion in morality has to be faced squarely. Furthermore, we do not, of course, face only the social conditioning of our early development. It is the natural and enduring tendency of persons to absorb and identify with admired and loved persons. Value osmosis is a constant fact of human relating, and it is a fact of which we are not usually very conscious. Socialization, in other words, is ongoing.

Because of all of this, it is a mark of wisdom in considering any issue of morality to attempt to get some critical view of the forces that are conditioning us. It is chilling to think of the value judgments that persons in the past were able to accept and then to wonder what malignant assumptions undermine us now, however strong our avowed commitment to civilized behavior. The examples I now offer illustrate the negative side of group influence. This will serve a salutary purpose, since the negative examples bear blunt witness to the strength of group influences, and awareness of baneful cognitive influences is required for properly critical thought. After discussing these negativities, however, I will turn to the positive uses of group experience.

Lessons from History . . .

It is a chilling reality to note that if one grew up during the period of the Crusades in Christian Europe, there is every reason to say that we would have believed that the highest moral option offered us was to sally forth to the East and slaughter persons who did not share our religious beliefs. We would like to think that we would have been able to rise above the reigning consensus of that time and choose more sanely, but the history of the period is not encouraging. With all the pacifistic content that the books of the Christians contained, which might have stimulated dissent, few dissenters to the militancy of that time emerged. The odds are enormous that we would have felt as almost all felt and would have displayed no critical resistance to the barbarity of the period.[6]

We can look to more recent history and see the comfort of American society with slavery for a long period, even in the presence of the foundational traditions and repeatedly avowed ideals of this nation which were generated in a revolution motivated by the love of freedom and the dignity of man. Like the Crusaders who went forth to rapine and murder with the Gospels of love at hand, Americans managed for almost a century to live with both slavery *and* the Declaration of Independence. This would be branded implausible if it were not historically true. The plausibility is found not only in our enduring ability to exploit others for gain with the most improbable rationalizations but also in the fact that when our moral evaluation is set into a particular social context, it becomes "natural" to think and act in accord with the social momentum of that cognitive context. A Crusader or slaver value structure is the natural issue of a Crusading or slaving time.

Now that our cultural milieu has changed and found room for more sensitive moral appraisals, the idea of slavery becomes abhorrent to most. We can look with disapproving frowns at the apartheid form of slavery in South Africa because our social sense of reality has shifted somewhat. It is now in closer accord with our ideals, and thus we judge it more realistic and more humane. As a simple matter of understanding the human way, however, we must admit that if we had been born white South Africans, we might today be offering subtle and tortuous reasonings about how the "separate development" of blacks and whites is really a goodly thing. The absorbing power of our social context is a fact of cognitive life of which ethics must take account. Awareness is the first step toward relativizing this power and equipping us to criticize it and transcend it to a degree. Systematically taking account of it is part of the redemptive work that makes straight the way for the creative mind.

It is all well and good to say we have transcended slavery and the debacles of Crusading religious wars, even though an argument could be made that we have not fully transcended either and that Western war-making still bears the slightly disguised insignia of the Crusaders, and that our racism still points us toward the goals of slavery. Still the cognitive influence of society must press us to ask where our minds are gripped today. What are the socially ensconced seductions that are leading contemporary evaluations astray?

Class and Nation as Conditioners of Consciousness . . .

Class consciousness and nationalism, to give two major examples, are still important shapers of the human mind. One need not be a Marxist—one need only be a realist—to be concerned with class and its influence on human development. In a nation like the United States, class differentiation is not as salient as it has been in other societies. It would be naïve, however, to suppose that we in any way approach a classless society where equity and equal justice are wed. Reinhold Niebuhr perceptively observed "that inequalities of social privilege develop in every society, and that these inequalities become the basis of class divisions and class solidarity."[7] Class-engendering privilege normally has an economic base. But whatever its base, class consciousness unfolds into a rationalization for maintaining its privileges over against the claims of those not similarly endowed. A person born into a particular class is heir to a special outlook suited to the perceived needs of that class. The implications of this for ethics are clear. As Niebuhr says: "The moral attitudes of dominant and privileged groups are characterized by universal self-deception and hypocrisy."[8] These are rather stark tidings, but Niebuhr argues powerfully that the social and ethical outlook of members of given classes "is invariably colored, if not determined," by the privileges and economic prerogatives of the class.[9]

At this early point in human moral development, it remains true that nothing spurs our genius more than self-interest. Thus, the self-interest of the class tends to be ingeniously disguised. Raw interest in its naked rawness cannot be faced, even by those whose interest it is. And so the protective "tissue of lies" is woven out of the stuff of eternal verities, grand ideals, and religious and moral posturings. Vernon Louis Parrington wrote something of another age that can find exemplification in any time:

> Compressed in a sentence [the Tory philosophy] was the expression of the will to power. Its motive was economic class interest and its object the exploitation of society through the instrumentality of the state. . . . much ingenuity in tailoring was necessary to provide it with garments to cover its nakedness. Embroidered with patriotism, loyalty, law and order, it made a very respectable appearance and when it put on the stately robes of the British constitution it was enormously impressive.[10]

This kind of Toryism is not dead; it is natively human. And ethics should look for its influence wherever economic and social privilege accrue whether in a democratic or a socialist political setting. Also, the category of class need not be limited to very broad and merely economically delimited groupings. In an extended but valid sense it refers to professions and to any group marked out by its privileges. The attitudes of professions toward those not within the corps or toward those who aspire to enter therein, shows some fairly raw and narrow self-interest at work in spite of the elaborate plumage of self-justification and high-mindedness. Disputes between management and labor represent a conflict that can also be fruitfully interpreted in terms of class. One class is more privileged than the other, yet both are normally acting out of class concerns and not in terms of the common good. Moral language will abound in these disputes, but hard analysis would direct light to the rationalizations of class interests that have nothing to do with nobility or passion for the common weal, but have everything to do with the inheritable value structures of class consciousness.

Class has taken on a new form in American life in the phenomenon of suburbanization. What has developed here is a king of geographic classism that is highly relevant to the ethics of racism. Suburbanism shows the self-deception and hypocrisy that are characteristic of class ideology. Suburbanites are camp followers. They are of the city but not in it. The suburban enclaves are there only because the city is there. The etymology of suburb implies that. Most would not have been built nor would they survive if they could not feed upon the economic and social resources of the city. The city provides jobs, a work force, customers, cultural and service facilities, and entertainment. It is a fiction to think of a suburb as an independent social entity. The legalism of separate incorporation gives form to this fiction and lends a special kind of legitimation to what can be called suburban class consciousness.

Class formation, of course, is always "interested," and motivated by the desire for advantages in terms of economics, social privilege, and status. This applies generously to suburban classism. Class is a kind of apartheid that goes beyond mere considerations of color. It is segregative by nature. American suburbanism is utterly characteristic of this. The gains are economic. Whatever laments there are about the taxation required to build new school systems, services, and utilities for these para-urban strategic enclaves, the suburbanites are usually spared direct financial responsibility for the host city where the needs might be at a crisis level. Status and privilege also accrue to suburbia. Segregated "status" is usually achieved in the suburbs; suburbia is largely white. Passports to the suburbs, however, are acquired more along economic than racial lines. A black person may move to the suburbs, but in so doing, he steps into another class. His acceptance depends upon the degree of his identification with the geographic and economic class into which he has migrated. Suburban class consciousness is made of sturdy stuff. It is supported by the Anglo-Saxon proclivity to confuse legality with reality and morality. The separate legal identity of the suburban unit is perceived as very righteous grounds for the shirking of moral responsibility to the urban center, which is actually the heart of the local community—however that community is legalistically subdivided. The desegregation of schools, for example, is not just an urban problem; it is a local community problem, and that community includes the suburbs. It is only class thinking in the suburbs that supports the view that it is proper and moral to avoid responsibility for the human integration of schools through the legalistic stratagem of separate incorporation. Here is where group thinking in the form of class consciousness joins legalism in befouling moral discourse. Moral experience is based upon the perceived value of persons in community. The artificial and self-serving division of the community, which developed largely to evade responsibility for the urban plight, is not morally sensitive, although it might make a case for being legally correct. A truly moral consciousness hears the moral claim of other persons. There are human problems within the urban-suburban complex that cannot be solved by only one part of that complex. In fact, the cause and the solution to the city's problems might lie more in the suburbs than in the city.

The point here is not that we are responsible for everyone else's problems. The point is that the urban-suburban community is a community of persons, linked together by a number of the facts of social and economic life. These facts are the basis of relationships which, like all human relationships, generate moral obligations. One cannot avoid those obligations simply by moving across an arbitrarily drawn line within the actual greater community. The legal immunity of the suburbs does not make this moral fact any less real. Certain fiscal and integration problems do not abide by the city limits in their causes or potential solutions. Persons who are related to those problems by their relationship to the urban center are deterred by class consciousness from seeing that on some issues, there are no moral boundaries between city and suburb. This exemplifies the absorbing power of toxic group thinking. One important dimension of this power merits comment.

Consciousness of the moral dimension of human life is the badge of civilization. It is also a burden and an affront to our egoism because moral consciousness is other-regarding as well as self-regarding. It involves a sense of one's own value that does not negate the value of the other either conceptually or by the behavioral choices we make. If our attitudes or choices do imply a negation of the value of the other by blotting out the just claim of the other within a given urban-suburban community, the terms "immoral," "wrongful," and "evil" apply. However, no one can bear to think of himself as evil. Through rationalization, we withdraw from a sense of guilt as instinctively as does a hand withdraw from excessive heat. Class consciousness makes it easy to do that. This is because there is solidarity within the class and rationalizations that are finely embroidered, in the manner of the Tories of old, with such things as "patriotism," "loyalty," "law and order." Class consciousness longs for and usually gets the mantle of respectability. Therefore, because it is serving a deeply felt need for preserving the perquisites of the class and because it appears to have socially proper credentials, it is a powerfully seductive force. To be in a class is a fact of one's history; it is also a fact of one's operating epistemology. Again, this must be recognized before it can be transcended, and it is to this end that ethical analysis must take careful note of class as a social influence on evaluation.

Nationalism and Social Evaluation . . .

Another example of negative group influence on evaluation is suggested by this question posed by Hans J. Morgenthau:

> How, then, does it come about that the great mass of the individual members of a nation, whose individual power is not affected by the vicissitudes of national power, identify themselves with the power and the foreign policies of their nation, experience this power and these policies as their own, and do so with an emotional intensity often surpassing the emotional attachment to their individual aspirations for power? By asking this question, we are posing the problem of modern nationalism.[11]

Nationalism, which has much common ground with classism, is still an important conditioner of human consciousness. Certain developments have tamed nationalism a bit: communications, mobility, the perception of problems that can only be solved internationally, and the development of bonds based on common transnational interest in things such as science, religion, or even the so-called youth culture. But the fervor of nationalism endures as a major political and cognitive force.

Nationalism has been described as "an emotion that regards the quality of one's own nation as superior to all others, and its interests as predominant over those of all others (my country, right or wrong)."[12] The importance of nationalism shows in the fact that it has the emotional strength to convince the mind of two illusions: first, that one's nation is superior to all others, even those that we do not know or only dimly know, simply on the basis of *their* otherness; and, second, that the nation is superior to right and wrong. Edgar N. Johnson spells out the enormous ethical import of nationalism: "It is willing to falsify both past and present to make what was inglorious seem glorious, or it is quite indifferent to public morality, arguing that might makes right or that the end justifies the means. . . . [it] is often irresponsible and reckless in its use of state power to enhance the prestige or increase the wealth of the nation or the governing class."[13]

Nationalism also provides a prism through which the other is perceived. We can look to the ugly European to see nationalism at work in assessing others in a colonial relationship. The ruling assumption of the colonizers was that their own culture, race, and custom were superior. As one historian sums up the effect of this on cognition:

> If the natives did not share his religion, they were "heathens," if they did not have his sex complexes and taboos, they were "immoral," if they did not have his compulsion to work, they were "lazy," if they did not share his opinions or possessed a different kind of knowledge, they were "stupid," if they behaved in ways that he could not predict because of his own ignorance of their culture, they were "childlike."[14]

This outlook did not end with the colonies. It is still visible in the view that both Europeans and Americans have of non-Europeans and is a significant factor in contemporary racism. It is of interest to see even briefly why nationalism has such enduring strength, strength that is so great that persons will even give their lives in its causes. And once again, it helps us appreciate the social dimensions of our thoughts and moral evaluations.

For one thing, the nation as a group has been knit together by a number of shared experiences. The people of a nation have a common history with all of its political, cultural, religious, linguistic, and literary elements. Through selective memory, a common pride develops and is sustained by the memory of great events, especially mili-

tary victories, which have a peculiar intensity. Nationalism also feeds
on economic interests, since the nation provides and protects opportunities for achieving economic security and even affluence.[15]

Nationalism also feeds on a primitive need for barbarians—for persons clearly defined as inferiors and even as evil and threatening. The
presence of the palpably inferior reassures us of our virtue and value,
and if the inferior and evil force is also threatening, we have an
added gain in the increased sense of unity this produces among us.
Perhaps this is what the poet Cavafy tells us when he writes: "Night
is here but the barbarians have not come. Some people arrived from
the frontiers, and they said that there are no longer any barbarians
. . . These people were a kind of solution."[16]

Beyond this, the strange strength of nationalism has sacral origins.
As Arnold Toynbee observes, "Human beings are inclined to worship
the greatest powers that are within their ken. . . ."[17] So it was that
food-gathering man worshiped those things upon which he was so utterly dependent; his gods were earth, water, sun, moon, and those animals that either threatened him or were his food. When the wandering of the hunter and gatherer yielded to the collectivization of
civilization, religious as well as economic changes occurred. Man became enormously impressed with his collective power. Collective
man could convert the savage jungle swamps by building canals and
dikes, thus liberating land for agriculture. A new outook was born
when, in Toynbee's words, "the unprecedented productivity of these
reclaimed wildernesses had raised the wealth and populousness of a
local community from the level of a Neolithic village to the level of
a Sumerian city-state."[18] Toynbee notes the impressive evidence that,
at the dawn of civilization in Sumer, the nature-gods became the
deification of Nippur; as did Nanna the moon-god for Corinth, Baal
the vegetation-god for Tyre. In Toynbee's words: "The local communities have become divinities, and these divinities that stand for
collective human power have become paramount over the divinities
that stand for natural forces. The injection of this amount of
religious devotion into nationalism has turned nationalism into a
religion, and this a fanatical one."[19] In Toynbee's view, the nationalism that is the bane of the atomic age is an intensified and
universalized form of the Sumerian nationalism of the third millennium B.C.[20]

Toynbee saw the importance of subsequent historical influences
on modern nationalism. For example, he believes that nationalism

imbibed deeply from the messianic spirit of Christianity, which from its Judaic origins is inclined to exclusiveness, intransigence, and "proneness to resort to violence in order to impose on other people what [its] own adherents believe to be true and right."[21]

Other historians also have stressed that the receding influence of Christianity and the onset of the Enlightenment caused a shift of devotion from Christian doctrines to the new gospel of human progress of which the nation-state became the prime sacrament. The state, in fact, adopted even the tactics of organized religion, demanding unquestioning loyalty from the citizen-devotee. Thus the divine right of kings became the divine right of nations.

Because of all that nationalism has going for it, it tends to be victorious in competition with other powerful ideologies and religious beliefs. Joseph Stalin is reported to have said during World War II that he wished his armies were fighting so valiantly for the cause of communism, but that this was not the case. They were fighting for Mother Russia. And, in fact, the nationalism of both Russia and China has proved stronger than the communistic ideology that has for so long been drummed into those peoples. Similarly in time of war, coreligionists of different nations will kill one another in the cause of the nation.

The result of this is catastrophic for social morality. A narrow nationalism (or tribalism) animates the politically prominent concept of "the national interest." The Commission on International Development reached the conclusion that "we live in a time when the ability to transform the world is only limited by faintness of heart or narrowness of vision."[22] Both the faintness of heart and the narrowness of vision relate to nationalism. The perceptual powers of the nationalist tend to be constrained by the false absolutes of the nationalistic interest. As a result, aid is given parsimoniously and unimaginatively, in a way that broader vision would allow us to see as ultimately even self-defeating.

Nationalism does not have to be tribal and narrow. It can be the prism of generous thoughts. There is the broad vision of Giuseppe Mazzini, for example, who saw nations not as islands of collective egoism, but as "the workshops of humanity." Nationalism he saw as sacred because it can be "the instrument of labour for the good and progress of all men." In Mazzini's view, "no nation will ever develop the highest and most enduring forms of national life while it is contented to remain the passive and uninterested spectator of the onward and upward struggles of kindred peoples."[23] Mazzini's thoughts involve both idealism and realism as these terms have been used in political theory. His vision rises above the tribe to humanity. He perceives all peoples as "kindred." There is an ideal in this which our still primitive civilization has not yet embodied. But Mazzini also sees the advantage of noting the gain for individual nations in transcending their own constricted nationalism. This fact of interdependency, which can be expressed in the utilitarian terms that nations most naturally harken to, is more visible today than it was when Mazzini wrote over a century ago. The nationalists of his day jailed Mazzini and threatened him with death. The new facts of our planetary life might now open the way to a transformation of nationalism along the lines of Mazzini's prophecy. This is a tender but true possibility. In that event, nationalism would function as a positive factor in our social cognitive matrix. This is a sanguine thought, and it can serve to lead us into some of the more positive considerations of socially influenced evaluation.

On Knowing Better Socially . . .

Each of the spokes of the wheel model of ethical method being developed in these pages is presented as a primarily positive force in evaluation. Each of them also, as has been noted, can be abused and misused. Given the tendency of man to consume unreflectively the value gospels of his society, I have lingered on the negative potential of this social influence on evaluation. This must not cancel out the fact that thinking man cannot hide from society, since thought is to a substantive degree a social product. Also, we cannot think or evaluate *well* unless we deliberately appropriate the value appreciations that have arisen in our society and learn from those that have arisen in other societies. It is in these two ways that I shall urge the positive value of group experience for ethics. Moral knowledge and acuity profit from the trusting appropriation of the wisdom and experience of our own society *and* from comparisons and contrasts with diverse social experiences.

On the first point, it should be obvious that we really have no choice but to accept the values of our society to a substantial degree. As moralist Robert Springer says, "No human lifetime suffices for an individual methodically to question all the values of his culture." To do so would put us in emotional and personal jeopardy. "Behavioral science, then, warns us of precipitous or total questioning of value systems."24

What this points to is our finitude. The moral universe is comparable to the physical universe in scope and mystery. No single person can explore it, and even together, our reach is limited. So, naturally and inevitably, we tune in to the knowing processes of others. Knowing is an ecumenical and shared process by nature and sheer necessity. However, we are not merely charting the necessities but also speaking normatively of what ought to be done. Communal appreciations should be tapped, whether they exist in the present or whether they can be partially retrieved from history. The reason for this is our finitude and the concomitant and humanizing exigency of trust. Here group experience relates to what was said regarding authority in moral experience. Complementarity and reliance are integral to our social being. Trust is an essential ingredient in the process of becoming more human. This trusting pattern that is a noble trait of human life enters into evaluations and conjoins us to the moral achievement of humankind.

My lengthy stress on the pernicious possibilities of absorption into group consciousness was not intended to supplant trust and install cynicism. It was rather geared to urge that our trust retain a critical edge. Without that, it would deteriorate into naïveté.

Related here, too, is my treatment of principles, since it is through principles that group consciousness and moral sensitivity is significantly articulated. In appropriating (critically) the principles and other moral testimony of our society we are acknowledging that that society, for all its lingering barbarity, has not been entirely unmoved before the exquisite and mysterious values of personal and terrestrial being.

The second value of group experience for ethics relates to the comparison of diverse group experiences and the resultant relativization of one's own cultural perspectives. Absolutism is the bane of sensitive intelligence. Making sense of things is the consuming libido of the mind. Sometimes when we have had some sense-making success, we tend to freeze our insight, forgetting that it is only partial and forgetting too that truth for us is a process of atunement and never a completed product. This freezing into absolutes happens in every field of thought. Dogmas develop and are defended by a priesthood of those whose status depends on those dogmas. The central moral faculty of creative imagination is regularly blocked in every intellectual discipline by the difficulty of penetrating those dogmatic group orthodoxies. Sensitivity to what other groups think or have thought on matters that concern us can be effective solvents of false orthodoxies. For example, rather than simply being immersed in the kind of particular ethical issues that emerge in our system, ethics should press us to look at the different kind of moral presuppositions that may emerge in some other system. The reason for this is that if you do not check your presuppositions, you may, for example, end up spelling out with punctilious ingenuity the rights and duties that slaves have instead of questioning the institution of slavery. Drawing another group experience into view can yield perspective.

Frank Bray Gibney, a student of Japanese society, writes of the entirely different views that operate in Japanese law. For one thing, the comparative number of lawyers is illuminating. The United States, with a population of 215 million, is served by an estimated 350,000 lawyers, while Japan, with a 115 million people, has fewer than 10,000 attorneys. The difference is that in the American system, the stress is on justice; in the Japanese system, the accent is on harmony. As Gibney puts it: "The Japanese legal system sets out at the beginning to harmonize the views of the antagonists."[25] The stress, therefore, is on compromise and mediation. There is, in fact, strong social pressure to achieve an out-of-court settlement. Gibney gives the example of a squatter suing a farmer for possession of ten acres which he would like to claim. In the West a court would probably rule up or down on the squatter's rights. An approved solution in Japan would be to concede the squatter two acres even if he has been shown to have no rights to any land. The goal is not so much to determine narrowly the presence or absence of a right as it is to restore harmony to the society. Beyond the question of rights, harmony has been disturbed, and the restoration of peace is the supreme goal. This same spirit is seen throughout the society. As Gibney says, in business "there is rarely any formal judgment against the incompetent or the actually destructive persons."[26]

Clearly, harmony has no such prerogatives in the United States. The point is not that we should convert to the Japanese system. Their way of doing things may be utterly impractical in the culturally diverse situation of the United States. The point is that in this litigious American society, where persons go to court at the drop of any hat, it is well to see that our customs are surely not the laws of nature. The contrast with Japan's experience *relativizes* and raises questions about the American approach to conflict resolution. In the absence of all contrast, questions about our system could remain unasked, leaving us incapable of moral criticism. Having seen a major modern nation functioning in a markedly different way, we can go on to ask whether our rather abstract delineation of rights best serves the human good. Since right, abstractly conceived, is indivisible, the American contesting squatter will get either ten acres or none, leaving bitterness behind in one party or the other. Is this the best that the human imagination can achieve in the circumstances of American life? Perhaps it is. But one way of testing that is to seek out contrasting experiences. Such experiences can stimulate critical and relativizing questions regarding our dominant social mind-set. The discovery of such question-breeding social contrasts is a necessary task of ethics.

Anthropology has done a major service to ethics by discovering the wide variety within human mores and thus providing us with many contrasts. Historically, much of the ethics of sex has had an essentialist cast, discovering what should or should not be done by the very nature of the sexual encounter. Usually, this amounted to a rationalization of what were the accepted norms of a culture. Anthropology revealed that these norms were not necessarily so, since other cultures, with apparently felicitous results, behaved very differently in sexual matters. The Trobrianders, for example, "begin their acquaintance with sex at a very tender age. The unregulated and, as it were, capricious intercourse of these early years becomes systematized in adolescence into more or less stable intrigues, which later on develop into permanent liaisons."[27] This is the acceptable way of life among the Trobrianders.

The experience of variety presses us to look to the roots of our own standards. It raises the questions of whether the Trobrianders are to be judged adversely for their lack of Puritanism, or whether the American sexual tradition is to be criticized for its many hedges on sexual freedom. More basically it prompts us to ask how we and the Trobrianders came to think the way we do about sexual behavior. Comparisons press us to go deeper. Let me illustrate further how compared group experiences can move us more deeply into particular ethical issues.

In contrast to the Trobrianders, Margaret Mead found the Manus in New Guinea to have a highly regulated sexual life, marked out by distinctly puritanical rules.[28] This attitude seems to be related to the

strong business interests of the Manus. They tilt from the more
disorderly Dionysian approach to sex to the Apollonian concern for
efficiency. Free sexual attitudes would distract from business and
hence are socially banned by the Manus.

One might conclude that the Trobrianders and the Manus have
no relevance to the discussion of sexual ethics in the modern West.
Obviously, the relevance is limited; it is not, however, lacking. Again,
we are faced with a human experience that allows us to raise questions about our own folkways, since it reminds us that our ways were
developed in a particular history, more or less suited to our contextual reality. The question of whether they are still more or less suited
is the key question that is of concern to ethics. Maybe our current
standards reflect a distortion that was caused by some undue emphasis in another area. Margaret Mead does not hesitate to note "a curious analogy between Manus society and America."

> As in America, work is respected and industry and eco-
> nomic success is the measure of the man. . . . Artists they
> have none, but like Americans, they, richer than their
> neighbours, buy their neighbours' handiwork. To the arts of
> leisure, conversation, story telling, music and dancing,
> friendship and lovemaking, they give scant recogni-
> tion. . . . The ideal Manus man has no leisure; he is ever
> up and about his business turning five strings of shell
> money into ten.[29]

The comparison is not simply neat, but there are booming
similarities. American society deferred to Apollo, the god of order
and achievement, and restrained Dionysus, the god of ecstasy and
revelry. Dionysians could not have carved out the wilderness into the
metropolitan complexes and tidily divided farms that one sees when
flying over these United States. In this land, clearly, Apollo has
reigned.

Contemporary sexual ethics does not take place outside the reach
of that history and the culture nurtured therein. A shift in sexual
mores is now going on, but as we theorize ethically about what does
or does not befit our human reality within this time, the example of
societies which were not utterly dissimilar gives perspective. In ethics
as in art, contrast allows for depth perception.

For example, a discussion of the use of surrogate partners in sex
therapy cannot fruitfully transpire by merely focusing on the conceptualized duties and expectations of spouses. We should be able to

see a bit of the Manus at work here. The ruling paradigm is business. If the orgasm enterprise is not successful, stage a workshop in proper Apollonian fashion. Purchase the designated manuals, experiment with other systems (or partners), and hire system analysts. Orgasmic profit should show on the bottom line. Ethical analysis of this contemporary question, which is replete with moral implications, cannot be unmindful of the culture in which it appears and which, in many ways, it typifies. That there is sexual maladjustment is a fact, and that certain kinds of therapy can be fruitful seems clear. The approaches to the problem, however, bear the marks of Apollonian man working hard to have fun. The employment of a surrogate partner may increase the yield of orgasms, but the success is superficial. Dionysus could not only look and laugh, and tell us that Trobrianders and others, in all their simplicity, know what Manus and Americans have yet to learn.[30] Consciousness of diverse group experiences in any area of morality can liberate us from the constricting grip of tenured bias.

A Caution on the Demonic Comparison . . .

Comparison and contrast yield perspective. Comparison, however, to only *one* other experience may obsess our minds and paralyze us. For example, discussions of the morality of mercy death in extreme situations usually become impaled on Nazi analogy. The argument is advanced that if we were to allow the morality of even one instance of mercy death, the dominoes would fall one after another and we would find ourselves in the world of Nazism where hundreds of thousands of persons may have perished in "euthanasia centers." With remarkable persistence, this analogy is raised in both popular and scholarly literature to counter the proposition that in certain situations—such as a situation of unmanageable pain in a terminal illness—death might be accelerated by positive means.

Here is a case where the experience of one group is stamped as definitive. Two contentions are implicit: first, if any mercy killing is seen as moral, by some kind of a physical law, a process will thereby be initiated which will carry through to a Nazi-like situation; second, other group experiences with mercy death are ignored or treated as not relevant. This is a serious misuse of group experience which absolutizes rather than relativizes. The paralyzing absolutism is overcome by seeing the deficiencies of the analogy and by inducing other group references. For the Nazis, " 'euthanasia' was only a code name which [they] used as both camouflage and euphemism for a program of murder—killing various categories of persons because they were regarded as racially 'valueless'; deformed, insane, senile, or any combination thereof."[31] The German experience at this time is limited as analogy in other ways: There the state was normally the deciding agent; the announced concern was utilitarian, the elimination of "useless eaters"; neither individualism nor moral pluralism were facts of German society in the way that they are facts of American life; and finally, the question is rising in our day in an entirely different way. The question for us is the value of death in certain circumstances for an individual. The Nazi analogy is valid for any proposal to give to a state, with an avowed and promulgated racist philosophy, totalitarian powers of decision over life and death. It is not an analogy that can be offered as decisive and leading in the contemporary discussion of the morality of mercy death in certain extreme cases.

The demonic grip of the Nazi analogy can also be relaxed by studying other experiences. Uruguay allows for judicial review of each instance of what is alleged to be a mercy death, and full exoneration, if the person who accomplished it was honorable and compassionate in his motivation and induced by repeated requests of the deceased.[32] The Swiss Penal Code provides that the judge "may mitigate the punishment . . . where the actor was induced to commit the act (acted) by honorable motives. . . ." In cases of compassion, this may lead to total exoneration. Neither of these societies has degenerated into Nazi-like abuses.[33] Fixated attention on only one historical human experience is a block to moral discourse.

Anticipatory Revisionism and the Pendulum Effect . . .

Any discussion of group consciousness must take account of the pendulum effect in the history of human thought. The pendulum is a fitting symbol for human knowing. Knowledge develops in a field of action and reaction. In reaction against certain errors, the pendulum shifts and can easily swing too far in the other direction. Puritanical rigidity with its patterned modes of behavior regarding sexual conduct can give way to an antinomian intuitionism and hedonism. Trust in the established canons and authorities in society can yield to asocial conceptions of freedom and glorification of doing one's own thing. Confidence in the general principles and reliance on that which is commonly true can produce a counterreaction in which validity of the unique and unrepeatable is loudly championed. Depending on where the pendulum is, rules or exceptions may be on trial. In reaction against the toothless and naïve efforts for peace at the beginning of this century, where florid hopes abounded for the success of the Hague Tribunal, the League of Nations, and the Kellogg-Briand Pact, there ensued an overreliance on violent power and a resultant depression in the art of diplomacy. To and fro, then, is the way of thought.

After a strong swing of the pendulum, the revisionists often appear to point out what was missed in the rush from one extreme to the other. In performing this service, the revisionists often veer off to a new extreme, overreacting against an overreaction. Still the revisionists' role is important. It exercises a conservative role of recovery and its service can be considerable if it does not overlook the values in that which it seeks to revise. Otherwise a new revisionism would be needed to correct the first.

Developing an acute sense of the pendular movements of thought is essential to critical judgment. The critical thinker must always check to see where the pendulum is carrying him with forces that he did not create. In the face of all of this, ethics should act as a weight on the pendulum, to keep it from flying off too far in extreme reaction. One way of doing this is to attempt to achieve anticipatory revisionism and not to wait while extremism completes its swing. What is needed is a discipline of the mind whereby we force ourselves to consider the values in that against which we are reacting.

It could be taken as a working rule that if anything has been held by a large number of persons for a long period of time, it is probably not valueless. It may in the main be erroneous and in need of drastic criticism. However, if we may assume that pure error is unimaginable, there is probably something worthy of retrieval even in highly erroneous group positions. Again, this is stated not as an absolute principle, but as a guiding assumption.

An example from history may illustrate this. If we go back to the middle of the fifteenth century, we find that under Christian auspices all interest-taking was considered immoral. Even a modest percentage of interest to compensate for the risk of a loan was deemed immoral. The prevailing position was this:

> On a loan to a poor man or a rich man, to help the starving
> or to finance a mercantile enterprise, nothing could be

sought or even hoped for. The risk inherent in lending was
not a ground for taking interest; that would have been to
circumvent the prohibition and destroy the normal gratui-
tousness of the loan. Interest could never be lawfully
sought as profit.[34]

One would be hard-pressed to find a moralist to defend that position today. Yet it was a consensus position at one time. Is there any
way in which the guiding assumption mentioned above could apply
to this consensus? What value could be contained in such an unnuanced position? It is not difficult to find the major causes for this
position. Christian moralists found seemingly clear prohibitions in
the Jewish and New Testament Scriptures. Yet no position that becomes established in a society is explainable merely on the basis of a
handful of texts, however authoritative the source. It is to be expected that a variety of perceived needs were being attended to in
the historical maturing of this social ethic. Professor of Law John T.
Noonan, Jr., notes the opinion that in the medieval village economy,
this moral rule served to concretize the needs of justice and of char-
ity. Many of its effects were good.

Western Europe never knew the plague of village usurers
that stifled ancient Greece or twentieth-century China.
Money was channelled into risk ventures. The poor were
helped in gratuitous ways. The usury rule was a good rule
for this society.[35]

The absolute prohibition of interest no longer obtains. However,
in rejecting it, some of the goals achieved in the social manifestation
of that prohibition were lost. Maintaining the prohibition would not
be the answer, since so blunt an error could not endure. Rather, in
the criticism of it, a lookout for the values hidden in this social experience should have been alertly maintained.

The ethics of interest-taking provides a useful parable for moral inquiry. The older position was wrong, but not valueless. An untenable
prohibition nurtured tenable goods. In contemporary ethics the pendulum is swinging rapidly away from some older positions. Civil dissent has acquired a new respectability as the state is stripped of its
aura of almost absolute authority. Sexual ethics is in a revolutionary
mood as fewer and fewer ethicists are willing to draw a line called
the ceremony of marriage and say, indiscriminately, that all sexual

exchange on one side of that line is immoral. A majority of Americans now believe that mercy death is moral in certain circumstances. In most things, the conventional, the traditional, and the "established" are in the dock, and the exceptional and unique enjoys a new presumption of favor. There is value in each of these reversals, but let the critic make room in his soul for the angel of anticipatory revisionism. Criticism of old errors has a naturally narrow focus which leaves peripheral values unillumined. We live in an age when nothing is beyond criticism. In the zeal of such a time we must be missing much. Revisionists will have a deserved field day on us—unless we anticipate them.

A Word on Small Group Witness . . .

Consensus is tyrannical. Dissent leaves you open to ridicule and excommunication. Consensus, after all, does carry with it a lot of precious satisfaction—"What everyone thinks must be right." "Fifty million Frenchmen can't be wrong." Dissent is unsettling and to a degree insulting. The beneficiaries of consensus take poorly to it. Because of all these factors favoring consensus, it is the better part of wisdom to pause at length before the moral value dissent of even a few. The opinion may indeed be an upstart going nowhere. But it might also be the vanguard pointing to a better way. Moral dissent may represent the first shoots of a humanizing insight whose time of growth is upon us. Its apparent dimness may be the early dark of a new dawn. The minority opinion, after all, has a distinguished past.

Among the outcast minority views of the past, we find positions such as the immorality of slavery; the nonsacrality of civil government; the immorality of torturing a prisoner to get a confession; the right to conscientious objection; ecological conservationism; and, indeed, democracy itself. Minority views should be deliberately sought out. The outcast might have royal blood.

In Defense of the Living Intellect . . .
Individual Experience . . .

An ethical system may supply laws, general rules, guiding principles, a number of examples, suggestions, landmarks, limitations, cautions, distinctions, solutions or critical or anxious difficulties; but who is to apply them to a particular case? Whither can we go, except to the living intellect, our own, or another's?[36]

These are the words of John Henry Newman, a philosopher who became a cardinal of the Roman Catholic Church. His ecclesiastical status makes his continuing remarks all the more striking. "The authoritative oracle, which is to decide our path, . . . is seated in the mind of the individual, who is thus his own law, his own teacher, and his own judge in those special cases of duty which are personal to him."[37]

His words introduce our consideration of the unique credentials of the individual discerning subject. This spoke obviously overlaps with others in this model of ethical method. That there is shared ground here and elsewhere in this model is recognized and admitted. In treating creative imagination, affectivity, and authority, for example, the special prerogatives of the individual's knowing capacity have been acknowledged. For this reason, I may treat this particular spoke more concisely. Special status is given to individual experience, however, to supply an emphasis that should be corrective of a common distortion.

Trust in one's own unique powers of knowing is not commonplace. Henri Bergson, in fact, writes very pessimistically about our ability to accept our capacity for original perception. Bergson notes that we belong both to ourselves and to society. Much of our mental stability is found by clinging to others. This represents the socialized self, in which "on the surface of life we are in continuous contact with other men whom we resemble." Bergson asks, however, if we need always take refuge in that part of us which is socialized. Is there not, the deeper we delve into our personal consciousness, "an ever more original personality, incommensurable with the others and indeed undefinable in words"? Could we not rely more on this original center of our personality? Bergson illustrates the situation with a helpful comparison.

> . . . in our innermost selves, if we know how to look for it, we may perhaps discover another sort of equilibrium, still more desirable than the one on the surface. Certain aquatic plants as they rise to the surface are ceaselessly jostled by the current: their leaves, meeting above the water, interlace, thus imparting to them stability above. But still more sta-

ble are the roots, which, firmly planted in the earth, support them from below.[38]

The original center of the self is the root, which has an inherent and solitary stability unlike the interlacing firmness achieved by the surface leaves. At this point in his comparison, Bergson's pessimism shows through. He wonders about our capacity to reach for the roots and concludes: "If possible at all, it is exceptional: and it is on the surface, at the point where it inserts itself into the close-woven tissue of other exteriorised personalities, that our ego generally finds its point of attachment; its solidity lies in this solidarity."[39]

Bergson may have yielded too much to his Gallic pessimism here. To work from the original center of our personalities may truly be exceptional; it is hardly impossible. Those creative geniuses who have turned us inside out with their vision surely exemplify the originality and confidence in the self of which Bergson speaks. Even in less extraordinary and history-turning ways, we are all graced with some persons who exhibit a freshness in their value consciousness that comes from their ability to be something other than faithful mirrors. Still, let us certainly grant the rarity of the original mind. Given our social nature, no mind is purely original. Originality is more a matter of degree. But some minds are almost completely strapped to their social props; others, less so. This is a point that must be of interest to ethics. Ethics seeks to point the way to a value awareness that is fully alive. If persons choke on their own unique perceptive powers and timidly repair to crowd-think, the community of valuing animals is to some degree crippled. Such huddled thinking must yield something of a blur. In order to hang together it must rely heavily on stereotypes and generalizations. To preserve itself, crowd-think must shy away from the singularity that can be discerned by "the living intellect."

Two things must be kept in mind in championing the prestige of individual cognitive experience: the uniqueness of the individual and the uniqueness of every situation. It is no poetic license to say that each human being is unique and unrepeatable. Even physiologically, the very structure of our brain suggests this uniqueness. Erich Fromm refers to the "truly fantastic number of interneuronal connections" that distinguish the brain of man. As one study of the brain puts it: "If a million cortical nerve cells were connected one with another in groups of only two neurons each in all possible combinations, the number of different patterns of interneuronic connection thus provided would be expressed by $10^{2,783,000}$." In point of fact, the actual intercellular connections "would far exceed the $10^{2,783,000}$ already mentioned as the theoretically possible combinations in groups of two only."[40] For comparative purposes, it is pointed out that the number of atoms in the universe is estimated to be about 10^{66}.[41] The very structure of the brain symbolizes the unique veins of experience possible for us. Build on this the fact that no two persons have identical experiences or histories. Nor do any two persons react to the same reality in an identical way. Since affectivity is also one of the ways in which we are aware, another infinitely variable source of uniqueness presents itself.

Five artists looking at the same scene will produce five different paintings. A painting, it has been said, is nature seen through a temperament. And temperament is molded from a personal history that is unprecedented and unrepeatable. Moral insight, like a painting, gives a view of reality refracted through the prism of a unique temperament and cognitive structure. We will look for no perfect sameness in the knowing experience if we relinquish the simplisms of a mirror image of knowledge. A mirror inertly and indiscriminately reflects the physical objects before it. In the conscious awareness that we call knowledge, a vital and multidimensional process of attunement, interpretation, filtering, accenting, and imagining is going on. The process reflects the complex uniqueness of the knower (*actio sequitur esse*). This is true to an extent in knowledge of *things*; it is especially true in the knowledge of *values*.

Attention has to be drawn to this, since, as Bergson saw, our confidence in our own perceptive powers is slight. We fly to that which is similar, unsure of that which is unique in us. Socially endorsed positions seem more reliable. One result of this is practical and can be tragic; we can lose our confidence in our own "common sense." As a result, we slight the wisdom of "the common man" who, using his reasoning and affective powers, and steeped in traditions that may be heavy with insight, is well equipped to be the simple one who can confound the wise. He may be well qualified to see the lie in the current crowd-think and in the utterances of the socially revered oracles of the day. But the chances are that he would not dare, nor would his contribution be valued if he did.

It is a sad fact of intellectual life that persons will sacrifice their best insights to the canons of the group. They may basically know that the emperor is stark naked, but they will join the crowd in discussing his clothes. A lesson that the Buddha gave his followers is forever apropos. The Buddha was speaking to the Kalamas, an intelligent people who were questioning the teachings that they had received. Said the Buddha, "Do not accept a thing merely because it has been handed down by tradition or from generation to generation or from hearsay. . . . you should reject a thing when you know for yourself that a thing is harmful and will bring misery to yourself and to others."[42] The common tragedy is that we will bear the misery more readily than we will follow the simple advice of the Buddha.

The plight of insecure man is seen in the fact that he is "the primate that emerged at the point of evolution where instinctive determination had reached a minimum and the development of the brain a maximum."[43] We have very little by way of instinctive equipment. As Erich Fromm puts it: "Aside from some elementary reactions, such as those to danger or to sexual stimuli, there is no inherited program that tells him how to decide in most instances in which his life may depend on a correct decision."[44] We are the deciding animal, blessed and pained by responsibility. We shrink from this noble burden when we place excessive reliance on social sources of insight. As Josef Pieper says, "No one can be deputized to take the responsibility which is the inseparable companion of decision. . . . The strict specificity of ethical action is perceptible only to the living experience of the person required to decide."[45] Like persons, situations are also unique and in a state of flux. Ethics always swims in crosscurrents, where new patterns and new problems are always emerging. For judging that which is new, the established wisdom drawn from past experiences, is not enough. The burden again falls on the living intellect of the individual.

As the French philosopher René Le Senne writes of moral duty:

> At the same time as it is the same for everybody, in the sense that no concrete duty can be a duty without applying the imperative universally, it is true, because of the inexhaustible fecundity of duty, that this duty, which imposes itself upon me, at such and such an instant, is an historical duty, that no other person is called upon to face, and which is incumbent upon me only by reason of what I am and what I want.[46]

The responsibility for individual assessment does not just extend to concrete behavioral decisions. It also imposes the burden of criticism of the values—which we have inherited from our society—as far as this is possible. We are not free to be controlled by crowd-think in the same way that lesser animals are controlled by instinct, though it would appear that crowd-think is our substitute for the instinctive apparatus that we would, in our pusillanimity, prefer to freedom.

There is an irremediable loneliness to moral knowledge and moral decision. Our knowing transpires amid the structures and strictures of group knowing, but we are never wholly melted into an unindividuated group consciousness. In line with Teilhard's notion that true union differentiates, group experience should deepen and consolidate our individuality. It should not blot out our unique cognitive resources, but should rather release them. It is to this end that the model spoke *individual experience* is directed.

Religious Experience . . .

Religion is an important bearer of moral attitudes and judgments, and the moral content of religious experience relates to both individual and group experience. Religion, of course, has not always been tied to morality. Some ancient religions saw it as their business to cope with the gods as best as one could, and the gods were not always distinguished for their ethics. Thus the Babylonian woman, who was required to serve as a temple prostitute once in her lifetime, may have been personally offended at this from the viewpoint of her own morals, but if this was what the gods required, so be it. Similarly, the ancient Egyptian who took with him to the tomb written formulas calculated to deceive Anubis, the god of judgment, may have been committed to honesty in his dealings with humans throughout his life.[47] In dealing with the gods, one might have to leave one's morals aside and do what one had to to assuage the divinities.

The major religions that are represented in contemporary society, however, blend their moral and religious perspectives and are rich in moral content. The prophet Amos, for one example, signals the centrality of morals in Hebrew religion:

Seek good and not evil
so that you may live,
and that Yahweh, God of Sabaoth, may really be with you
as you claim he is.
Hate evil, love good,

maintain justice at the city gate . . .
let justice flow like water
and integrity like an unfailing stream.[48]

Religious literature abounds in moral teaching, often in very specific terms that easily become dated and encrusted in a contextually insensitive orthodox code of conduct. The value of this, of course, is little or nothing. In other ways, however, religious experience serves the "valuing animal" in such wise that any theoretician of ethics ignores it to his own impoverishment. Philosophical ethicists of our day are inclined to disdain the moral content and ethical service of religious experience, feeling, perhaps, that these sources are tainted with whatever it is that "theology" might be, and are thus unworthy of the philosophical enterprise. This is intellectually myopic and, from the view of ethical method, unsound. Good ethical method is sensitive to all the sources of moral valuation, whether those sources are religiously or otherwise affiliated.

There are two principal ways in which moral insight derives from the major religious traditions. First of all, these traditions significantly affirmed the validity and prerogatives of individual experience in valuation. Arnold Toynbee notes that our forebears moved from primitive nature religion to man-worship about 5,000 years ago at the dawn of "civilization." After some 2,500 years, Toynbee says, the "higher religions," represented in their earliest form by the Judaism of the Prophetic Age and Zoroastrianism and Buddhism, directed man's instincts for the sacred beyond humankind to "ultimate spiritual reality."[49] If Toynbee is right, what this did was free men from the worship of collective human power, laying the foundations for a potentially healthy individualism. Other forces operated to bring about this release from sacral collectivity, but the role of religion was significant. Eric Voegelin, for example, notes that the idea that society was not so much the cosmos written small as "man written large" (in Plato's oft-quoted phrase) took form during the period from 800 to 300 B.C. under such diverse influences as Confucius and Lao-tse in China, the Upanishads and the Buddha in India, Zoroastrianism in Persia, and in the philosophers of Greece.[50] This advance in human self-understanding represents a major contribution to ethics, and the reinforcement of this idea by either religious or other influences should be discerned and appreciated.[51] Insights borne by religious carriers need no special passports to enter an open mind.

Also, and necessarily, one can be eclectic in learning from the religious traditions. There is no long-tenured tradition, religious, political, or other, that is not encumbered with unhappy and even absurd accretions. We can learn from these traditions, however, without becoming tied to their errors.

Religions are also major vehicles of group experience containing as they do a good deal of the moral appreciations and discoveries of groups. The great religions constitute a particular vision or, rather, a number of harmonized (or partly harmonized) visions of what the shape of the good life is. The notion of God, in fact, often recapitulates the basic notions of what moral goodness entails, as perceived by a particular people. Each religious tradition was forged on the anvil of a particular time in history, marked by unique and unrepeatable challenges. Its moral vision and interpretations will be distinguished by its tense, dominant gender, geography, history, mood, myths, analogues, symbols, and saints. Different things will be cared about, and, again, caring is intrinsic to knowing. The result is that each religious tradition should be looked to as a unique locus of moral interpretation, where distinctive perceptions of what does or does not befit the mysterious phenomenon of personhood have been achieved. Irrelevancies are also to be anticipated, reflecting the unique aspects of the original experience. But valid insights may also be awaited, wrought from the experiences of a reflective people and enshrined in the literary and oral traditions of that people.

There are certain inevitable dialectical tensions that present themselves to moral understanding. We must all somehow take our stand on the conflicting claims of pessimism and hope of the individual and the common good, of creativity and conformism, of authority and initiative, of ecstasy and order. We must fashion or assume a conception of what power, justice, love, nobility, etc., imply. The various religious traditions have done this in ways that have *potentially* universal benefit. What this means for ethics is that, to give a particular example, Jewish ethics is not just for Jews. Many persons, Jewish or not, will not want to identify with every aspect of the Jewish visions of personhood, but there is no one who cannot be instructed by those visions, in some way. And so on for the other major religions. This is another area in which traditional ethics has been remiss, treating the significant anthropologies of the various religions as having meaning only for the devotees of the particular faith. Religious ethicists from the particular traditions have also erred by behaving in an exclusivist mode, as though all world views outside of their own were irrelevant or "pagan." The ethicist of a particular religious tradition does indeed have a duty to explore his tradition, clarify it, and apply it. Each of us, like the travelers in *The Canterbury Tales*, has a story to tell, and it is our business to know our story.[52] Because of our story, we can teach what others do not know, and then we can listen to learn something of what we have missed that others found. This ecumenical openness can also be commended regarding the various philosophical traditions, but I here stress the religious sources of moral wisdom, since they are so regularly neglected in the ethical treatment of group experience in this age of adolescent secularism.

NOTES—CHAPTER TEN

1. Arderne, *Treatises of Fistula in Ano*, edited by Power, p. 23; quoted in *Chaucer's World*, compiled by Edith Rickert, edited by Clair C. Olson and Martin M. Crow (New York: Columbia University Press, 1948), p. 177.
2. Karl Mannheim, *Ideology and Utopia* (New York: Harcourt, Brace & World, Inc., A Harvest Book, 1936), p. 3.
3. Clifford Geertz, "The Impact of the Concept of Culture," in John R. Platt, ed., *New Views of the Nature of Man* (Chicago: University of Chicago Press, 1965), pp. 112–13.
4. Peter L. Berger and Thomas Luckmann, *The Social Construction of Reality* (Garden City, N.Y.: Doubleday & Co., Inc., Anchor Books, 1967), p. 3.
5. Ibid., p. 131.
6. For an interesting study of the collapse of the ideal of peace in historical Christianity, see Stanley Windass, *Christianity Versus Violence* (London: Sheed & Ward, 1964). Windass quotes a witness of that period: "The word of God was scattered plentifully, and every day increased the number of 'Jerusalemites'; those who stayed were ashamed, and those who were preparing to leave gloried of it publicly. Everyone encouraged his neighbour, and eager discussions went on in public places, at the street corners and at the crossroads." Even subtler enthusiasms can exercise similar constraints on our thinking and decision-making and draw us passively in their wake.
7. Reinhold Niebuhr, *Moral Man and Immoral Society* (New York: Charles Scribner's Sons, 1960), p. 114.
8. Ibid., p. 117.

9. Ibid., p. 116. He laments that this fact, which is regarded as axiomatic by economists, still had not made much impression on moral theorists. The point still has·to be pressed years after Niebuhr wrote of it. It is still a significant factor in contemporary racism, where class interests are also at issue along with undifferentiated bias in terms of mere color.

10. Vernon Louis Parrington, *Main Currents in American Thought*, Vol. 1, *The Colonial Mind* (New York: Harcourt, Brace & Co.), p. 197.

11. Hans J. Morgenthau, *Politics Among Nations*, 3rd ed. (New York: Alfred A. Knopf, 1962), p. 102.

12. Edgar N. Johnson, *An Introduction to the History of the Western Tradition* (Boston: Ginn & Co., 1959), Vol. 2, p. 460.

13. Ibid.

14. A. F. K. Organski, *World Politics* (New York: Alfred A Knopf, 1958), p. 224.

15. For a treatment of some of the causes of nationalism, see Johnson, *Introduction to the History of the Western Tradition*, Chap. 8.

16. C. P. Cavafy (Kavaphis), quoted in Edmund Stillman and William Pfaff, *The Politics of Hysteria* (New York: Harper & Row, 1964), p. 5.

17. Arnold J. Toynbee, *Change and Habit* (New York and London: Oxford University Press, 1966), p. 104.

18. Ibid., p. 106.

19. Ibid., p. 107.

20. Ibid., p. 108.

21. Ibid., p. 110.

22. Lester B. Pearson, *Partners in Development: Report of the Commission on International Development* (New York, Praeger Publishers, 1969), p. 11.

23. Quoted in Johnson, *Introduction to the History of the Western Tradition*, pp. 476–77.

24. Robert H. Springer, "Conscience, Behavioral Science and Absolutes," in Charles E. Curran, ed., *Absolutes in Moral Theology?* (Washington, D.C.: Corpus Books, 1968), p. 36.

25. Frank Bray Gibney, "10,000 Lawyers vs. 350,000" *Center Report 8*, No. 4 (Oct. 1975), p. 8.

26. Ibid., p. 9.

27. Bronislaw Malinowski, *The Sexual Life of Savages* (London: George Routledge & Sons, 1932), p. 44.

28. Margaret Mead, *Growing up in New Guinea* (New York: William Morrow & Co., 1975).

29. Ibid., p. 9.

30. Trobriander ways cannot simply translate into another culture. What is good for the Trobrianders might wreak only havoc in

Dubuque. It would also have to be shown that what the Trobrianders do is good for them.

31. Lucy Dawidowicz, "The Nazi Experience: Origins and Aftermath,"
Hastings Center Report 6, No. 4 (Aug. 1976), special supplement,
p. 3.
32. Penal Code of Uruguay, Art. 37 (Law No. 9155), cited in Helen
Silving, "Euthanasia: A Study in Comparative Criminal Law," *University of Pennsylvania Law Review* 103 (1954), p. 369, note 74.
33. Swiss Penal Code, Art. 64, cited ibid., p. 367.
34. John T. Noonan, Jr., "Authority, Usury and Contraception," *Cross
Currents* 16, No. 1 (Winter 1966), pp. 55–56.
35. Ibid., p. 72. Noonan offers this as one possible way to understand
theologically the Church's older position on usury.
36. John Henry Newman, *A Grammar of Assent* (Garden City, N.Y.:
Doubleday & Co., Inc., Image Books, 1955), p. 277.
37. Ibid., p. 278.
38. Henri Bergson, *The Two Sources of Morality and Religion* (Garden
City, N.Y.: Doubleday & Co., Inc., Anchor Books, 1956), pp.
14–15.
39. Ibid.
40. C. Judson Herrick, *Brains of Rats and Man*, quoted in Erich
Fromm, *The Anatomy of Human Destructiveness* (New York: Holt,
Rinehart & Winston, 1973), p. 224.
41. Ibid.
42. J. Kashyap, "Origin and Expansion of Buddhism," in Kenneth W.
Morgan, ed., *The Path of the Buddha* (New York: Ronald Press
Co., 1956), pp. 16–17.
43. Fromm, *Anatomy of Human Destructiveness*, p. 224.
44. Ibid.
45. Josef Pieper, *The Four Cardinal Virtues* (New York: Harcourt,
Brace & World, 1965), p. 28.
46. René Le Senne, *Le Devoir* (Paris: Presses Universitaires, 1930), p.
270. Translation, Vernon J. Bourke, Vol. 2, p. 71.
47. See Bruce Vawter, *The Conscience of Israel* (New York: Sheed &
Ward, 1961), pp. 39–40.
48. Amos 5:14–15, 24.
49. Toynbee, *Change and Habit*, pp. 26–27.
50. Eric Voegelin, *The New Science of Politics* (Chicago and London:
University of Chicago Press, Phoenix Books, 1952), p. 60.
51. Those who work out of a Christian perspective should be very open
to the special prerogatives of the individual. (Historically, this has
not been the case.) Christian theology contains the revolutionary
doctrine that the new law which binds Christians is not anything
written but is rather the grace of the Holy Spirit. In other words,
moral wisdom written in the "books" of church, state, and culture is

secondary to the illuminating spirit of God. "Whence even the letter of the Gospel would kill if there were not present interiorly the
healing grace of faith." *Summa Theologica* I II q. 106, a. 2, in corp.
This doctrine obviously is not congenial to the idea of infallibility in
morals, an idea that is not held by many Catholic thinkers today and
not theologically developed by those who cling to it in some fashion.
See Daniel C. Maguire, "Moral Absolutes and the Magisterium," in
Curran, *Absolutes in Moral Theology?* Clearly, any church teaching
is secondary to the illumining grace of the spirit. This obviously
called for criteriology, and the theology of the discernment of the
spirit attempted to supply this. This doctrine also would provide a
base for civil disobedience and would temper the notion of loyal citizenship. Unfortunately, this teaching was neglected in common
teaching and has been rediscovered in somewhat exotic form by
some of the anti-intellectualistic Pentecostal movements today who
use it with little concern for criteriology.

52. For two examples of my contributions to Christian and Catholic self-
understanding, see Daniel C. Maguire, "Credal Conscience: A Question of Moral Orthodoxy," *Anglican Theological Review*, Supple-
mentary Series, No. 6 (June 1976), pp. 37–54, and Daniel C.
Maguire, "Catholic Ethics with an American Accent," in Thomas
M. McFadden, ed., *America in Theological Perspective* (New York:
Seabury Press, 1976), pp. 13–36.

CHAPTER ELEVEN

THE COMIC AND THE TRAGIC IN ETHICS

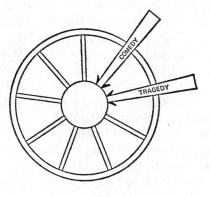

Sense in Nonsense . . .

Unfortunately, theologians and moralists have had much to say about man's responsibility to work, but little about his responsibility to play: many words about seriousness and sobriety, few about nonsense and laughter.[1]

Clearly, the history of ethics shows that humor has not been given a prominent place in the systematic study of morality. It is not that humor has been ignored by all philosophers. The bibliography of J. Y. Greig's *Psychology of Laughter and Comedy* mentions 363 works devoted wholly or partially to the subject. The authors range from Plato and Aristotle to Kant, Bergson, and Freud. Still, with all of this, the interest in humor has not led to its inclusion as an integral part of ethical method. I submit that this represents a serious omission in ethical method.

There are many modes of moral consciousness, and one of the ways in which we come to awareness of moral truth is through the phenomenon of amusement. If it is seen what humor is and what it achieves, it should be clear that it has a major role in the evaluational resources of moral man. As to what humor is, I will suggest that it involves (1) a response to incongruity within human life, (2) surprise, (3) creative imagination, (4) affectivity.

Human Incongruity. At the outset, humor appears as something of a delightful anomaly. Man is the only animal to be amused, and he is amused at nothing but himself. He is, as the ancients called him, the "laughing animal" (*zoion gelastikon*) or the "animal capable of amusement" (*animal risibile*). Humor is utterly human, achieved by man alone, and focused on man alone. The hyena may make laughing sounds, but he is not amused. Hilarity is a peculiarly human blessing. And its object is ourselves. We laugh only at that which is human or humanlike. As Peter Berger says: "The biological as such is not comic. Animals become comic only when we view them anthropomorphically, that is, when we imbue them with human characteristics."[2] Most theories of humor agree that it is provoked by some incongruity or inconsistency. However, it is *our* inconsistencies and incongruities that evoke our laughter; the inconsistencies and incongruities in inorganic and subhuman nature do not amuse us. If we laugh at the orangutan or the bear at the zoo, it is because human qualities and emotions can be imaginatively attributed to them. The same is true of household pets whom we personalize in our imaginations. The distinguished man wearing a derby who slips and plops down in the snow can stir amusement. A falling brick is not funny unless its falling can be related to a potentially funny human cause.

Humor, from childish jokes to sophisticated witticisms, lives on discrepancy or incongruity. In the humorous view, something is seen in a different, comic light which could be seen in a serious or even tragic way. Bergson seems correct when he says that the humorous situation "is capable of being interpreted in two entirely different meanings at the same time."[3] The humorous interpretation collides in its own unique and delightful way with a possible serious interpretation. Thus the statement that "Kansas will remain 'dry' as long as the voters can stagger to the polls" has a claim to being funny. Without humor, the probable reaction would be disgust at the hypocrisy of the citizens who manage to have their drink and ban it too. The humorous view of this does not miss the discrepancy that could, in another kind of reaction, feed our disgust. Indeed it feasts upon it, and may even succeed in drawing attention to it more sharply than would a dour judgment on the inconsistency of the Kansans.

The fact that we are the unique subjects and objects of laughter should have sent initial signals to ethics. If ethics is concerned with the distinctively human, it should be alert to any reaction which is wholly centered on humanness. This fact alone raises delicious suspicions of relevance. Beyond that, humor involves an intellectual reaction. It represents an appraisal of incongruities within human experience. No specific intellectual manifestation should be ignored by the art-science which seeks to understand and evaluate the whole phenomenon of humanness.

Surprise. Humor also involves surprise. The surprise element is visible all the way from the peekaboo laughter of the baby to the satires of Mark Twain. It appears clearly in Twain's remarks, "It is by the goodness of God that in our country we have those three unspeakably precious things: freedom of speech, freedom of conscience, and the prudence never to practice either of them." The initial piety of the comment sets us up for the surprising ending. Again, the humor here comes from inconsistency between the professed love of freedom and the practiced cowardice that enslaves.

The surprise element is obvious again in the cartoon that depicted Mary and Joseph kneeling beside the manger in which Jesus lay and saying with much disappointment to the shepherds: "We had been hoping for a girl." (This also illustrates, as we shall discuss further, that nothing within human experience is beyond the purview of the comic—even the sacred.) Humor, then, involves a *new* twist. The repeated joke fails. It may provoke renewed laughter, but it is of a different commemorative sort whereby we imaginatively relive the pleasant shock of the original amusement. Surprising newness is of the essence of humor. The joke that has to be explained fails. The explanation, however well achieved, takes away the surprise factor and the humor perishes.

Creative Imagination. Humor is a work of creativity. That is why it surprises. Humor involves the discovery and sharing of some hidden likenesses brought out in a pleasant and fresh interpretation. It is understandable that Part One of Arthur Koestler's study *The Act of Creation* is devoted entirely to laughter and amusement, since humor is a signal work of creative wit. As Koestler says, the jester's humor provides a back-door entry into the inner workshop of creative originality.[4] The creative mind perceives connections and similarities that are missed in more literal and blunt views of the facts of life. This is precisely the achievement of the humorist.

American humorists during the Vietnam War did much to disarm the reasonings offered for that peculiar enterprise. Seizing upon a degree of likeness, Arthur Hoppe took the pacification and resettlement ideas that were operating in Vietnam and applied them as a solution to our inner-city ghetto problems. He wrote wryly of removing all persons from the ghettos, calling on B-52s to level those areas, mining the entrances to the ghettos, and then resettling the former residents in municipal parks or other such areas.[5]

The humorous comparison may be made with a broad brush, but if enough hidden likenesses are discovered, the humor is a success. The discovery of previously hidden likenesses is an intellectual event. And when the subject under view is heavy with moral value considerations, the creative humorous response might discover and communicate more than tedious analytical discourses on the same situation. Often enough, the "back-door entry" is the only door that is not locked. The humorous discovery of morally significant incongruities in the field of human behavior may then become a force for further intellectual conversion. With the mind thus painlessly pried ajar, further serious reflection of an enlightening nature might follow. Humor, therefore, is not just a respectable and normal avenue for the growth of moral awareness; it may at times be the only avenue open to moral insight and moral imagination. To bypass this, because it does not suit our pompous rationalistic conceptions of how proper ethics should be done, is unintelligent.

Moralists should have taken the lead from psychologists who have sensed the important revealing power of humor. As Gordon Allport says: "We have grounds for supposing that a person's sense of humor is also an important variable in relation to prejudice. In the syndrome of a prejudiced personality, humor is a missing ingredient just as it is an ingredient that is present in the syndrome of tolerance."[6]

Psychologist Harvey Mindess makes the point that the sense of humor that is significant psychologically is not found merely in the capacity to deliver a number of witty one-liners or in the ability to enjoy jokes and contrived comic routines. The sense of humor that is salvific "must constitute a frame of mind, a point of view, a deep-going, far-reaching attitude to life."[7] The cluster of qualities that characterizes this frame of mind shows the relationship of humor to creative imagination. Mindess lists these qualities as *flexibility*, a readiness to consider every side of every issue; *spontaneity*, the capacity to leap from one mode of thinking to another; *shrewdness*, a refusal to take anything or anyone, self included, at a face value; and *playfulness*, bringing a sense of gaming to life and an openness to enjoy his tragicomic existence and humility. "A man who can shrug off the insufficiency of his ultimate wisdom, the meaninglessness of his profoundest thought, is a man in touch with the very soul of humor."[8]

These qualities seem not just to describe a humorous frame of mind but to be applicable also to the creative mind in general. Even the scientist to be creative must have a touch of all of them. He must even have a kind of playful readiness to test and play with hypotheses in a way that the reigning common sense in his field does not encourage. In ethics the humorous frame of mind then would seem a necessary flowering of moral imagination, that supreme faculty of the valuing animal. Humor's fully fledged citizenship in ethics should not be in question.

Humor as Affectivity and Delight. There is some truth in the saying that life is a tragedy for those who think and a comedy for those who feel. There is also some error in it, since tragedy and comedy, as we shall discuss, can no more be separated than can thought and feeling. The truth of the saying, however, is in the linkage of humor and feeling. Humor is a species of delight. As the felicitous phrasing of Christopher Fry has it: "In tragedy we suffer pain; in comedy pain is a fool, suffered gladly."[9] There are many aspects to the joyous effervescence which is humor's delight. Part of what is delightful is at the level of the physical, quasi-orgasmic release of laughter. This is one of the fascinatingly unique things about humor. As Koestler says, humor "is the only domain of creative activity where a complex pattern of intellectual stimulation elicits a sharply defined response in the nature of physiological reflex."[10] This reflex was happy results. Again Koestler: "The peculiar breathing in laughter, with its repeated, explosive exhalations, seems designed to 'puff away' surplus tension in a kind of respiratory gymnastics. . . ."[11] The delights, however, are also of a more spiritual sort. For one thing, humor is a friendly experience. It is social and socializing, and this in two ways: First, it calls for sharing. Laughing alone, like a meal alone or like

sex alone, is an incomplete and abortive experience. Full-hearted
laughter calls for company; we must imagine ourselves or actually be
in the company of others to indulge fully in humor, and if we do
laugh alone there is a natural desire and urgency to share the moment. Laughter is social and socializing.

There is a deeper sense, however, in which laughter presupposes
society. The joke is ultimately on all of us. My folly is everyman's
and everyman's folly is mine. Laughter reflects the human condition
and not just my condition. It presupposes agreement on what the
human condition is and ought to be. This is the backdrop that
makes the funny discrepancy both noticeable and funny. Humor
plays upon the possible and the actual and celebrates the discrep-
ancies between what is and what might be. But the common denom-
inator in all of it is our consciously shared human condition. This is
a major source of humor's delight. There is, of course, a sour humor
which lacks social fullness. This is the experience of those who cannot laugh at themselves, whose humor, therefore, is short-circuited
and ultimately hostile. It is turned on others, but it misses the ecstatic joy of celebrating our infirmities together, which is the liberating delight of genuine humor.

This, then, is another source of delight in humor. True humor has
implicit reference to self; to laugh at others is to laugh at self, since
we are in this thing together. And laughter at self is delightful. It
releases us from our own pretenses and relaxes the burden of our defensive pomposities. It also strikes a blow at our unnatural inhibi-
tions. As M. Conrad Hyers writes, "In comedy the superego is either
granted a leave of absence . . . or made the object of comic withdrawal and aggression."[12] In either case the superego and its inhibi-
tions are relativized, set in perspective, and made less formidable.
And this is both a relief and a delight.

Humor is delightful, too, because it is a sabbatical from purposive
adulthood, "a holiday of innocence"[13] in which we return to both
the simplicities and joyous rebellion of our youth. Obviously it is fun
to rebel against the oppressive proprieties that gird us about. Somehow, in laughter, our weaknesses and debits become a source of
strength; suddenly we can pick ourselves up by the boots, or, in other
imagery, we are provided in laughter with a delicious sort of alchemy
that turns misfortune into joy. Laughter is ecstasy in the literal sense
of the term. When we are amused, we stand outside of ourselves. It
is a moment of releases from all the "normal" ways of seeing things.

All of this has the stuff of "holiday" about it. There is refreshment in this experience, and delight.

Laughter delights also because it fulfills our insatiable need for newness. Our minds are always restlessly in motion from the known to the not yet known. Humor fulfills this hunger for newness. It is thus a treat for the mind as well as for the body. A "good laugh" is good in so many ways.

Finally, though not exhaustively on the subject of humor's delight, humor is based on hope, and hope is the fountainhead of all delighting. True humor is not destructive but re-creative. In a sense we tear down in humor, but it is not a tearing down that is unto death. Perverted humor, of course, can represent despair. Its purposes can be vindictive and malicious. But genuine humor strikes benignly at that which it loves. It prunes that for which it has high hope. That is why nothing is beyond laughter. Even the sacred is within the province of the humorous, and there is no sacrilege in this since the disrespect in humor is only apparent. We need relief from all our imperfect and domineering images, even those that we have of God. Otherwise, comedy would become tragedy of the darkest kind. Without hope, there would be nothing to laugh at. To quote again M. Conrad Hyers:

> . . . comedy is a prefiguration of anticipated joy, a return to chaos as a prelude to a new cosmos, a comic suspension of meaning and plunge into irrationality as a transition into a fuller meaning and higher rationality that is to come.[14]

Perhaps our hope can be said to be vindicated in humor, since there is a strong sense of reality in the humorous perspective, and a depressing sense of unreality in humorlessness. To a degree, reality is hilarious. He who lacks a sense of humor is missing that. In other words hilarity and laughter are among the appropriate responses to reality. This has got to be reassuring. It means that tragedy does not have the final and only word. Hope perdures. And that is delightful, as well as relevant to ethics.

Humor as the Bane of Absolutism . . .

From simply seeing what humor is, much appears to show that comedy is germane to ethics. Humor is concerned with the human and that which relates to the human, and so is ethics. Humor is a work of intelligence, creative imagination, and affectivity, and so too is ethics. Humor points to and promotes communion among persons, and so does ethics. These bedfellows should obviously regularize their natural relationship.

To assist further in this, we can look to one of the problems that beset ethics as it does every other form of human thought. My reference is to what has been called "the absolutizing instinct."[15] In discussing this instinct, psychologist William F. Lynch concludes that the most difficult proposition in this world for all of us is that there is but one God and no more than that.[16] In fact, we are all polytheists and idolaters, fashioning gods indiscriminately from such delicate clay as our own egos, ideas, authorities, and evaluations. What this does is to give divine and absolute status to bias and imperfection. Fighting this by breaking idols is, as we have stressed, a major goal of ethics. Humor is an important force in relativizing false absolutes. Since humor gives what has been called "a God's eye view of life," it is in a good position to spot pretenders to divinity. It is of value to see how humor serves its relativizing function in the face of the absolutisms of rationalism, power, demonic images, and tragedy.

Rationalism. Rationalism, as I argued above, overestimates our ability to capture truth in the blueprints of the mind.[17] It involves an immodest respect for our knowing efforts and an inadequate respect for the reaches of the real which we do not know. It forgets that in our service of the truth we are at best unprofitable servants who know only in part. Rationalistic man is not open to surprise. He bends over when he thinks and becomes more and more mesmerized with his own squinting view. His symbol is the transfixed navel-gazer, not the *orant* of the Roman catacombs who stands reaching for the truth that he has not as yet touched. The rationalist's fussy need to make sense of things consumes him and he will not let anything, including reality, distract him from his goal.

The rationalist is not a rare bird. Rationalism claims at least a corner in every soul. Basically this is due to our horror of the incongruous, of that for which our way of viewing things has not provided. When data that does not suit our conceptions presents itself, we tend not to see it. If there is no place on our blueprints for this data, then either the blueprints or the data must go. Rationalistic man prefers his blueprints.

Studies have been done to show the perceptual denial of the incongruous. We develop expectations of what the real has to offer, and we are controlled in our interpretations by those expectations, not by the signals from reality. In one study, subjects were asked to identify a red six of spades. Ninety-six per cent of the subjects failed at first to identify the anomalous card for what it was. And it took four times longer to perceive the incongruous cards as it did to identify the normal cards. The conclusion of the researchers was that ". . . for as long as possible and by whatever means available, the organism will ward off the perception of the unexpected, those things which do not fit his prevailing set. . . ."[18]

Thus the rationalist is everyman, clinging to the inadequate sense he has made of things, and shying from surprise. Solutions are available for his plight; humor is one of them. Humor jolts our bowed head back and makes us look up to discover that the little plot of reality on which we had been gazing with fixed vision is bounded by a universe. Humor bespeaks *more*. In humor we leap beyond the limits of our reasonable conceptions and taste something of the more that is always beckoningly beyond.

In his celebrated theory of knowledge, Bernard Lonergan notes "the profound significance" of humor and contends that "proofless, purposeless laughter can dissolve honored pretense; it can disrupt conventional humbug; it can disillusion man of his most cherished illusions, for it is in league with the detached, disinterested, unrestricted desire to know."[19] The "unrestricted desire to know" can get restricted in the rationalist. Humor can break up that bondage. It brings to the rationalistic mind precisely what is needed—release and expansion. It introduces the affections in their cognitive role. The rationalist is closed to this, since the affections are full of surprises and cannot be contained in the rationalist's constrained categories. The affections are less manageable than concepts. In humor the affections appear in the posture of delight, and in delight we stretch and grow to contain the good not heretofore included in our experience.

A humorous mind-set also comports a habit of anticipating newness. Humor is bred of novelty and surprise. In a mind where it is at home, therefore, there will be less rigidity and more suppleness of spirit, qualities that well befit a "living intellect."

Humor also thrives on paradox and on the recognition that there are times when we simply cannot "get it together," when we are left with the likeness of truth on both horns of an intellectual dilemma. Humor, as Lonergan says, "blushes with humility."[20] Puffy rationalism does not, and so it is that it needs redeeming humor. Rationalism wants to explain everything. Humor knows that that cannot be done, and that there is understanding that transcends explanation. As we have seen, a joke will evanesce if it must be explained to the unamused. Humor is a healthy reminder of how variegated and ultimately mysterious understanding is. It is thus a force for modesty and intellectual realism. Humor does not fight rationalism by going against reason. It is not antirational so much as preter-rational. It presents another way of viewing the same facts and so is a native and primordial force for the expansion of the mind. René Dubos writes: "Ethical attitudes and intellectual creativity depend in part on the ability to hear 'the voice of the deep' and to tap resources from regions of man's nature which have not yet been explored."[21] Humor is a voice from the deep, and though it is fun, the intellectual need for it is serious.

Power. There is an old Latin saying that says: "Once a year it is permissible to go mad!" (*Semel in anno licet insanire!*) It seems that cultures instinctively provide for that. From the Dionysian celebrations to the cavortings of Mardi Gras, from the Maypole dancers to the somewhat forced revelries of New Year's Eve, some place for madness is allowed. Such phenomena, appearing as they do transculturally, are the expression of deep and usually unnamed needs. One of these days of madness is particularly revealing about what needs are being met and about the role of humor in meeting them. I refer to the "Feast of Fools," a holiday that was a vigorous part of life in parts of medieval Europe.[22] This was a day when only humor was sacred. All that was customarily sacred was open to mockery and lampooning. Schoolboys and even clerics dressed as prelates and magistrates and made fun of all "the powers that be." Whatever was mighty and great was the natural target of the day. The mighty and the great did not always take well to it, and so the feast was often visited with indignant condemnation. Nevertheless, it stubbornly managed to stay around for a long time. As Harvey Cox says, ". . . despite the efforts of fidgety ecclesiastics and an outright condemnation by the Council of Basel in 1431, the Feast of Fools survived until the sixteenth century."[23]

The "Feast of Fools" corresponds to another important tradition, that of the jester. Societies institutionalize that which they find important, and the jester was an institution. A man of sufficient skill and talent could acquire a jestership in the court of prince or bishop.

In his role he enjoyed an outstanding immunity and could make fun of everything including his lordly master. The jester was not just a harmless comedian. He performed a further humanizing and serious service. He relativized the pomp and the power of the court and brought redemption to those who might otherwise have choked on their own importance. Though he was looked down upon by many of the great, he earned his place at the throne. He worked at preventing power from losing all sense of human limit. He relativized the strutting absolutes that were everywhere about him. In a word, he was a source of refreshing profanation, and a living symbol of the role of humor in moral consciousness.

The Feast of Fools and the jester show the ethical role of relativizing power. Power, unfortunately, has a bad name, although it is a rudimentary reality which, unabused, is beautiful in all its forms. It is power that enables the blade of grass to break through the soil and live, and it is power that pushes the stream of life forward in all of its manifestations. In the world of persons, it is power that can enlighten minds or create beauty from clay or sounds or words. And it is power that directs the affairs of men harmoniously and creatively. But power does corrupt, and that absolutely, when it itself is absolutized and cut off from the essential human task of building community among persons. The power that operates among persons, to remain human in kind, must be intertwined, related, and thus relativized by its service to other human values. Power that becomes an end in itself is corrupt. The jester and the Feast of Fools remind power of its human station. They tell power that it is a means validated by its service to human ends.

The message here is important in interpersonal life and even more important in centers of political power and in centers of learning. The inability to laugh corrodes the quality of mercy. The work of the jester is there waiting to be done in the White House, the Kremlin, the Board Room, and in a religious power center like the Vatican. If all of these centers seem singularly humorless, then that is a danger signal that power unredeemed by humor has probably been absolutized and dehumanized.

There is an intellectual as well as political danger in this, since the centers of collective power—states, corporations, and organized religion—are potent symbols which display and tend to legitimize a particular system of moral values. Power is always a pedagogue and so there is all the more reason to keep it human. It always needs the ministry of those who embody "the philosophy of the jester." As one philosopher put it, "The philosophy of the jester is a philosophy which in every epoch denounces as doubtful what appears as unshakable; it points out the contradictions in what seems evident and incontestable; it ridicules common sense into the absurd—in other words, it undertakes the daily toil of the jester's profession along with the inevitable risk of appearing ludicrous."[24] Absolute pedagogical power in whatever form arrogates to itself the badge of self-evidence. Shattering this badge is the jester's work. In every line of human intellectual endeavor and expertise, the instinct of absolutizing power is at work forming, when possible, dynastic clubs which would banish unsanctioned novelty and rule upon what can be considered truth. In few fields of thought are such clubs not in evidence. Jesters are thus badly needed in the courts of the academy as well as in the courts of politics and corporate power.

Demonic Images. The human mind is easily captured by a particular image which can wrap up all our clever reasonings and leave them dangling helplessly under the control of the dominant image. Sometimes a word can function as an image that demonically captures a whole history of venom and hate. "Nigger" is a word like that. And Dick Gregory, the prophet-jester, gives an example of what humor can do to relativize that vicious image. He has told hundreds of rollicking audiences that he used that word as the title of one of his books so that whenever his children heard the word, they could say: "Somebody is talking about Daddy's book!" Here Gregory was acting also as an exorcist, driving out the devil that possessed a word.

Humor can go to work also on other demons like the work ethic, male dominance, and the myths of woman, class, and nation. Also, it is not necessary to take on with supine obedience all the imperiously established values of one's profession, class, time, or place. Humor is one of the forces that can bring liberation from the demonic images that come to us from a thousand sources and shackle the mind in disgraceful servitude.

Demonic images can easily attach to the most serious things in our life. The more serious things are, however, the more need there is for comic perspective. G. K. Chesterton put it this way: "Life is serious all the time, but living cannot be. You may have all the solemnity you wish in your neckties, but in anything important (such as sex, death, and religion), you must have mirth or you will have madness."[25]

Tragedy. Tragedy is a somber fact of human living. In speaking of it here I am not yet treating tragedy as one of the spokes of the wheel model. When I do that, as I shortly shall, I will be stressing the potential for moral illumination through one's response to tragedy. Here I am speaking of the tragic dimension of our existence and its need for redemption through comedy.

That tragedy will ever be with us is grounded in two intrinsic problems of the human condition: our finitude and our capacity for deep love. As to our limits, we are the only animal that knows its own mortality and we live in the shadow of this privileged knowledge. In our early days, the aging process is called growth, but for most of our lives it is seen for what it becomes, movement toward death.[26] And so death, the supreme limit, hovers over our consciousness, symbolizing the many lesser limits that fill our world. Crisscrossing this knowledge of death, the unavoidable and complete limit, is our boundless affectivity which can desire and love *without limit.* This too relates to our burden of tragedy. As the Irish poet William Butler Yeats said: "A pity beyond all telling, is hid in the heart of love."[27] The "pity" that he finds is in the fact that when one loves, he extends his vulnerability. All kinds of things that were formerly no hazard to me now, in Yeats's words, "threaten the head that I love." Love prompts us to possess the beloved with a security that our limit will not permit. We love in a perilous world in which menacing chaos has not been routed. Pain and loss are our portion. There is no way of getting ready for this. Most emerge from childhood with ebullient expectations of bliss. Only slowly can we comprehend the tragedy that marks our being. Yeats, who felt acutely the tragic dimensions of life, wrote in another poem of the delicate innocence of youth in the face of tragedy:

> Come away, O human child!
> To the waters and the wild
> With a fairy, hand in hand,
> For the world's more full of
> weeping than you can understand.[28]

When we begin to "understand," tragedy can and often does crush. Tragedy at its depths dissolves the essential filament of hope and so undoes the human spirit. Hopeless, senseless tragedy can break the mind or drive us to lonely suicide. To be unaware of tragedy is to be superficial. To yield to its grimness is deadly. What is needed is what has been called a tragicomic sense of life. Comedy relativizes tragedy without trivializing it. As Peter Berger observes, "At least for the duration of the comic perception, the tragedy of man is bracketed."[29] With its power to reveal other dimensions, humor broadens our gloomy focus. It is a harbinger from the *more* that reality promises, a kind of blessed augury which says that tragedy, however real, is not the name of God.

When Humor Goes Amuck . . .

As an ancient saying has it, "The corruption of that which is best, is the worst" (*Corruptio optimi pessima*). Humor is among the best of the graces. The ways in which it can go awry must not be missed. For one thing, strained humor might be a work of despair—a collapse before oppression. As psychologist Gordon W. Allport writes, "If the master wants to be amused, the slave sometimes obligingly plays the clown."[30] Humor might be used to underwrite the pain that seems inexorable fate. Again in Allport's words, "There is often a flavor of pathos in the self-directed humor of minority groups. They seem to be saying, with Byron, 'if I laugh at any mortal thing, it is that I may not weep.' "[31] We could laugh when we should be weeping or doing battle with courageous indignation. Such laughter is a weak retreat. It trivializes that which it should attack.

Laughter can also take the terrible form of ridicule and derision. Ridicule is a force for social conformism. It is closer to hostility than humor. It is relevant to ethics, since many of our skewed valuations are driven into us by way of ridicule and derision. Racism, for example, is re-enforced this way. Deviations from racist folkways are derided. How instructive it is to see in children that blackness or whiteness is of no significance. The natural concentration of the child is on the human qualities. Little black hands reach spontaneously for little white hands . . . until society instills its perverse message. Derision and the fear of derision are a major part of society's teaching power. Laughter's service is not always holy.

Where Tragedy and Comedy Meet . . .

"In all the wild imaginings of mythology a fanciful spirit is playing on the border-line between jest and earnest."[32] In humor which is not simply frivolous (there is of course room for the simply frivolous), the humorous spirit plays on the border line not only between jest and earnest but also between comedy and tragedy. We saw this in Dick Gregory's calling his book *Nigger*. Black parents looking at their children know that this word is more full of weeping than their little ones can as yet understand. This was no light matter for Gregory to joke about. His humor was, as humor often is, contiguous to tragedy. He took this painful word and doused it with cleansing laughter, but in this laughter, comedy and tragedy kissed, with comedy managing to set the mood. The tragedy here was not denied, but it was for the moment at least upended by comedy. And indeed the tragic side was not likely to be affected only for a moment. Such a dramatic humorous transformation could never allow the reality to be experienced in quite the same way. In such humor the tragedy is to a significant and permanent degree conquered by its better half.

The close relationship of the tragic and the comic appears in the historical fact that some groups that have suffered the most are outstanding in their intuitive sense of comedy. Professor James Lynwood Walker points out that Jews and blacks who have encountered an undue share of the tragic have both produced "cogent thinkers and sensitive comics, who fear neither serious nor light-hearted analysis of the contemporary state of man and society."[33] (With admitted bias, signaled by my name, I would add the Irish to this list.) Walker goes on to comment on "the relative lack of profundity and gaiety in many, perhaps most, contemporary white Americans. Profoundly thinking and genuinely comic whites seem rare. . . ."[34] In what must be the oddest of relationships, the tragic and the comic go together. The tearless will also be the laughless, and vice versa. Those who cannot take reality as it is with its inexorable tragedy will not have the depth or breadth for a comic vision.

One can turn to Dick Gregory again to see the contiguity of the tragic and the comic. Though Gregory is best known for his gift of comedy, there are strong elements of poignancy and pathos in his work. For example, he tells about his grandmother's memories of slavery. She remembered a slave woman who had to give up her children for immediate sale. Only if the child was deformed could she keep her baby. After having two children taken from her like this, she then prayed that when she became pregnant again, her child would be deformed. When I heard Gregory tell this story to a large university audience, he paused at this point and that distinctive silence that attends the hearing of some horror struck the entire auditorium. Gregory broke the silence to comment that if white men would understand black men ("us niggers," in Gregory's parlance) they should think about that prayer for a deformed baby. The story, however, was not yet finished. The woman's child was born, and it was "deformed." The mother received it lovingly into her arms, saw its deformity, and said: "Thank God!" And Gregory urged his silent audience again to "think about *that* prayer."

Gregory was here the tragedian, who was able to get into the consciousness of his almost entirely white audience in a way that a thousand well-formed syllogisms could never achieve. There are many roads to moral truth. Tragedy is one of them. Like its fair sister, comedy, it ruptures cold complacency and offers our moral consciousness a chance for healing. This leads us very naturally to our consideration of:

The Positive Value of Tragedy . . .

I have listed tragedy as one of the spokes of my wheel model of ethics, thus saying that it has a potentially positive value for the expansion of moral consciousness. Each of the spokes represents a personal or cultural resource through which moral understanding is advanced. What I have said so far might suggest that tragedy can only have a value if it is redeemed by comedy. In a sense this is true, and in a sense, false. The mating of tragedy and comedy into a tragicomic sense is the wholesome goal. One without the other would lead to the destruction of the person by way of either despair or superficiality. However, even within the tragic experience itself there is potential for light.

At a conference on behavior control through the use of drugs, Dr. L. Jolyon West made the following comment:

> Let us assume the development of a "happiness" drug which is relatively safe. It would make it possible for a human being to go from birth to death without having encountered suffering, tragedy, and anxiety. Trauma could be swiftly counteracted with drugs. What kind of people are those going to be, those who grow up without having suffered, without undergoing the trauma of "normal life"—as *we* know it? To what extent are our ideas of maturity, nobility, sympathy, and so on, dependent on the experience of suffering? That, after all, is the point of Huxley's

Brave New World: that the non-sufferer is somehow inhuman.[35]

It may seem impossible to speak in praise of suffering without lapsing into sadism or masochism. Perhaps this is why ethicists have done little thinking about this subject. However, it is possible to admit that suffering is intrinsic to living and also that it is the crucible from which significant influences on our moral consciousness emerge, and still work to eliminate suffering whenever we can. Medical science, for example, has eliminated many tragedies from life by limiting infant and maternal death and by controlling so many diseases. This is an obvious good. Wherever tragedy can be contained it is a moral duty to contain it. Suffering has no per se value. Whether tragedy and suffering contribute positively to our growth depends entirely on our response to them. What is special about persons is their ability to transcend suffering and to transform it into something positive. Other animals do not have this capacity to any discernible degree. A horse, for example, that was born deaf and blind would be best put to death. Helen Keller, however, was born with these terrible disabilities, and yet she was a person and as such was able to transcend them marvelously and bring much fulfillment to her own life and much hope to the lives of others. Suffering thus borne is a moral teacher. It draws our consciousness more deeply into the foundational moral experience of the marvels of personhood. It sharpens our appreciation of our human capacities and deflates the word *impossible.* Helen Keller's own consciousness had to take on heroic dimensions to rise up and meet the prodigious limits that afflicted her. Her greatness related to her tragedy.

One way of sensing the positive potential of a growth through tragedy is to consult our own experience of what positive things it can do to people. The Belgian philosopher Jacques Leclercq goes so far as to say: "We can take it as a general rule that when we meet a man in whom we discern some profundity of character, that is to say a strong personality, we almost always find when we come to know him well that he has been scarred by suffering."[36] H. Richard Niebuhr also comments that "everyone with any experience of life is aware of the extent to which the characters of people he has known have been given their particular forms by the sufferings through which they have passed." Niebuhr insists, further, that it is not so much what has happened to people that changes them so much as how they responded to what happened to them. With this understood, he asserts that "it is in the response to suffering that many and perhaps all men, individually and in their groups, define themselves, take on character, develop their ethos."[37] It would seem indeed to be within the experience of all of us that deep suffering can bring greater depth and sensitivity to persons who were, before that, overly self-assured and superficial. (It is also true, of course, that suffering can break a person, and this too is revealed by even a little of life's experience.)

What is being said here, then, in terms of ethical method, is that our response to suffering can bring moral depth to our character and can make our affective response to moral truth more sensitive. Both Niebuhr and Leclercq turn to the word "character" to find the place of impact where suffering met in a fitting way ennobles. As I discussed above,[38] it is within character that the data of moral experience resonate. The affective and characterological orientation wrought by well-met tragedy touches at an essential component of moral knowing. This is why tragedy can be listed as one of the spokes of the method model.

Niebuhr's point is also not to be missed when he says that suffering affects the development of an ethos for individuals and for groups. "It has often been remarked that the great decisions which give a society its specific character are functions of emergency situations in which a community has had to meet a challenge."[39] Thus the American national character[40] was fashioned not so much by its professed ideals or its system of laws, as by the way it met situations it did not want, but through which it had to suffer. The Civil War, the Depression, the world wars, the challenge from communism, the depletion of resources, etc., were the tragic situations that led to growth or decline in moral awareness and sensitivity. To know how a person or a society has responded to suffering is to know much of the good or the bad of the person and the society. Knowing this calls attention to the importance of suffering. It also helps in analyzing the individual and group experiences that must be consulted in a moral method.[41] The question must be asked as to whether the suffering has soured or ennobled the sufferer. Thus attention to the tragic elements in individual and group histories is important.

How Can the Tragic Be Good? . . .

Some suggestion can be made about how our response to suffering may have a positive effect on our moral character and consciousness.

In speaking of tragedy and suffering, and I am using the words interchangeably here, I refer to a painful experience that is not of our own choosing, one that cuts athwart our plans and hopes, which we would avoid if at all possible. I do not make reference to the pain that we may inflict on ourselves for ascetical, aesthetic, or other purposes.[42] Tragedy is the hurting experience that we would do anything to avoid. So the obvious question is, What good could such a thing possibly do? Why is it that we look to it for positive contributions?

Bernard Lonergan sees a positive cognitive role for tragedy. He views man as a being whose existing lies in developing. He is a creature gripped by a need which "heads him ever towards a known unknown." His mind is marked by "a need to respond to a further reality than meets the eye and to grope his way towards it." Man is driven by intimations of the more that he has not as yet seen. What this amounts to is a kind of "indeterminately directed dynamism" which has its ground in potency. It is not an easily analyzable dynamism. It lacks "the settled assurance and efficacy of form. . . ."

Lonergan is not speaking of some kind of a directed instinct that keeps us sniffing sure-footedly in the direction of truth, our inevitable quarry. The knowing dynamism of man is nothing so chartable as that. It is a force that makes itself felt most notably in certain circumstances such as in tranquil solitude or *"in the shattering upheavals of personal or social disaster."*[43] Disaster is obviously something to be avoided, and yet it can be the avenue to profundity in our knowing process. It is in the unsettlement of disaster that we might best catch a glimpse of that further reality that lures the eye of the questing human knower.

To understand something of how suffering can do this, it is well to know what suffering is not. First of all, suffering is not unhappiness any more than pleasure is happiness. As Leclercq says: "Suffering and pleasure correspond to particular goods and partial states of consciousness. A man may suffer from hunger, ignorance or solitude and still be happy, if his life is dominated by a consciousness of fulfillment.[44] Suffering, of course, can lead to unhappiness and depression, in which event it submerges the powers of the person, arrests growth, and can even break the mind and the spirit. This is when suffering becomes absolute and overwhelming. Leclercq appears to be correct in saying that "suffering is never absolute, as long as man is conscious of pursuing his end."[45] If there is meaning that endures in spite of the suffering, then the tragic dimension will not blot out hope or stifle the processes of growth. Personal and cognitive growth might occur during the suffering, and for reasons which we will discuss, it might occur even precisely because of the suffering. If tragedy inevitably produced unhappiness, we could only look for the gradual extinction of the personal powers of the sufferer.

Second, the positive evaluation of suffering is also not a collapse into masochism. Ethical method takes a positive view of tragedy only because persons are such that they can grow in their reaction to suffering. The value is in the sufferer, not in the suffering itself. Masochism involves a sick and debasing glorification of pain. On the contrary a sense of what a person can do in response to suffering takes note of one of the glories of personhood, our ability to advance in the worst of times. It is this alchemic potential of persons to bring value from the apparently valueless that gives tragedy possible entree into the realm of the good.

Tragedy works as an antidote to smugness. I do not speak of smugness merely as one of the more obnoxious manifestations of pride. I speak of it more in an epistemological sense as a kind of master myth of omnipotence that can imbue the mind with undue confidence in its assessments of reality. Tragedy attacks the arrogance and superficiality of the intellectually smug. It does this in an obvious way when the tragedy strikes directly at a moral blind spot. For example, the Don Juan who moves from one romantic conquest to another with no feeling for the expectations that he engenders and then leaves cruelly unfulfilled might take instruction only from tragedy and pain of the sort that he has regularly caused. Only when he goes through the sequence of promising intimacy followed by rejection could he possibly learn the value implications of his behavior. Similarly a nation like the United States, which grew arrogant in its sense of power and abundance, would seem to be learning the reality of limit through the route of tragedy. As recently as a decade ago, warnings of limits to our resources or our military capacities seemed unreal. Then we felt the weight of the oil cartel at the very time that we were coming to see that our own supplies were not infinite. We failed to achieve what we wanted in a long and costly war. No "invisible hand" can be seen benevolently operative in our economic story as city after city deteriorates to the brink of chaos. Nuclear destruction, that great ghost of the modern mind, haunts at least the outer regions of our consciousness. America's naïve belief that it could turn its back on the tragic dimension of life is coming to an end. The sense of limit that this brings could be the gateway to a new wisdom. Having been forced to look tragedy in the eye, we cannot sustain our traditionally smug view of the state of things. Many of our treasured symbols of self-understanding have been upended. The possibility of unhappy endings now enters into our consciousness, and that is a whole new and potentially less superficial mind-set.

Tragedy, however, may also be instructive even when it is not focused on a critical moral blind spot. Tragedy shakes the foundations of the mind. Nothing is quite the same after the quake of a major tragedy. Tragedy always involves a surprise. We are at least surprised at how terrible something can be. Suffering occurs when that to which we are not inured accosts us. There is something new and rattling about this. It cannot but touch our complacent patterns of interpretation. Tragedy enters with its shocking newness and tears at our psychic structures and habitations. It is a powerful reminder that all is not as we had imagined. It does this even if we had to some degree anticipated the tragedy. Anticipation is not an adequate cushion. Tragedy is always to some degree shocking.

Because we learn in tragedy that reality can produce such terrible shocks, we are less disposed to take reality for granted or to trust our conceptions of what reality truly is. The tragic experience introduces a new horizon. The banalities with which our mind was beclouded are exposed to new and searching light as a new and undesired experience forces itself into the center of our conscious existence. Tragedy brings us into direct and unmistakable contact with the concrete world from which we manage to hide through our abstractions and myths. We do not tend to take reality as it is. Rather, we condition and filter our perceptions in our effort to make sense of things. We can thus come to live in an unreal world. Tragedy is a voice from the real world. It breaks through our intellectual sensoring equipment which works to keep out what is new and threatening to our current view of reality. In this sense, tragedy is an opportunity and may be an opening to creativity.

It is often said of someone who has experienced great tragedy that "he was never the same after that." Different things are meant by that expression, but here I use it for its epistemological meaning. Tragedy acquaints us with reality in a new way. It changes us. Perception, however is conditioned by our state of being. We are not the same after tragedy, nor do things appear to us afterward in the same light.

The change in consciousness that attends tragedy is not necessarily beneficial. One's view can be distorted by pain. There is, however, a genuine opportunity that is missed when this happens.
Healing possibilities await us when the waters are stirred. The literature of tragedy points to this saving possibility. As James Walker
writes: "Usually, as the tragedy unfolds toward the denouement,
the hero, often admirable in many ways, achieves insight into the
meanings of his conflicts, and the tragic act signifies an achievement
for the hero of some sense of unification of an inner self."[46] This
inner unification and the deepening and sharpening of perspective
are among the possible fruits of tragedy well borne.

Tragedy and the Activation of the Will . . .

Two of the other evaluative capacities of man represented as
spokes in my wheel model of ethical method are *affectivity* and *creative imagination*. Suffering and tragedy relate to these moral faculties
in two ways: First of all, tragedy is a form of resistance. It can, of
course, break our will and reduce us to passivity. But it can also be
received as a challenge and a summons to the mobilizations of all of
our responsive feelings and imagination. Without challenge we can
become listless and stagnant. It is when our affectivity rises that we
become fully alive.

Tragedy involves challenge and challenge stimulates. As René
Dubos writes: "Wherever life is without challenge and too comfortable, as supposedly in the Polynesian islands, the best that can be
hoped for is an arrested or static civilization rather than one that is
innovating and on-going."[47] Indeed, the remarkable enlargement and
development of the human brain seems related to the need to meet
challenges in a hostile world.[48] The fierce Ice Ages which ended
much life forced man into a flurry of inventiveness. We can speculate on what the development of man might have been had he not
been forced to meet the tragic challenges of the Ice Ages. Tragedy
stirs the affections in which creative imagination is nourished.

Tragedy invites courage, and courage is a quality of the will which
has important influence on the operation of the intellect. "Fear has
large eyes," says a Russian proverb. It sees with painful keenness all
that is a threat. But courage has larger eyes. It sees beyond the
overwhelming circumstances of distress and reaches for the possibilities that the timid do not even admit. It is the courageous mind

that can be creative. Courage represents a flourishing of the human spirit, and it is the fairest possible response of persons beset by tragic experience.

There is a second way, however, in which suffering relates to affectivity and creativity. In the first way, suffering calls forth affective sensitivity and creative response. But there is also a way in which strong affective commitment and creative activity call forth suffering. The effect may also be a cause. Anyone who loves and attempts great things will not be unacquainted with suffering. Love, first of all, extends our vulnerability by extending the area of the precious. It enlarges the area in which we face and feel risk. Love also relates to creativity, and the creative will never be alien to tragedy. Pusillanimity is the breeder of slight expectations, and from these proceed those rigid canons of mediocrity that tend to prevail and shackle human society. The persecution of excellence is a prominent and persistent reality in human history. The creator may make it into the pantheon, but he is likely to stimulate resentment before he stimulates praise. The technological inventor is less likely to feel the resentment of reigning mediocrity if what he has produced is appealing to ease and pleasure. Even in this case, however, good ideas can be resisted for a long time. But if someone would move creatively in society to work for justice and criticize injustice, tragedy and suffering may always be expected. Society does not readily entertain challenges to its low standards of justice and fairness. Criticism is not welcomed.[49]

With this chapter, I have completed my discussion of the nine spokes of the wheel model of ethical method. These spokes represented the evaluational resources and faculties through which moral consciousness may unfold and grow. Incompleteness and insensitivity are the basic hazards of ethical inquiry. The method suggested here hopes to counter these failings. The reality-revealing questions in the hub of the wheel are geared to increase empirical sensitivity and thoroughness, to preclude the rush of fallacies that follow the unasked question. The spokes signify ways in which our pluriform consciousness can evaluate the reality unveiled by the expository, questioning process.

It should be clear that the several spokes are diverse in nature. In assessing a particular problem, it is not possible to sit down and systematically summon these evaluational elements as one might call in a group of witnesses, each in its assigned turn. Some of these spokes may have limited use in certain morally adjudicable cases. There are, for example, heroic situations which call for unique and more intuitive solutions for which no principles can adequately prescribe. Sometimes when principles seem to collide irreconcilably, we are cast more upon our affective appreciations. Similarly, there are situations of impasse where old solutions clearly will not do and creative imagination must of necessity strain to find the answer.

It is, of course, possible to press the mind in a fairly systematic way to turn to seven of the evaluational modes that I discussed. Thus we can insist upon attention to the potential contribution of *principles, affective insight, authority, reason and analysis, creative imagination, individual* and *group experience*. We can check for neglect in each of these areas and seek to avoid the pitfalls of a too unilateral and one-rubric approach. We cannot, however, in an equally systematic way invoke the tragic and the comic perspectives while assessing a particular case of moral concern. Awareness, however, of the positive aspects of comedy and tragedy in one's world view can introduce perspective. Often a comic perception or tragic experience will be the immediate avenue of moral insight. But even when this is not so, a sense of the significance of the comic and tragic view can function influentially at the level of presupposition. Openness to the salubrious role of the comic and the tragic can create a mental climate which leaves us less likely prey to the raging absolutisms that stymie and deter the processes of knowing and evaluating.

It should also be noted that one's method should not be explicit in all cases of ethical analysis. Method is not technique or tactic. But the spelling out of a method is a way of charting out with self-conscious modesty the manifold aspects of the phenomenon of knowing. Following the method suggested here does not mean that when studying some moral problem, one need always have bobbing at the surface every one of the explicitated elements of this method. Nevertheless, if the method has validity, as I submit it does, it should be detectably implicit in all of one's particular analyses of normative issues. One should always "do ethics" with alertness to the various ways in which moral truth is attained. One need not stop and say: "See, I have not forgotten spoke number four in my discussion of this corporate merger." But when the discussion is completed, it should not show neglect of what that spoke symbolized of our knowing potential.

With this said, it is now timely to admit that nowhere in this model of ethical method is there place for the obviously important fact of conscience. One would think that any model would find a place for conscience. Why it does not appear is a matter to which I will now attend.

NOTES—CHAPTER ELEVEN

1. M. Conrad Hyers, "The Dialectic of the Sacred and the Comic," *Cross Currents* 19, No. 1 (Winter 1968–69), p. 72.
2. Peter L. Berger, *A Rumor of Angels* (Garden City, N.Y.: Doubleday & Co., Inc., Anchor Books, 1970), p. 69.
3. Henri Bergson, "Laughter," in W. Sypher, ed., *Comedy* (Garden City, N.Y.: Doubleday & Co., Inc., 1956), p. 123.
4. Arthur Koestler, *The Act of Creation* (New York: Dell Publishing Co., Laurel Edition, 1967), p. 28.
5. Gordon W. Allport, *The Nature of Prejudice* (Garden City, N.Y.: Doubleday & Co., Inc., Anchor Books, 1958), p. 409. See also Gordon W. Allport, *Personality: A Psychological Interpretation* (New York: Henry Holt, 1937), pp. 200–25.
6. Ibid. See Chapter 25, on "The Prejudiced Personality."
7. Harvey Mindess, "The Sense in Humor," *Saturday Review* (August 21, 1971), p 10.
8. Ibid.
9. Christopher Fry, "Comedy," in Robert W. Corrigan, ed., *Comedy: Meaning and Form* (San Francisco: Chandler Publishing Co., 1965), p. 15.
10. Arthur Koestler, *Act of Creation*, p. 95.
11. Ibid., p. 59.
12. M. Conrad Hyers, "*Dialectic of the Sacred and the Comic*," p. 75.
13. Ibid., p. 73.
14. Ibid., p. 76.
15. For an interesting treatment of this from a psychiatric point of view, see William F. Lynch, *Images of Hope* (New York: New American Library; Mentro-Omega Book, 1966), pp. 90–108.

16. Ibid., p. 108.
17. See Chapter 8 for examples and further description of rationalism.
18. J. S. Bruner and L. Postman, "On the Perception of Incongruity," in M. D. Vernon, ed., *Experiments in Visual Perception* (Baltimore: Penguin Books, 1966), pp. 285–92. I am indebted for the reference here to Robert E. Neale's superb article "Surprise: The Horrible, The Humorous, and the Holy," in George Devine, ed., *New Dimensions in Religious Experience* (New York: Alba House, 1971).
19. Bernard J. F. Lonergan, *Insight: A Study of Human Understanding* (New York: Longmans, Philosophical Library, 1957), p. 626.
20. Ibid.
21. René Dubos, *So Human an Animal* (New York: Charles Scribner's Sons, 1968), p. 103.
22. Harvey Cox used this historical custom to introduce and entitle his book on festivity and fantasy: *The Feast of Fools* (Cambridge, Mass.: Harvard University Press, 1969).
23. Ibid., p. 3.
24. Leszek Kolakowski, "The Priest and the Jester," *Dissent* 9, No. 3 (Summer 1962), p. 233.
25. G. K. Chesterton, *Lunacy and Letters*, edited by Dorothy Collins (New York: Sheed & Ward, 1958), p. 97.
26. On the two faces of aging, see James Lynwood Walker, "The Here and the Hereafter: Reflections on Tragedy and Comedy in Human Existence," in *To Live and to Die* (New York: Springer-Verlag, 1973), pp. 160–68.
27. *The Collected Poems of W. B. Yeats* (New York: Macmillan Co., 1956), p. 40.
28. Ibid., pp. 18–19.
29. Berger, *Rumor of Angels*, p. 70.
30. Gordon W. Allport, *The Nature of Prejudice* (Garden City, N.Y.: Doubleday & Co., Inc., Anchor Books, 1958), p. 144.
31. Quoted ibid.
32. Johan Huizinga, *Homo Ludens* (Boston: Beacon Press, 1950), p. 5.
33. Walker, "The Here and the Hereafter," p. 167.
34. Ibid.
35. Dr. L. Jolyon West, quoted in *Hastings Center Report* 2, No. 5 (Nov. 1972), p. 6.
36. Jacques Leclercq, *Christ and the Modern Conscience* (New York: Sheed & Ward, 1963), pp. 263–64.
37. H. Richard Niebuhr, *The Responsible Self* (New York: Harper & Row, 1963), pp. 59–60. Niebuhr comments that suffering is "a subject to which academic ethical theory, even theological ethics, usually pays little attention." Ibid., p. 59.
38. See Chapter Nine.

39. Niebuhr, *Responsible Self*, p. 59.
40. Though a common enough expression, the notion of national character is imprecise, especially when applied to an incorrigibly pluralistic society such as the United States. More properly it should be said that there are many group characterological orientations within the American people. Still there are some general trends which affect most Americans due to those elements of our history and affect all of us more or less, thus justifying this admittedly loose usage. Finding the right symbols to discuss social consciousness is never a wholly profitable enterprise.
41. For the discussion of individual and group experience in ethical method, see Chapter Ten.
42. The term "suffering" lends stress to the subjective element and this coheres with my emphasis on the response of the sufferer.
43. Lonergan, *Insight*, p. 625. Emphasis added.
44. Leclercq, *Christ and the Modern Conscience*, p. 261.
45. Ibid., p. 268.
46. Walker, "The Here and the Hereafter," p. 162.
47. Dubos, *So Human an Animal*, p. 165. Dubos is here summarizing the challenge-and-response theory of ideal human development.
48. Ibid., p. 124.
49. See Reinhold Niebuhr, *Moral Man and Immoral Society* (New York: Charles Scribner's, Sons, 1932, 1960), pp. 88–89.

CHAPTER TWELVE

CONSCIENCE AND GUILT

Conscience is a term that suffers from overfamiliarity. As Augustine said of "time," one knows exactly what it is until asked to define it. So too, it would seem, for conscience. As the Oxford English Dictionary says of it: "Opinions as to the nature, function, and authority of conscience are widely divergent, varying from the conception of the mere exercise of the ordinary judgment on moral questions, to that of an infallible guide of conduct, a sort of deity within us." Milton saw it as an "umpire," Aquinas saw it as the pedagogue of the soul," Locke as simply our own opinion in moral matters, and Byron called it "the oracle of God." Some reduce conscience to the Freudian "superego" or to a mere echo of the social mores.

Most persons would agree with the eighteenth-century philosopher-bishop Joseph Butler that "we have a capacity of reflecting upon actions and characters, and making them an object to our thought; and on doing this, we naturally and unavoidably approve some actions, under the peculiar view of their being virtuous and of good desert; and disapprove others, as vicious and of ill desert."[1] Different common folk and philosophers take this to mean that we have within us an innate moral faculty or an intuitive moral sense, a voice within the soul which operates as a kind of instinct to achieve instant ethics. Many deny that we have any such mysterious evaluative capacities as standard equipment and see conscience as having a simpler meaning.

However variegated its definition, conscience carries with it a prodigious weight and authority. "Freedom of conscience" is a kind of sacred shibboleth in our culture. Doing something "for the sake of conscience" (which is a very old phrase in our language) implies an inherent and mighty sanction. It is almost self-justifying. Something done "in good conscience" has a *prima facie* case going for it, whereas something done "in bad conscience" portends corruption. The word "conscience," then is a strong word in our moral vocabulary, and systematic ethics must obviously attempt to bring some clarification to it.

Regarding the etymology of the word, "conscience" comes to us from the Latin *conscientia*, a word that is translated in two distinct ways in English: as "conscience" or as "consciousness." This dual meaning of *conscientia* evolved gradually in English as we came to reserve "conscience" for the moral sphere, devising the term "consciousness" for the nonmoral field of awareness. As Eric D'Arcy writes: "In Greek, as in Latin and French, a single word serves both purposes; one is left to decide from the context whether or not in a given place it has a moral connotation."[2] In English, then, moral awareness has its own unique verbal standing. The failure of such a word to appear in my wheel model would therefore seem all the more a glaring lacuna.

Conscience as Self . . .

Conscience is the conscious self as attuned to moral values and disvalues in the concrete.[3] Conscience is not just one phase of an ethical method, neither is it a "faculty" or a "superego"—a precipitate of our psychosexual history. It is rather the person in his actual state of sensitivity or insensitivity to the worth of persons and their environment. The term "conscience" does not describe the activity of persons as they speculatively contemplate moral issues in which they are not involved. The term has a reference to the concrete and to the order of experience in which the self is existentially implicated. One does not have a conscience problem about someone else's moral quandary unless one is involved in that quandary in some way.[4]

The key, then, to understanding conscience is to see it as the morally conscious self in his actual state of moral awareness. This necessitates both an understanding of the moral history of the self and a critical assessment of how the elements of good ethical method are represented in the workings of conscience. Conscience, in a sense, is method incarnate in a person. With my wheel model of method in mind, it can be said that conscience should with increasing sensitivity and thoroughness represent all of the evaluational elements of

that wheel appropriated and embodied in a valuing person. Berdyaev
is correct when he says that ethics should be "a critique of pure conscience."[5] Conscience is not so much one of the parts of ethics as it
is that which ethics should serve, critique, and seek to perfect. Ethics
should seek to purify not just reason but all that a morally evaluating
self is . . . and that means more than reason. It means conscience
with all that that entails.

It must be made clear from the outset that conscience is not innate. We can no longer naïvely so conceive it in view of what we
know of cultural and moral variation among different peoples. If
conscience were innate or proceeded from some single divine source
of inspiration, one could look for a sameness among the conscientious orientation of all peoples of all times. Such does not obtain.
The error in thinking conscience innate verges on that of the intuitionist philosophers. The intuitionist H. A. Prichard, for example,
wrote: ". . . the sense of obligation to do an action of a particular
kind, or the sense of its rightness, is absolutely underivative, or immediate. . . . This apprehension is immediate, in precisely the sense
in which a mathematical apprehension is immediate, e.g., the apprehension that a three-sided figure, in virtue of its being three-sided,
must have three angles."[6] All that is needed, according to Prichard,
is not "any process of general thinking" but rather "getting face to
face" with the situation and then "directly appreciating" the moral
value involved.[7]

The same simplism is found in Butler's statement regarding conscience.

> Let any plain, honest man before he engages in any course
> of action, ask himself, Is this I am going about right or is it
> wrong? Is it good or evil? I do not doubt in the least, but
> that this question would be answered agreeably to truth
> and virtue, but almost any fair man in almost any circum-
> stances.[8]

The facts rather are that fair men will be found on almost any side
of any question. Innatists and intuitionists are involved in a kind of
naturalistic perception of ethics which would see moral values as perceptible in the manner that natural objects are. This misses the rela-
tionality and the cultural and historical complexity that are the hall-
marks of moral reality and moral knowledge.

Conscience is also not purely superadded like a graft on the *psyche:* It is not a simply extraneous imposition on our subjectivity. There are, in other words, the seeds of conscience in every person. Conscience is rooted in the foundational moral experience into which no person who approximates normalcy is wholly uninitiated. This humanizing experience points to the socializing nature of persons. As was seen above, the foundational moral experience consists of an appreciation of the value of self, the value of others, and an awareness of the connection between the two. Conscience is grounded in this experience. It grows out of the process of this experience. No two processes of this experience and no two persons will be identical. Neither will any two consciences be identical.

Conscience always bears the distinguishing marks of each person's unique moral odyssey. It is historically conditioned and developed. But what each conscience will have in common with all others is its roots in the core of the foundational moral experience. Conscience will always give form to our natural status as social beings. What is innate in all of this is that we are born persons, naturally geared to relate harmoniously and fruitfully with other persons. The shape and activity of our individual conscience is not innate. It is the product of our decisions, our education, our formative personal encounters—in a word, of our history. As I said above, conscience is incarnate method. It reflects in its being the evaluative orientation of the person. To exemplify this, I return to the method I have been proposing in the pages of this book. If the method has validity and completeness, then the ideal conscience would reflect its various elements. This is not to say that conscience could ever be the result of critical thought alone. As I have said, the conscience is the moral self and the self comes into being amid the always somewhat chaotic vicissitudes of life. No self, no person, is unscarred by its journey. No conscience will be free of the inevitable debits and distorting influences of one's life story. In the course of our development, we will introject unworthy attitudes, identify with persons whose moral vision will be in significant ways skewed. We will at times have been punished for good things and rewarded for the bad, and our natural proclivity for imitation will have established unfortunate habits of thought and conduct. All forms of life bear witness to the struggles that are the price of survival. This is why Berdyaev's call for "a critique of pure conscience" points us to a task that will never be complete. Conscience will never be pure.

It is well at this point to relate conscience to character (discussed above in Chapters Eight and Nine). These phenomena are very close. Both bespeak the moral orientation and timbre of the person. Both signify the kind of person you are; thus, both are ways of speaking about the qualities of the moral self. Conscience, however, is a broader notion, since it implies the application to judgment and action of one's characterological orientation.[9] Like character, however, conscience has all the complexity and ingrained stability that derive from the innumerable variables of a long history. Thus one can say that conscience is educable, but instantaneous conversions are not to be anticipated. The critique of conscience must be an eternal fact in human existence.

One's method in ethics offers the groundwork for such a critique. And so to the method that I have proposed.

Conscience, first of all, relates to the reality-revealing questions that give form to the expository phase of ethics (the hub of the wheel). The specific nature or quality of a person will be marked by greater or lesser empirical sensitivity. If a person has had considerable experience and has acquired a habit of inquisitiveness in the face of moral decisions, it means that this aspect of moral evaluation has become ingrained. It enters into the dynamism of the moral self; it becomes an aspect of conscience. Many decisions of conscience are nearly instantaneous; they are evaluative reactions within the swirl of life's processes. They do not allow for the leisure to sit down and begin to ask what? why? how? etc., and to inquire after the foreseeable consequences and alternatives. Someone who has made a habit of pursuing the right questions will have a *skill*, and a sharp conscience can in fact be called a kind of skill. That shows that it is an acquired, permanent reality and that it includes an ability to react without elaborate preparation.[10] Comparison can be made again to an able lawyer, who, even before he has had a chance to study a case in depth, has a certain feel for and insight into the main thrust of a case upon its first presentation. Similarly, an inept conscience is comparable to the "skill" of an inept lawyer who might well miss the main point right from the beginning. Poor conscience, like poor lawyers, are educable. The education, of course, may not be easy, since poor consciences, even more than poor lawyers, tend to be possessed of a stubborn and unwarranted self-confidence.

Conscience should also embody the main import of each of the evaluational resources (spokes in the model). For example, the attitude of *creativity* is ideally reflected in one's conscience. A developed conscience is not just a judge that sits and passes verdicts of licit or illicit on situations as they arise. Included also should be a developed "instinct" for the possible. If human consciousness is distinguished by its capacity for perceiving the possible that is latent within the actual, the conscious moral self (conscience) should exemplify this. Ruth Anshen's definition of conscience comes down strongly on this. Conscience, she says,

> is the pressure within man of all that has not yet existed but pleads for existence, of all that is potential, yet unknown, begging for actualization and life. Man has the capacity through conscience and reason to enhance those conditions which develop a nostalgia for the good and bring about its realization.[11]

Good conscience has the skill of discovery and inventiveness. A conscience animated by a creative spirit will discern alternatives in moral situations where the less imaginative would be blind. This aspect of conscience is neglected by many ethicists. The reason for the neglect is clear. When one treats conscience, one's method shows through, and many rationalistic ethicists bypass the signal position of creative imagination in cognitive moral experience. Thus, it will not be in evidence in their tell-tale treatment of conscience.

Conscience will also reflect one's established knowledge of the meaning of *principles* and one's habits of *reasoning and analysis*. Principles do not serve moral consciousness merely as a kind of reserve intellectual knowledge. All moral knowledge has an affective dimension. And the affections draw what is known into the interior of the personality. The values contained in principles with which we have sufficiently identified enter into our cognitive framework and into conscience. They are at our service not merely when we view them in propositional form but they become enfleshed in conscience. Just as we are aware of the rules of grammar when we speak but do not have to keep formulating those rules mentally as we go along, so, too, moral principles which condition the climate of the moral self also condition the reaction of conscience . . . even if we do not think of them explicitly. Likewise patterns of *reason and analysis* leave their mark on conscience and are thus influential even in decisions that are made with little or no time for the reflective processes of reasoning. A habit of thorough reasoning endows conscience with what the ancients called *solertia*, a quality of the mind implying a certain nimbleness and adroitness in reaction to new situations.[12] Again, the skillfulness of the seasoned lawyer is an apt comparison.

Though he does not discuss it in this specific light, John Dewey's notion of "conscientiousness" relates to this habit of the soul. Dewey says that conscientiousness "is constituted by scrupulous attentiveness to the potentialities of any act or proposed aim. . . . The good man who rests on his oars, who permits himself to be propelled simply by the momentum of his attained right habits, loses alertness; he ceases to be on the lookout." Genuine conscientiousness means "intelligent attention and care to the quality of an act in view of its consequences. . . ."[13] This idea of conscientiousness seems also to involve creative imagination and affective perception as well as ingrained habits of reason and analysis.

Evaluative *affectivity* will also be an aspect of a good conscience. He who loves the good will be sensitive to its presence. Love renders our perceptive powers delicate and keen. The loving eye sees far. It is alert to all that befits and enhances what is loved. The classical doctrine of "prudence," which did not have any of the undertones of timid cautiousness, such as characterize modern "prudence," was equivalent in many ways to the discussion of conscience.[14] Thus it is significant to see Augustine referring to prudence as "love discerning well" (*amor bene discernens*).[15] Good conscience is imbued with the *votum* of the heart. Indeed this gives meaning to Augustine's often abused phrase: "Love, and do what you will." Genuine love has its own inherent divining instincts for the good, and a love-informed conscience will have the special sharpness that corresponds to these powers. It will be filled with the practical wisdom of the heart. In this sense it can be said, "Have a good conscience and do what you will."

Authority is another way to moral truth, and it too affects the shape of conscience. The perception of truth has a social dimension. We depend on one another also in knowing. Given the limits of the mind and the infinity of the knowable, we are compelled to rely on various authorities to fill out our knowledge. If one knows and accepts this, his conscience will show a docile attitude of reliance. This is not the docility of the weak-minded, but rather the open-mindedness of the intellectually realistic. Here is where Pieper's phrase applies: "A closed mind and know-it-allness are fundamentally forms of resistance to the truth of real things. . . ."[16] An attitude of openness to the supplement that authority proffers is a mark both of a mature conscience and of genuine intellectuality.

Individual experience and group experience also should show through in the living conscience. Understandably, *individual experience* has special relevance to conscience. This calls for more extensive comment.

In treating individual experience I spoke of the capacity of a person to perceive moral truth from the depths of his own originality. As Berdyaev says, we live in a world in which "falsity is pragmatically justified, while truth is often regarded as dangerous and harmful." Because of this there surges forth from the depths of personal consciousness a protest "in the name of pure truth and reality." Beleaguered as we are by entrenched falsity, "there arises a longing for ontological truthfulness, a desire to break through to freedom and purity of judgment—to what I should call *original and virginal conscience*." What this issues into is a "will to originality," not in the sense of a will to be peculiar, but rather in the sense of a "desire to derive one's consciousness from its primary source."[17]

The healthy moral self is in touch with its own depths. It reaches for the relief of originality; it tries to move as far as possible from the conditioning influences that would engulf and dominate, and it attempts to express its own unique contact with reality. Good conscience hungers for Berdyaev's "original and virginal conscience." Such a hunger gives a special probing and straining orientation to conscience when it becomes an abiding aspect of one's moral awareness.

Individual experience, then, points to the original center of moral identity and consciousness. It points us, therefore, to the sacred core of personality and the center of integrity. Conscience embodies the splendors or inadequacies of this center and of the foundational moral experience. Persons may communicate at many levels. The contact may be at the level of business, social service, or almost purely physical sex. But when person relates to person *qua* person, the meeting is at the level of conscience. When valuing animals meet, their most intimate contact is at the point of conscience. Conscience speaks to conscience in genuine personal encounter. Here is where the sacredness of persons is most accurately located. Love of any sublime sort penetrates to this center of personality. There is much along the way that can fascinate and draw, but enduring love comes to rest here. Even though we are not inclined to speak of it that way, due to narrow and incomplete conceptions of conscience, to love a person means to respond appreciatively to that person's conscience. Not to commune at this level is not to commune. True *meeting* occurs here.

There is also political significance in the individual center of moral consciousness that conscience is. It is in individual conscience that the claim of *the one* is staked out against the powers of *the many*. Here is the permanent bastion against the spirit of totalitarianism. Were it not for this lonely center of moral identity and awareness, social conscience would be all. Personal man would be herd man. It is in conscience that the dignity and rights of the individual moral self are manifested. Conscience, in a word, gives relief from the abstract strictures of "positive law" and dominant custom. It endows us with the power of dissent. Through the medium of conscience, moral obligation is personalized; in it we can find refuge from the inevitable insensitivities of generalization that mar the rule of fleshless law.[18] As Martin Buber says: "The more or less hidden criteria that the conscience employs in its acceptances and rejections only rarely fully coincide with a standard received from the society or community."[19] There is more to us than our society. That is the mystery of the individual and the secret of his worth.

If, then, conscience is so sacred and central, is it always right to follow one's conscience? This is a question that has bothered ethicists for centuries. It also surfaces implicitly in a lot of contemporary rhetoric about the rights of conscience, rather absolutistically conceived. In a sense the question is a bad question, since it is misleading. Obviously it can be said in a general way that one must act in accord with one's conscience. If conscience is the conscious moral self, contradicting it in behavior would be violative of one's own identity and integrity. If we are conscientiously convinced that something is wrong, we should avoid it or we would be assaulting our own convictions. This would create that painful fissure within the personality which goes by the name of guilt. From this point of view, then, the answer must be that it is always right to follow one's conscience.

There are misleading implications, however, in the notion of always following one's own conscience. First of all, it might not suggest sufficient cognizance of the fact that conscience is fallible. Ethics is fallible; man is fallible; and so, obviously, conscience is fallible.

This should prompt some reservations about conscience's leadership. Conscience should not be conceived of as an independent supreme court which can be judged by no man and which merits naïve loyalty from the part of the individual and uncritical respect from everyone else. There is what could be called a conscience hedonism implicit in much talk about the rights of conscience. Hedonism is a species of intellectual despair about the possibilities of attaining truth. In championing conscience one might equivalently be saying that whatever turns one's conscience on is fine. The anti-intellectualism here is braced also by a strong dose of heady individualism. We are intrinsically social beings and conscience should reflect that.

This is where *group experience* comes into the understanding of conscience. Good conscience has good antennae and is regularly alerted to the signals available to it from our counterparts in the community of persons. Conscience is not individual or social in persons. It is both. It is not a center of moral judgment which is atomistically cut off from other centers. Genuine conscience lives in dialogue and mirrors our social nature. It is indeed in conscience that *the one* takes its stand vis-à-vis *the many*, but it is not mechanically or merely contiguously related to *the many*. For us, action is interaction and that rule of existence will be visible within the workings of healthy conscience. The individual and supremely personal nature of conscience does not mean *me* against *them*; it means *me* distinct from *them* but intrinsically *with them*. To the general statement that one should always follow one's conscience should be added that one should also always question one's conscience. The autonomy of conscience is not absolute. It would be inhuman if it were.

Though conscience is primarily a term of personal moral consciousness, one may speak of the conscience of a society. This adaptive use of the term would refer to those distinguishable traits in a society or a culture which mark it with notable sensitivities or insensitivities. (In a similarly extended fashion, one could speak of the character of a people.) Certain values are more highly prized in some societies than others. Freedom, for example, enjoys extraordinary esteem in American society, whereas in socialist nations, the equitable distribution of goods will command superior commitment. In looking to the conscience of affluent nations, one would naturally seek to discern their attitudes toward the unaffluent peoples of the so-called third and fourth worlds. This study of group conscience is of considerable usefulness, since individual conscience will to a great extent reflect the strengths and weaknesses of the group. Also, it is sometimes easier to get perspective this way and to admit one's moral weaknesses when we see them in their communal context.

The evaluative contributions of *comedy* and *tragedy* are also felt in the stable center of moral awareness that is conscience. As I said above, comedy is important for ethics not so much for individual instances of applied humor, but more for the relativizing effects of the comic perspective of life. The self that has this perspective will have a conscience that is all the better for it. The conscience that is naturally amenable to the comic view will not be easy prey for the absolutizing penchants that we encounter within and without. A sense of tragedy can also add delicacy and sensitivity to conscience. Tragedy adds to conscience a telling sense of limit and fallibility. It leaves the moral self less naïve about the actual malleability of the real, and more readied and equipped for surprise. It brings the peculiar strength of scar tissue to the perduring human task of moral inquiry.[20]

Conscience in Three Tenses . . .

Conscience looks forward and backward; it also takes on the challenges offered in the present tense. Probably, though, it is in looking back in pain that we experience conscience so vividly, and so we will give the backward look of conscience special attention here. The guilty conscience is the most perceptible manifestation of conscience. The term "remorse," from the Latin *mordere*, meaning "to bite," is a term often used to describe the experience of guilt. It is not a subtle experience and it is a painful one, as the etymology of "remorse" suggests. Guilt is the product of a split between what we are and what we do, between what we basically know to be good and what we will in its place. It is a fundamental human experience. Since the Freudian revolution in psychology, guilt is often treated as a symptom of illness. There is a crude error in this. There can, of course, be a sick guilt. We can feel the agony of remorse when there is really nothing objective that we should be regretting or feeling responsible for. Such guilt is like the red light on the dashboard of a car that flashes when nothing is wrong. That requires therapy. Real guilt compares to the light which flashes when something is wrong.

The car is overheating or is out of oil. We ignore this at our peril. Bernard Häring puts it this way. He says that intellect and will

> can part ways in their activity, but not without unleashing the most profound grief in the depths in which they are united, not without creating a rift in those very depths. . . . The most agonizing cry wells up from the depth of the soul itself, for as root and source of unity of the powers, it is directly wounded by their dissension. Here is the profound reason for the first elemental agony of conscience . . . a spontaneous unreflecting pain.[21]

To feel this type of split through what we call conscience is healthy, not sick. It is a diagnostic pain. Thus Häring describes conscience as a kind of "instinct for self-preservation arising from the urge for complete unity and harmony."[22] The loss of this unity is the first cause of the pangs of remorse. A saying of Goethe gives further insight here. "All laws and rules of conduct may ultimately be reduced to a single one: to truth." Untruth is jarring. The ancients used to say that "the liar pays a price" (*nemo gratis mendax*). This is the principle behind the imperfect mechanism of the "lie detector" or polygraph. The truth is ultimately native to us; falsehood is a disturbing alien. Without underestimating the human capacity to naturalize this alien and give him almost indigenous status, we can appreciate the natural congeniality of truth to human consciousness. When untruth is lived and realized in behavior and in the attitudes that spawn that behavior, it is all the more jarring. This is what happens in guilt. What we do is not true to the exigencies of what we are and must become. The process of humanization is "shorted," and this is part of the jolt of objective guilt.[23]

Guilt also involves a sense of dread and threat. This is understandable if we see guilt as a reaction to a felt contradiction of our foundational moral experience. The foundational moral experience involves an appreciation of the value of others and the value of self and sees these as linked. Thus in guilty behavior—that is, behavior involving conscious and unnecessary harm—we always attack ourselves as well as others. The offended value is our value *as well as* that of the person(s) directly affected by the guilty behavior. The ominous impressions that attend guilt relate to this self-destructive element that is always present in guilty behavior. Martin Buber says: "Existential guilt occurs when someone injures an order of the human world whose foundations he knows and recognizes as those of his own existence and of all common human existence."[24] The dread that would naturally flow from the recognition of such an injury may be neuroticizing if unattended, but it is not of itself neurotic. It is a realistic reaction to that personal crisis that we call guilt.

Conscience, however, is not merely a source of pain. It can also react with joy and exuberance when behavior realizes the rich potentials of personhood. And it can do this in any tense . . . that is, in reacting to past, present, or prospective behavior. Again, the relationship to the foundational moral experience is clear. Behavior which enhances this radical appreciation of what is truly good has its own exhilaration. It complements our ultimately indestructible kinship with the true and the good. Morality has been so distorted by preachers, so abstractly and unattractively explained, that it is hard for us to see that morality has its special beauty. Its aesthetic side has been slighted by dons and deans and common folk. We do not expect it to sing. Neither do we normally realize that morality—and with it conscience—is the natural ally of that master virtue: enthusiasm.[25] Again conscience is the tell-tale. If one's view of morality is dry and cool, this would be reflected in one's view of the critical category conscience.

On the Nature of Realistic Guilt . . .

Psychiatrist Karl Menninger has written a book entitled *Whatever Became of Sin?* In it he observes that the notion of sin has been transformed. Sin is seen either as symptom or as crime. Psychiatrists have set a strong symbolic tone in society in this matter by shying away from the notion of sin and by treating it as a symptom. Menninger comments: "Psychoanalysts do not use the word 'sin' because of its strong reproachful quality, its vague or nonspecific quality, and its corollaries and implications of guilt, reparation, and atonement."[26]

I would urge that the psychoanalysts are not to be entirely faulted for this. "Sin" is a battered word, connoting diverse things to different people. It has distinctly religious connotations and easily evokes the simplistic lists of moral "don'ts" proclaimed as self-evident by some religionists. These "don'ts" are often in the genre of taboo—absolutistic and unnuanced. In much fundamentalist vocabulary, sin has primary reference to deviations in the use of sex or alcohol. To many the term denotes very little of matters such as social neglect, racism, sexism, or other violations of justice. The word is also linked by its linguistic history to pietistic calls to repentance and undeveloped understanding of religious experience.

On top of this, many forms of undesirable behavior were called sin and condemned in terms of righteousness when they should have been seen as personality disorders requiring treatment. At the level of vocabulary, sin is not the most useful of words. Some of the blame does indeed fall on psychiatrists who were obsessed with the perspectives of their own discipline when treating of the phenomenon of guilt. However we describe the reality that "sin" as a wounded word was seeking to express, it cannot be simplistically conflated into symptomology. And indeed most psychologists today would concede that and find little to disagree with in the comment Abraham Maslow made in an interview while president of the American Psychological Association: "If you think only of evil, then you become pessimistic—hopeless like Freud. But if you think there is no evil, then you're just one more deluded Pollyanna."[27]

Seeing sin as a crime is another historical development that tended to banish sin as a meaningful term. As Menninger points out, a different reality came into being when the state was thought to have major responsibility for the cataloguing and management of misbehavior. There was a veritable rush in the face of almost any moral transgression to say that "there ought to be a law," and thus to change the status of the misdeed into a crime. Menninger writes:

> After the reign of Henry VIII in England many sinful acts were formally declared to be not only immoral but illegal. . . . Remaining to the domain of the moralists (churches) were the seven cardinal sins of anger, greed, pride, sloth, envy, lust, and gluttony. Even some of these, in special forms, were pre-empted by the law. Perhaps the transfer of authority for major social offenses from the home and church to the crown or state was less a matter of seizure than a matter of forcible gift. In colonial days the parish authorities were prevailed upon to enact into law many details of the moral code in order to make sure that there would be a democratic enforcement of virtue in the community.[28]

Sometimes this led to ludicrous enactments forbidding drinking, smoking, spitting, hanging out laundry on Sunday, or using profanity in the presence of the mayor. The main effect, however, was more subtle. The criminalization of sin depersonalized and juridicized moral failure, distracting us from its true significance within the moral realm. The juridical paradigm, for all of its utility, will not lead us to a knowledge of what Buber has called "the abyss of guilt."

When a word is brutalized with so many inappropriate understandings, the reality it would describe can easily be overlooked. Connotations have a way of becoming denotations, and when too many fallacies attach to the word, the word needs either careful and explicit redefinition or retirement as a linguistic tool. My preference is to retire "sin" when possible in favor of "guilt," a word that has been jostled somewhat by usage but which is still serviceable. It too has juridical connotations and strong psychological meaning, but as a word, it is considerably less encumbered with debits.

The renewed interest in guilt is not limited to psychologists and psychiatrists such as Menninger and Maslow. We are suddenly and newly faced with overwhelming evidence of our iniquity in society. It is accurate to say that guilt is coming out of its temporary hiding and is attaining a high visibility. Reinhold Niebuhr observed:

> Actually the view that men are "sinful" is one of the best attested and empirically verified facts of human existence. It has been obscured by those philosophies having their rise in the Enlightenment. Such philosophies either derived the evils of human history from specific causes (as for instance the Marxists, who derived it from the institution of property) or regarded social evil as due to the inertia of ignorance or natural passion or social institutions.[29]

There is a greater readiness today to follow Niebuhr in his belief that it is naïve to say that the problems grouped under the term "social evil" will pass peacefully away when reason breaks free from the bondage of such "inertia." The guilt of free persons is no corrigible misfortune which could have been otherwise had history made a few different turns. The naïveté of a young liberalism which could think that a little dickering with education and reform will cure what ails us is with difficulty entertained in the compounding crises of today's world. We do not know all of what is going on; our confusion makes us more humble. But we know with growing certainty that guilty and wrongful behavior is a fundamental fact of human life. The evasions we used to use to avoid this recognition are increasingly futile.

Frances Moore Lappé, writing about world hunger, says: "Historically, people have tried to deny their own culpability for mass human suffering by assigning responsibility to external forces beyond their control."[30] The Black Death of the Middle Ages was blamed on "divine retribution," whereas it was undoubtedly related to the unwillingness of the class society of that day to provide sanitation for the masses. Lappé urges that world hunger today is similarly misattributed. The problem is allegedly due to changes in climate, to our finally touching bottom on resources, and to the inexorable swell of population. These are all "natural" laws and agencies, not behavioral problems. There is a perverse comfort in such analysis. It takes humans off the hook and opens the door to Garret Hardin's "lifeboat ethic," which concludes, with gesticulations of innocence, that the death of the disadvantages is the sensible solution. Lappé's conclusion is that "world hunger is now, above all, a political and economic problem to which we directly contribute."[31] Malthus did not see in the late eighteenth century that economic imbalance and not the number of people would create the terrible crunch. He could scarcely have foreseen that economic imbalance would become such that the rich would with profligate abandon begin feeding agricultural resources to animals. Lappé notes, relevant to the United States: "Today we feed at least 85 percent of all of our corn, barley, oats and grain sorghum, and over 90 percent of our nonexported soybean crop to livestock."[32] Close to half of our agricultural acreage is now devoted to crops fed to livestock.

This indictment of the free human causes has been buttressed in a variety of ways by those writing today on the contemporary human problem. More and more people are ready to point the finger at human guilt, rather than at natural disasters, to explain present and impending calamities.

Robert L. Heilbroner argues that the dangers that now threaten the human habitat

> do not descend, as it were, from the heavens, menacing humanity with the implacable fate that would be the consequence of the sudden arrival of a new Ice Age or the announcement of the impending extinction of the sun. On the contrary . . . all the dangers we have examined—population growth, war, environmental damage, scientific technology—are *social* problems, originating in human behavior and capable of amelioration by the alteration of that behavior.[33]

What these writers are stressing is that we do have a choice. And the dark side of their view is that we have made bad choices, wrong-

ful choices of the sort that leave us guilty. Hamlet does not speak
with the voice of modern man when he effuses: "What a piece of
work is a man! How noble in reason! How infinite in faculty! In
form and moving how express and admirable! In action how like an
angel! In apprehension how like a god! The beauty of the world!
The paragon of animals!"[34] Closer to our new malaise and awareness
of guilt is Blaise Pascal, who, though not despairing, had a hope that
was severely chastened by insight into human moral failing. "What a
chimera then is man! What a novelty! What a monster, what a
chaos, what a contradiction, what a prodigy! Judge of all things, im-
becile worm of the earth; depository of truth, a sink of uncertainty
and error; the pride and refuse of the universe!"[35]

Three Understandings of Guilt . . .

There are at least three ways in which guilt is understood; it may
be used in a taboo sense, in an egoistic sense, or in what I will argue
is the realistic sense. Each of these ways also reflects a different conception of ethics and conscience, since one's view of guilt will also
reflect the presuppositions of one's ethics.[36]

Guilt at the taboo level is a primitive appreciation which sees
something as wrong because it is forbidden. Guilt here is the violation of a prohibition. The prohibition may or may not make sense.
Making sense is not of the essence for the taboo mentality. Neither
is it essential that the behavior judged wrong be productive of harm.
Guilt as taboo simply involves transgression which leaves one liable
to the sanctions of "the powers that be," however these may be perceived. As Louis Monden says of this: "It is an almost physical occult sense that one has strayed beyond a safe boundary and is now
threatened with the vengeance of the mysterious power that guards
it."[37]

The so-called technical virgin may be used to illustrate this. The
term is used to refer to a woman who will engage in sexual intimacy
even to the point of orgasm but will not have intercourse so as to
preserve her "virginity." The taboo mentality shows through here if
the abstention from intercourse is not based on fear of pregnancy or
some other defensibly realistic consideration, but is rather the result
of cultural conditioning that has attached enormous moral prestige
to the mere material fact of nonintercourse. The abstention here is
not rationally motivated. Such abstention might be rationally ar-

gued; in taboo it is not. There is no thought-out evaluation with a resultant decision against intercourse. There is rather an almost instinctive withdrawal from this act *regardless of the good or harm that it might do*. This "regardless" is the crux of taboo. The behavior is wrong not because it harms, but because it is forbidden. The forbiddenness comes from without, not from within the situation. The action is not wrong because of the circumstances that orient it more toward disvalue than toward value, but because it is banned. It might be good and reasonable to do that which is forbidden, but this is radically irrelevant to taboo. That which is under taboo is not open to nuance or distinction. Taboo is sweeping and undiscriminating in its scope.

What I have said thus far refers to the workings of the mind under the controlling spell of taboo. Such a mind does not do ethics. It simply shies away from certain areas which have been designated by the culture as dangerous. Taboo in its origins, however, might represent a great deal of discernment. We are accustomed to think of taboo in association with the inexplicable prohibition of primitive peoples. There can be two mistakes in this: Taboo is not limited to illiterate cultures. It occurs also in modern dress. The "technical virgin" is just one example of this—I shall suggest others. And, second, taboo is not entirely inexplicable in its origins. Some particular prohibitions among peoples with whom our acquaintance is imperfect may remain unexplained. Some taboo also appears to be the product of ignorant superstition and nothing more. This, however, is not to be presumed. The taboos of primitive people are reflective of what society judged necessary for its survival and welfare. Many taboos which forbade certain foods or activities were literally lifesaving and the fruit of long and dire experience. Other taboos, such as the almost universal incest taboo, for example, seem to arise from a recognition of the biologically and socially disruptive force of intrafamilial sexual relationships. Elements of a realistic ethics can be discerned in the development of taboo. The problem is that the taboo is undiscriminating. Once it is established, the door is closed to the making of distinctions where there are differences. Thus taboo becomes a substitute for ethics.

We find another somewhat modern example of taboo in the sexual ethics of the German Catholic moralist Heribert Jone: "All directly voluntary sexual pleasure is mortally sinful outside of matrimony. This is true even if the pleasure be ever so brief and insignificant. Here there is no lightness of matter. —Even the individuals in whom the sex urge is abnormally intense (sexual hyperesthesia) can and must control themselves."[38]

In this view the elements of taboo are in full bloom. Thus there is serious guilt even if the pleasure is "brief and insignificant." Also, the accent is not on harm done but on the pleasure, which was consciously accepted. It is this pleasure which is taboo; hence there is no need to enter into an analysis of what harm a particular instance of sexual pleasure might do. The guilt is still serious. The essentially unreasonable nature of taboo shows up in the judgment that even individuals who have pathologically intense sex drive can and must refrain from sexual pleasure in thought, word, and deed. Having placed sexual pleasure under taboo, Jone goes on to make the following remarkable classification: "Because of the varying degrees of influence they may have in exciting sexual pleasure, the parts of the human body are sometimes divided into decent (face, hands, feet), less decent (breast, back, arms, legs), and indecent (sex organs and adjacent parts)."[39] Here again the taboo mentality is present in full vigor. In prosecutorial pursuit of the sexual pleasure which is under taboo, Jone is drawn to using negative value terms to designate the parts of the body most likely to produce that pleasure. This is very illustrative of the inability of the taboo mentality to think relationally or with sensitivity to contextual variables. The physical act itself in its simple materiality becomes wrong. With Jone, even the organs that produce the physical phenomenon merit negative judgment.

Jone represented a low point in Catholic moral theology. Most Catholic thinkers today have moved away from a taboo approach to sexual behavior. Taboo, however, still reigns in certain quarters of Catholicism. For example in the Vatican document on sexual ethics issued in January 1976, we read that "the moral order of sexuality involves such high values of human life that every direct violation of this order is objectively serious."[40] As Theologian Richard McCormick accurately comments: "This is a reassertion of a traditional theological thesis that states in technical language that there is no so-called 'parvity of matter' in directly voluntary sexual acts."[41] All voluntary sexual acts outside of marriage incur serious moral guilt. The Vatican document goes on to apply this explicitly to premarital sex, homosexuality, and masturbation, and, with the grand sweep of taboo, sees all directly voluntary sexual pleasure in these areas as gravely immoral *regardless of the circumstances.*[42] Once again, the "regardless" of taboo.

The taboo in this case is, of course, highly rationalized. It does not, as in primitive societies, exist as a simple given. The Vatican document alleges that it has discovered "the essential order" of human nature, with the "immutable principles" and the "eternal, objective and universal" laws thereof. An attempt is made to buttress this position with religious and ethical arguments. In essence what they produce is a kind of intuitionism which purports to perceive with unquestionable self-evidence the exceptionless principles of human moral behavior. The result is an undiscriminating ban on certain kinds of behavior with all significant differences swept aside and treated as meaningless. This is the stuff of taboo that underlies the superstructure of rationalization.[43]

This kind of crypto-taboo puts the Vatican ethics close to that of Immanuel Kant. His categorical imperative, once perceived, must be adhered to should the whole world perish. As discussed above (see Chapter Seven), once one perceives that truth-telling is a duty, the truth must be told. "Truthfulness in statements which cannot be avoided is the formal duty of an individual to everyone, however, great may be the disadvantage accruing to himself or to another."[44] Thus one would have to reveal secrets held in confidence or reveal the whereabouts of an intended victim to someone intent on murder. Not telling the truth is, in effect, taboo, marked by the unnuanced universalism of the taboo mentality.

Kant does offer arguments for his position, as did the Vatican, but in this case, too, the arguments do not support the universalized judgment offered. In a utilitarian mode, Kant argues that "mankind generally" would be hurt by individual untruths, even those that seem to achieve some proximate good. The credibility of declarations and contracts would be imperiled even by the seemingly benevolent untruth. This is gratuitously asserted, just as it is gratuitously assumed that the needs of "mankind generally" could be so assurately assessed that a very specific duty that is transculturally applicable could be deduced from that assessment. When taboo is operating, we can anticipate that unlikely arguments will be brought forth in attempted justification.

Sometimes when the shallowness of an argument that is attempting to shore up a taboo is all too obvious, appeal will be made to

religious authority. Moralist Gerald P. Kelly, for example, was working with the idea that certain types of actions can be "intrinsically
evil" . . . that is, there is no possible circumstance that could justify
them. One of these, he argued, was the intentional taking of the life
of innocent persons—"innocent" meaning persons who were not
unjust aggressors. He writes: "Only God has the right to take the life
of the innocent; hence the direct killing of the innocent, without the
authority of God, is always wrong." Kelly, however, shows some
awareness that his decidedly confident assertion might not seem certain or even true to many: "The reason for this difficulty seems to be
that to those who really believe in creation and the supreme dominion of God, the principle is too obvious to need proof; whereas for
those who do not believe in creation there is no basis on which to
build a proof."[45]

Though Kelly comes out of a tradition that makes frequent ap-
peals to reason, he has to lodge his universal negative judgment banning all such things as abortion, mercy death, or even killing the
baby to save the mother in the absence of all alternatives, in an
unspecified faith experience. His position is all the more untenable,
since many persons who do believe in creation and the supreme dominion of God do not share his very specific and unbending conclusion. They believe that being a created person implies the responsible pursuit of the good and the reasonable even in such cases as
abortion and mercy death. Thus again, we see the implausible argument used to support a position which reductively represents a taboo
placed on a particular kind of action—regardless of what that action
might mean in really different circumstances.

Modern taboo will not always come equipped with elaborate rationalizations. It is a phenomenon, however, to which we should be
intellectually alert. One should look for it in patterns of conduct
which are well ensconced in history. A full analysis of issues such as
sexism, racism, the moral rights of homosexuals, or the ideologies of
nationalism or classism would uncover a number of unnatural and
gratuitous prohibitions within socially accepted moral perspectives.

Beyond the levels of taboo, guilt may also be conceived of in an
egoistic way. This involves a kind of antiseptic concern for one's own
moral purity and integrity. "Nice girls don't do that" . . . the implication being that my niceness is the all-controlling rubric. Guilt is
here perceived as a disfigurement. A person who does something
wrong has damaged himself in some fashion. The concern is "me-

centered." An obvious example of this is Ayn Rand's ethics of selfishness. Lacking a genuinely altruistic conception of virtue, she naturally could not have any elements of altruism in the guilt that would be incurred by immoral conduct. Her prime ethical consideration is concern for survival, and this is basically an individualistic concern. Guilt would mean acting unreasonably against survival needs. Such guilt is therefore radically egoistic. A person is morally guilty if he defaults in his pursuit of his own happiness, since that happiness is the moral purpose of his existence.[46]

What Rand illustrates here is that ethics based on happiness, or eudaemonistic ethics, *can be* a theoretical cast for egoism. Eudaemonism is not necessarily egoistic, since it may include an essential reference to the claim of others and may give direction to a genuine social conscience. An ethics that recognizes the need for happiness and the moral normalcy of self-love might still appreciate the moral normalcy of self-transcendence. But eudaemonism can be disguised hedonism.

Hedonism in any of its forms could only yield an egoistic conception of guilt. Even the hedonism of a utilitarianism that seeks the greatest happiness of the greatest number, for all of its apparent magnanimity, is tendentially egoistic. Utilitarian thinking can yield a kind of group egoism or tribalism where the well-being of one's tribe becomes the ultimate. Utilitarianism, of course, is not a complete theory of ethics. It can be animated by a variety of spirits, not all of them mean or narrow. But utilitarianism can also be a way of saying that guilt occurs when I do not act in a way that produces happiness for me and mine. Guilt could be that which is counterproductive from an egoistic viewpoint.

Egoistic guilt proceeding from egoistic ethics is what can be seen in the professed ethics of many businessmen. Egoistic business ethics would involve a desire to do what one must do to avoid getting hurt. It is an effort, in effect, to stay within the law in such wise that no actionable claims are generated by one's practices. Such a narrow concept of guilt would not consider the neglect of creative possibilities presented by the power of a business enterprise. In the often cynical business ethos of today one would be thought naïve if he suggested that business ethics means any more than staying out of trouble. This is a minimalist ethics which only asks what must be avoided and does not ask what might be done by way of enriching the framework of human commerce within the perspectives of a posttribal consciousness. This is an ethics that is one step above barbarism, and, clearly, even its low standards are not met by many of the practitioners of business. The notion of guilt that would obtain in such a climate would be no more subtle or profound than the image of a bad investment. Ironically, those who philosophically believe that government should do less and business more, often seem the least likely to be ready to transcend the harsh confines of ethical egoism. They seem content to believe with an extraordinary faith that an "invisible hand" will bring good things out of the untrammeled and unrestrained impulses of greed in the market place. Their notion of guilt has its grounds in egoism.

Finally there is an understanding of guilt that I would call realistic. Its definition is this: Guilty behavior is *conscious and free behavior (active or passive) which does real unnecessary harm to persons and/or their environment.* First, to the details of this definition: In speaking of conscious and free behavior, I acknowledge the number of subconscious and unconscious determinisms that are a fact of our psychic life. We are free only to a point. "Conscious and free" simply refers to the fact that behavior that cannot be linked to any conscious control or any freedom does not merit moral evaluation.

Behavior can be active or passive—that is, it may take the form of omission or commission. Omission can be quite voluntary and influential. Describing it as passive behavior should not give the impression that it denotes nonbeing or the complete opposite of activity. There was, for example, the case in Germany a few years ago when a husband and a wife had a serious quarrel. In a rage the husband hanged himself in the presence of his wife. The case went to law. On the face of it, it would seem that the wife could not be charged with anything. She had simply witnessed a suicide. However, the court did not stay with this surface rendition of the facts. It noted that the wife could easily have cut her husband down and that she was "satisfied with the course of events—events which had occurred without any action on her part." She was convicted of the crime of "failure to render assistance."[47] As a subsequent court consideration put it: "In omitting to act, contrary to duty, she failed to interrupt the chain of causation started by her husband; she thereby participated in causing his death."[48]

The difficulty of delineating how this lady "participated in causing his death" in the course of events "which had occurred without any action on her part" strains the minds of jurists and moralists. Yet the direction of German law in this regard seems sound. When we do not do anything about something that we *can* do something about, it is distinctly different from situations in which we do not do anything about something that is beyond our influence. The question then becomes whether we *should* do something when we *can* do something. The answer to that will reflect a number of things but will always reflect one's basic anthropology—that is, how one conceives persons and the relationships and duties that emanate from what persons are.

An omission may of course represent momentary psychological paralysis so that it would scarcely qualify under the rubric of conscious and free behavior. It may also represent heightened and intense personal decision. The wife who would like to be married to someone else and who *omits* going for the medicine when her husband manifests signs of a heart attack is not really in the position of "having done nothing." What she had "done" is an act of refusal that is free and highly significant. This refusal might in fact be the most voluntary action of her life. In most actions we are buoyed by habit, social expectations, or inner determinisms. In this instance the woman might be summoned to an agonizing activation of her freedom of the sort which she may have rarely if ever before experienced. Her own deliberate volition will be called for in a unique way. Her behavior is *passive* in the sense that it is not active as it would be if she were to shoot her husband, but it is *active* in the sense that it is free and effective volition. Deliberate omission is not outside the circle of human moral responsibility.

Not all omission is as deliberate as that of the wives who let their spouses die. Their omissions were distinguished by a high degree of conscious awareness of what they were in a position to do and of what they were not doing. Sometimes morally significant omissions are clouded by some ignorance or diminished consciousness of what is being left undone. Older moralists distinguished vincible and invincible ignorance. Invincible ignorance is that which should not be dispelled by any reasonable amount of diligence. Thus, our omissions regarding problems we know nothing of and could know nothing of are simply amoral. We could have no moral responsibility for that of which we are invincibly ignorant.

The idea of vincible ignorance, however, is more subtle and significant. There is a way in which we can have what moralists of the past called a *conscientia larvata*—that is, a masked conscience. Ignorance can be contrived and self-servingly sustained. It is then not so much ignorance as avoidance. It represents a choice. The morally demanding reality is dimly perceived and then instinctively commended to the shadows of the mind. This may be illustrated by many of the Germans who claimed to know nothing of the Nazi genocidal programs. Affluent Americans who claim to be unaware of the deep poverty existing in various places in this country are another example. The "ignorance" of "good" white people of the indignities visited still upon black Americans is also suspect. Our broad unawareness of world hunger—and consequent uninvolvement—illustrates the same problem.

In a crucial way, this kind of affected ignorance falls under the broad rubric of "conscious behavior." It has its own kind of determined deliberateness, even though it is obviously not that of a first-degree murderer. If the ignorance involved is invincible, there is no guilt. We are outside the area of conscious behavior. But the ignorance of the examples cited above is more likely devious and vincible. It would be naïve to deny the possibility of such a crass ploy.

Certain classical moral traditions are especially sensitive to the amount of harm that is done by way of omission. The Christian tradition is strikingly attuned to this. In fact, omission seems to constitute the substance of the definitive moral assessment known as "the Last Judgment." Those rejected in this judgment are the omitters who "never gave me food . . . never gave me a thing to drink . . . never made me welcome . . . never clothed me . . . never visited me."[49] And the condemnation of the Pharisees, those ogres of the Gospels, is also in terms of omission. The punctiliously elaborate behavioral codes of these self-consciously virtuous gentlemen were impressive to the point of heroism, but they were indicted for *omitting* "the weightier matters of the Law—justice, mercy, good faith!"[50] The opposite of the good Samaritan were those who "passed by" leaving the wounded man untended.[51] There is sharp insight in this stress on guilt through omission. I would even submit that most harm that comes to the world of persons derives from what is undone.[52] The question of collective guilt, to which we shall return, inevitably entails considerations of responsibility for omissions.

Omissions are morally significant too because they "show where the heart is." They reveal the morally crucial center of sensitivity that shapes attitudes and character. No one can bear the thought of being evil or of being thought evil. The things we do are often posturings to support the character image that we wish to project. But the undone deed speaks loudly of how much caring animates one's moral existence and of how deeply one is into the foundational moral experience. A barbaric society (and I see the term as having modern as well as ancient meaning) is not characterized mainly by the active practitioners of cruelty. These, in any surviving society, will be a minority. The soul of barbarism is the undergirding apathy of the many, the collective nonresponse to the legitimate moral claims that confront that society. It is this which "legitimates" the barbaric propensities of any social entity. In the realistic definition of guilt, then, "behavior" refers to both omission and commission.

According to the definition, guilty behavior also does real, *unnecessary harm*. Harm is the critical term here. If we do no real harm, we incur no guilt. In speaking of taboo, I noted that taboo often has realistic origins. If often represented an aversive reaction to perceived harm, even though it finds expression in an absolutized way that allows for no discriminating judgment. It is because it does not allow for distinctions where there are differences that taboo becomes unreal, banning whole classes with no regard for differentiation. Thus some modern taboo has put all gambling, all drinking, or all divorce under the same negative judgment—even though in certain instances these activities do no *real, unnecessary harm*. This is the central failing of taboo, or of any kind of ethics that abstractly condemns all behavior of a certain class.

The prolonged conviction that all contraceptive intercourse is immoral, which derived largely from Stoic ethics, is a classical example of this. As one ancient writer imbued with Stoic doctrine put it: "It is particularly well established that we have intercourse not for pleasure but for the purpose of procreation. . . . The sexual organs are given man not for pleasure, but for the maintenance of the species."[53] What happened here was that an abstract definition of the intrinsic finality of sex was taken as fully exhaustive of what the sexual encounter means to persons. Such abstraction involves a decision to consider only one aspect of sex—in this case the procreative aspect —as real. Thus all nonprocreative sex was deemed immoral—not because it would be judged as harmful, but simply because it would offend the chosen conceptualization of what sex means. This kind of abstracting happens in many areas. The stress on harm brings relief from this kind of thinking, because it draws you back to the empirical order where the wrongfulness will be manifested if it is real. It spares you the nominalism present in most cultural codes of ethics which label as evil that which is harmless and potentially good.

The point here is not that you cannot theorize about guilty action. To do just that is a prime task of ethics. The problem arises when the theory has no empirical base. Then that which is called wrong might be harmful only to our theory. Hence the need to insist on *real harm* in the definition of guilty behavior.

The objection, of course, can be raised that this puts too much freight on the simple notion of harm. In response, I would say that harm to persons is the nether side of the good, and the whole of ethics is geared to the exploration of this bipolar reality. Ethics is concerned with the systematic discernment of what does or does not befit the mysterious and complex reality of personal life. To say that it explores good and evil is to say the same thing. To assess the real, unnecessary harm involved in a particular business deal is exceedingly difficult. It admits of only imperfect success. It is, however, a task from which the valuing animal cannot hide. The alternative would be to surrender powerful forms of collective human activity to caprice. The difficulties involved in doing ethics and assessing harm amid the boggling complexities of collective life have driven many to treat moral concern and ethics as though it had meaning only amid the home and hearth issues of interpersonal life. This is an intellectual and moral defection that has always been congenial to the interests of political and commercial despots.

The term *unnecessary* has to qualify harm in the definition of guilty behavior because it is sometimes moral and necessary to cause harm. Killing in self-defense when there are no less drastic alternatives is obviously harmful to the deceased. It may, however, be judged *necessary* harm. The apportionment of goods and bads in a society may do necessary harm to certain citizens. When young males are drafted into military service and compelled to take capital risks, the harm is profound and ultimate to many of them. The circumstances, however, may show it to be necessary. Similarly, the quota system which gives preferential treatment to groups that have suffered unfair discrimination can be another example of justifiable necessary harm to some.

That wrongful behavior is so because it is harmful to *persons* is obvious. Less obvious is the *and/or their environment* of our definition. This environment includes the animals, vegetables, and minerals that make up our terrestrial context. Like a man who strikes it rich and arrogantly abandons his kith and kin, *Homo sapiens*, having evolved into a conscious and somewhat free animal, treated the earth as though it were a stage that had no intrinsic connection with the drama played upon it. He forgot that he grew up out of the material of that stage and that it is truly flesh of his flesh and blood of his blood. The animism of primitive man that we easily scorn as naïve was an imperfect symbolization of our identification with our environment. Within the excesses of animism can be discerned a reverence for our roots and for the parent earth. It is only of late that we have been forced to admit that we have much to learn from men whom we call primitive.

From this definition of guilty behavior, therefore, it should be obvious how dangerous and intellectually vacuous it is to treat guilt as though it were neurotic. Rather, as J. Glenn Gray writes: "If guilt is not experienced deeply enough to cut into us, our future may well be lost."[54]

The Possibility of Collective Guilt . . .

Various notions of collective guilt have come to the fore in the past decade. With the realization that a good deal of corporate and political agency is wrongful, the question of assigning guilt is with us. Who was guilty of the cruel extravagances of the Vietnam War? Who, more specifically, was guilty for the massacre at My Lai? The generals, Lieutenant Calley, the Congress who provided the monies to wage the war, or we who provided the Congress? Who is guilty for the wasting of the earth wrought by corporate power? The board of directors, the stockholder, those who buy the products of those corporations? Who is guilty for the old and new violence at Wounded Knee? Can guilt be inherited? Do we bear the guilt of our fathers who in centuries of dishonor drove the Indians from their homelands and slaughtered many of them? Do we owe reparation to women and blacks because we all have been in some way responsible for damaging discrimination that has been visited upon them? In an incisive article entitled "Guilt: Yours, Ours, and Theirs," Theodore R. Weber analyzes the dangers that may attach to the rhetoric of collective guilt. He points out that "in the latter years of World War II and in the decade following, the concept of collective guilt was widely discussed—particularly in liberal academic and ecclesiastical circles—and overwhelmingly repudiated."[55] Weber recalls the "war guilt" clause of the Versailles Treaty, the "guilt" of the Jewish people, wartime propaganda stereotyping, the Japanese-American relocation, and the guilt by association of the McCarthy period. A bill of indictment against the concept of collective guilt arose including the following particulars:

> "—It linked people to deeds with which they had no proximate and/or volitional connection.
> —It brought innocent people and moral monsters under a common judgment.
> —It dissolved the necessary distinctions between minor transgressions and major crimes.
> —It reduced the complexity of intergroup claims and counterclaims to simple and unarguable moral judgments and demands.
> —It erased the faces and histories of unique individuals.
> —It ignored the historic diversity and social plurality of designated collectivities.
> —It predisposed groups to unrelenting, indiscriminate, unlimited warfare.
> —It placed a summary judgment on human beings at conception and left them vulnerable to the execution of sentence at the option of the 'offended party' and at a time and in circumstances of the latter's choosing."[56]

Given the weight of these charges, one should move with careful step to any attempted revalidation of the idea of collective guilt. We can, in fact, even add to these charges that it is the individual who acts even if he is acting in a group with other actors. There is the further problem that when everyone is guilty, no one is guilty. Collective guilt can be something for people to wallow in, comforted by the conviction that there is nothing much that can be done about it since responsibility is such a morass. Collective guilt can be a species of self-serving rationalization. In spite of all of this, a proper conception of collective guilt seems indicated and feasible.

. The basis of a notion of collective guilt may be found in our social nature. We are not in society because of its utility or by arbitrary contract. We are in society because we are social beings. We do indeed agree to certain kinds of social structuring and we do find utility in social living, but all of this is subsequent to our constitutional sociality as persons. This intimates that our conception of guilt cannot be atomistically individualistic. Our natural relatedness to others must show through in our guilt as well as in our virtue. Some meaningful conception of communal guilt can be properly anticipated. Also, at the behavioral level, as Weber acknowledges, "we support a system of attitudes, values, and power which perpetrates injustices by reason of its systemic strength and its innate disposition and dynamism. . . . We are not passive or neutral toward the social housing we inhabit. We receive it, use it, reinforce it, and pass it on."[57] This does not mean that we can say that we killed Martin Luther King, Sitting Bull, or Malcolm X, but it does allow a judgment of complicity in systemic arrangements that are discriminatory.

Some understanding of this guilty complicity can be gained by referring back to the discussion of the three kinds of justice that mark our relationship with others: commutative, legal, and distributive. Again, commutative is between individuals or discrete groups, legal refers to the debt of the individual to society, and distributive to the obligations of the social whole to the individual. (See Chapter Three.) A grossly individualistic view of personhood would allow only for commutative justice and a purely individual notion of guilt. You have no claims on me if I did nothing to you. Exaggerated collectivism would leave little ground for the claims of one individual to another since the individual is only an ephemeral wave; it is the ocean (the state) which subsists and endures. Guilt in such an extreme view would have collectivist meaning.

A proper conception of person integrates the three kinds of indebtedness implied in the three kinds of justice. Guilt, correspondingly, could occur at any level, since we can violate justice at any level.

Lest we get lost in terminology here, let us apply the discussion to American guilt in the matter of racism. Though specific legislation and new policies have begun to correct the situation in certain ways, the fact still is that black persons in our society face a situation of insult and deprivation in many significant ways. How are those of us responsible who have never engaged in active discriminatory behavior and who might even have worked actively for civil rights? In other words, is this an example of collective guilt?

First of all, collective guilt arises from what is undone. Albrecht Haushofer, a determined opponent of Hitler who was imprisoned and executed near the end of the war wrote a sonnet entitled

"Guilt." He admits that he is guilty in the way that the Nazi court views his case. He did resist the government. But he goes on to say

> Yet I am guilty otherwise than you think
> I should have known my duty earlier
> And called evil by its name more sharply—
> My judgment I kept flexible too long . . .
> In my heart I accuse myself of this:
> I deceived my conscience long
> I lied to myself and others—
> Early I knew the whole course of this misery—
> I warned—but not hard enough or clearly!
> Today I know of what I am guilty. . . .[58]

Here was the sensitive voice of a man who risked all and paid in full for his courage. Yet he was painfully aware of his early compromising hesitations, his "prudent" flexibility, his circumvention by way of contrived obscurity, his protestations about how complicated it all was—all the stratagems that make up the tangled defenses of the cold conscience. Certainly all of us who were alive and mature before the civil rights movement—and in their own way, those who are younger—can make their own the sentiments of Haushofer. We all take part even now in segregation. Segregation is not just a matter of real estate. There is psychological and social segregation also, and this is more basic. It shows up, for a significant example, in the low statistics of interracial marriage and dating. Biologically there is no reason why we should not intermarry. Whites do not hesitate to marry persons who have very different backgrounds and cultural influences—as long as they are white. Segregation also appears in the customs of social relating and even in the condescension of supposedly "liberal" whites. He who claims to be without sin here is surely a liar. Who could say that they warned enough, or called evil and the unholy by its name with a clear voice?

The violations here are at the several levels of justice. At the level of *commutative justice*, it can be argued that black and white societies are like separate nations. Some passports are granted to blacks but they come slowly and for most they do not come at all. The reason for affirmative-action programs is to force that which we would not yield voluntarily. In this way there is a group debt such as one nation owes another. Debts between discrete social groups come under the first form of justice. The guilt will not be equal for all members of the group, and theoretically there could be a person who could be guiltless, a person whose sensitivity and response were entirely ideal. This is not a practical possibility, however.

Communal guilt can also be understood in this regard in terms of *legal justice*, or our obligations to the good of the social whole. We owe society some contribution to equity and fairness and to an atmosphere free of tolerated insult. We owe it to society to work for conditions in which friendship and not minimal justice will be the critical social energy. Obviously, we are a long way from such an achievement. Again, to say guiltless is to say that one has been sensitive enough, has cared enough, been creative enough, etc.

Distributive justice also explains communal guilt. The onus of distributive justice would seem to fall only on the officials of government. Recall that Thomas Aquinas sees this as a virtue that resides also in the citizenry. He says that this kind of justice is primarily in the prince who distributes the common goods of the society. But, he says, distributive justice "is also in the subject to whom the good are distributed inasmuch as they are pleased [*sunt contenti*] by a just distribution."[59] Inversely it can be said that the subjects violate distributive justice and incur guilt when they are "pleased" or content with an unjust distribution. Such contentment is a product of freedom. As J. Glenn Gray says, "Freedom is possible . . . not only in the power to do or prevent, but also in inner assent and consent to action by others. With a relative criterion like this it is, of course, impossible to be exact in estimating even one's own guilt. Yet the jubilation in evil deeds allows little room for doubt that inner consent is often forthcoming."[60] This inner consent, which may rise even to the point of "jubilation," not only indicates that one might well do what the officials are doing if he had a chance but also serves to "legitimate" and endorse what the officials are now up to. It gives a socially important mantle of respectability to the current policy.

Communal or collective (or political) guilt, therefore, is primarily to be understood in terms of omission, the failure of appropriate response. This is something that the individuals in the group are responsible for. It is not something attributed to them by some nominalistic use of "collective guilt." It is also not something that one could try in a court of law. Its proper forum is conscience. In certain instances, as we have seen, in European law, the failure to render assistance in a particular case can be made a matter of judicial concern when the opportunity to aid is clear and individualized. Communal guilt allows for no such precision. Hence, the legal or paralegal harassment of Japanese-Americans during World War II or the historical persecution of Jewish people because of their "guilt" for the crucifixion of Jesus are crudities to which all considerations of communal guilt need not descend.

A final point on collective guilt relates to the hostility of entrenched egoism. In Arthur Miller's play *Incident at Vichy*, to which I referred earlier, the Jew Leduc, who is awaiting interment in a Nazi camp and probable death, is trying to explain to the decent Von Berg that he, Von Berg, in spite of his decency is implicated in the hatred that is about to condemn Leduc. Says Leduc: "I have never analyzed a gentile who did not have, somewhere hidden in his mind, a dislike if not a hatred for the Jews." Von Berg protests: "That is impossible, it is not true of me!" Then Leduc addresses Von Berg with special earnestness, with, in the playwright's directive, "a wild pity in his voice."

> Until you know it is true of you, you will destroy whatever truth can come of this atrocity. Part of knowing who we are is knowing we are not someone else. And Jew is only the name we give to that stranger, that agony we cannot feel, that death we look at like a cold abstraction. Each man has his Jew; the black, the yellow, the white, it is the other. And the Jews have their Jews. And now, now above all, you must see that you have yours—the man whose death leaves you relieved that you are not him, despite your decency. And that is why there is nothing and will be nothing—until you face your own complicity with this . . . your own humanity.[61]

Leduc's cynicism may be excessive, as even the play suggests, since after this conversation, Von Berg gives his pass to Leduc allowing him to escape while he remained to face the consequences. Still there is the scent of some truth in Leduc's outburst. Egoism is still so strong in the species that we can bear the ills of others with "a cold abstraction." As Leduc says pointedly, another man's death "leaves you relieved that you are not him, despite your decency." Egoism also encourages particularized hostilities. "Each man has his Jew. . . . And the Jews have their Jews." Insecure in our sense of our own worth, we almost seem to need to downgrade others. We need the barbarians, or the Jews, or the Communists, or the blacks as alien others whose imputed inferiority or malice sets our value in a more favorable light. There is nothing new about this. In India, centuries ago, we see the rise of groups of people who were known as untouchables or outcasts. As A. L. Basham writes, the practice of social ostracism appeared even among the outcasts: "The outcasts themselves had developed a caste hierarchy, and had their own outcasts. In later India every untouchable group imagined that some other group was lower than itself. . . ."[62]

It would seem that the enthusiastic malevolence of the lynch mob appears in subtle disguise in human society more often than we would care to admit. This grim side of our psychic history is something that must be included in an estimate of collective guilt. We have an instinct not just for grouping, but for grouping against. The group gives strength to our baser proclivities. In a face-to-face encounter with all of its chastening immediacy, we feel ourselves on the spot. Our reactions are likely to be more benign. But group experience dilutes individual conscience. Egoism finds freer rein. Blurring abstractions develop which give a sense of cohesiveness and comfort to the group. From such a base it is easier to do real, unnecessary harm to persons. To speak only of individual guilt is to miss this influential aspect of our many-leveled reality.

In conclusion, therefore, there is such a thing as healthy guilt—guilt that is not neurotic and that calls not so much for therapy as for moral conversion. We are capable in diverse ways of seeing evil and doing it with some conscious deliberation. The widespread neglect of the basic phenomenon of guilt is the sorry badge of cultural vacuity. Moral insight that does not extend to the subject of guilt is truncated. Guilt must be faced for the terrible reality that it is. We do no know ourselves if we do not know our guilt.

NOTES—CHAPTER TWELVE

1. Joseph Butler, *The Analogy of Religion*, quoted in Richard B. Brandt, *Value and Obligation* (New York, Chicago, and Burlingame: Harcourt, Brace & World, Inc., 1961), p. 169.
2. Eric D'Arcy, *Conscience and Its Right to Freedom* (New York: Sheed & Ward, 1961), p. 4.
3. In speaking of conscience as a manifestation of the "conscious self," I do not imply that its roots do not reach into the regions of the subconscious. Affectivity runs deep, and conscience, rooted in the foundational moral experience, touches these depths.

4. One's conscience, of course, may become involved simply by considering an ethical case. It is easy and natural for persons to be implicated in value questions when they study them and feel the relevance of the case to their own moral situation. Pure detachment from any human problem is unlikely.

5. Nicolas Berdyaev, *The Destiny of Man* (New York and Evanston: Harper & Row, Harper Torchbook, 1960), p. 16.

6. H. A. Prichard, "Does Moral Philosophy Rest on a Mistake?" *Mind* 21 (1912); reprinted in W. T. Jones, F. Sontag, M. O. Beckner, and R. J. Fogelin, *Approaches to Ethics*, 2nd ed. (New York: McGraw-Hill Book Co., 1969), p. 474.

7. As philosopher Harry K. Girvetz comments: "One suspects that intuitionist philosophies flourish among individuals so supremely confident of their values that they find it difficult to take alternative value schemes seriously enough to contemplate the possibility of genuine challenge and conflict." Girvetz adds pointedly: "The self-assurance of Cantabrigians and Oxonians is notorious. Could intuitionism be a product of the serene and placid atmosphere of Cambridge and Oxford?" Harry K. Girvetz, *Beyond Right and Wrong* (New York and London: Free Press, Collier Macmillan Publishers, 1973), pp. 113–14.

8. Joseph Butler, *Works*, edited by S. Halifax (Oxford, 1874), Sermon III, Vol. 2, p. 32.

9. Since I spoke of character in my treatment of the cognitive potential of affectivity, I was giving character an epistemological significance. Still, character is not the same thing as the spontaneously judging moral self which is conscience. The knowing function is primary in conscience; secondary in the denotative meaning of character.

10. In his discussion of conscience, Eric D'Arcy suggests that *habitus* in the vocabulary of Aquinas can be translated as skill. *Conscience and Its Right to Freedom*, pp. 34–35.

11. Ruth Nanda Anshen, "The Conservation of Family Values," in Ruth Nanda Anshen, ed., *The Family: Its Function and Destiny*, rev. ed. (New York: Harper & Brothers, 1959), p. 520.

12. See Thomas Aquinas, *Summa Theologica* II II q. 49, a. 4, where he says that *solertia* implies a facile and prompt response to sudden and unexpected situations. "*Solertia est habitus qui provenit ex repentino, inveniens quod convenit.*"

13. John Dewey and James H. Tufts, *Ethics*, rev. ed. (New York: Henry Holt & Co., 1932), p. 300.

14. Josef Pieper, for example, says: "This primary and fundamental cognitive aspect of prudence is, incidentally, confirmed by the direct meaning of the Latin *con-scientia*, which includes knowledge (*scientia*); and as we have said, conscience and prudence mean, in a certain sense, the same thing." *The Four Cardinal Virtues*, (New

York: Harcourt, Brace & World, 1965), p. 12. See also pp. 11 and 30.

15. Augustine also calls prudence "love . . . sagaciously choosing" (*amor . . . sagaciter eligens*). *De moribus Eccles.* C. 5: ML 32, 1322. Commenting on these passages, Aquinas seems to do some violence to the forthright meaning of Augustine, saying that prudence is love only in the sense that love moves to the act of prudence. This is not what Augustine said. Thomas need not have treated the text this way, since his notion of practical reason discussed in the article following his comments on Augustine's text can be understood as having an essentially affective component. Also, his notion of knowledge by way of connaturality (see *Summa Theologica* II II q. 45, a. 2) could have given a better interpretation of Augustine. For Thomas' comments see *Summa Theologica* II II q. 47, a. 1.

16. Pieper, *Four Cardinal Virtues*, p. 16.

17. Berdyaev, *Destiny of Man*, p. 163.

18. In this sense, conscience relates to the discussion of "natural law." Natural-law thinking, by insisting on the possibility of discovering the tracings of the good within concrete reality, gives us ground from which to challenge these conceptualizations that are established as law or custom.

19. Martin Buber, "Guilt and Guilt Feeling," *Cross Currents* 9 (Summer 1958), p. 202.

20. It should be clear as stated above that tragedy well borne can adduce these favorable cognitive effects. Poorly met, it is crushing. At times it may be overwhelming for its victims, and the resources to meet it well might simply not be had.

21. Bernard Häring, *The Law of Christ* (Westminster, Md.: Newman Press, 1961), p. 143.

22. Ibid.

23. In speaking of "objective guilt," I admit the ambiguities that accrue to the terms *objective* and *subjective*. Subjects with their subjectivity are part of the objective order and there is not objectivity where that is ignored. Here I use the term "objective" to stress against some psychiatric and common usage that guilt is merely a subjective malfunction without reference to reality.

24. Buber, "Guilt and Guilt Feeling," p. 197.

25. It should be all too obvious at this point that the idea of conscience cannot be collapsed into the superego or ego ideal of Freudian psychoanalytic theory. As Louvain professor Joseph Nuttin writes: "According to psychoanalysis this *super-ego* or *ego-ideal* is the starting-point for religion and the moral conscience, and indeed for human culture as a whole." *Psychoanalysis and Personality* (London: Sheed & Ward, 1954), p. 20. The superego is said to have grown out of the Oedipal crisis. A boy represses his erotic desire for his mother

and yields to identification with the father after experiencing the futility of his Oedipal love. Out of fear of castration and encouraged by adulation, he develops an internal value system. See Paul W. Pruyser, A *Dynamic Psychology of Religion* (New York: Harper & Row, 1968), especially pp. 306–8. As R. R. Sears comments: "Freud's notion of the universal Oedipus complex stands as a sharply etched grotesquerie against his otherwise informative description of sexual development." "Survey of Objective Studies of Psychoanalytic Concepts," *Social Science Research Council Bulletin* 51 (1943).

26. Karl Menninger, *Whatever Became of Sin?* (New York: Hawthorn Books, Inc., 1973), p. 23.
27. Mary Harrington Hall, "Conversation with the President of the American Psychological Association, The Psychology of Universality: Abraham H. Maslow," *Psychology Today*, July 1968, p. 35.
28. Ibid., pp. 24–25.
29. Reinhold Niebuhr, "Sin," in Marvin Halverson and Arthur A. Cohen, eds., *A Handbook of Christian Theology* (Cleveland: Meridian Books, 1958), p. 349.
30. Frances Moore Lappé, "The World Food Problem," *Hastings Center Report* 3, No. 5 (Nov. 1973), p. 11.
31. Ibid.
32. Ibid.
33. Robert L. Heilbroner, *An Inquiry into the Human Prospect* (New York: W. W. Norton & Co., Inc., 1975), p. 61.
34. William Shakespeare, *Hamlet*, Act II, Scene ii, lines 315–19.
35. Blaise Pascal, *Pensées* (New York: Washington Square Press, 1965), No. 434, p. 127.
36. For a tri-level treatment of sin that takes a different tack, see Louis Monden, *Sin, Liberty and Law* (New York: Sheed & Ward, 1965), pp. 4–18.
37. Ibid., p. 5.
38. Heribert Jone, *Moral Theology*, "Englished and Adapted" by Urban Adelman (Westminster, Md.: Newman Press, 1955), p. 146. For a history of the development of this see José M. Díaz, "La Doctrina Moral Sobre la Parvedad de Materia in re Venerea Desde Cayetano Hasta San Alfonso," *Archivo Teologico Granadino* 23 (1960), pp. 5–138
39. Jone, *Moral Theology*, p. 154. Jone argues that moralists are justified in making such a classification, since civil authorities in the interest of public morality may ban the exposure of certain parts of the body.
40. "Declaration on Certain Questions Concerning Sexual Ethics," S. Congregation for the Doctrine of the Faith, first published in *L'Osservatore Romano*, January 22, 1976.
41. Richard McCormick, "Sexual Ethics: An Opinion," *National Catholic Reporter* 12, No. 14 (Jan. 30, 1976), p. 9.

42. The term "directly" in this discussion means that the sexual pleasure was willed in itself, that it was intentional. The idea was that if it occurred incidentally and not intentionally in the performance of one's duty as a physician, for example, it would not be immoral if it was not sought or voluntarily welcomed.

43. See Daniel C. Maguire, "The Vatican on Sex," *Commonweal* 103 (Feb. 27, 1976), pp. 137–40.

44. Immanuel Kant, "On a Supposed Right to Lie from Altruistic Motives," in *Foundations of the Metaphysics of Morals*, translated by Lewis White Beck (New York: Liberal Arts Press, 1959), p. 347.

45. Gerald Kelly, *Medico-Moral Problems* (Dublin: Clonmore and Reynolds, 1955), pp. 165, 167.

46. Ayn Rand, *The Virtue of Selfishness: A New Concept of Egoism* (New York: New American Library, Signet Books; copyright © 1961, 1964 by Ayn Rand; 1962, 1963, 1964 by the Objectivist Newsletter, Inc.), p. 46.

47. See Helen Silving, "Euthanasia: A Study in Comparative Criminal Law," *University of Pennsylvania Law Review* 103 (1954), pp. 372–73. The case had a complicated history on appeal where it was held that manslaughter or negligent homicide might be the applicable categories. The problems that German and French law encounter in determining responsibility in cases of "failure to render assistance" illustrates the complexity of omission as behavior. Their advances in this area, however, are laudable.

48. Ibid., p. 373, note 94.

49. Matthew 25:41–46.

50. Matthew 23:23.

51. Luke 10:29–37

52. For an interesting study of the ethics of omission, see Eric D'Arcy, *Human Acts* (Oxford: Clarendon Press, 1963), pp. 40–56. For a treatment of the ethical and legal problems in assessing specific instances on harm-producing inaction, see John Kleinig, "Good Samaritanism," *Philosophy and Public Affairs* 5, No. 4 (Summer 1976), pp. 382–407.

53. *The Nature of the Universe*, Sec. 44. This is a Pythagorean treatise spuriously ascribed to Ocellus Lucanus. Quoted in John T. Noonan, Jr., *Contraception* (Cambridge, Mass.: Belknap Press of Harvard University Press, 1965), p. 47. Stoic influence is seen in this aspect of Pythagorean thought.

54. J. Glenn Gray, *The Warriors: Reflections on Men in Battle* (New York, Evanston, and London: Harper & Row, Harper Torchbook, 1959), p. 212.

55. Theodore R. Weber, "Guilt: Yours, Ours, and Theirs," *Worldview* 18, No. 2 (Feb. 1975), p. 15.

56. Ibid.
57. Ibid., p. 18
58. Albrecht Haushofer, "Schuld" (Guilt), quoted and translated by Gray, *The Warriors*, pp. 204–5. The English loses some of the force of the German.

> *Doch Schuldig bin ich anders als ihr denkt,*
> *ich musste früher meine Pflicht erkennen*
> *ich musste scharfer Unheil Unheil nennen—*
> *mein Urteil hab ich viel zu lang gelenkt . . .*
>
> *Ich klage mich in meinem Herzen an:*
> *Ich habe mein Gewissen lang betrogen*
> *Ich hab mich selbst and andere belogen—*
>
> *Ich Kannte früh des Jammers ganze Bahn*
> *Ich hab gewarnt—nicht hart genug and klar!*
> *Und heute weiss ich, was ich schuldig war . . .*

59. Thomas Aquinas, *Summa Theologica* II II q. 61, a. 1, ad 3.
60. Gray, *The Warriors*, p. 200.
61. Arthur Miller, *Incident at Vichy*, Dramatists Play Service, Inc., pp. 48–49. Copyright © 1966 by Arthur Miller.
62. A. L. Basham, *The Wonder That Was India: A Survey of the Culture of the Indian Sub-Continent Before the Coming of the Muslims* (London: Sidgwick & Jackson, 1954), p. 145.

CHAPTER THIRTEEN

THE HAZARDS OF MORAL DISCOURSE

Myth
Cognitive Mood
False Analogues
Abstractions
Selective Vision
Role
Banalization

Myth

The great enemy of the truth is very often not the lie—deliberate, contrived and dishonest—but the myth, persistent, persuasive and unrealistic. Too often we hold fast to the clichés of our forebears. We subject all facts to a prefabricated set of interpretations. —John Fitzgerald Kennedy

Reality is not transparent. It is a supreme fallacy to think of the mind as a docile camera or a mirror that obediently and accurately reflects things back to us as they are. Human knowing is an event in which the knower both receives and gives. Human knowing is interpretive. The word "interpretation" comes from the Latin *interpres*, which means a broker, a negotiator, an agent who arranges a bargain between two parties. This is in fact what goes on in the interpretive act of knowing. A kind of bargain is struck between the knower and the known. Within the knower, the bargain is controlled by the mind's need for meaning. The mind cannot stand a vacuum of meaning. It must make sense of things. Thus when knowable reality comes before us, it is not just simply ingested. To be received into knowledge, that which becomes known must be related to the already known. In that sense, knowledge is relational; we know by relating. When an object or situation becomes known, it is brought into a community of other knowns.

Things known are not stored up like photographs that do not relate to other photographs kept in the same drawer. To be known is to be related, to be set in a meaning-giving, already familiar context. The experience of meaning derives from seeing things as fitting into and relating to the over-all universe of our knowledge. Even if something new is known, it is given meaning, and it makes sense only when we see that it somehow relates to the already known. Otherwise the new candidate for knowledge is like the proverbial man from Mars, meaningless and disturbing. He does not fit into the established interpretive scheme and so he appears as a threat to the mind. He triggers a rejection mechanism. It is even possible that we will not see him at all. We can actually be blind to the presence of that which seems unrelatable to the already known and accepted. We notice this in others more than in ourselves. We wonder how they can be so blind! And others who have different filters and interpretive structures have similar wonderings about us.

What this implies is that the mind values meaning above knowledge. We would rather not know that which appears meaningless. Meaning is the oxygen of the mind. A person arrives at intellectual maturity when, in his search for meaning, he has so extended his relational field of knowledge and has achieved such security in knowing that he can welcome even that which shakes his current universe of knowing.

Openness of mind is the mark of such maturity. No minds, however, are fully open. There are limits to how much any of us will dare in our mission into the unknown. Our hunger for meaning is such that we may impose more than we receive in our search for it. The necessary receptivity may be lacking. The knowledge that results may not so much be an image of the real as it is an image we have projected. In such a situation we do not discover meaning; we fabricate it.

Myth as a Bargainer for Meaning . . .

There is some truth in Herbert Marcuse's characteristically blunt statement that "epistemology is in itself ethics, and ethics is epistemology."[1] Ethics must know how we know, and that is the passion of epistemology. Knowing how we know, in fact, is the beginning of all wisdom. Foolishness, an amalgam of volitional and intellectual defects, is the state of not knowing and not caring how we know. It is characteristic of the fool that he never feels foolish. Only the wise man knows this feeling, for it is this that makes him wise. When we set out to know how we know by checking the underpinnings of our certitudes and presumptions, we discover some of the limits of our knowing and see what fools we can be. That is the pain of wisdom and it is a pain that ethics cannot do without.

In order to know the ways of moral understanding, ethics must chart out a method. Having done that, however, it remains an unprofitable servant if it leaves the matter at that. The best method in the world will do little for someone whose vision of the real is captivated by an obsessive and distorting myth. Or, better, method is only fulfilled by the recognition of the hazards of moral discourse. We do not know "from the neck up"; all that we are is involved in our knowing. We also know out of a history and a social setting. There are filters, socially and intrapersonally derived, that stand between us and what is. True method accosts those filters in the hope of minimizing their distorting effect.

Myth is the first of such silent but busy filters. Immediately, it is necessary to explain what myth means in this context since it is a polyvalent word. Words are like people in that they have many relatives and hangers-on. When you decide to marry one to your particular purpose, it is wise to make clear in advance that it is the word you want and not the whole family of associations. Myth in my usage is this: *It is a complex of feelings, attitudes, symbols, memories, and experienced relationships through which reality is refracted, filtered, and interpreted.*[2] By that definition, knowledge is always to some degree mythic. Interpretation will always be affected by the complex of our feelings, attitudes, etc. Sometimes this will be gainful. Buoyed by a creative myth, persons may rise to heights they never would have aspired to in the absence of the myth. The confidence-inspiring myth of "American know-how" has historically served to keep our technologists working to the point of success when those working without the myth would have given up at an earlier more "reasonable" point. The myths surrounding patriotism and parenthood often bring forth generosity and imagination from the most unlikely subjects. Myths may be the vehicle of ideals that

keep persons and societies moving forward. Benito Mussolini realized
the power of myth to draw people on. He said in one of his
speeches: "We have created a myth. This myth is a faith, a noble
enthusiasm. It does not have to be a reality, it is an impulse and a
hope, belief, and courage. Our myth is the nation, the great nation
which we wish to make into a concrete reality."[3] If the ideals are
good, then, the myth can be described in very positive terms. As
Mussolini himself illustrates, however, the bad myth can be blinding,
and all the thinking that is done under its sway will be impaired. My
concern here is with myth in its pejorative sense—with myth as a
warping and limiting force in cognition.

The myth springs first of all from our horror of a vacuum of meaning. Some sense must be made of things, and myth fills the bill.
Myth is also social and historical in its roots. We might think of a
private myth developed in the history of one person, but this is not
the common usage of the term. Normally when we speak of myth we
refer to a phenomenon which is present in the culture waiting for us
to fall under its spell.

The Myth of Woman . . .

The myth of woman is one that is finally being brought under the
searing light of social criticism. If we look at it closely, it can instruct
us on many of the basic properties of myth.

Often historical exigencies lay the foundations for myth. Because a
man does not get pregnant and cannot nurse a baby, he was often
the more natural candidate to leave the cave and go forth to meet
the challenges of the hunt or of self-defense. Growing out of this,
there emerged in history the myth that a woman is essentially a creature of "die Kuche und die Kinder." Cooking and children are the
realities that define her, and when she is engaged in these contexts
her true being is accurately reflected. Domesticity, then, became
woman's identifying essence in the view that this deep-rooted myth
communicates.

The belatedly obsolescent word "spinster" shows the force of the
myth, especially when compared to "bachelor." The bachelor, provided he is not prissy and effeminate (another myth-laden concept),
may be admired for the very absence of marriage. His male friends,
married or not, are less likely to be anxious to "find somebody for

him." He is not a truncated person because of his single state. Although this is changing slowly, the unmarried woman cut off from the child-filled kitchen is a creature exiled from her natural habitat. She lacks the reality that symbolizes her meaning. As the Epistle to Timothy puts it, "She will be saved through motherhood."[4] Even in Catholic spirituality where virginity was in high esteem, nuptial imagery was often employed to explain the nun's dignity—she was "the spouse of Christ."

Sexual ethics reflects this too. In ancient Israel, for example, infidelity for a woman was punishable by death, whereas her husband had broader sexual freedom as long as he did not offend the rights of another husband. As Scripture scholar Kenneth Grayston writes: "Since everything centered on the man, polygamy was the natural type of marriage for Israelites, for several wives do more than one to satisfy the demand for children. If a wife gave her husband insufficient children he might take secondary wives and concubines and be encouraged by his wife to do so."[5] Augustine drew all this to its ultimate conclusion writing: "I do not see what other help woman would be to man if the purpose of generating was eliminated."[6] Here the definition-by-myth of female persons was complete.

Myths, of course, are never simple, as the woman myth also illustrates. Thus, women are often also associated with the origins of evil. In this sense they enter into a cosmology or mythic explanation of historic reality. In their imaginative and poetic accounts of the origins of their race many ancient peoples gave women a vicious role. In this type of work, as Arnold Toynbee observes, "the great catastrophes are apt to be women's work, even when the woman's role is ostensibly passive."[7]

Woman as the root of all evil had extensive currency. Simone de Beauvoir cites some examples of it. "Eve, given to Adam to be his companion, worked the ruin of mankind; when they wish to wreak vengeance upon man, the pagan gods invent woman; and it is the first-born of these female creatures, Pandora, who lets loose all the ills of suffering humanity. . . . Woman is thus dedicated to Evil. 'There is a good principle, which has created order, light, and man; and a bad principle, which has created chaos, darkness, and woman,' so says Pythagoras."[8] Hannah Arendt points out another aspect of the understanding of woman. She notes the striking fact that from

earliest history, there has been a perceptible need for the bodily part
of human existence to be hidden.

> Hidden away were the laborers who "with their bodies
> minister to the bodily needs of life" (Aristotle) and the
> women who with their bodies guarantee the physical sur-
> vival of species. Women and slaves belonged to the same
> category and were hidden away not only because they were
> somebody else's property but because their life was "labori-
> ous," devoted to bodily function.[9]

The complex myth of woman exercised its blinding influence even
in physiology. Thomas Aquinas, for example, relying on Aristotle,
wrote, with a view to "particular nature," that woman is something
deficient and misbegotten, the result of a lapse in the generative
process. His argument is an epic of "male chauvinism." The active
strength which is in the sperm of the male would naturally tend to
produce something "like unto itself . . . perfect and masculine." Obviously, sperm does not always succeed in doing this, since women
are generated. Thomas has several possible reasons for this: It could
be due to intrinsic weakness in the active strength of the sperm, or
because of some indisposition of this material. Extrinsic causes
would also be responsible for the generation of a woman. Thomas,
referring to Aristotle, cites the possible causal influence of the humid
winds that come in from the south. These might so affect the internal environment that a woman would be conceived instead of a
man.[10]

One might be inclined to say that we know well now that woman
has been offended by the myths, and this only goes to prove how corrigible myth is. The lesson, however, lies not in the slow process of
demythologizing which is taking tenuous hold but in the long and
tranquil tenure the myth enjoyed. The historic and ongoing atrocities now being documented in the literature of women's liberation
have long been with us, visible but unseen. That we were so inured
to them illustrates the power of myth. Even now we are inured to
the de facto segregation of women from government and many professions where males predominate with a lopsided majority.

As the woman myth illustrates, myths are stubborn. They are re-
sistant to data that does not square with the thrust of the myth. The
reasons for this are many. To mention a few: Myths are often a
shield for guilt. If they are challenged, some ugly facts might be un-
covered requiring painful moral conversion. To attack a myth is to

attack well-established vested interest. Not only will guilt be exposed but privileges will be lost. Beyond this, myths interlock with other myths and other patterns of interpretation. The fear of a domino effect within our mental universe stimulates defensive reactions and consolidates the myth. With all the gains myths provide, there are strong effective commitments to them in a society. They will not be unsettled simply by logical criticism. Even in a world marked by rapidation in the area of technology it remains true that myths nourished by many centuries of living will not be undone by fiat or even by exposure to the truth. That exposure is, of course, part of the cure, since truth has its own marvelous energy. Some deeply planted cultural myths will only yield to correction over several generations of personal encounters in an atmosphere in which truth is kept sufficiently visible.

Part of the power of myth such as the woman myth is that it is tinged with religious faith. As I have said, the mythic understanding of woman became part of the accepted cosmology. The myth entered into the understanding of the shape of reality itself. Woman was part of our explanation of evil and materiality. Such grand cosmological views are always "full of gods." When we attempt to explain the ultimate shape of the real, we feel ourselves awesomely close to the divine sources of the real. The next step is to assume that the role assigned to woman in these cosmologies was God's idea, not ours. This adds enormously (as religion always will) to the emotional freight of the myth. For similar reasons, the religious element is prominent also in political myths, as we will see.

The myth of woman shows the social and historical origins of this phenomenon. In many societies, it may have been a practical necessity to apportion the roles in such a way that woman bore most of the burdens of domesticity. But out of this functional necessity a myth was born which did not present the situation as functional but rather as ontological. This was not a rational conclusion, but myth is not a product of logic. With woman thus assigned to many of the more menial tasks, other considerations (her association with evil and the "shameful" side of life) would easily move in to deepen and complexify the myth of her inferiority.

The etiology of the woman myth is more complex than I could suggest in this brief illustrative treatment, but clearly this myth shows how profoundly the mind can be bewitched by myths. Good minds under the influence of the myth reached preposterous conclusions with no qualms. The temptation is to say that we would have done otherwise, but the story of myth in this instance and in others shows such confidence unwarranted. The power of myth is frightening, and some deliberate fear of it is the mark of the wise. A critical consciousness of myth is essential to ethics. The task here for ethics is never-ending, since even if we manage to critique and dislodge a deleterious myth, we are likely to substitute another for it. As we demythologize, we remythologize. Despair is not the response due to this proclivity of ours. Fruitful myths may succeed bad ones. Criticism may at least yield better myths. But since all myth is marked by stereotypical thinking and, therefore, the failure to make distinctions where there are differences, all myths call for criticism.

Myths and the Psychopolitical Universe . . .

Jacques Ellul is obsessed with the special problems that confront modern man's political self-understanding. His concerns can be instructive regarding the nature of myths in modern political life. Ellul feels that political facts have different characteristics than they had in simpler times. Formerly the facts which people knew were of immediate interest and were directly ascertainable. So a case of local bankruptcy, or famine, or a succession crisis in the local lord's family could all be observed directly by everyone interested and affected. There was no global or national solidarity, and local events were only remotely connected with national political affairs. At that level a political elite operated and their doings were normally far removed from the little burgher who heard little about them and that largely from ballads and troubadours.

Today, however, global interconnectedness has been established by a network of communications systems. A sense of interdependency and interrelatedness is widely felt at least to some degree. As Ellul says, "A war in Laos, a revolution in Iraq, or an economic crisis in the United States will have direct consequences for the average Frenchman."[11] The facts of these matters therefore are important even though they cannot be obtained directly. They are known through "verbal knowledge conveyed by many intermediaries."[12] What is taken now for important fact can be experienced *directly* by very few people. The facts are colored and distorted somewhat in the network of their communication, but only those who know them directly could test this.

This leads Ellul to some gloomy conclusions which cast dark shadows on modern political intelligence. First of all, there is the emergence of the "nonfact"—that is, something which *does* indeed exist, but which never manages to register on public consciousness. Ellul cites the Nazi concentration camps. Thousands of people experienced the reality of these camps, but there is good evidence that they did not really register in the "psychopolitical universe" of Germany. Ellul notes that Admiral Karl Doenitz's diary reveals quite convincingly that he did not know what went on in these camps even as late as 1945. Many would say that Doenitz was guilty of a contrived naïveté. Not so, says Ellul. Many disagreeable facts do not register in the political world of indirect knowledge. Indeed, many agreeable facts do not register in the public mind. Public opinion "obeys mysterious rules, secret motives and forms and deforms itself irrationally. . . ."[13]

Ellul's conclusion is that "a fact is of no importance except when it collides with a well-established social stereotype, or when by the use of the mass media, public opinion is led to give it great importance."[14] It is the stereotypes of propaganda that have the greatest success in the psychopolitical universe. In this universe symbols have replaced experience. In these symbols prejudice and ignorance become firmly ensconced. Facts which jeopardize the reigning symbol system simply dissolve. There is the equivalent of concentration camps in every society the reality of which will not be evidenced in the diaries of the people.

What is interesting in Ellul's viewpoint is that he seems to have reached a conclusion similar to that of philosopher George Berkeley in another sphere of thought. Berkeley came to the conclusion that *esse est percipi* (to be is to be perceived). This coheres with Ellul's position that events which do not become expressed in public opinion may have local significance but they are as nonbeing in the political arena. The assassination of Archduke Francis Ferdinand was enough to trigger the initial events of World War I. The fact entered into public opinion immediately. In another time the death of such an archduke may have passed with only a whimper of sympathy at most. In the circumstances of Europe in 1914 this shooting would have a terrible echo in the slaughterous unfolding of "the Great War." Events and statements in Russia and China today do not produce the same reaction they did fifteen years ago in the United States. Public opinion has changed. In my terms, the myths have changed.

Ellul seems to overstate his case when he says that "a fact that does not command attention and does not become a political fact ceases to exist even as a fact, whatever its importance may be."[15] But the substance of his thesis seems true. Knowledge in the political universe is heavily mediated. Abstract images and stereotypes have better access to the mind than concrete realities. The "psychopolitical universe" is a natural breeding ground for distorting myths.

It is an obvious fact that persons *en masse* can change with such rapidity and to such contradictory positions that an individual who did the same would be recommended for psychiatric care. For example, our attitude toward the Germans in the beginning of this century was quite benign. They were perceived as industrious and clever folk. The Wright brothers got help from Germans for the technology of their first airplane. The Germans looked fine at this time in our psychopolitical universe. Then came the war. The *Lusitania* was sunk, and even though it became known later that it was carrying munitions, this fact became an unambiguous symbol of German perfidy.[16] Suddenly, all the symbols changed. The Germans were Huns. Killing them was redemption for the earth. Even the German language became taboo in many parts of this country and sauerkraut had to be called "liberty cabbage." Then the war ended, and with the imposition of unrealistic reparations on the Germans, our crusading spirit was sated, and gradually the Huns left and the Germans returned—even the sauerkraut came back. We were slow to react to the demonic qualities of Hitler, but when we did the Germans became Huns again. Today they are once again revered international partners, more respected than many of those who were our allies in the war.

In studies done in 1942 and again in 1966 respondents in the United States were asked to choose from a list of adjectives those that best described the people of Russia, Germany, and Japan. In 1942 the Germans and the Japanese, who were then enemies, were seen as "warlike," "treacherous," and "cruel." None of these adjectives was chosen for the Russians, who were then allies. By 1966 the Germans and Japanese were no longer treacherous or warlike or cruel. These adjectives now described the Russians.[17]

In a similar study a Russian-speaking American psychologist did some interviews in Russia to see how the people viewed the United States. He found that the Russians felt that the Americans were the aggressors in the international sphere, that the American government exploited and deluded its people, that the American people did not fully support the government, and that American leaders could not be trusted since their foreign policy bordered on madness.[18] Parallel images were, of course, common in the United States vis-à-vis the Russian situation.

Toward the end of World War II, Harry Hopkins, an adviser to President Roosevelt, reflected the sanguine view of the Russians, and of Stalin in particular. "The Russians had proved that they could be reasonable and far seeing, and there wasn't any doubt in the minds of the President or any of us that we could live with them and get along with them peacefully for as far into the future as any of us could imagine."[19] Mr. Hopkins reported "that we could not foretell what the results would be if anything should happen to Stalin. We felt sure that we could count on him to be reasonable and sensible and understanding—but we could never be sure who or what might be back of him there in the Kremlin."[20] Within six months, at Potsdam, while Stalin was still the chief negotiator, a different message was heard. President Truman had never seen "such a pig-headed people."[21] In January of 1946 he wrote to Secretary James Byrnes: "Unless Russia is faced with an iron fist and strong language, another war is in the making. Only one language do they understand—'how many divisions have you?' "[22]

By this time Russia had begun to extend its control over Eastern Europe. In the mythic euphoria reflected by Hopkins, no sound estimates were made as to what Russia was likely to do to establish its security after the devastation of the war. Myths of diabolic messianism succeeded the euphoric myths projecting on the Russians' intentions that exceeded both their possibilities and their needs. The diabolic myths were the myths of which the cold war was made. Now these have waned and a new Russia is in sight. *and we have returned to the old myths*

Times of crisis seem to make mythic thinking even more unreliable. In April of 1942, 112,000 Americans of Japanese descent were shipped to the interior of the country and installed (literally) in abandoned stables. All of this was done on two weeks' notice, without any reference to due process, and, in fact, not one of the 112,000 was at that time or thereafter accused of an act of disloyalty. The claims of one of these persons, Korematsu, were tested all the way to the Supreme Court in what Milton Mayer calls "one of the most disconsoling cases ever brought to the bar in America."[23]

The right to seize a citizen without trial, deprive him of his property, and imprison him indefinitely was upheld by the Supreme

Court in an opinion written by Justice Hugo Black—a man who has been described as "that single-minded advocate of individual liberty." Black held with the majority that "we cannot reject as unfounded the judgment of the military authorities and of Congress that there were disloyal members of that population, whose number and strength could not be precisely and quickly ascertained. . . ."[24] One dissenting opinion pointed out that Korematsu was judged a criminal for belonging to a race from which there was no way to resign. The majority of the Court, however, missed the point, as did the majority of those in the nation. Aside from the nebulosity of the term "disloyal" it can be noted that no one today would argue that Americans of Russian, Chinese, or Latvian descent could be similarly dispossessed of their rights on the grounds that some unascertainable number of them might be "disloyal." The Korematsu story cannot, I submit, be understood apart from the category of myth. Were we dealing here with an intemperate decision of a battlefield commander, it could be explained in terms of stressful conditions that permitted no reflection. But that it could be blessed even in the reflections of the highest court of the land in the face of eloquent minority dissent shows the capacity of the mind to be utterly beguiled by the power of myth. Potent myths were still in control of American consciousness at that time, and even the best-trained minds fell prey. This illustrates the inadequacy, in ethics as in law, of a method of discernment which takes no account of the realities of social psychology. Here was a case where it could be said that "to be is to be perceived." Korematsu's rights were not perceived in the myth-heavy darkness of that time. For most people, even high levels of legal and ethical sophistication were not enough to dispel that darkness. In such a time, the normal skills of discernment are as nothing; the myth is as all.

The myths surrounding communism offer similar examples of blindness. Americans have long held in the highest esteem the principles of the Bill of Rights and the ideal of freedom. Nevertheless, as late as 1963, the American Institute of Public Opinion and the National Opinion Research Center found that "68% of Americans would not allow a Communist to make a speech; 66% would remove his books from the library; 91% would fire him from a high school teaching post; 89% would fire him from a college professorship; 68% would fire him from a clerk's job in a store; 61% would put him in jail; and 64% would allow the government to eavesdrop on his or on anyone else's telephone conversation in order to get evidence against Communists."[25]

This does not mean that myths are to be viewed as inexorably overwhelming. There was a minority that saw through the myth enveloping the Korematsu case, and the myths surrounding communism have been eased. What is required first of all by sound ethics is consciousness of the mythic bent of our knowing. Acknowledgment is the beginning of criticism. Jacques Ellul yields to too much gloom in noting the favorable conditions for distorted thought in the collectivity. The very forces that enhance the creation of myths can demythologize. The shrinkage of the planet through communication and mobility thrusts us against competing cultures and world views. The kind of soporific enclosure that nourishes and preserves myths is now hard to come by. Myths in collision are less secure. Still myths do retain their stubborn fiber in any context. Just as our forebears could outgroup other world views by calling them heathen or barbaric, we too are endowed with an enduring facility for confident excommunication. A critical awareness of the obsessive and distorting influence of myth is the precondition for discernment.

Myth and the Understanding of History . . .

Historical consciousness is a requisite safeguard against naïveté. In human affairs we must know something of the whence to know the where and the whither. Myth is an important analytical category for the perfecting of our historical knowledge. The data of the past is raw and confusing if ripped out of its mythic context. And since the past lays heavily upon the present shape of things, our own self-understanding is at peril if we do not look into the mythic forces that helped give us our actual form. Had the myths been different, we too would now be different.

One of the most striking examples of the historic presence of myth centers on the person and the work of one Joachim of Flora. Though Joachim is not a household name today, the respected scholar Eric Voegelin argues that "Joachim created the aggregate of symbols which govern the self-interpretation of modern political society to this day."[26] Joachim broke with other conceptions of the course of history and applied the symbol of the Trinity as a master rubric. He speculated that the history of mankind had three periods corresponding to the three persons of the Trinity. The first period in history was the period of the Father. The second period, beginning with Christ, was the age of the Son; and the final period will be the age of the Spirit. The three ages will be characterized by intelligible increases in spiritual fulfillment. The leader of the first age was Abraham, the second, Christ, and the leader of the third and final age was due to appear in 1260, given Joachim's calculation of the prototypical length of the first age.

Joachim's trinitarian symbolism had an unlikely but prodigious impact. In effect, he gave birth to a myth in which history would be adequately understood as a sequence of three ages in which the last would be the ultimate in fulfillment. Voegelin mentions some of the applications of Joachim's master rubric that have extended into our own time.

> As variations of this symbol are recognizable the humanistic and encyclopedist periodization of history into ancient, medieval, and modern history; Turgot's and Comte's theory of a sequence of theological, metaphysical, and scientific phases; Hegel's dialectic of the three states of freedom and self-reflective spiritual fulfillment; the Marxian dialectic of the three stages of primitive communism, class society, and final communism; and finally, the National Socialist symbol of the Third Realm. . . .[27]

Voegelin sees further reflections of Joachim's vision in the Franciscan revival which saw St. Francis of Assisi as the leader of the final spiritual age. It also shows through in Dante's speculation on the leader of the new spiritual age, in Machiavelli's Prince, and in the secularized supermen of Condorcet, Comte, and Marx. Joachim's final age would be marked by the withering away of the Church and the development of men into a community of the spiritually perfect who can live together without dependence on institutional structuring. Voegelin finds traces of this in medieval and Renaissance sects, in the Puritan churches of the saints, and, in secular dress, in the "Marxian mysticism of the realm of freedom and the withering-away of the state."[28] It is also a discernible component of the contemporary faith in democracy.

Joachim, in his most egotistical moment, could scarcely have dreamed that his shadow would be so long. What he might be said to have done, aside from the particular references of Voegelin, was to give a special tilt to the myth of modernity. *Modern* is a weighted word. Etymologically, it comes from *hodiernus, hodie*—that is, it refers to today, to that which is now existing. It was originally a term to distinguish present realities from the past, as in the expression "our most gracious queen modern" where it did not signify that the queen was "up to date" but that she was the queen at this time. Gradually, however, the term picked up normative connotations. Not to be modern is to be imperfect. The related word is *passé*, which carries strong impressions of turning one's nose up at that which is so described. Direct lineage to Joachim could not easily be established in this linguistic development, but it can at least be said that the contemporary usage of "modernity" is filled with Joachimite presuppositions.

Modern does not just mean that which is most recent; it means, further, that which is in some way definitive in its excellence. It certainly imports a denial of our relative primitivity. Morally speaking, judging from the chaotic and inequitable distribution patterns that exist among the human species, it could be said that primitive describes us well. Geologically speaking we are, on a scale, in the early beginnings of a twenty-four-hour day. Temporally, the earth has some twelve billion years to go before it is swallowed up in the solar apocalypse—that is, if we behave and do not induce premature planetary calamity. The sense of qualitative or temporal ultimacy, therefore, implied in "modern" is certainly mythic. We are only modern in the sense that the term is used in geology and zoology— that is, as belonging to a comparatively recent period in the life history of the world.

Furthermore, when you marry the mythic content of "modern" to the mythic belief that technology is the badge of human development (witness the loaded term "underdeveloped peoples"), an unconscionable moral complacency can ensue. If we have reached the definitive phase of human development, the "third realm," why not rest a bit and wait for its blessing to unfold? Moral imagination and sensitivity could only atrophy in the false peace of these myths.

Much of the well-received political rhetoric in the United States about our being "the greatest and best country in the world" has more than a hint of Joachim in it. Why should the saints of the final days curtail their extravagances! Americans are disinclined to see themselves as one small segment of the human race which is at the early stages of building community upon this precious earth. Our disposition, rather, is to see ourselves as a blessed culmination of human

destiny. A comparison of the American mind to a religious sect of
the saved is not without fruit. And the need for a discerning ethics
to be aware of this infectious mentality should be obvious. Otherwise, our ethics, however ingenious in its unfolding, will be done in
an atmosphere of unreality.

Myth and Morals in the American Political Experience . . .

It is no simple matter to get a critical view of one's own myths.
Since the myth defines reality for us, it is a major critical achievement to discover wherein it is unreal. History is an indispensable critical tool. When we see the operation of the myths of another time,
we can get a clearer idea of the dynamics of the myth. Then too, if
yesterday's myths are still with us in clever disguise, we may be able
to get to their influence in the moral discernment of today.

On March 13, 1842, the Reverend Sylvester Judd delivered a discourse to the people of his Unitarian Church in Augusta, Maine.
Judd's words were published under the copious title: A Moral Review of the Revolutionary War or Some of the Evils of That Event
Considered. As the title can suggest, Judd was accosting a heavily
mythologized event. In his address he criticized the motives of the
colonists for going to war, suggested that the goals of the war could
have been peacefully achieved, deplored the barbaric behavior of the
American freedom-fighters, and excoriated our genocidal treatment
of the Indians. When he gave the address, Judd was the chaplain of
the House of Representatives and the Senate of the state of Maine.
One day later, he received the following communication:

> State of Maine,
> House of Representatives, March 14, 1842
>
> Ordered, That Rev. Mr. Judd be dismissed as chaplain
> of this House.
>
> Read and Passed. Attest: Wm. T. Johnson, Clerk.[29]

Judd adds that "a note of similar import was received from the
Senate."[30] Judd was charged with libeling the patriots of the revolution. In the published introduction of his discourse he says in his
own defense (writing in the third person): "In the conduct of the
discourse, he has confined himself chiefly to facts; facts which are a

matter of historical record, facts which in the copiousness of the references are open to every ones revisions. If there be any sentiments in the discourse, they are the sentiments of facts . . . if any libel it is the libel of facts. He took the facts as he found them, too stubborn things to be winked out of sight, and he presented them as he found them, hoping that the facts, and the *facts alone*, would have weight with his hearers."[31] Judd would discover, in the language of a later day, that the facts would not be perceived as facts in the psychopolitical universe of his time.

It is illuminating to rehearse just a few of the things that Judd recounted in his rather heavily footnoted discourse. He first of all pointed out that the British contracted huge debts as a result of the Seven Years' War with France. The taxes that so aggrieved some of the colonists were, he argues, within reasonable limits in view of the great expanses of rich land that the colonists got after the French defeat. He speaks of the "dictatorship of Washington" and the absolute despotism that reigned in this country for the space of six months."[32] During this period and beyond it, the army was empowered to take what it wanted from people and to arrest and confine anyone who would appear to be "disaffected to the American cause."[33] He quoted accounts of the torture of soldiers and civilians by the revolutionary army, the popular weaknesses of support for the revolution, and the corruption of the officers and political leaders.

Judd was particularly emphatic about the abuse of the Indians. "They did not tax the Indians, without representation, but exterminated them and planted themselves in their territories."[34] He describes the treatment of the Six Nations of Indians who lived in New York. These Indians were "in the way of the western lands that had been promised to such Americans as would join the war." It was determined in the language of the times to "chastize these savages." General Washington ordered some troops under General Sullivan on this expedition. Judd relates the story:

> "The Six Nations," says De Witt Clinton, "were a peculiar and extraordinary people, contra-distinguished from the mass of the Indian nations, by great attainments in polity, in negotiation, in eloquence and in war." They inhabited the beautiful and fertile valley of the Genesee River. They had several towns, and many large villages, laid out with considerable regularity. They had framed houses, some of them well finished, having chimneys and painted. They had

broad and productive fields, orchards of apple, pear and peach trees. . . . Churches to the true God had been erected in their villages. Some of them were attached, as well as they could be, to the Americans. Sullivan, as I have said, started against them with peremptory instructions from General Washington not to listen to propositions of peace until he should have "very thoroughly completed the destruction of their settlements." . . . The American army approached the valley of the Genesee, which, says the historian, they beheld with astonishment and delight. "The town of Genesee contained one hundred and twenty-eight houses, mostly large and quite elegant. It was beautifully situated, almost encircled with a clear flat, extending miles around, over which extensive fields of corn were waving, together with every kind of vegetable that could be conceived. But the entire army was soon engaged in destroying it, and the axe and the torch soon transformed the whole of that beautiful region from the character of a garden to a scene of drear and sickening desolation. Forty Indian towns . . . were destroyed . . . the Indians were hunted like wild beasts till neither house, nor fruit tree, nor field of corn, nor inhabitant remained in the whole country. . . . I would add that General Washington after this received among the Indians the name of town destroyer, and in their bitter complaints against him they say, when "your name is heard, our women look behind them and turn pale, and our children cling close to the necks of their mothers."[35]

Judd's revisionist history fell with drastic suddenness upon the beautiful people of Augusta. His facts might, as he admitted, be contested by some on certain points. This, however, would imply a rational debate—something which obviously did not take place between the delivery of the address on March 13 and the reaction of the legislators on March 14. Judd was attacking the sacral myths of the people. He was also speaking to persons who were to some degree beneficiaries of the Indian repression. The actual historic facts had become irrelevant. Thus he could be dismissed with an expeditiousness that is hardly typical of the performance of any legislative body.

I have said that these myths were sacral. This compounded Judd's problems because of the peculiar power that accrues to the sacred and the religious. Religion, even in its perverted manifestations, has phenomenal power. As Huston Smith says, ". . . wherever religion comes to life it displays a startling quality; it takes over. All else, while not silenced, becomes subdued and thrown without contest into a supporting role."[36]

The myths that surround a nation's self-image are always limned with sacral hues. This religiosity is especially visible in the mythology of American patriotism. The American Revolution was credal in nature, consisting of events "under God." The foundational documents of the nation articulated this idea. The Puritan experience imbued America with notions of the promised people in the Promised Land. Early America was not just founding a nation but fulfilling a destiny. This land would be a saving sign to the aching monarchies of Europe of the freedom and democracy that were God's will for all men. The new Zion was in this nation, and energetic preachers drove home the idea that God was initiating a new era in the new world. The nation said *Amen* when Nathaniel W. Taylor preached with confidence that this nation was the one "on which the Sun of Righteousness sheds his clearest brightest day. . . ."[37]

Even the Civil War did not dispel this predestination complex. The war was seen as an expiatory event which further demonstrated our divine calling. Evidence of divine blessing in Union victories was traced out by George S. Phillips of Ohio in his literally incredible book, *The American Republic and Human Liberty Foreshadowed in Scripture*. Phillips averred that God's Old Testament promise to found a nation fully obedient to him was fulfilled when he established the United States. Phillips found our story in the pages of Sacred Scripture. According to him, Isaiah and Daniel clearly foretold the day and the hour of the Declaration of Independence; Isaiah predicted the Boston Tea Party and even the coming of Chinese immigrants to California. Phillips roared on to this conclusion: "The United States is to fill the earth . . . so to occupy the place of government in the world, as to leave room for no other government."[38] If Phillips were an outrider in the American tradition, he could be studied as a curiosity. In fact, as William A. Clebsch says of his work: "The patent unoriginality of Phillips' book signifies its representing a major body of religious and nationalistic sentiment in the north."[39]

The American mythology, with all of its religious underpinnings, can be seen in vigorous bloom in the words of President McKinley when he explained his decision to hold the Philippine Islands after our war with Spain. We had not wanted these islands, he avowed, but "they came to us, as a gift from the gods." He said that he sought help from Republicans and Democrats as to what to do with them, "but got little help." Then, he said, "I went down on my knees and prayed Almighty God for light and guidance more than one night." God apparently was not unresponsive. Late one night the answer came, according to McKinley. The islands could not be returned to Spain, for "that would be cowardly and dishonorable." Neither could we turn them over to our commercial rivals, France or Germany, for "that would be bad business and discreditable." (One wonders whether God is still speaking at this point and, if so, one must credit him with a keen sense of business—at least for American business.) Our duty, as McKinley saw it, was to "uplift and civilize and Christianize" the people of the Philippines and "by God's grace do the very best we could for them as our fellowmen for whom Christ also died."[40]

Later Warren G. Harding while still a United States senator would look back on our work in the Philippines and dub it "the most magnificent contribution of a nation's unselfishness ever recorded in the history of the world." Comparing our heady new imperialism to no less a personage than Jesus Christ, Harding professed "that we ought to go on with the same thought that impelled Him who brought a plan of salvation to the earth. Rather than confine it to the Holy Land alone, He gathered his disciples about him and said, 'go ye and preach the gospel to all nations of the earth.' "[41] These words were uttered in the Senate and addressed to "Mr. President and Senators."

Either one of two things might be appearing in such utterances: hypocrisy or myth. It could be that McKinley and Harding knew better. There is evidence that at one point McKinley did. When Spain was ready for peace, he had instructed the Secretary of the Navy to investigate "the desirability of the several islands; the character of their population, coal and other mineral deposits; their harbor and commercial advantages; and in a naval and commercial sense, which of the islands would be the most advantageous."[42] Still even at this same time he was filled with notions of "benevolent assimilation," and the myth of our "manifest destiny" weighed heavily upon him. It would seem simplistic to explain his description of his prayerful decision to hold the Philippines simply as lying.

As to Harding, according to his biographer, W. F. Johnson, he maintained his pious interpretation of the seizure of the Philippines to the day of his death. And there is no doubt that the pious interpretation was common among the American people. The evidence permits us to say that reality was being "refracted, filtered, and interpreted" through myth in a way that is significant for history, politics, social psychology, and ethics. George F. Kennan has faced the question of why we annexed the Philippines and reached the conclusion that "the fact of the matter is that down to the present day we do not know the full answer to this question."[43] Nevertheless, I would say that without the category of myth we cannot even address that question intelligently. Myth is not the only tool we can bring to an analysis of such a period; it is, however, indispensable. The use of it does not excuse us from hard and patient analysis of the power and interests of nations. Political analysis and political ethics are not just myth-analysis. The point here is that myth, especially when its presence is unsuspected, is a serious hazard for moral inquiry, and its influence must be critically calculated.

Kennan's study illumines the mythic elements in our decision to enter the war in the first place. The causes regularly cited for this war are the extreme harshness of Spain's Cuban policy, the leaked and published letter of the Spanish minister in Washington that insulted President McKinley, and the sinking of the *Maine*. These causes, however, do not explain the consequent military outburst. A new government had just come to power in Spain that seemed more moderate in its attitudes toward Cuba; the imprudent minister was immediately removed with proper apologies; and, as Kennan says of the *Maine*,

> . . . there has never been any evidence that the Spanish government had anything to do with the sinking of the vessel. . . . Spanish authorities, as well as our own consul-general in Havana, had begged us not to send the vessel there at that time for the very reason that they were afraid this might lead to trouble. The Spanish government did everything in its power to mitigate the effects of the catastrophe, welcomed investigation, and eventually offered to submit the whole question of responsibility to international arbitration—an offer we never accepted.[44]

Possibilities of fruitful negotiations with Spain were ignored. Alternatives to war were bypassed. Something other than a direct perception of the reality of the situation was operating.

Myth and Ideology . . .

The notion of myth as I am using it is obviously related to *ideology*. Ideology, however, is a broader term. It is also a highly ambiguous term, and the literature of social science and history reveals that it can have a large number of meanings. It is, I believe, accurate to say that, normally, the term has a broader meaning than myth and that it does imply more systematized thought than does myth. André Dumas, for example, sees ideologies as "methods of thought." Ideologies, he says, "are based on a scientific interpretation . . . [and] on a human awareness which has power to organize."[45] And, again, "ideology is a rational system of collective needs."[46] Dumas argues, and I disagree, that ideologies have replaced myths. I believe they contain myths and, to some degree, marshal them into the work of understanding and organizing collective movements. But, more than myth, ideology imparts a rational and organizing element. It also carries its own historically derived pejorative connotations. After its first popularization in the beginning of the nineteenth century, it came quickly to be associated with highly abstract thinking. Napoleon said that all the misfortunes of France were due to ideology, and for Marx it was a pathology of human knowledge that would be eliminated in a classless society. It was the "tissue of lies" that societies drape over their actual purposes. However, given the linguistic facts of life, one must be judged on how he chooses to use these verbal vagabonds which are, it seems, inevitably with us, at least for a time.

Ross Terrill, for example, relates ideology to myth in a way that I find more congenial. He refers to the ideology of "American messianism" which is "based upon the myth of New World virtue that attached to the founding of America, free from the corruptions of Europe, and upon the myth of New World mission. . . ."[47] Myth in this usage is something within ideology and it is something upon which ideology may build.[48]

With this clarification in mind, then, we can return to the presence of myth in the American political experience. Terrill cites the messianic myth in the words of President Johnson when he left for Asia in October of 1966 announcing in a way that could scarcely have edified the Asians: "I have a great many objectives . . . for the people of that area of the world." Terrill sees it too in the voice of

the New York *Times* after Britain announced its withdrawal from
Asia. "The arc from Arabia to the China Sea becomes virtually our
responsibility." And again, the editors of *Look* magazine said in May
of 1967: "The Far East has now become our Far West."[49]

Given the facts of life that are only coming to light in our consciousness now, another statement of Johnson's made in 1965 seems
almost ill in its unrealism. He said: "History and our own achievements have thrust upon us the principal responsibility for protection
of freedom on earth. . . ."[50] We paid an unacceptable price to
break out of that myth which convinced us that we had the power
and mission to protect "freedom" all over the world and to "make
the world safe for democracy" regardless of the preferences or possibilities of individual nations. While this myth was in full flower,
however, today's somewhat more modest foreign policy goals would
have struck most Americans as proximate to treason. Such is the
might of myth. Myths reject unwelcome and contradicting facts as a
body repels a foreign substance and ideologies are filled with myths.
The facts, however, remain facts. Therein lies the hazard.

Rollo May refers to the "second Copernican revolution" in modern thought achieved by Immanuel Kant. He writes: "Kant held
that the mind is not simply passive clay on which sensations write, or
something which merely absorbs and classifies facts. . . . Kant's revolution lay in making the human mind an active, forming participant in what it knows. Understanding, itself, is then constitutive of
its world."[51] This basic insight is one that must be advanced so as to
see the specific and varied ways in which the mind is an active participant in what it knows. This participation becomes a hazard when
the interpretive aspect of knowing barters away our reality contact
and confuses the figment for the fact. This is what happens in the
hazard of myth. We can prefer our conceptualization of the reality
to the reality itself. The Flemish Vesalius turned the study of anatomy around in 1543 with his book *The Structure of the Human
Body*. Before this time, in what is a sorry lesson on human epistemology, "anatomists had generally held that the writings of Galen,
dating from the second century A.D., contained an authoritative description of all human muscles and tissues. They had indeed dis-
sected cadavers, but had dismissed those not conforming to Galen's
description as somehow abnormal or not typical."[52] Galen's views
had functioned as a myth functions by becoming a data-resistant in-

terpretive screen. Vesalius broke through to reality and thus becomes the symbol of the myth breaker, as Galen was the symbol of myth. In other ways we should presume that there are upon our minds the effective ghosts of more than one Galen, blocking discoveries and thus preventing the growth of moral consciousness.

Myth lives, for example, in economics in those who believe that growth is an inbuilt characteristic of society and that the alternative to it is decay. This myth conceals the morally and economically relevant fact, in André Dumas's words, that "growth has no qualitative aim. It is the rule of means which have no collective ends."[53] Myth also hovers over the establishment of education, giving prestige to the fact of education regardless of its direction and effects. Myth can convince us that progress is inevitable or impossible, that Euro-American civilization is paradigmatic for humanity, that violence is the most reliable form of power, that industrialization and success are as one, etc. Morality is based on reality, and discerning ethics, to get to that reality, must work through myth. Attending to it, therefore, is not an optional exercise for ethics.

Cognitive Mood

The same event or the same physical object will not look the same to a child, a dying person, a lover, a businessman, a poet, a Wisconsin farmer, or a Stone Age tribesman. Neither will any of these persons view that same reality in the same unchanging light. Each of them represents a different mood, and even the mood each represents will vary. Mood affects how we see, and its influence might at times be controlling. Even a child learns early that there are times to ask for something and times when the request is best postponed. From our childhood we sense the impact of mood on how one will see and evaluate. Mood is a conditioner of our subjectivity. It can sharpen our vision, or place a veil between us and reality. It can also induce a darkness that sends us back apologizing later when another mood ensues and lends light. The cognitive effect of mood, then, is not always negative. But since it can be and since mood is such an omnipresence, it merits consideration among the hazards of moral discourse.

To move toward a descriptive definition of this large and complex category of human subjectivity, the observations of a thoughtful traveler might provide a key. The traveler is in Morocco and he writes of what he experiences there.

A dazzling sun falls on the whitewashed dwellings of Tangiers. The sea is turquoise, and behind the dwellings rise high and noble palms. The Mediterranean clime inspires a feeling of timelessness. Tomorrow is just an extension of today; it has no separate, threatening identity. It would be a strange man or woman who could live principally by calculation in Tangiers. These people wait long periods for each other and are patient with nature. They give themselves fully to the present moment. The future does not mortgage them; the past sits naturally upon them and grows within them. In the peace of Morocco, life and the world seem fully embodied in the tangibles that can be felt in the present moment. A line of Camus hangs on my mind: "I am learning that there is no superhuman happiness, no eternity outside the curve of the days." . . . The morning mood on Tangiers' main boulevard has no throb or rush. People move as languidly as in the hours after lunch. The shops open desultorily one by one. . . .[54]

Our astute observer senses something here that is more easily described than analyzed. But much of what struck the author of this gracious description can be captured in the word "mood." Obviously in the background is an experience of another mood and another place and clime, where the shops do not open desultorily one by one and where impatient achievers, mortgaged to the future, rush through the present almost as though they were in flight from it. The mood of Tangiers is different; it is easier to say that than to say what makes it so. The weather, the degree of cultural homogeneity, the animating religious faith of the people, hard-learned historical lessons about the futility of spastic activism, a sense of hope, or maybe its opposite. All of the above and more may enter in some part into the mood so sharply felt by the foreign visitor to Morocco. But whatever the causes of the mood, the effects are many and significant. Different things are prized and different expectations reign over human affairs. Tracing the impact of all of this would not just be a cultural study of ethics, but a study of economics, politics, art, and psychology in Morocco. Mood casts long shadows over all our valuing whether those values be aesthetic, commercial, or specifically moral.

What we touch on when we speak of mood is the spirit of the
people and the complete atmosphere in which they work and do
their valuing. It is not just the thinking animal that evaluates; it is
the thinking, feeling, sensing, believing, reacting, geographically and
culturally situated animal that responds to value. He does not operate in a void but in an enormity of internal and external contex-
tualizing factors. Mood is a large category of this valuational context.
How precisely can we describe it?

Mood is broader than myth (and indeed includes myths) and cannot be as neatly defined. In fact it is description rather than definition that we can bring to this rich term. Mood is an affective and intellectual mode of attunement to an environment.[55] It signifies a
certain bent of mind, or mind-set, reflective of one's personal and
cultural orientation. Unlike myth, mood can refer to a private and
intrapersonal or social and cultural reality. The mood of the person,
however, could not be entirely unrelated to the cultural moods that
are his vital matrix. A mood reflects the accents within the psychic
air. Certain things are cherished and certain things are ignored. Certain doors are open while the existence of others is unsuspected. The
mood of most American blacks before the 1950s was one in which
some aspirations were simply excluded by what was seen to be the
nature of things. Paolo Freire's work on *conscientization* opened up
the minds of the poor in South America to the fact that their
deprivation was not an ontological and immutable datum. For this
reason, the forces of oppressive government were instinctively shrewd
enough to challenge and ban his work, since he would transform the
mood of the passive poor.

Mood also arises from salient decisions or commitments that have
been made. The Declaration of Independence in some significant
ways changed the mood of the colonies, and even those who had little enthusiasm for rebellion could not be entirely immune to the lure
of the new mood. A deeply felt decision to become committed and
loyal to a person or a cause transforms one's mood and frame of perception.

Sometimes the collection of our deeds creates a consuming mood.
Hannah Arendt notes a fundamental change in attitudes resulting
from the successes of science. She writes: "The radical change in
moral standards occurring in the first century of the modern age was
inspired by the needs and ideals of its most important group of men,
the new scientists; and the modern cardinal virtues—success, indus-

try, and truthfulness—are at the same time the greatest virtues of modern science."[56] Similarly, the heady discoveries of science in the nineteenth century created a mood filled with airs of infallibility that affected the men of science, state, and church. Even our sense of history was adversely affected by the mood that science made. The scientific West came to believe that history was as malleable as laboratory materials—that it was controlled by calculation and strategy and marked by predictable results. Those caught in the pull of such moods and the accompanying myths are as handicapped as prisoners unless they know of such a force and are disposed to test for its presence.

Religion is also a mood-maker. The framers of our Constitution, for example, were not just pragmatic students of social planning. They were that, but they also were animated by a religious conception of what man is and what he needs. As Horace White put it years ago, the Constitution of the United States "is based upon the philosophy of Hobbes and the religion of Calvin. It assumes that the natural state of mankind is a state of war, and that the carnal mind is at enmity with God."[57]

Belief is a normal state of man, whether it amounts to religious faith or not. As Tocqueville declared: "Unbelief is an accident, and faith is the only permanent state of mankind."[58] And belief is not limited to formal religion. Even the philosopher and the man of reason is filled with it. Again Tocqueville: "There is no philosopher in the world so great but that he believes a million things on the faith of other people and accepts a great many more truths than he demonstrates."[59] We have neither the time nor the power to demonstrate all that we need to accept to make life feasible and possibly good. And, therefore, we believe. There is nothing irrational in this, as I have argued above (see Chapter Three): Belief is an achievement of discerning affectivity. Though it may be utterly misguided and foolish, it may also have access to truth that reason cannot reach. This fact of our cognitive nature is important for an understanding of mood. What we believe and what we then dare hope for set the tone and make the mood in which we know and evaluate. Those who believe little and hope little will see life through dark eyes. Their mood will be chill and self-preservative. Creativity will not be their forte, for creativity proceeds from mood—not inexorably or without that discontinuity that is the mark of genius—but mood relates to those preconditions that set the stage for the creative leap.

In the words of an Irish poet, there are those who are "born of homes that never bred a dream." Moods too can be like those sterile dreamless homes.

Though it is true that our decisions and commitments can importantly affect our moods, it must be said that mood is never entirely of our making. To some degree it comes upon us for good or for ill. Certainly we cannot reason ourselves into one or out of one. The arrival and the departure of the mood have their own pace. Mood is, after all, affected by other people and even by such unmanageable things as weather and climate. When Montesquieu published his *Spirit of the Laws*, in 1748, he reported his conclusion of seventeen years of work: that a large variety of factors had to be considered to understand the laws of any people. One had to look to the economic facts of those people as well as to what could be called their character. Beyond this Montesquieu said it was necessary to look at their climatic conditions, for as he saw it, the climate helps to form the character and passions of a people. The British are simply not like the Sicilians, and laws fitted for one would hardly serve the good of the other. Montesquieu did not see the climate factor as utterly determinative of the spirit of their laws and institutions, but as a clear influence. Similarly, I would say that climate and geography are factors that may enter in and shape mood. Climate can influence the tempo of life, as well as our choice of symbols, our closeness to or alienation from the earth, and our dependence on technology. All of these factors have resonance in the thinking and feeling subject.

Mood also relates to the action-reaction pendulum in human values. Though we are always in search of the elusive center that we call balance, human history is marked by broad and eccentric swings. We move from Victorian discomfort with sex to contemporary pornography in all of its frantic forms. We can move from global messianism to isolationist nationalism, from comfort with established values to suspicion of all that is socially structured. So the symbol of the pendulum must again be recalled to understand mood. What we are reacting against is often most revealing of why we are for what we are for. What we are reacting against, as we ride the pendulum from one unbalanced view to another, is also a mood-setter of which we cannot afford to be unaware.

Finally, it can be said of mood that it may be transient and ephemeral or enduring, just as it may be personal or somewhat settled into a culture. Sometimes mood will be of little relevance to our evaluation and represent a very minor epistemological consideration. At times it can be controlling. Ethics must maintain a critical awareness of the reality and strength of mood. It must remind the valuing animal that he is not a smoothly meshing reasoning machine but a buffeted beast who is caught in the swirl of myriad enveloping influences. To ignore all of this and not attempt to get some critical assessment of it represents an unacceptable naïveté.

One of the most common human failings is simplistic epistemology. Part of the original sin of everyman is to think that reality is there and we see it with mirrorlike immediacy and reliability. The chastening gospel that ethics must preach is that even mirrors can deceive and that, mirrors aside, we tend to see only what we are willing to see. Myths and moods condition our willingness to see. We are substantially limited by the language and symbols available to us in our time and culture. Individually and collectively we are prone to infatuation. Knowledge is a process full of hazards which are especially damaging to those who think their path is clear. It is only when we know how we know that we can begin to be free.

False Analogues

All knowing is analogical and comparative. As we know, we relate the unknown to the known. This is not a hazard for moral understanding; this is simply a fact of our cognitive life to which I referred in the beginning of this chapter. Our experience gives us a fund of references to which the mind turns for enlightening comparison when something new presents itself. No two persons will have the same fund of experiences. The Trobriander tribesman and the vacationing heiress will not bring the same ensemble of recollects to bear when they see an impression in the sand. We know out of our histories, and since our histories are unique, there is a unique character to the way each of us knows. (Hence the advisability of consulting many minds in complex moral matters.)

The problem arises when our analogical knowing is based on false analogues. When we are coming to know something new, an ensemble of what I have called recollects is instinctively summoned. Not all of our recollects will be called forth—only those which appear to have similarity to that which is now being known. Herein lies the hazard. We can be so impressed with how similar the new candidate for knowledge is that we overlook the differences. The analogical aspect of our knowing process can easily dull our perception of what is new and unique. In fact, this is what regularly happens, and it is for this reason that false analogues must be given special attention.

Our proclivity to draw too much from comparisons is understandable in view of the gains that are temptingly offered by this indulgence. For one thing, the mind's gnawing hunger for making sense of things is quickly satisfied if the new is exactly like the old. Our minds are comfortable with the familiar, and this comfort can give rise to the level of passion in those whom we classify imperfectly as conservative. Many persons are so committed to conflating the new into the old that they will reject the new if this cannot be conveniently done. "I have never heard of such a thing" will be seen by such persons as a disqualification and invalidation of that about which they are now for the first time hearing.

Tying in to this is our natural wariness of surprise. Too much surprise is unsettling and we are inclined to minimize it. False analogues are a natural way to do this. Their use, however, entails no slight hazard. What it does is commit us to a cyclic view of history, or in the words of William Stringfellow: "It reduces history to redundancy."[60] Stringfellow notes the limits of the saying that "history repeats itself." Of it he says: "I reject this view of history as false, misleading, escapist. I esteem history as ambiguous, versatile, dynamic."[61] Without denying that we are likely to repeat history's blunders if we do not know history, it must be said, with a view to the point we are stressing here, that whether we know history or not, we will not entirely repeat it. In its totality as well as in its details, it cannot be perfectly replicated. Thus in assessing the present or projecting for the future, history is an essential but partial aid. An appeal to history can actually be the last firm bastion of a closed mind.

Like all that touches on morality, the effects of false analogues are practical and often crucial for persons. President Truman had a great fondness for history and undoubtedly it often stood him in good stead. His use of history, however, also reveals the perils of false historical analogues. Glenn D. Paige says that Truman believed that today's problems were thrust forth from the past and that the past also revealed appropriate solutions for those problems. "Thus he held that for 'almost all' present problems there were precedents that would provide clear guides to right principles of action. With history as an unambiguous moral teacher, decision making became an exercise in applying its lessons. An occasion for decision became a stimulus to search for past analogy."[62] Richard Barnet writes that as the Truman Doctrine took shape along with our decision to stop the uprising in Greece, "no one in the national-security bureaucracy appears to have ventured a political analysis of the Greek rebels, their relations with Russia, Yugoslavia, or the other Balkan neighbors. The fifth-column analogy from World War II dominated official thinking."[63]

This mind-set was also prominent in the President's decision leading to our entrance into the Korean War, a war in which more than 33,000 Americans were killed. Truman felt that the North Korean attack was the same in nature as the German, Italian, and Japanese aggressions that had led to World War II.[64] He also saw the Korean situation as an exact analogue of the Greek situation that he had already misinterpreted. Pointing to Korea on the large globe in his office, he announced: "This is the Greece of the Far East. If we are tough there now there won't be any next step."[65]

The reactions of senators showed the same uncritical reliance on past analogues. Senator Styles Bridges in Senate debate invoked the fateful memories of Manchuria, Poland, Czechoslovakia, Romania, and Bulgaria. Senator William F. Knowland, in facing the question of how quickly we should react in Korea, said: "We must constantly keep in mind that Holland was overrun by Nazi Germany in five days and Denmark in two."[66] Senator Abraham Ribicoff exclaimed: "What difference is there in the action of northern Koreans today and the actions which led to the Second World War? Talk about parallels!"[67]

Though not meant that way by Ribicoff, his question is *the* question: "What difference is there in the action of northern Koreans today and the actions which led to the Second World War?" Clearly there were differences. However one may view the ultimate values and disvalues of the Korean War, it is clear that the North Korean attack could not have made Korea the Greece, Manchuria, Poland, Czechoslovakia, Romania, Bulgaria, Holland, and Denmark of the East! Yet these analogues had significant influence not only on the decision to go to war but on the timing.

Concerning another event—the decision to go into Vietnam—Arthur M. Schlesinger comments: "The generalizing compulsions in our political rhetoric were reinforced by an uncritical addiction to historical analogy."[68] President Johnson, defending the decision to fight in Vietnam, said in a speech in Beaumont, Texas:

> In 1940 with most of Europe in flames, four Democratic senators . . . said that President Roosevelt could negotiate a just peace—that is, with Hitler—if he would only make an effort. Sounds kind of familiar doesn't it? . . . We are not going to be Quislings and we are not going to be appeasers, and we are not going to cut and run. . . . We do believe that if Hitler starts marching across the face of Europe that [sic] we ought not wait until the last minute to let him know that might doesn't make right.[69]

The remarkable thing about Johnson's statement was that by the end of it he was only speaking about Hitler. If that one sentence was taken out of the context and one were asked to date it, the date would certainly have to be in the 1930s and not in the mid-1960s. This illustrates the pernicious power of the false analogue. In judging X, we note that it is similar to A, B, and C. With that, attention shifts to A, B, and C and we might even turn our backs on X, which is what we started out to discuss. This phenomenon will not always appear in the blunt form displayed by Johnson in his Beaumont address. It is, nevertheless, even when well disguised, the basic difficulty of the obsessive analogue. In Johnson's more formal speech at Johns Hopkins, which in many ways marked the crystallization of the government's resolve to go for a victory in Vietnam, the European analogy was ruling: "We must say in Southeast Asia, as we did in Europe, in the words of the Bible: 'Hitherto shalt thou come, but no further.'" As to our responsibility for freedom in Vietnam, "We have it for the same reason we have a responsibility for the defense of freedom in Europe."[70] Another analogue made an interesting appearance in this speech. Referring to the principle of freedom, Johnson saw connections with early America: "This is the principle for which our ancestors fought in the valleys of Pennsylvania. It is the principle for which our sons fight in the jungles of Vietnam."[71]

Not all analogues are historical. For example, in the commitment to Vietnam the "domino theory" played a major role. The theory was that if Vietnam fell to the Communists, then all the other nations in the area would fall with a collapsing effect that might extend from Burma all the way to the Philippines. Here again is the baneful path of false analogy which does not make distinctions where there are differences. The analogy obscured Chinese interests and economic and military possibilities, as well as the very notable internal differences that marked each of the prospective "dominoes." Our analogies and metaphors can imprison us, deceptively convincing us that they encapsulate for us the actual stuff and data of the real.

The false analogies that I have employed as examples thus far are all political. Though it is true that "the feeble mind of a nation" is most susceptible to the compulsive simplisms of false analogizing, this mental hazard can also befall us in private and interpersonal contexts. Thus parents might easily use their first child as an analogue for their second without realizing the unique dynamism of this second child. If the reality of the first child becomes the domineering analogue, the authentic potential of the second child might be stunted and serious psychic wounds may be inflicted. Similarly, one business venture might be sidetracked by comparison to an earlier one that is similar but, of course, not identical with the present one. I have already noted the Nazi analogy which beclouds much of the discussion of our moral dominion over our dying, implying that any instance of mercy death in extreme circumstances, where death is deliberately accelerated because of unmanageable pain, is perfectly comparable to the events that produced the Nazi euthanasia slaughter. Historically, Stoic philosophers, and many Christian thinkers depending on the Stoa, taught that intercourse during pregnancy was wrong. A farmer, after all, does not sow seed in a field that is already planted and growing. The ancients were also generally confident in the sexual continence of pregnant animals and applied this analogy to persons. Pliny observed that "except for women, few pregnant animals copulate."[72] And so the Christian Origen condemned those women "who, like animals, serve lust without any restraint; indeed I would not compare them to dumb beasts. For beasts when they conceive know not to indulge their mates further with their plenty."[73]

The use of false analogies is obviously telling not only for ethics but for any logical discourse and any discipline. What it does in ethics is to block the expository phase wherein all the empirical data is brought before the discerning subject for analysis and comparison and contextually sensitive judgment. When false analogy has gained control, it will short-circuit this process and the moral judgment will be based more on figment than on fact.

Abstractions

Abstractions, like analogies and metaphors, are essential means of thought. To condemn abstract thinking in one sense is impossible and contradictory, since one could not do so without using abstractions. Abstraction is the soul of theory. As Marcuse says, ."Critical philosophic thought is necessarily transcendent and *abstract*. Philosophy shares this abstractness with all genuine thought, for nobody really thinks who does not abstract from that which is given, who does not relate the facts to the factors which have made them, who does not—in his mind—undo the facts. Abstractness is the very life of thought, the token of its authenticity."[74]

In this sense abstractness is the beginning of creativity. If we cannot abstract from the grip of the currently given, we will never perceive what might be. We could discover no ideals. If we could not abstract, we could only like animals register what is and live as prisoners of the status quo. Abstract comes from the Latin *ab*, "from," and *trahere*, "to draw." If we could not draw or pull away from the particulars that surround us, we could develop no generalizations or standards for critical judgment. Abstracting is a quest for the epitome of that which we know, beyond the particular manifestations of the individual reality known. It enables us to discover what constancies exist in this infinitely variegated universe. These constancies undergird our generalizations and give us a framework for judgment of particulars.

However, we must recall, again in Marcuse's words, that "there are false and true abstractions. Abstraction is an historical event in an historical continuum. It proceeds on historical grounds, and it remains related to the very basis from which it moves away. . . ."[75] Our abstracting power is such that we can move away too far; we can cut the essential ties that link realistic abstractions to the reality about which one is thinking, albeit abstractly. False abstractions have lost their chastening contact with the concrete and the historical. They become so detached from a chastening sense of the particular that they are unreal. It is this unreal sense of "abstract" that lexicographers are noting when they list as possible meanings of this term such things as impersonal, removed, separate, abstruse, or insufficiently factual.

It is always enlightening to see the gains behind such mental aberrations as false abstractions. Ease in the pursuit of meaning is the first and most obvious gain. It is obviously tempting to soar above the gritty complexities of the empirical order and impose meaning through detached abstractions from on high. To perceive reality through empirically innocent generalities is surely more commodious than learning what one is talking about. (One thinks of the comfortable churchman who commented confidently: "I know poverty. I have driven through it!") What is even more delightful is that the abstract presentation of truth can often sound impressively learned. Is not abstraction the hallmark of intellectuality! Here then is a form of reality avoidance that enjoys the sweetness of prestige. Only the facts could serve to embarrass it. And if the cognitive mood of the time is not all that concerned with the facts, and if the attendant myths add their special luster to the deceptive abstractions, the abstractions may long endure and flourish.

A related gain of false abstractions is that they serve as masks of our actual purposes. "Law and order," for example, is an abstraction. Adolf Hitler's use of the term in seeking election shows its value as an abstract mask:

> The streets of our country are in turmoil. The universities are filled with students rebelling and rioting. Communists are seeking to destroy our country. Russia is threatening us with her might, and the Republic is in danger. Yes, danger from within and from without. We need law and order. Yes, without law and order our nation cannot survive. Elect us and we shall restore law and order.[76]

The Ought-to-Is Fallacy

False abstractions illustrate the ought-to-is fallacy. In this fallacy, we can see how abstractions relate to the will and enter the service of its errant purposes. From the willful impression that this is the way things "ought to be," we can abstractly leap to the judgment that this is the way things are, or, in an inverse form of this fallacy, we can be so consumed by what we deem ought to be that we reject what is. The wish, then, is father to the abstraction. A young man (or an old one) may leave the concrete reality of his friend's genuine preferences and conclude—quite abstractly: "She ought to want to have sex with me. Therefore, she does." Subsequent pain and embarrassment may illustrate the rueful process of exorcism in which demonic abstractions are routed by forced immersion in concrete reality. At the political level we might similarly suppose that a nation should want a democratic system of government, and therefore it does. With such abstraction in control, it may take a long time to realize that the nation may be no more ready for democracy than the lady of our previous example was ready for sex—however regrettable this may appear to the abstracting minds in either case. This, however, is the way of the ought-to-is fallacy; it is not easily or painlessly undone.

Dostoevski uses the expression "abstract and therefore cruel." The ought-to-is fallacy of abstractness often justifies this conjunction, especially when it takes the form of our being so taken by what ought to be that we cannot cope with or accept what is. Parents of a genetically damaged child, for example, may fail to appreciate what the child is, obsessed as they can be with their stricken hopes of what he might have been. Their abstract conception of what he should be will overshadow the gentle beauties that may still be his. The vigor of personal life is such that we can anticipate that lovely forms of personality may even break through the frost of tragic genetic damage and come to blossom. Parents of children afflicted with Down's syndrome are now becoming aware that these children need not be relegated into oblivion as though no precious personal life could manifest itself in spite of the debits. It would, of course, be abstract in the worst sense, to say that the birth of a Down's baby is not normally tragic or that abortion could not be a moral option when an affected fetus is discovered by amniocentesis. Nevertheless, when the child is born, his concrete possibilities must be accepted and brought to full potential. What he *is* must not be sacrificed to what he "ought to" be.[77] The ought in that case is abstract; the child is real.

It should be noted that in good abstractions, the ought-to-is process is praiseworthy. When we abstract from the inadequate present and envision better possibilities, we are moving our perception of what ought to be toward creative being in a new *is*. In proper abstraction the *ought* is a pressure for transcendence to a better *is*. It proceeds from a vision of realistic ideals.

The ought-to-is fallacy shows something that is prominent in the misuse of abstraction—the stereotype. The stereotype generalizes even that which is not generalizable. In the stereotype, as in all false abstractions, the specific is blurred in the generic. The existence of genuine variety is ignored. For example, there was the example of the great American stereotype hidden in the symbol of the "melting pot." Now it has been discovered that the various cultural and ethnic branches have not homogenized into some stereotypical "American." Behind the idea of the melting pot was an abstract notion of nation and community which could not brook cultural pluralism and the real diversities that characterize humanity.

Abstractions then can be creative or beguiling. It is their negative potential that pertains to the theme of this chapter. False and detached abstractions are seductive—to some minds, it would seem, almost irresistibly so. Such abstractions also can be cruel or even lethal. Ethics must repair again to Sartre's insight that the greatest evil of which man is capable is to treat as abstract that which is concrete.

Words, Words, Words—and Abstractions

Thucydides, describing the conditions preceding the Peloponnesian War, complained that the meaning of words no longer had the same relation to things. This he saw as a major mark of the unrest of that time. Words are the houses of our thoughts and abstractions, good and bad, and a study of the use of words is an analytical necessity. Understanding is not limited to words. We know, feel, and intuit more than we could ever say. But words are the outstanding common symbols of what it is we mean.

Falstaff spotted this in Shakespeare's *Henry IV*. He saw that the good word "honor" was being asked to cover over abstractly some realities that he was not ready to bear. When battle with all of its call to glory and honor was imminent, the unimpressed Falstaff was reminded by the Prince.

PRINCE: Why thou owest God a death. (Exit) FALSTAFF: 'Tis not due yet, I would be loath to pay Him, before his day. What need I be so forward with him that calls not on me? Well, 'tis no matter. Honor pricks me on. Yea, but how if honor prick me off when I come on? How then? Can honor set to a leg? No. Or an arm? No. Or take away the grief of a wound? No. Honor hath no skill in surgery, then? No. What is honor? A word. What is in that word

honor? What is that honor? Air. A trim reckoning! Who
hath it? He that died o' Wednesday. Doth he feel it? No.
Doth he hear it? No. 'Tis insensible, then? Yea, to the
dead. But will it not live with the living? No. Why? De-
traction will not suffer it. Therefore I'll none of it. Honor is
a mere scutcheon. And so ends my catechism.[78]

Falstaff was well advised to check the key words used in time of
war or any other crisis. At such times words function even more than
usually as abstract shields covering much that is unsavory and brutal
in the concrete. The flight to abstraction is distinguished by a hesitancy to call a spade a spade. "Nuclear deterrence policy" means a
readiness to incinerate millions of people. It means genocide, and it
also means a bankrupting military budget to finance research, production, and deployment. Deterrence, however, mutes the acerbity
and irrationality of all this. The word, after all, implies that something will not happen. It does not immediately suggest that unless
we are really ready to perpetrate nuclear genocide, the "deterrence"
will not deter.

Again in the same insidious vocabulary, "taking out a city" means
reducing it and its inhabitants to radioactive ash. "Taking out," however, has a clean sporting ring to it. A good block in football is described as "taking out" the other player. This helps us to abstract
from what we really intend. Bombing in Vietnam was described as
"a defensive ordnance drop." A confused and chaotic retreat was
called a "retrograde action" by a Pentagon spokesman. "Invasions"
became "incursions." Escape and surrender became "peace with
honor." What would Falstaff say?

"National interest" and "national security" are extremely abstract
terms. Though the term national interest is not useless, it is only useful if its crucial limits are acknowledged. How much precision should
we pretend to when we base a particular decision on "the national
interest." The term signals an extraordinary paternalism whereby a
small elite decide upon the needs and priorities of a very varied mass
of people and interests. When, for example, it is seen to be "in the
national interest" to maintain co-operative relations with nations
who have stepped beyond the pale of normal governmental inequities and have begun to torture and kill political dissidents in large
numbers, "national interest," like Falstaff's "honor," begins to cover
a multitude of sins. The argument is offered that "stability," another
temptingly abstract term, is vital to our foreign policy goals. Also, it

is alleged with posturing innocence that it is improper to interfere in the internal affairs of another nation, although nations, in accordance with their power, are involved in "interference" in multiple ways all the time. The fact that persons are being hideously tortured and that we are providing economic and political support to the torturers in direct and/or indirect ways is a reality that hides under "national interest," "stability," "foreign policy goals," and other abstractions.

The abstractionists claim that it is naïve and unrealistic to say that nations can discipline other nations for their internal misbehavior. But it is also naïve to say that nations can do nothing with the myriad forms of power to which they have access to mitigate blatant practices which are violative of the most fundamental human rights. Chile, of course, is a case at point. There is now evidence that the United States had no scruples about interfering in their internal affairs when a "destabilizing" Communist government was in power. Now with evidence of atrocities mounting, how is it that we have grown so impotent and so still? That question addressed to the tenders of the state would surely evoke a torrent of abstractions, just as a plethora of abstractions once explained why we could do nothing about the apartheid and other violations of blacks in southern Africa —until it was suddenly decided that we could.

Verbal abstractions, then, are to be watched. They can serve as a basic medium of intelligence and communication, but they can also be fonts of rascality. Not all abstract circumlocutions are mischievous. If I speak of "accelerating the dying process" rather than "killing" when I speak of administering a heavy and probably lethal dose of barbiturate to an agonized patient who is already near death, the circumlocution is not necessarily an abstract cover-up. "Killing" is too unnuanced a term to describe the truth of the situation. "Killing" normally means terminating life as a complete and adequate cause of death. When a person is already in a dying process and when other killing causes are already inexorably in operation, the reality is different. The human intervener joins a conspiracy of fatal causes which are already at work. The *what*, therefore, is different. Different phrasing is called for.

On the other hand, there may be reasons to refer to an abortion as "interrupting the pregnancy" or as "inducing the birth process." There is also the possibility that the terms could represent dishonest euphemism intent on rendering abstract that which is concrete.

Abortion in my judgment may be moral and good, however tragic. The determination of this, however, should not be based on obfuscation and unnecessary abstracting from the reality of feticide. Abstract cushioning language may be dictated by the needs of delicacy and compassion in many situations where clinical verbal precision would be crude. The mischief occurs when it is used to cover up the seriousness of what it is we are about—when it is conscience that is being cushioned, not the appropriate sensitivities of involved persons.

The moral problems in all of this relate most directly to the center of the wheel in my model of method. This is the questioning, expository phase of ethics, and false abstractions cut it short. While we remain detached from the empirical goriness of capital punishment in any of its forms, it is easier to find abstract grounds to justify it. Deterrence is a common argument for capital punishment, even though it is unprovable, given the infinity of variables that underlies either a decrease or increase in "capital" crimes. The accumulated data of studies and surveys do not relieve the deterrence argument of its unacceptable abstractness. The killing of an unarmed prisoner who has been rendered harmless by captivity remains more impressive than all the briefs and calls for what is reductively a primitive act of blood vengeance. The abstractness with which we view this particular act of the state would be relieved if we were to return to the custom of ancient Israel. Execution there was not sanitized and reported secondhand in the clean print of news media. There the condemned person was taken outside of the town. The witnesses for the prosecution cast the first stones and then all the people joined in the stoning until their victim collapsed and died. Nothing cushioned them from the brutality of what they did.

Now we have agents do it for us, and filming of the preliminaries and the actual event are prohibited. We do not see the electrocution; we hear about it. Our contact with it is mediated and abstract. We do not have to smell the body as it literally cooks. Neither need we look at the eyes as the lenses fracture from the electrical jolt. We need not witness the body snapping back and forth like a whip as every muscle is pulled in gruesome distortion. Some witnesses are invited in to observe, but a hood over the victim's head spares them from looking at what happens to the face when the shock hits. The hood becomes the ultimate symbol of devious abstraction. It spares us from seeing what it is we are actually doing.[79]

A clue to the abstractness of our approach to capital punishment is our inconsistent unreadiness to admit to less drastic alternatives. We would not allow physical torture, even though the jail system now usually constitutes just that, and even though the experience of "death row" is an infallible form of psychological torture. We would judge public flogging uncivilized and offensive. Dismemberment is even more repulsive to the strange public conscience. Yet if deterrence is our game, the removal of one or both arms would deter this criminal and make him a living witness to the grim determination of the state not to tolerate crime. Ideas such as dismemberment are, of course, grotesque, and because we are not accustomed to them we can appreciate their grotesqueness. Their stark empirical reality does not escape us. In capital punishment, most persons are inured to the physical starkness of it and this leaves the mind liable to the easy beguilement of abstraction.

There is more to the institution of capital punishment than the insidious influence of misused abstractness. It is rooted in our history, and our cultural addiction to it is intelligible only in and through that complex history. However, it does conspicuously illustrate the kind of abstractness that can afflict moral consciousness by detaching us from the empirical reality that must ground genuine moral judgment.

Abstractions concern ethics in another way. They also open the way to deviant uses of imagination. Hitler, after all, was imaginative in his plans for the *Dritte Reich*. He was, however, abstracting from the humanity of the Jewish people and from most of the civilizing political processes that have won acceptance from men of good will. Plato's vision of what the ideal state would be was certainly imaginative, but Marcuse's criticism in terms of its false abstractness is well aimed. "Plato's 'ideal' state retains and reforms enslavement while organizing it in accordance with an eternal truth. . . . Those who bore the brunt of the untrue reality . . . were not the concern of philosophy. It abstracted from them and continued to abstract from them."[80]

Furthermore, abstractions can boggle ethics because they *impose* meaning, whereas ethics should be the humble seeker after meaning. Ethics is the response of persons standing in awe before the mystery of their own ineffable humanity. Modesty befits the ethical enterprise. Bad abstractions do not befit it since they are by nature arrogant. They represent a refusal to render the due service of patiently

unraveling the empirically distinctive and often surprising problems
that characterize a world where dilemma, conundrum, and paradox
are persistently at home. Finally, false abstractions are the natural
refuge of hypocrisy and bad faith. The concealment that they practice is often basely motivated, and the spurious security they promise
is seductive. The phenomenon of false abstractions, therefore, is another necessary concern of a sensitive ethics.

Selective Vision . . .

In treating these various hazards of moral consciousness, I am citing some of the mental mechanisms and instinctive stratagems that
can distract the vision of even the best of minds. It is my contention
that any system of ethics that does not take account of them is too
high and mighty to do its complete job. Were we disincarnate intel-
lects perceiving readily in the way that the medievals thought the angels did, these hazards would not be a concern. To our subangelic reality, they are a concern. The one of which I now speak might best
be introduced by discussing a historical development which might at
first blush seem only curious. It is, however, introduced, not as a curiosity, but as a caricature of a common trick of the mind. I turn to
Hebraic history for the example.

In one way or the other, almost everyone in the West and many
in the East are indebted to Jewish moral and religious experience.
This exuberantly rich tradition has had broad impact. One of the elements in the Jewish tradition that was most refreshing was the Sabbath. The institution of the Sabbath struck a major and early blow
against drudgery and the natural obsessions of the work ethic in a
tough world. The Sabbath was to be a day of rest, and delight, and
expansion. The best of food and clothing were to ceremonialize the
day. The genius of the Sabbath was to realize that the meaning of
morals and God's arcane purposes were not best perceived amid the
tumult and draining busyness of the working day. Wisdom does not
come to fruition amid bustle. Being means more than doing—a point
that can be missed in a world that demands so much doing. For this
reason, work was to stop on the Sabbath. "The Sabbath was given
for enjoyment," the rabbis said.[81] The work of good deeds was permitted on the Sabbath on the grounds that "Scripture forbids '*thy*
business,' but *God's* business is permitted."[82] Religious, moral, and
personal fulfillment were the goals of the Sabbath. Such fulfillment

would bring delight. The Sabbath was more precisely a day of delight than a day of rest. Jewish literature illustrates this with a story.

> The Emperor asked R. Joshua B. Hannaniah, "What gives your Sabbath-meat such an aroma?" He replied, "We have a spice called Sabbath, which is put in the cooking of the meat, and this gives it its aroma." The Emperor said, "Give me some of this spice." He replied, "For him who keeps the Sabbath the spice works, for him who does not keep it, it does not work."[83]

This shows the intended destiny of the Sabbath and in many ways it was realized. The aberrations, however, concern us here in our search for typically deviant mental behavior in the face of moral values. And aberrations there were! If one observed the Sabbath in its fullness, it would bring him face to face with all the value demands of the Jewish moral tradition. An avoidance mechanism, therefore, appeared. Instead of focusing on the positive aspects of the Sabbath day, a heretical tradition developed which became obsessed with the no-work clause. The results were that some of the rabbis went to work defining licit and illicit sabbatical work. The conclusions reached were that the Sabbath would be violated by such things as: tying or untying a knot, putting out a lamp, sewing two stitches (one was permissible though obviously not very helpful), writing two letters of the alphabet, etc.[84] One could rinse a tooth with vinegar licitly so long as he swallowed it. If he did not swallow it, it would be taking medicine which was forbidden; if he swallowed it, it would be taking drink.[85] Similarly, he could put an injured foot in cold water but he could not move it around or that would be forbidden medicinal bathing.[86] Things so deteriorated that it even reached the point where it was debated whether or not it was permissible to eat an egg laid on the Sabbath, based presumably on the observation that it took the chicken some work to lay the egg and so there was a question of guilt by association.[87] Carried to this extreme, as Giuseppe Ricciotti says, this view of the Sabbath "would have meant abstaining from any form of manual effort whatever, hence even from defending one's life when threatened by armed force (as some Jews did during the persecution of Antiochus Epiphanes, 1 *Mach.* 2:31–38), and also from all that might be necessary to satisfy the needs of the body (as the Essenes did, cf. *Wars of the Jews*, II, 147)."[88]

Here then is another case of the corruption of the best being worst. The temptation is to say that this is a single case of misdirection, something that was the unique problem of some Jews many years ago. I submit that it would be unwise not to see this particular development as a caricature of a common human failing which is another prevalent hazard of moral discernment. This perversion is a complex psychological phenomenon. In a central way, however, and in a way that concerns us here, the legalistic perversion of the Sabbath represented a syndrome whereby attention was fixated on nonessentials while the essence was passed by.

No one can think himself entirely evil. Therefore if he is unwilling to match up to the essential demands of goodness he will fixate on the area of less essential or nonessential matters and there chart out the pattern of his rectitude. The noble Englishman who, in the days of the British Empire was punctiliously careful to curb his dog and mind the queue, was able to participate in the exploitation of colonized peoples with the same ease that the heretical Jew was able to restrain the number of steps he took on the Sabbath and exploit some of his helpless neighbors. Catholics in the recent past who were able to carefully abstain from meat on Fridays or even from frying an egg in bacon fat could still indulge in blatant racism with an untroubled sense of moral well-being. Businessmen who would never break a local ordinance at home by burning their leaves or not shoveling their walks can go to work and make and cover up decisions that will pollute the air we breathe and the water we need—and all without compunction and indeed with an aura of civil propriety. Spouses can justify themselves by noting their fidelity to little things even though they are avoiding the great demands made of those who would really build marital friendship. And even the Mafioso who bequeaths money copiously to the pastor of the little, struggling downtown church is another unsubtle manifestation of the syndrome of selective value reponse.

A snobbish ethics would say that the problem here is a practical matter of concern only to moral counselors. This is an error. The problem is not limited to those who need special counseling. Ethics, with all of its impressive theoretical structure, can also fall prey. The history of ethics shows that it has often been in the company of the Jewish ethicians who pondered the eligibility and moral edibility of the egg laid on the Sabbath. There are more than a few Sabbath eggs in history that have claimed the vigorous attention of ethicists.

The German chaplains in the Nazi army who were busy warning their troops against sinning with Dutch prostitutes were the products of highly elaborated moral systems. Their apparent ability to miss the moral meaning of the invasion can be seen as all too typical of an ethics which has specialized in the picayune to the neglect of collective and political action where the most important moral decisions are made. Preoccupation with Sabbath eggs is, in fact, a permanent human problem. And it is a problem with which the theory and not just the practice of ethics must contend, since the theorists can be its most influential victims. It is a problem of theory because it is a problem of vision. It is only a rationalistic and unrealistic theory that could contemplate the methodic unfolding of moral consciousness as though cognitive filters and hazardous mental mechanisms did not exist and could therefore be ignored.

Role and Banalization . . .

This list of the indigenous hazards of moral discourse is illustrative, not exhaustive. Before concluding it, I will touch briefly on two other natural hazards: *banalization* and the uncritically accepted code of ethics that can go with a *role*.

The notion of role is related closely both to myth and to cognitive mood. Role refers to the kind of life style associated with a particular function or life situation. Its implications for ethics lie in the fact that a particular code of ethics may come along as an unsuspected stowaway when one embarks on a new role. A role is powerful because it is socially and mythically endorsed. This has great positive potential. Selfish persons may rise to unpredicted heights of altruism when they assume a new role that implies a new way of life.

It is not hard to think of the rather dissolute student who becomes serious and responsible when given a position (and role) which seems to call for this. The psychology is as simple as that used in making the bad boy a patrol leader in the scout troop. However, a new role may contain a poor code of ethics. The role of soldier, for example, dictates the compliance patterns of an automaton. A citizen may become a conscientious objector; a soldier who has the opportunity to see the nonabstract reality of the war may not. Such use of conscience has been excluded by the social expectations attaching to the role.

The role of the businessman may make it "natural" to engage in

many questionable practices. The role mentality simply prescribes
that this is the way things are done. A lawyer may be convinced by
his established role that idealism is incompatible with his calling. As
a boy begins to play the role of "a man," he may inertly accept the
expectations that he will show no fineness or delicacy of taste and
that he will, in sorrow, abandon the natural resource of tears. The
student may see his role as passive receptacle of information, not as
active participant in a process of discovery. The intellectual may see
himself as above manual labor. The father may not pause enough before the ecstasies of his child's infancy. In every case, the bad ethics
that may go with a role is a problem that rationalistic ethical theory
will leave intact.

Regarding banalization, the words of Teilhard de Chardin are instructive. "What too closely envelops us automatically ceases to as-
tonish us."[89] The truth of this is illustrated by the story of two men
laying bricks. One was asked what he was doing and he replied:
"Laying bricks!" But when the second man was asked the same question he exclaimed: "I am building a cathedral!" Banalization is a loss
of crucial perspective. It is a blunting of our sense of wonder, our
ability to find "eternity in a grain of sand." According to the old saying, Consueta vilescunt—meaning that things that we have grown
accustomed to became banal and tawdry in our eyes. I would add to
this old saying, Et semper minus capiuntur—meaning that the more
this happens, the less we understand. Banalization obstructs understanding especially in matters moral. Banality is the opposite of ecstasy, and the moral life is built on the ecstatic discovery of value.
Even our routines can sing. Ethics is hampered by those who are
deaf to any part of the human song.

In conclusion, regarding these various modes of reality avoidance,
I repeat that the list is not exhaustive. There are many ways in
which human knowing goes astray. As I have mentioned above, each
of the evaluative processes and resources represented by the spokes of
my model of ethics can be abused and serve to diminish our contact
with reality. Some of these hazards overlap with others and with
problem factors treated in the development of my method. I do not
apologize for the overlap if it served, as I intended it, to show an un-
disclosed side of a large question. The important thing if for ethics
to resist the temptation to view its enterprise as transpiring in a
chaste vacuum. It transpires in the maelstrom of social and personal
history.

In Fine . . .

Justice Holmes used to say that science makes major contributions to minor needs. Ethics is the attempt to make at least minor contributions to major needs. Modern man has been little attracted to the work of ethics even though his technological genius has caused exponential increases in the number of questions requiring ethical judgment. The decline of ethics relates to the rise of science. Science has become a symbol of an age that takes its minor needs more seriously than its major needs. The major needs, however, are being newly felt. Scientist René Dubos declares that people are beginning to doubt "that Galileo, Watt, and Edison have contributed as much and as lastingly to human advancement and happiness as Socrates, Lao-tze, and Francis of Assisi."[90] A renewed interest in the formal investigation of the deepest human problems is a renewed interest in ethics. No professional ethicist who seeks to serve this renaissance dares deem himself "a profitable servant." I do not so deem myself. What I have done in these pages is to present the fruit of many years of professional effort to discover how the valuing animal should best do his valuing. I have not sought to solve all the problems I have introduced, but I have attempted to show how those problems can best be addressed.

The ethics that will meet civilization's needs will call Socrates and Galileo, Lao-tze and Watt, Francis of Assisi and Edison into a community of discernment. There is no area of human experience that is not the bearer of moral meaning. Ethics can only seek to bring method and some completeness to that human conversation on moral values from which no one is dispensed. If it does that even somewhat well, it has served a world which is, thus far, more clever than wise.

NOTES—CHAPTER THIRTEEN

1. Herbert Marcuse, *One-dimensional Man* (Boston: Beacon Press, 1966), p. 125.
2. See Daniel C. Maguire, " 'Myth' in Politics," *Worldview* 13, No. 10 (Oct. 1970), pp. 15–17.

3. Quoted in Karl Mannheim, *Ideology and Utopia* (New York: Harcourt, Brace & World, Inc., A Harvest Book, 1936), p. 139, note 32.
4. I Timothy 2:15.
5. Kenneth Grayston, "Marriage," in Alan Richardson, ed., *A Theological Word Book of the Bible* (New York: Macmillan Co., 1962), p. 139. Grayston refers to Genesis 16:1ff; 30:1ff.
6. Augustine, *On Genesis According to the Letter* 9-7 (Vienna: Corpus Scriptorum Ecclesiasticorum, 1866), 28:275.
7. Arnold Toynbee, *A Study of History*, abridgments of Volumes VII–X by D. C. Somervell (New York and London: Oxford University Press, 1957), p. 142.
8. Simone de Beauvoir, *The Second Sex* (New York: Bantam Books, 1961), p. 74.
9. Hannah Arendt, *The Human Condition* (Garden City, N.Y.: Doubleday & Co., Inc., 1959), p. 64.
10. Thomas Aquinas, *Summa Theologica* I q. 92, a. 1, ad 1. . . . *virtus activa quae est in semine maris, intendit producere sibi simile perfectum, secundum masculinum sexum.* . . . Thomas does say that in reference to "universal nature" the generation of woman is not something accidental but is of the intention of nature and God for the work of reproduction. This strange distinction does not get him off his chauvinist hook.
11. Jacques Ellul, *The Political Illusion* (New York: Alfred A. Knopf, 1967), p. 98.
12. Ibid.
13. Ibid., p. 104.
14. Ibid., p. 108.
15. Ibid., p. 98.
16. See Roland H. Bainton, *Christian Attitudes Toward War and Peace: A Historical Survey and Critical Re-evaluation* (New York and Nashville: Abingdon Press, 1960), pp. 208–10.
17. See Jerome Frank, *Sanity and Survival* (New York: Vintage Books, 1968), pp. 134–35.
18. U. Bronfenbrenner, "The Mirror Image in Soviet-American Relations: A Social Psychologist's Report," *Journal for Social Issues* 17 (1961), p. 46.
19. Robert E. Sherwood, *Roosevelt and Hopkins* (New York: Harper & Brothers, 1948), p. 870.
20. Ibid.
21. Harry S Truman, *Memoirs: Year of Decisions* (Garden City, N.Y.: Doubleday & Co., Inc., 1955), Vol. 1, p. 402.
22. Ibid., p. 552.
23. Milton Mayer, "On Liberty: Man v. the State," Occasional Paper of the Center for the Study of Democratic Institutions, Santa Barbara, California, December, 1969, p. 54.

24. Quoted ibid., p. 55.
25. Cited ibid., p. 86.
26. Eric Voegelin, *The New Science of Politics* (Chicago and London: University of Chicago Press, Phoenix Books, 1952), p. 111.
27. Ibid., pp. 111–12.
28. Ibid., p. 113.
29. Sylvester Judd, *A Moral Review of the Revolutionary War, Or, Some of the Evils of that Event Considered* (Hallowell, Me.: Glazier, Masters & Smith, Printers, 1842), p. 5.
30. Ibid.
31. Ibid., p. 4.
32. Ibid., p. 27.
33. Ibid.
34. Ibid., p. 38. The discussion of the Indians to which I refer runs from pp. 38 to 40.
35. Ibid., pp. 38–39. In this passage, Judd is quoting *Stone's Life of Brandt*.
36. Huston Smith, *The Religions of Man* (New York: Harper & Row, Perennial Library, 1965), p. 11.
37. Nathaniel W. Taylor, *Concio ad Clerum: A Sermon Delivered in the Chapel of Yale College, September 10, 1828* (New Haven: Hezekiah Howe, 1828), p. 22; quoted in William A. Clebsch, *From Sacred to Profane America* (New York: Harper & Row, 1968), p. 32.
38. George S. Phillips, *The American Republic and Human Liberty Foreshadowed in Scripture* (Cincinnati: Poe & Hitchcock, for the author, 1864); quoted in Clebsch, *From Sacred to Profane America*, pp. 189–91.
39. Clebsch, *From Sacred to Profane America*, pp. 191–92.
40. Quoted in Charles A. Beard, *The Idea of National Interest* (New York: Macmillan Co., 1934), p. 368.
41. Quoted ibid., pp. 380–81.
42. Quoted ibid., p. 395.
43. George F. Kennan, *American Diplomacy: 1900–1950* (New York and London: New English Library Ltd., A Mentor Book, 1951), p. 17.
44. Ibid., p. 14.
45. André Dumas, "The Ideological Factor in the West," in Harvey G. Cox, ed., *The Church Amid Revolution* (New York: Association Press, 1967), pp. 208–9.
46. Ibid., p. 225. Dumas is using myth in a very narrow sense when he says that "critical science has reduced them to the level of legends" (p. 207). Also, when he says that contemporary societies are not concerned about their mythical origins, he is not only narrowing the

term but overlooking the fact that myths have a way of not dying but of only fading away into other still active forms. The archtypal symbols that fill the subconscious mind of man are not without links to the myths of our early history.

47. Ross Terrill, "Pax Americana and the Future of Asia," *Cross Currents* 18, No. 4 (Fall 1968), p. 484.

48. For an example of an ideological effort to muster the available American myths, especially the religiously charged ones for a particular purpose, Ford's statement on pardoning Nixon is a classic. Here he is clearly the successor of Harding and McKinley. In that brief statement he spoke of God five times, used four other religious terms, referred to conscience seven times, and used twenty-seven specifically moral terms excluding the nine religious terms, which are also moral by implication.

49. Quoted in Terrill, "Pax Americana," p. 484.

50. Quoted in Arthur M. Schlesinger, Jr., *The Crisis of Confidence* (New York: Bantam Books, 1969), pp. 133–34.

51. Rollo May, *Love and Will* (New York: W. W. Norton & Co., 1969), p. 226.

52. R. R. Palmer, *A History of the Modern World*, 2nd ed., revised with collaboration of Joel Colton (New York: Alfred A. Knopf, 1960), pp. 265–66.

53. Dumas, "Ideological Factor in the West," p. 222.

54. Ross Terrill, "North Africa Notebook," *Atlantic* 234, No. 4 (Oct. 1974), p. 17.

55. Immediately it should be noted that mood is such a broad term, just as environment is, that it could also be said that mood is part of the environment. Nevertheless, for purposes of specifying the meaning of mood the usage in the text can be understood in a helpful way.

56. Arendt, *Human Condition*, p. 253.

57. Quoted in Richard Hofstadter, *The American Political Tradition* (New York: Vintage Books, 1960), p. 3.

58. Alexis de Tocqueville, *Democracy in America*, edited by Phillips Bradley (New York: Alfred A. Knopf, 1945), Vol. 1, p. 310.

59. Ibid., Vol. 2, p. 8.

60. William Stringfellow, "Does America Need a Barmen Declaration?" *Christianity and Crisis* 33, No. 22 (Dec. 24, 1973), p. 274.

61. Ibid.

62. Glenn D. Paige, *The Korean Decision* (New York: Free Press, 1968), p. 23.

63. Richard Barnet, *Intervention and Revolution* (New York: World Publishing Co., 1968), p. 121.

64. Ibid., p. 115.

65. Quoted ibid., p. 148.

66. *Congressional Record*, Vol. 96, Pt. 7, June 26, 1950, pp. 9157ff. On Bridges comments see p. 9146.
67. Ibid., June 27, 1950, p. 9269.
68. Schlesinger, *Crisis of Confidence*, p. 116.
69. Quoted ibid., pp. 116–17.
70. "A Pattern for Peace in Southeast Asia: The Johns Hopkins Speech," reprinted in Marvin E. Gettleman, ed., *Vietnam: History, Documents, and Opinions on a Major World Crisis* (Greenwich, Conn.: Fawcett Publications, Inc., 1965), pp. 323–30.
71. Ibid., p. 324.
72. Pliny, *Natural History*, 7, 11, 43.
73. Origen, *Fifth Homily on Genesis* 4, *Die Griechischen christlichen Schriftsteller der ersten Jahrhundert* (Leipzig, 1897), 29:62. See John T. Noonan, Jr., *Contraception: A History of Its Treatment by the Catholic Theologians and Canonists* (Cambridge, Mass.: Harvard University Press, 1956), p. 77 and pp. 47, 79, 80, 85.
74. Marcuse, *One-dimensional Man*, p. 134.
75. Ibid.
76. Quoted in Arthur Cochrane, "Barmen Revisited," *Christianity and Crisis* 33, No. 22 (Dec. 24, 1973), p. 269.
77. My discussion of genetically damaged children is not abstract. My four-and-a-half-year-old son, Danny, is afflicted with Hunter's syndrome, a rare genetic disease that normally involves the gradual deterioration of the central nervous system. In his case, that deterioration has begun.
78. William Shakespeare, *Henry IV*, Part I, Act V, Scene 1, lines 126–43.
79. See Louis Nizer, *The Implosion Conspiracy* (New York: Garden City, N.Y.: Doubleday & Co., Inc., 1973), pp. 478–82, for a detailed and depressing description of the actual execution of Julius and Ethel Rosenberg.
80. Marcuse, p. 135.
81. R. Hiyya b. Abba, Pes. R. 121 a. in C. G. Montefiore and H. Loewe, eds., *A Rabbinic Anthology* (New York: Meridian Books, 1963), p. 195.
82. Sab. 150 a. fin. (cp. Tanh., Bereshit, No. 2 f. 82), quoted ibid., p. 193.
83. Sab. 119 a., quoted ibid., p. 192.
84. Sav. VII, 2, quoted in Giuseppe Ricciotti, *The Life of Christ* (Milwaukee: Bruce Publishing Co., 1947), p. 64. Ricciotti, reflecting his concerns with the New Testament, does not develop the positive aspects of the Sabbath to which I have alluded. He does, however, note that the Sabbath was to be a day of "spirituality and joy," but he is preoccupied with the reaction of Jesus against the legalistic abuses of the Sabbath.

85. Tosephta, Sab. XII, 9, quoted ibid., p. 65.
86. Sav. Sab. XXIII 6, quoted ibid.
87. Besah, I, I; Edduyyoth, IV, I, quoted ibid., p. 249.
88. Ibid., p. 64.
89. Pierre Teilhard de Chardin, *The Vision of the Past* (New York: Harper & Row, 1966), p. 202.
90. René Dubos, *So Human an Animal* (New York: Charles Scribner's Sons, 1966), p. 221.

INDEX